T0220761

Communications
in Computer and Information Science   **977**

Commenced Publication in 2007
Founding and Former Series Editors:
Phoebe Chen, Alfredo Cuzzocrea, Xiaoyong Du, Orhun Kara, Ting Liu,
Krishna M. Sivalingam, Dominik Ślęzak, Takashi Washio, and Xiaokang Yang

More information about this series at http://www.springer.com/series/7899

Paolo Mori · Steven Furnell ·
Olivier Camp (Eds.)

Information Systems Security and Privacy

4th International Conference, ICISSP 2018
Funchal - Madeira, Portugal, January 22–24, 2018
Revised Selected Papers

 Springer

Editors
Paolo Mori
IIT-CNR
Pisa, Italy

Steven Furnell 🆔
Plymouth University
Plymouth, UK

Olivier Camp
MODESTE/ESEO
Angers Cedex 02, France

ISSN 1865-0929   ISSN 1865-0937   (electronic)
Communications in Computer and Information Science
ISBN 978-3-030-25108-6   ISBN 978-3-030-25109-3   (eBook)
https://doi.org/10.1007/978-3-030-25109-3

This Springer imprint is published by the registered company Springer Nature Switzerland AG
The registered company address is: Gewerbestrasse 11, 6330 Cham, Switzerland

Preface

The present book includes extended and revised versions of a set of selected papers from the 4th International Conference on Information Systems Security and Privacy (ICISSP 2018), held in Funchal, Madeira, Portugal, during January 22–24, 2018.

The ICISSP 2018 aims at creating a meeting point for researchers and practitioners that address security and privacy challenges in information systems, especially in organizations. ICISSP 2018 focuses both on technological issues and social issues. The conference welcomes papers of either practical or theoretical nature, presenting research or applications addressing all aspects of security and privacy, that concern to organizations and individuals, thus creating new research opportunities.

ICISSP 2018 received 71 paper submissions from 25 countries, of which 21% were included in this book. The papers were selected by the Event Chairs and their selection was based on a number of criteria that included the classifications and comments provided by the Program Committee members, the Session Chairs' assessment, and also the Program Chairs' global view of all papers included in the technical program. The authors of selected papers were then invited to submit a revised and extended version of their papers, having at least 30% innovative material.

The papers selected for inclusion in this book contribute to the understanding of relevant trends of current research on Information Systems Security and Privacy. These include technology-level contributions such as enhanced approaches for user authentication and access control, and improved methods for understanding attacks and intrusions, alongside more human-focused issues such as techniques for privacy control and management, and alternative approaches to end-user security education. The discussions also span topical application areas, including smart technologies and online voting.

We would like to thank all the authors for their contributions and also the reviewers who have helped ensure the quality of this publication.

January 2018

Paolo Mori
Steven Furnell
Olivier Camp

Organization

Conference Chair

Olivier Camp   MODESTE, ESEO, France

Program Co-chairs

Steven Furnell   University of Plymouth, UK
Paolo Mori   Istituto di Informatica e Telematica, Consiglio
                            Nazionale delle Ricerche, Italy

Program Committee

Habtamu Abie   Norwegian Computing Center, Norway
Ahmad Ahmadi   University of Calgary, Canada
Ali Al Mazari   Alfaisal University, Saudi Arabia
Mario Alvim   Federal University of Minas Gerais (UFMG), Brazil
Thibaud Antignac   CEA, DRT, LIST, France
Man Au   The Hong Kong Polytechnic University, SAR China
Montserrat Batet   Universitat Rovira i Virgili, Spain
Cătălin Bîrjoveanu   Al.I.Cuza University of Iasi, Romania
Reinhardt Botha   Nelson Mandela Metropolitan University, South Africa
Christos Bouras   University of Patras, CTI&P Diophantus, Greece
Francesco Buccafurri   University of Reggio Calabria, Italy
Olivier Camp   MODESTE, ESEO, France
Luigi Catuogno   Università di Salerno, Italy
Rui Chen   Samsung Research America, USA
Thomas Chen   City University London, UK
Feng Cheng   Hasso-Plattner-Institute at University of Potsdam,
                            Germany
Yannick Chevalier   Université Paul Sabatier Toulouse III, France
Hung-Yu Chien   National Chi Nan University, Taiwan
Stelvio Cimato   Università Degli Studi di Milano, Italy
Miguel Correia   Universidade do Porto, Portugal
Gianpiero Costantino   Consiglio Nazionale delle Ricerche, Italy
Mathieu Cunche   INSA-Lyon, Inria, France
Rafael de Sousa Junior   University of Brasilia, Brazil
Hervé Debar   Télécom SudParis, France
Andreas Dewald   Friedrich-Alexander-Universität Erlangen-Nürnberg,
                            Germany
Josep Domingo-Ferrer   Universitat Rovira i Virgili, Spain
Isao Echizen   National Institute of Informatics, Japan

David Eyers	University of Otago, New Zealand
Mathias Fischer	University Hamburg, Germany
Stephen Flowerday	University of Fort Hare, South Africa
Alban Gabillon	Laboratoire GePaSud, Université de la Polynésie Française, French Polynesia
Clemente Galdi	Universitá di Napoli Federico II, Italy
Debin Gao	Singapore Management University, Singapore
Bok-Min Goi	Universiti Tunku Abdul Rahman, Malaysia
Mario Goldenbaum	Princeton University, USA
Dieter Gollmann	TU Hamburg, Germany
Ana González-Tablas	University Carlos III of Madrid, Spain
Gilles Guette	University of Rennes, France
R. Hansdah	Indian Institute of Science, Bangalore, India
Martin Hell	Lund University, Sweden
Guy Hembroff	Michigan Technological University, USA
Fu-Hau Hsu	National Central University, Taiwan
Dieter Hutter	German Research Centre for Artificial Intelligence, Germany
Rafiqul Islam	Charles Sturt University, Australia
Mariusz Jakubowski	Microsoft Research, USA
Christian Jensen	Technical University of Denmark, Denmark
Jens Jensen	STFC Rutherford Appleton Laboratory, UK
Mark Karpovsky	Boston University, USA
Anne Kayem	University of Cape Town, South Africa
Christoph Kerschbaumer	Mozilla Corporation, USA
Zubair Khattak	ISACA, Pakistan
Hiroaki Kikuchi	Meiji University, Japan
Dong Kim	University of Canterbury, New Zealand
Elisavet Konstantinou	University of the Aegean, Greece
Hristo Koshutanski	Atos, Spain
Nadira Lammari	Conservatoire National des Arts et Métiers, France
Andrea Lanzi	University of Milan, Italy
Gianluca Lax	University of Reggio Calabria, Italy
Gabriele Lenzini	University of Luxembourg, Luxembourg
Shujun Li	University of Kent, UK
Flamina Luccio	Università Ca' Foscari Venezia, Italy
Ilaria Matteucci	Istituto di Informatica e Telematica, CNR, Italy
Vashek Matyas	Masaryk University, Czech Republic
Catherine Meadows	US Naval Research Laboratory, USA
Francesco Mercaldo	National Research Council of Italy (CNR)
Mattia Monga	Università degli Studi di Milano, Italy
Paolo Mori	Istituto di Informatica e Telematica, Consiglio Nazionale delle Ricerche, Italy
Charles Morisset	Newcastle University, UK
Kirill Morozov	Tokyo Institute of Technology, Japan
Paliath Narendran	State University of New York at Albany, USA

Vivek Nigam	Federal University of Paraíba, fortiss, Brazil
Antonino Nocera	University Mediterrana of Reggio Calabria, Italy
Mehrdad Nojoumian	Florida Atlantic University, USA
Donal O'Mahony	Trinity College Dublin, Ireland
Aida Omerovic	SINTEF, Norway
Carles Padro	Universitat Politecnica de Catalunya, Spain
Yin Pan	Rochester Institute of Technology, USA
Mauricio Papa	University of Tulsa, USA
Günther Pernul	University of Regensburg, Germany
Kenneth Radke	Information Security Institute, Queensland University of Technology, Australia
Wolfgang Reif	University of Augsburg, Germany
Karen Renaud	Abertay University, UK
Jean-Marc Robert	ETS Montreal, Canada
Roberto Rojas-Cessa	New Jersey Institute of Technology, USA
Christophe Rosenberger	Ensicaen, France
Neil Rowe	Naval Postgraduate School, USA
Antonio Ruiz-Martínez	University of Murcia, Spain
Michaël Rusinowitch	Laboratoire Lorrain de Recherche en Informatique et Ses Applications, France
Nader Safa	University of Warwick, UK
Hossein Saiedian	University of Kansas, USA
David Sanchez	Universitat Rovira i Virgili, Spain
Antonella Santone	University of Molise, Italy
Andrea Saracino	Consiglio Nazionale delle Ricerche, Istituto di Informatica e Telematica, Italy
Michael Scott	Certivox Ltd, Ireland
Kent Seamons	Brigham Young University, USA
Qi Shi	Liverpool John Moores University, UK
Abdulhadi Shoufan	Khalifa University of Science, UAE
Boris Skoric	Eindhoven University of Technology, The Netherlands
Angelo Spognardi	Sapienza Università di Roma, Italy
Paul Stankovski	Lund University, Sweden
Rainer Steinwandt	Florida Atlantic University, USA
Hung-Min Sun	National Tsing Hua University, Taiwan
Iraklis Symeonidis	APSIA, University of Luxembourg, Luxembourg
Cihangir Tezcan	Middle East Technical University, Turkey
Yasuyuki Tsukada	Kanto Gakuin University, Japan
Sylvestre Uwizeyemungu	Université du Québec à Trois-Rivières, Canada
Adriano Valenzano	Consiglio Nazionale delle Ricerche, Italy
Rakesh Verma	University of Houston, USA
Artemios Voyiatzis	SBA Research, Austria
Edgar Weippl	SBA, FHSTP, Austria
Bing Wu	Fayetteville State University, USA
Ching-Nung Yang	National Dong Hwa University, Taiwan
Ping Yang	Binghamton University, USA

Alec Yasinsac   University of South Alabama, USA
Meng Yu   University of Texas at San Antonio, USA

Additional Reviewers

Lake Bu   Boston University, USA
Jean-Francois Lalande   CentraleSupélec, France
Mario Larangeira   Tokyo Institute of Technology, Japan
Martin Loesdau   Université de la Polynésie française, French Polynesia
Dayana Spagnuelo   University of Luxembourg, Luxembourg

Invited Speakers

Ueli Maurer   Swiss Federal Institute of Technology (ETH),
                                    Switzerland
David Jacoby   Kaspersky Lab, Sweden
Ross Anderson   University of Cambridge, UK

Contents

Fine-Grained Privacy Control for Fitness and Health Applications Using the Privacy Management Platform

Christoph Stach[✉]

Institute for Parallel and Distributed Systems, University of Stuttgart,
Universitätsstraße 38, 70569 Stuttgart, Germany
stachch@ipvs.uni-stuttgart.de

Abstract. Due to the Internet of Things, novel types of sensors are integrated into everyday objects. A domain that benefits most is the fitness and health domain. With the advent of the so-called *Smartbands*—i. e., bracelets or watches with built-in sensors such as heart rate sensors, location sensors, or even glucose meters—novel fitness and health application are made possible. That way a *quantified self* can be created. Despite all the advantages that such applications entail, new privacy concerns arise.

These applications collect and process sensitive health data. Users are concerned by reports about privacy violations. These violations are enabled by inherent security vulnerabilities and deficiencies in the privacy systems of mobile platforms. As none of the existing privacy approaches is designed for the novel challenges arising from Smartband applications, we discuss, how the **P**rivacy **P**olicy **M**odel (*PPM*), a fine-grained and modular expandable permission model, can be applied to this application area. This model is implemented in the **P**rivacy **M**anagement **P**latform (*PMP*). Thus the outcomes of this work can be leveraged directly. Evaluation results underline the benefits of our work for Smartband applications.

Keywords: Smartbands · Health and Fitness Applications ·
Privacy Concerns · Bluetooth · Internet · Privacy Policy Model ·
Privacy Management Platform

1 Introduction

The *Internet of Things* has significantly revolutionized our daily lives. As sensors, microprocessors, and memory became smaller, more powerful, and, above all, cheaper, this technology is increasingly integrated into everyday objects which we carry with us permanently. Examples for such *Smart Devices* are *Smartphones*, *Smart Watches*, or *Smart Bracelets*. These devices can run small third-party applications called *apps*. Perhaps the most important feature, however, is that these devices can be connected with each other. This way, the Smart

ⓒ Springer Nature Switzerland AG 2019
P. Mori et al. (Eds.): ICISSP 2018, CCIS 977, pp. 1–25, 2019.
https://doi.org/10.1007/978-3-030-25109-3_1

Devices can provide their gathered sensor data to other devices and applications. Due to energy-efficient connection and transmission technologies such as Bluetooth LE, this interconnection has little to no impact on their battery life. As a result, novel application cases are constantly arising from different domains, which make use of these accumulated data stocks.

The consumer market is currently dominated by *Smartbands*. These hardware devices are equipped with GPS and a heartbeat sensor. Therefore, they are ideally suited for fitness apps. The Smartband is only used for data collection, while the actual fitness app is run on a connected Smartphone. This means that data processing (including data preparation, data analysis, and data presentation) is completely handled by the Smartphone. Since the smartphone carries many additional information about its user, the fitness data can also be linked and augmented with this data. As a result, a lot of further insights can be gained. As *Wearables* such Smartbands are small and comfortable to wear, they virtually disappear from our awareness [66]. This means that they can also be kept on while doing sports or even while sleeping.

Innovative apps take advantage of this persistent data capturing. For instance, a fitness app can analyze data from acceleration sensors and orientation sensors to identify movement patterns and determine the current activities of a user [32]. Location data can be used to determine the distance traveled by a jogger as well as his or her running speed and thus calculate his or her calorie consumption [67]. Heartbeat data can even be used to analyze the sleeping behavior of a user [43]. Such a comprehensive health profile is not only beneficial for the user, but also for his or her physician and many other stakeholders [30].

Yet, a *quantified self*, i.e., a comprehensive mapping of our lifestyle to quantifiable values to assess our daily routines, does not come without a price. This permanent, self-imposed monitoring poses a threat to our privacy. Smartbands and other Smart Devices collect so many personal data that a great deal of knowledge about the user can be derived from it. Many research activities are therefore concerned with the concrete threats posed by such innovative apps as well as their vulnerabilities [35] and what measures can be taken to provide security for these apps [38]. Particularly as the economic value of personal data increases [19], a completely new app business model has emerged. Users pay the usage of an app with their data, which is then sold to third parties, such as advertising clients [36]. Therefore, new control measures are needed to enable users to decide which personal information they are willing to disclose in return for what service [42].

To that end, we address the following five issues in our work:

(1) We introduce a real world mHealth use case for Smartband apps.
(2) We provide a comprehensive overview of state of the art concerning the protection of private data in the context of Smartband apps.
(3) We adapt a privacy policy model which enables users to control the data usage of Smartband apps in a fine-grained manner. Our approach is based on the **Privacy Management Platform** (*PMP*) [59] and its **Privacy Policy Model** (*PPM*) [58].

(4) We introduce a prototypical implementation of a privacy mechanism for Smartband apps using our privacy policy model.
(5) We evaluate our approach and demonstrate its applicability.

This paper is the extended and revised version of the paper entitled "Big Brother is Smart Watching You: Privacy Concerns about Health and Fitness Applications" [55] presented at the 4th International Conference on Information Systems Security and Privacy (ICISSP) 2018. This extended paper is more detailed on a technical level. The structure of a Smartband app is outlined, requirements towards a privacy system are derived from that app, and considerably more related approaches are discussed.

The remainder of the paper is structured as follows: Initially, a use case for Smartband apps is outlined in Sect. 2. In Sect. 3, current privacy control mechanisms for mobile platforms are discussed and the prevailing connection standard Bluetooth LE is characterized. Requirements towards a privacy system for Smartband apps is derived from this analysis in Sect. 4. Section 5 looks at some related work, that is enhanced privacy control mechanisms for mobile platforms. Our approach for such a mechanism specifically for Smartbands and similar devices is introduced in Sect. 6. Following this, our generic concept is implemented using the PMP in Sect. 7. Section 8 evaluates our approach and reveals whether it fulfills the requirements towards such a privacy control mechanism. Finally, Sect. 9 concludes this paper and glances at future work.

2   mHealth Use Case

Modern wearable Smart Devices such as Smartbands are equipped with multiple sensors and accordingly more and more data about their users can be acquired by them. While built-in GPS receivers are great to archive outdoor positioning, these sensors are virtually useless for indoor positioning. Therefore, there is a lot of research going on to archive indoor positioning with other standard sensors available in almost any Smart Device. Hsu et al. [25] introduce an approach using accelerometers and gyroscopes for that purpose. Another approach for indoor positioning is the use of the barometric pressure sensor [70]. Finally, the position can also be determined based on earth's magnetic field—i.e., via the compass sensor within the Smart Device [68]. However, these simple sensors can be used for more than just (indoor) positioning. In particular, wrist-based Smart Devices such as Smartbands enable to recognize activities of a user with high accuracy [27,49]. Medical sensors are also increasingly being integrated in Smartbands. Whereas methods for monitoring the heart rate are already widely used [1], there are also attempts to collect medical data, such as blood sugar levels, via such devices [65].

Due to these features, it is little surprising that these devices are increasingly being used for medical apps [44]. So-called *mHealth* apps can facilitate patients' lives, relieve physicians, and reduce treatment costs [37]. Due to the versatility of Smartbands, there is an app for almost every health-related issue [50]. In the

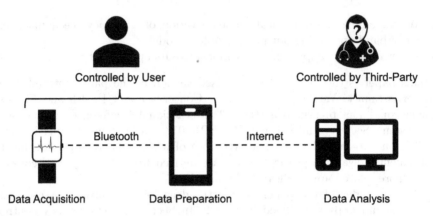

Fig. 1. Set-up of a Smartband app.

following, an app for children suffering from diabetes is outlined which is based on *Candy Castle* [20,33,54,61].

The aim of Candy Castle is to motivate children suffering from diabetes to check their blood sugar level regularly and keep their diabetes diary. To that end, the Smartphone app turns the children into a virtual owners of a castle. This castle represents their health condition. For this reason, it is regularly attacked by *dark forces*—i. e., the diabetes disease—and the children have to defend it with their *magic device*—i. e., their Smartband. This act of defense means that they carry out a blood sugar measurement. Apart from the actual blood sugar level, the Smartband also captures the child's most recent activities (e.g., to determine whether s/he did sports or took insulin) and his or her current location—it is assumed that the location has great influence on the health condition [34]. All this data is sent to the Smartphone and processed there: The player gets a reward (the castle gets repaired and upgraded) and a new entry is automatically added to an electronic diabetes diary. At some point in time this diary is sent to the physician, e.g., by uploading it to a *Hospital Cloud*. This approach enables to carry out comprehensive analyses on the health data and provide physicians with all required information [8,64].

Figure 1 shows the set-up of such an app. Most of the data acquisition is done on the Smartband. However, these devices are not powerful enough to process and combine all of this data. For this reason, they have to be sent to a Smartphone. This connection and data transfer is realized via Bluetooth. The data is then prepared on the Smartphone and provided to the Candy Castle. Even though Smartphone are becoming more and more powerful, they are not designed for comprehensive analyses. Therefore, data has to be sent to an external data processing unit via the Internet connection of the Smartphone. However, this implies that the user looses all control over his or her data. Especially, s/he cannot be sure about the identity of the recipient. Therefore, privacy actions have to be taken at the Smartphone.

3   State of the Art

Based on the aforementioned set-up, we explain, why especially the usage of apps for Smartbands and similar Smart Devices such as health or fitness apps constitutes a real threat to privacy. To this end, it is necessary to look at the privacy mechanisms implemented in mobile platforms as well as the modus operandi of how to connect a Smartband with a Smartphone.

Privacy Mechanisms in Current Mobile Platforms. The Smart Device market is currently dominated by two operating system, namely Apple's iOS and Google's Android [31]. Both of those mobile platforms apply a permission-based system to protect sensitive data [16]. This means that each app must specify which data it will process. Each time data is accessed, the system checks whether the respective permission can be granted. A permission does not refer to a specific type of data, but to a sensor or a potentially dangerous system functionality [5]. However, both mobile platforms implement this concept differently.

An iOS app requires Apple's approval before it is released. Automated and manual verification methods check whether the permission requests are justified. When Apple grants the permissions, the app is signed and released. The user is only informed about permissions concerning his or her personal data (e.g., the contacts) [40].

In contrast, Google does not intervene at all in the permission process. If an Android app is installed, the user is notified of any requested permissions and must grant them all to proceed with the installation process [6]. *Runtime Permissions* are therefore introduced in Android 6.0. A Runtime Permission is not assigned at installation time, but it has to be granted for each access to data that is protected by the corresponding permission [29].

However, studies show that users cannot cope with the multitude of different permissions—especially since they cannot understand the consequences of granting a certain permission [17]. Therefore Google divides the permissions in Android since version 6.0 into two classes: *Normal Permissions* no longer require the user's consent. Apps only have to indicate the usage of a Normal Permission in their Manifest. Only *Dangerous Permissions* (which are a superset of the Runtime Permissions) have to be granted by the user explicitly. For instance, the ACCESS_FINE_LOCATION (access to the GPS) or BODY_SENSORS (access to heart rate data) permission belong to this category. However, the BLUE-TOOTH and INTERNET permission are classified as Normal Permissions. Table 1 gives a comprehensive overview of Normal and Dangerous Permissions.

Figure 2 shows the effects of this decision. An app that needs to access GPS data, discover, pair with, and connect to Bluetooth devices, and open network sockets must declare the following four permissions: ACCESS_FINE_LOCATION, BLUETOOTH, BLUETOOTH_ADMIN, and INTERNET. In pre-Marshmallow Android versions (< 6.0), users must grant all permissions during installation. However, the installation dialog only informs the user about the Dangerous Permissions (see Fig. 2a). On devices with a higher Android version, Runtime Permissions are no longer shown as they have to be granted need-based

Table 1. Normal and Dangerous Android Permissions (excerpt) [based on [21]].

Normal Android Permissions	Dangerous Android Permissions
ACCESS_NETWORK_STATE	READ_CALENDAR
ACCESS_WIFI_STATE	CAMERA
BLUETOOTH	READ_CONTACTS
BLUETOOTH_ADMIN	ACCESS_FINE_LOCATION
INSTALL_SHORTCUT	ACCESS_COARSE_LOCATION
INTERNET	RECORD_AUDIO
NFC	READ_PHONE_NUMBERS
REQUEST_INSTALL_PACKAGES	CALL_PHONE
SET_ALARM	ANSWER_PHONE_CALLS
TRANSMIT_IR	READ_CALL_LOG
UNINSTALL_SHORTCUT	BODY_SENSORS
USE_FINGERPRINT	SEND_SMS
VIBRATE	READ_SMS
WAKE_LOCK	READ_EXTERNAL_STORAGE

(see Fig. 2b). Thus, each time the app attempts to access GPS data, a permission request pops up (see Fig. 2c). In any case, the user is not aware that the app is also granted to transfer this data to any Bluetooth device or the Internet.

Transmission Standard of Smart Devices. Bluetooth LE has become today's connection standard for Smart Devices. It uses consumes less power than Classic Bluetooth and has a longer operating range than NFC. The device manufacturer defines UUIDs that other devices can use to request services provided by the device. For example, a service of a Smartband could allow access to a built-in heart rate sensor. The manufacturer also specifies how the data is encoded by the device. A mobile platform therefore cannot determine which type of data is transferred between two Smart Devices, since it cannot know which services are addressed by which UUID. Moreover, without knowledge about the applied encoding, the platform cannot look into the transferred data. Therefore, the permissions only control the Bluetooth connection itself and not which data is transferred via this connection. The same applies to the forwarding of data to a server. Again, an app only needs to indicate that it needs access to the Internet, but the user does not know what data the app is sending or where the data is being sent to.

For instance, if a Smartband has a built-in GPS and heart rate sensor, then it can provide access to both, location and health data. An app only requires permission to discover, pair with, and connect to Bluetooth devices (BLUETOOTH and BLUETOOTH_ADMIN permission). However, both permissions belong to the Normal Permissions category. That is, the system grants these permissions automatically and the user is not informed about it. If the same app would

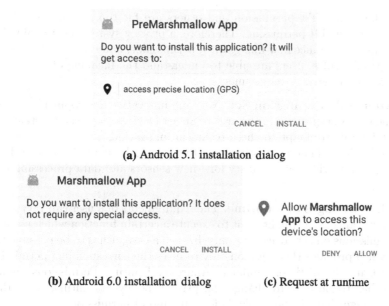

(a) Android 5.1 installation dialog

(b) Android 6.0 installation dialog   **(c)** Request at runtime

Fig. 2. Permission requests in different Android versions [55].

request the very same data directly from sensors which are built into a Smartphone, the ACCESS_FINE_LOCATION and BODY_SENSORS permissions are required. Both are Dangerous Permissions, i. e., the user must grant every access at runtime. As this kind of data is highly sensitive, that classification is reasonable. The use of a Smartband however completely override this protective measure. In addition, the app is able to share this information with any external sink without the user's knowledge. It only has to declare the INTERNET authorization in its Manifest—the INTERNET permission is also a Normal Permission. Therefore, a static, permission-based data privacy mechanism, as implemented in current mobile platforms, is not applicable to apps which access their data from Smart Devices such as Smartbands.

Since Android puts the user in charge of protecting his or her sensitive data, such a security vulnerability when dealing with data from Smartbands might have serious consequences. Therefore, this paper focuses on Android. However, the findings and concepts can be transferred to any other mobile platform.

4   Requirements Specification

Based on the identified deficiencies in current mobile platforms concerning privacy in Smartband apps, requirements for a privacy system can be derived. These requirements primarily focus on securing the two resources Bluetooth and Internet.

[R₁] Fine-Grained Privacy Rules. Although, Android provides a wide range of permissions, some of them are unnecessary (from a privacy point of view) such as the VIBRATE permission and others are far too coarse-grained such as the BLUETOOTH permission. Therefore, a privacy system has to split these permissions or introduce new fine-grained permissions. Only by introducing fine-grained privacy rules, users are able to understand the meaning of permissions and express their privacy requirements.

[R_2] **Extendable Permission Set.** New and innovative developments are constantly emerging, especially in the area of Smart Devices. A privacy system must therefore be able to adapt to these technical innovations in future generations of Smart Devices. That is, a privacy system has to be extendable in order to support—i.e., provide data security for—new sensors and data processing techniques.

[R_3] **Policy Changes at Runtime.** The requirements of a user can vary at any time. For instance, s/he might want to execute a certain function which require a lot of permissions on rare occasions only. In such a case, it has to be possible that an app which provides this function only receives the corresponding permissions for a short amount of time. Similar to Android's Runtime Permissions the user therefore has to be able to change the privacy policy at runtime—yet, these runtime changes have to be available for any kind of permission.

[R_4] **Context-Based Privacy Rules.** External factors can also influence a user's privacy requirements. For instance, an app may be granted more permissions in case of an emergency. Therefore, a privacy system must decide based on context data which privacy rules apply in the current situation.

[R_5] **Feedback.** In order for a privacy system to be effective, i.e., to enable the user to protect his or her interests with regard to data security, it is crucial that s/he is fully involved in the permission process. For this reason, a privacy system has to be designed to provide the user with comprehensive information about his or her options for granting permissions and also to make him or her aware of the possible consequences of his or her settings.

5 Related Work

As the prevailing privacy mechanisms applied in the current mobile platforms do not comply these requirements, there are a lot of research projects dealing with better privacy mechanisms for these platforms. In the following, we present a representative sample of these approaches and determine to what extent they are applicable for Smartband apps.

Apex [41] enables the user to add contextual conditions to each Android permission. These conditions specify situations in which a permission is granted. E.g., the user can set a timeframe in which an app gets access to private data or define a maximum number of times a certain data access is allowed. If the condition is not kept, a `SecurityException` is raised and the app crashes. Furthermore, as Apex is based on the existing Android permissions, it is too coarse-grained for the Smartband use case.

AppFence [24] analyzes the internal dataflow of apps. When data from a privacy critical source (e.g., the camera or the microphone) is sent to the Internet, the user gets informed. S/he is then able to alter the data before it is sent out or s/he can enable the flight mode whenever the affected app is started. However, AppFence does not knows which data an apps reads from a Bluetooth source. Thereby, it cannot differentiate whether an apps accesses trivial data from headphones (e.g., the name of the manufacturer) or private data from a Smartband (e.g., health data). Moreover, AppFence cannot identify to which address the data is sent to.

AppGuard [3] introduces a data protection system that integrates a monitoring component into apps which supervises apps from within. It consists of three components: (1) a pre-configured set of rules which are directly mapped to Android permissions, (2) an app converter that injects the monitoring component and the rule set into existing apps, and (3) a GUI, via which further, user-defined rules can be added. AppGuard also enables to describe how the control flow of an app should be modified if it violates any of the rules. However, as the rules are mapped to existing Android permissions, AppGuard has the same shortcomings regarding Smartbands. Moreover, the usage of the app converter violates copyright law [2].

AUDACIOUS [45] addresses this issue by introducing a program library via which experts are able to perform static and dynamic analyses on apps. As this library has to be integrated by the app developers themselves, this approach does not violate copyright law. The analyses reveal which data is used by an app and how it is processes. If any conspicuous data usage is detected, the app is stopped by AUDACIOUS. However, the rules are not defined by the user, but by experts who determine on their own which data usage is permissible.

Aurasium [69] introduces an additional sandbox which is injected into every app. This has to be done before the app is installed. The sandbox monitors its embedded app and intercepts each access to system functions. Thereby, Aurasium is not limited to the permissions predefined by Android. Especially for the access to the Internet, Aurasium introduces fine-grained configuration options, e.g., to specify to which servers the app may send data to. For every other permission, the user can simply decide whether s/he wants to grant or deny it. Moreover, Aurasium is not extensible. That is, it cannot react to new access modes as introduced by Smartbands where several data types can be accessed with the same permission. Also, the bytecode injection which is required for every app is costly and violates copyright and related rights.

CRêPE [11] is a context-based privacy system for Android. CRêPE uses a powerful situation recognition system to draw conclusions about the current activities of a user [12]. Via this technique, higher-level contexts can be described instead of simply linking single sensor values. Each privacy rule consists of a subject-object-permission triple. The subject is either a user or another app, the object represents any kind of data source, and the permission defines whether the given subject may access the object. A context is added to each triple and the rule is only active under that specific context. The access control is ensured

10   C. Stach

via *XACML* [39]. However, CRêPE is not designed for end-users and the privacy
rule creation is far too complex for common users.

Data-Sluice [47] considers solely the problem of uncontrolled data transfer to
external sinks. Therefore, Data-Sluice monitors the any kind of network activities. As soon as an apps attempts to open a network socket, the user is informed
and s/he can decide whether the access should be allowed or denied. Additionally,
Data-Sluice logs every network access and is able to blacklist certain addresses.
However, the user is neither informed about which data is sent to the network
nor is s/he able to limit the data access of an app from any other source, except
for the Internet.

Dr. Android & Mr. Hide [26] addresses the problem that many developers
are unable to handle the Android permissions and therefore unintentionally give
too many permissions to their apps [28]. To enable developers to assign permissions in a better way, Jeon et al. split the existing permissions into fine-grained
permissions. The novel permissions are based on the most common activities of
apps which require private data. The permissions are divide into four classes.
For each class, the user can apply different anonymization techniques. To enforce
the permission settings, the program library *hidelib* is provided which reimple-
ments the APIs of the Android app framework based on the new permissions.
However, Dr. Android & Mr. Hide manipulates the bytecode of each controlled
app, whereby it also violates copyright law.

IacDroid [71] does not directly address the issue of granting permissions, but
a related topic. As Android provides a wide range of possibilities for interprocess
communication (IPC), apps often exchange data and even permissions in an
uncontrolled manner [22,48]. Therefore, Zhang et al. introduce two components
that monitor and regulate data and permission exchange at runtime. All IPCs are
monitored for this purpose. This enables IacDroid to infer a sequence of process
calls. The user can then assign special permissions for each call. However, this
does not tackle the underlying issue of data collection in Smartband apps.

MockDroid [7] provides additional privacy settings for specific data sources
(including location data or the contacts) and system functions (including access
to the Internet or writing SMS messages). Via these settings, apps can reduce
the required permissions, e.g., by requesting Internet access to a specific address,
only. In addition, users can decide, whether apps have access to actual data or
whether MockDroid should provide them with fake data instead. However, all of
these settings are available for supported data sources and system functions, only.
While Internet access is protected by MockDroid, access to Bluetooth devices is
still unsecured.

Privacy Protector (No root) [23] is an Android app which promises a simple
privacy protection. However, the Privacy Protector only considers location data
and Internet access as safety hazards. Therefore, the user can specify which
apps should have access to it. Privacy Protector permanently monitors which
apps are currently running and if any of the regulated apps are among them,
the Internet or respectively the GPS tracking functions are deactivated system-
wide. This has an effect on all running apps. Moreover, since Android 5.0 the

`getRunningTasks` method has been severely restricted to prevent apps from spying on user behavior. This also reduces the functionality of Privacy Protector sustainably.

I-ARM Droid [14] is the most comprehensive approach. The user defines critical code blocks (i.e., a sequence of commands that accesses or processes private data) and specifies rewriting rules for each of them. A generic converter realizes the rewriting at bytecode level. However, this approach is much too complex for common users. As a consequence, its derivative *RetroSkeleton* [13] assigns this task to a security expert who creates a configuration according to the user's demands. Thereby frequent changes of the privacy rules are not possible— not to mention adjustments at runtime. Additionally, the expert has to know each conceivable code block that could violate the user's privacy. In other words s/he has to know every available Smartband, as each vendor defines a specific communication protocol.

SEAF [4] considers that the order in which permissions are requested might affect the risk potential of an app. For instance, an app that first gets access to the Internet and then accesses confidential data can do less damage than an app that performs these operations in reverse order. Banuri et al. therefore identify several operation sequences that indicate a potential data misuse and define the order in which permissions have to be requested to execute each of these operation sequences. SEAF monitors apps for such sequences of permission requests. If such a sequence is detected, SEAF informs the user and s/he decides whether the operations should be executed or whether the required permissions should be denied. However, SEAF is based on the coarse-grained Android permissions, and therefore it is not suitable for Smartband apps.

Sorbet [18] enables app developers to use IPC in a secure way. Sometimes it is required that apps exchange permissions via IPC. However, as the validity of Android permission is neither restricted in time nor in functionality, this leads to an almost unlimited and uncontrollable situation. Sorbet therefore enables controlled delegation of permissions and data. For this purpose, Sorbet records where the data or permissions originated from and to whom they were passed on. Each of these records is tagged with an expiration date which is specified by the permission originator, i.e., the app that received the permission in the first place. However, this does not solve the privacy problems of Smartband apps.

YAASE [46] introduces a new fine-grained permission model in order to reduce uncontrolled information passing between apps. In this model, the user has the option of tagging his or her data and thereby defining at a data level to which destination it may be sent to. Other apps as well as external recipients (e.g. Internet servers) can be used as targets. To monitor the inter-application information flow, *TaintDroid* [15] is used. In order to be able to monitor communication with Internet servers as well, YAASE also modifies the methods to establish Internet connections at a kernel level. This way, YAASE is always informed about the destination of any connection. As soon as a data transfer to an app via IPC or to an Internet server is detected that violates the privacy requirements of a user, any transferred data is concealed. However, YAASE provides no protection especially focused on Bluetooth devices.

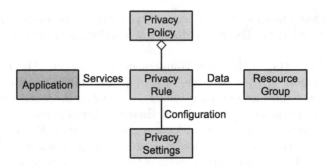

Fig. 3. Simplified representation of the Privacy Policy Model (untrusted components are shaded red and trusted components are shaded green) [based on [55,58]]. (Color figure online)

6   A Permission Model for Smartbands

None of the analyzed related work is applicable to restrict access to data from Smartbands as their permissions are too coarse. Moreover, they lack modular expandability. As a result, they quickly become obsolete as they cannot adapt to the privacy challenges originating from new device or data types. The **P**rivacy **M**anagement **P**latform (*PMP*) [53,58,59] provides these features. In addition, the PMP provides support for the connection of Smart Devices to Smartphones [63].

To this end, we add two components to the PMP: the *Smartband Resource Group* and the *Internet Resource Group*. These components enable the PMP to provide data gathered by Smartbands to apps in a privacy-aware manner and also restrict the spreading of sensitive data via the Internet. In the following, we introduce the **P**rivacy **P**olicy **M**odel (*PPM*), which forms the core of the PMP, and describe how we adapt it to the smart band setting (see Sect. 6.1). Then, we outline the mode of operation of the PMP (see Sect. 6.2). Finally, we present the concept of our two extensions (see Sects. 6.3 and 6.4).

6.1   The Privacy Policy Model

The PPM associates apps with data sources or system functions (labeled as *Resource Groups*). In the PPM, an app is subdivided in its *Features*. For each Feature must be specified, which data or system functions are accessed by it. An interface through which an app can interact with a Resource Group—i.e., access its data or functions—has to be defined for each group. In the *Privacy Rules*, the user specifies which Features of an app should be deactivated to reduce the usage of data or system functions. S/he can also refine any Privacy Rule by adding *Privacy Settings*, e.g., to reduce the accuracy of a Resource Group's data. The set of all Privacy Rules constitutes the *Privacy Policy*. The PPM assumes that apps are untrusted components, while Resource Groups are provided by trusted parties. The simplified model is shown in Fig. 3 as a UML-like class diagram. Further information on PPM can be found in the respective literature [58].

Fig. 4. Architecture of Resource Groups [55].

Only Resource Groups are of interest for the reminder of this work. Figure 4 provides insight into the architecture of a Resource Group. Each Resource Group defines an interface (**IResource**) and descriptors, how the provided data can be protected. The actual implementation of the interface is given in so-called *Resources*. Similar Resources can be bundled in a mutual Resource Group. This way, many alternative implementation variants for the interface can be provided. For instance, a *Location* Resource Group might provide a single method to retrieve the current location of the user. This method is implemented in two different ways, once via the GPS and once via the Cell-ID. Depending on the available hardware, user settings, and so forth, the Resource Group selects the appropriate Resource, when an app requests the data. Moreover, that Resource Group could define an *Accuracy* Privacy Setting that allows the user to define how accurate the location data is, i.e., up to how many meters the actual location should deviate from his or her current location. Of course, s/he can also completely prohibit access to the Resource Group for a certain app.

6.2 The Privacy Management Platform

The PMP is a privacy system that implements the PPM. Due to the structure of the PPM, the PMP has two characteristics that are very advantageous for work:

(a) On the one hand, the PMP is **modularly expandable**. This means that additional Resource Groups as well as Resources can be added at runtime. Therefore even the latest device models (by adding Resources) and completely new types of devices or sensors (by adding Resource Groups) are supported automatically by the PMP.

(b) On the other hand, the PMP supports **fine-grained access control**. Each Resource Group specifies its own Privacy Settings. These settings correspond to the requirements of the respective device. This allows users not only to turn a device or sensor on and off to protect their private data, but also to add numerical or textual restrictions. For example, a Location Resource Group may have a numeric Privacy Setting that can be used to reduce the accuracy of location data. Another example is an Internet Resource Group which provides a textual Privacy Setting to specify to which addresses an app is allowed to send data to.

To attain these properties, the PMP is an intermediate layer between the application layer and the actual application platform. For the sake of simplicity, the PMP can be seen as an interface to the application platform itself. Figure 5 shows the implementation model of the PMP in a condensed representation.

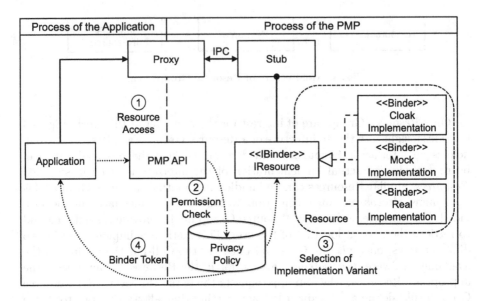

Fig. 5. Simplified implementation model of the Privacy Management Platform [55].

First, an app requests access to data sources or system functions—i. e., to a Resource Group—via the *PMP API* (1). The PMP checks whether this request complies with the Privacy Rules in the Privacy Policy (2). These rules also stipulate the restrictions (Privacy Setting) which apply to the respective app. When access is granted, a suitable implementation (i. e., Resource) is selected within the requested Resource Group (3). For each Resource, the PMP also has two fake implementations (*Cloak Implementation* and *Mock Implementation*) which provide only anonymized or fully randomized data. The proper implementation of the selected Resource is then linked to the *IBinder* interface as a *Binder*[1]. The PMP forwards a *Binder Token* to the requesting app (4).

Android's *Binder Framework* manages the actual access to a Resource: The IBinder interface of a Resource is materialized as a so-called *Stub*. *Proxy* components realize the interprocess communication (*IPC*) via which an app can pull data from these Stubs. Without the corresponding Binder Token, an app cannot communicate with a Stub. This ensures that any data request must be made via the PMP. So, the PMP is able to verify that each request complies with the Privacy Policy. Since all Resource Groups are implemented as subpackages of the PMP and run in the same process, they are executed in a mutual sandbox. In this way, the PMP can interact directly with Resource Groups.

These features qualify the PMP for our approach towards a privacy mechanism for Smartband apps. To achieve this goal, two novel Resource Groups are required, (*a*) a Resource Group for Smartbands that restricts access to the various data types of these devices (see Sect. 6.3), and (*b*) a Resource Group that

---

[1] See https://developer.android.com/reference/android/os/Binder.html.

restricts the data transfer of Smartband apps to the Internet (see Sect. 6.4). The specifications for these Resource groups are listed below.

6.3   Smartband Resource Group

The Smartband Resource Group must provide a unified interface to any Smartband model, including Smart Watches and related devices. For this reason, the interface is designed as a superset of data access operations supported by most of these devices. This includes access to personal data (e.g., age or name), health-related data (e.g., heart rate or blood sugar level), activity data (e.g., acceleration or orientation), and location data. Besides these receiving operations, most Smartbands have a small display for displaying short messages as well. The Smartband Resource Group also defines a send operation to display messages on the Smartband. However, not every Smartband model supports each of these operations. This has to be handled by the Resource implementing these functions for the respective Smartband model. The `UnsupportedOperationException` is introduced for this purpose. This exception is automatically caught and handled by the PMP, e.g., by passing mock data to the app.

The Smartband Resource Group defines several fine-grained Privacy Settings to restrict access to the data provided by a Smartband. Basically, there is a bivalent Privacy Setting for each type of data, via which the respective data access must be granted or denied. That way, the user can decide which app is allowed to access which data from the Smartband.

As already mentioned, this feature alone is a significant advance over the state of the art because Android supports only one Bluetooth permission for all types of devices and data—not to mention the fact that users cannot see whether an app needs this permission at all. Moreover, the Smartband Resource Group provides additional Privacy Settings for certain types of data. For example, the accuracy of location data can be reduced. In addition, any data source in the Smartband Resource Group can be replaced by a mocked implementation. All mock values are within a realistic range, so apps can't tell the difference.

Furthermore, Smartbands that provide location data can be integrated as additional Resources into the existing *Location Resource Group* as introduced in our previous work [51]. This allows the PMP to switch between the available resources if required (e.g., if the location data of the Smartband is more accurate than the location provided by the Smartphone).

6.4   Internet Resource Group

The Internet Resource Group provides a simplified interface for sending data to and receiving data from a network resource (e.g., a back-end server). Both functions essentially have two parameters, a destination address and the actual payload. The payload parameter is also used to store the response of the network resource. In the context of Smartband apps, such a simplified interface is sufficient. In order to support apps that require a lot of interactions with network

16   C. Stach

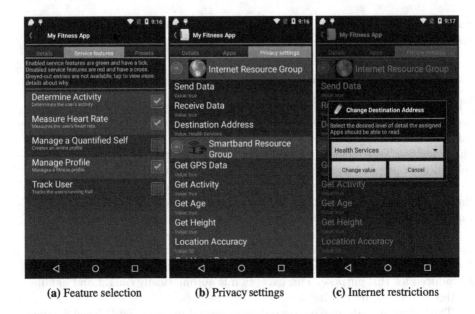

(a) Feature selection   (b) Privacy settings   (c) Internet restrictions

Fig. 6. PMP-based permission configuration [55].

resources, this interface can be extended by further generic I/O functions (e.g., to support several network protocols).

Similar to the Smartband Resource Group, the Internet Resource Group also defines bivalent Privacy Settings for both I/O functions. The user can decide for each app separately whether s/he wants to allow this app to send data to and/or receive data from the Internet. In addition, the permitted destination addresses can also be restricted. Theoretically, it is possible to do this via a textual Privacy Setting which indicates addresses to trusted network resources. However, the user's attention is limited and such a fine-grained address selection overburdens him or her [9]. For this reason, the Internet Resource Group categorizes addresses into different domains, such as the health domain or a domain for location-based services. There is also a category "public" which does not restrict the permitted destination addresses at all. In this manner, the user can see which domain a certain type of app should have access to. For experts however, the Internet Resource Group can still provide such a textual Privacy Setting described above to fine-adjust the permissible address space.

7   Prototypical Implementation

To verify the applicability of our approach, we have implemented a basic fitness app in addition to the two Resource Groups as described in Sects. 6.3 and 6.4. The fitness app creates a local user profile, including age, height, and weight. Workout data is collected by the Smartband's motion sensors (e.g., to determine current activities) as well as health data (e.g., the heart rate). These data are supplemented by location data from the Smartband to detect popular workout locations. To share this data with others (e.g., with an insurance company to document a healthy lifestyle) or to create a quantified self, this data can be uploaded to an online account.

The fitness app defines five Features that can be individually deactivated by the PMP. Once the app is installed, the PMP displays all these Features and the user can make an initial selection (see Fig. 6a). For example, a user wants to use the fitness app to record his or her workout progress in a local profile, only. However, the app should not track his or her locations in this process and by no means any data should be leaked to the Internet. This selection predefines which service quality the user can expect from the app. To find out what permissions are required for each Feature, the PMP can display additional information.

This interface via which apps are able to interact with the respective Resource Groups is described in the Android Interface Definition Language (AIDL). Listing 1 shows such an interface definition for the Smartband Resource Group in excerpts[2].

```
1   interface SmartbandResource {
2
3       // access to personal data
4       int getAge();
5       ...
6       // access to workout data
7       int getHeartRate();
8       ...
9       // access to location data
10      Location getLocation();
11      ...
12
13  }
```

List. 1. Interface Definition for the Smartband Resource Group in AIDL (excerpt) [55].

In addition, the user is able to adapt the Privacy Rules from a Resource Group's point of view as well. To do this, all Resource Groups requested by a respective app are listed together with the Privacy Settings defined by them (see Fig. 6b). Bivalent Privacy Settings such as "Send Data" can be switched on and off directly by simply clicking on them. For textual and numerical Privacy Settings such as "Location Accuracy", the user can enter new values in an input mask with a text field. Enumeration Privacy Settings such as "Admissible Destination Address" open an input mask with a selection box (see Fig. 6c). If the selected Privacy Settings are too restrictive for a particular Feature, the PMP informs the user that this Feature had to be deactivated due to conflicting Privacy Settings.

---

[2] The data type Location is not supported by AIDL. Additional type definitions are required to compile this interface definition.

The PMP introduces the so-called *Resource Group Information Set* (*RGIS*) to define Privacy Settings for Resource Groups. Like the Android *App Manifest*, this file contains the metadata required by the PMP about a Resource Group. Listing 2 shows an excerpt of the RGIS Privacy Settings definition for the Internet Resource Group. As can be seen in that listing, each Privacy Setting consists mainly of a unique identifier, a valid range of values, and a human-readable description. The PMP reads these XML files to compile the configuration dialogs for each Resource Group (see Fig. 6b).

```
1  <?xml version="1.0" encoding="UTF-8"?>
2  <resourceGroupInformationSet>
3    <resourceGroupInformation identifier="internet">
4      <name>Internet</name>
5      <description>Manages any network
       ↪  connections.</description>
6    </resourceGroupInformation>
7    <privacySettings>
8      <privacySetting
9          identifier="sendData"
10         validValueDescription="'true', 'false'">
11       <name>Send Data</name>
12       <description>Allows apps to send out data.</description>
13     </privacySetting>
14     <privacySetting
15         identifier="destinationAddress"
16         validValues="'PRIVATE', 'HEALTH', 'LOCATION',
       ↪     'PUBLIC'">
17       <name>Destination Address</name>
18       <description>Restricts destination
       ↪   address.</description>
19     </privacySetting>
20     ...
21   </privacySettings>
22 </resourceGroupInformationSet>
```

List. 2. Resource Group Information Set for the Internet Resource Group (excerpt) [55].

While the Feature selection is more suitable for normal users, the direct configuration of Privacy Settings is intended for fine-tuning by experienced users. According to the selected Features and the configuration of the Privacy Settings, the PMP adapts the program flow of an app, binds the required Resources, and carries out the configured anonymization operations. The user can adjust all settings at runtime, e.g., to activate additional Features. Neither apps nor Resource Groups need to deal with these data or program flow changes.

8 Assessment

As shown by prevailing studies, mobile platforms have to face novel challenges concerning the privacy-aware processing of data from Smartbands [19,42].

Table 2. Comparison of privacy systems for mobile platforms [based on [51, 52, 58]].

System	Feature				
	[R_1]	[R_2]	[R_3]	[R_4]	[R_5]
Android	✗	(✓)	✗	✗	✗
Apex	✗	✗	✓	✓	✗
AppFence	(✓)	✗	✓	✗	✗
AppGuard	✗	✗	✓	✓	✗
AUDACIOUS	✓	✓	✗	✓	✗
Aurasium	✓	✓	✓	✗	✓
CRêPE	✓	✓	✓	✓	✗
Data-Sluice	✗	✗	✓	✗	✓
Dr. Android & Mr. Hide	✓	✓	✗	✗	✗
IacDroid	✗	✓	✓	✗	✓
MockDroid	✗	✗	✓	✗	✗
Privacy Protector	✗	✗	✗	✗	✗
RetroSkeleton	(✓)	✓	✗	(✓)	(✓)
SEAF	✗	✗	✓	(✓)	✓
Sorbet	✓	✗	✗	✗	✗
YAASE	✓	✗	✓	✗	✗
PMP	✓	✓	✓	✓	✓

Since Android permissions are based on technical functions of a Smartphone, there is only a single generic BLUETOOTH permission restricting access to any kind of Bluetooth devices including headphones, Smartbands, and even medical devices.

On the contrary, our approach introduces a more *data-oriented permission model*. In this way the user is able to select specifically which data or function of a Smartband an app should have access to. Moreover, the PPM, which is the basis of our model, supports not only two-valued permission settings (grant and deny) but also numerical or textual constraints. Thereby, it enables a **fine-grained access control**, which is essentially for devices such as Smartbands dealing with a lot of different sensitive data ([R_1]). In addition, our model is **extendable** ([R_2]). That is, new devices can be added at runtime as Resources and are immediately available for any app. In conclusion, due to these three key features our approach solves the privacy challenges of Smartband apps. Any privacy rule can be **changed at runtime** ([R_3]). Moreover, due to the PPM, a *context can be added to each rule* in order to define a scope of app ([R_4]). Finally, the user is included in the configuration of the PMP all the time and s/he receives **feedback** so that s/he is able to express his or her privacy requirements in the PPM ([R_5]). A side-by-side comparison of PMP and the related work introduced Sect. 5 is shown in Table 2.

In addition, our approach also provides a solution for another big challenge in the context of Smartband apps: The **interoperability of devices** from different vendors is low. This means in effect, that each device uses its proprietary data format for the data interchange with an app [10]. So, each app supports a limited number of Smartbands, only. With our Smartband Resource Group, an app developer has to program against its given unified interface and the PMP selects the appropriate Resource which handles the data interchange.

Therefore, the usage of the PMP is particularly useful in an health context [60,62], as early prototypes of health apps have shown [20,54]. However, our approach is only able to protect the user's privacy as long as his or her data is processed on the Smartphone. Once the data is sent out, the user is no longer in control. Since many apps fall back on online services for data processing [8,64], it is part of future work to deal with this problem. In the following section, we give a brief outlook on a possible solution for this problem.

9   Conclusion and Future Work

The improvements in the area of the Internet of Things in recent years have been tremendous. Especially concerning wearable Smart Devices such as Smartbands, there are numerous innovations. An increasing number of sensors are integrated in Smartbands, enabling them to accurately capture the user's context. In addition to capture the user's location, these devices are also able to recognize activities as well as monitor health data. This makes innovative fitness and health apps possible by gather and analyzing all of these data in order to create a quantified self. As the processed data are highly sensitive, these apps require novel privacy mechanisms adapted to the latest innovations in the area of Smartbands.

As neither the prevailing privacy mechanisms applied in the current mobile platforms nor the latest research prototypes fully comply these special requirements, we come up with two extensions for the Privacy Management Platform (PMP) dealing especially with Smartband apps. One of these extensions does not only secure but also facilitate the connection to and data transmission from Bluetooth devices. The other one makes date transmissions to the Internet privacy-aware. This gives users full control over the access to and processing of private data by Smartband apps, as evaluation results show.

However, Smartband apps often do a lot of data processing and analyzing not directly on the user-controlled Smart Devices. Rather, most of the computation takes place at external computing clusters hosted by mainly unknown third-parties. These data stream processing systems have access to a large number of data sources and resources. Due to this huge amount of data and computing power, they can derive much knowledge about the users. Local privacy settings on the Smart Devices of the users restrict the knowledge extraction of these systems only slightly. Therefore, in addition to an effective privacy system for Smart Devices such as the PMP, an affiliated privacy system for stream processing systems is required. As *PATRON* [56,57] is highly effective in this area, future works has to investigate how privacy rules for the PMP can be deployed to PATRON. An initial step in this direction is the ACCESSORS permission model [60].

Acknowledgments. This paper is part of the PATRON research project which is commissioned by the Baden-Württemberg Stiftung gGmbH. The authors would like to thank the BW-Stiftung for the funding of this research.

References

1. Albaghli, R., Anderson, K.M.: A vision for heart rate health through wearables. In: Proceedings of the 2016 ACM International Joint Conference on Pervasive and Ubiquitous Computing: Adjunct, UbiComp 2016, pp. 1101–1105 (2016)
2. Alpers, S., Pieper, M., Wagner, M.: Herausforderungen bei der Entwicklung von Anwendungen zum Selbstdatenschutz. In: Informatik 2017: Digitale Kulturen, Tagungsband der 47. Jahrestagung der Gesellschaft für Informatik e.V. (GI), 25.9-29.9.2017, Chemnitz. LNI, vol. 275, pp. 1061–1072 (2017). (in German)
3. Backes, M., Gerling, S., Hammer, C., Maffei, M., von Styp-Rekowsky, P.: App-Guard – enforcing user requirements on Android apps. In: Piterman, N., Smolka, S.A. (eds.) TACAS 2013. LNCS, vol. 7795, pp. 543–548. Springer, Heidelberg (2013). https://doi.org/10.1007/978-3-642-36742-7_39
4. Banuri, H., et al.: An Android runtime security policy enforcement framework. Pers. Ubiquit. Comput. **16**(6), 631–641 (2012)
5. Barrera, D., Kayacik, H.G., van Oorschot, P.C., Somayaji, A.: A methodology for empirical analysis of permission-based security models and its application to Android. In: Proceedings of the 17th ACM Conference on Computer and Communications Security, CCS 2010, pp. 73–84 (2010)
6. Barrera, D., Van Oorschot, P.: Secure software installation on Smartphones. IEEE Secur. Priv. **9**(3), 42–48 (2011)
7. Beresford, A.R., Rice, A., Skehin, N., Sohan, R.: MockDroid: trading privacy for application functionality on Smartphones. In: Proceedings of the 12th Workshop on Mobile Computing Systems and Applications, HotMobile 2011, pp. 49–54 (2011)
8. Bitsaki, M.: An integrated mHealth solution for enhancing patients' health online. In: Lacković, I., Vasic, D. (eds.) 6th European Conference of the International Federation for Medical and Biological Engineering. IP, vol. 45, pp. 695–698. Springer, Cham (2015). https://doi.org/10.1007/978-3-319-11128-5_173
9. Böhme, R., Grossklags, J.: The security cost of cheap user interaction. In: Proceedings of the 2011 New Security Paradigms Workshop, NSPW 2011, pp. 67–82 (2011)
10. Chan, M., Estève, D., Fourniols, J.Y., Escriba, C., Campo, E.: Smart wearable systems: current status and future challenges. Artif. Intell. Med. **56**(3), 137–156 (2012)
11. Conti, M., Nguyen, V.T.N., Crispo, B.: CRePE: context-related policy enforcement for Android. In: Burmester, M., Tsudik, G., Magliveras, S., Ilić, I. (eds.) ISC 2010. LNCS, vol. 6531, pp. 331–345. Springer, Heidelberg (2011). https://doi.org/10.1007/978-3-642-18178-8_29
12. Conti, M., Zachia-Zlatea, I., Crispo, B.: Mind how you answer me!: transparently authenticating the user of a Smartphone when answering or placing a call. In: Proceedings of the 6th ACM Symposium on Information, Computer and Communications Security, ASIACCS 2011, pp. 249–259 (2011)

13. Davis, B., Chen, H.: RetroSkeleton: retrofitting Android apps. In: Proceeding of the 11th Annual International Conference on Mobile Systems, Applications, and Services, MobiSys 2013, pp. 181–192 (2013)

14. Davis, B., Sanders, B., Khodaverdian, A., Chen, H.: I-ARM-Droid: a rewriting framework for in-app reference monitors for Android applications. In: Proceedings of the 2012 IEEE Conference on Mobile Security Technologies, MoST 2012, pp. 28:1–28:9 (2012)

15. Enck, W., et al.: TaintDroid: an information-flow tracking system for realtime privacy monitoring on Smartphones. In: Proceedings of the 9th USENIX Conference on Operating Systems Design and Implementation, OSDI 2010, pp. 393–407 (2010)

16. Felt, A.P., Egelman, S., Finifter, M., Akhawe, D., Wagner, D.: How to ask for permission. In: Proceedings of the 7th USENIX Conference on Hot Topics in Security, HotSec 2012, pp. 1–6 (2012)

17. Felt, A.P., Ha, E., Egelman, S., Haney, A., Chin, E., Wagner, D.: Android permissions: user attention, comprehension, and behavior. In: Proceedings of the Eighth Symposium on Usable Privacy and Security, SOUPS 2012, pp. 3:1–3:14 (2012)

18. Fragkaki, E., Bauer, L., Jia, L., Swasey, D.: Modeling and enhancing Android's permission system. In: Foresti, S., Yung, M., Martinelli, F. (eds.) ESORICS 2012. LNCS, vol. 7459, pp. 1–18. Springer, Heidelberg (2012). https://doi.org/10.1007/978-3-642-33167-1_1

19. Funk, C.: IoT Research - Smartbands. Technical report, Kaspersky Lab, March 2015. https://securelist.com/analysis/publications/69412/iot-research-smartbands/

20. Giebler, C., Stach, C.: Datenschutzmechanismen für Gesundheitsspiele am Beispiel von Secure Candy Castle. In: Tagungsband der 15. GI-Fachtagung Datenbanksysteme für Business, Technologie und Web, BTW 2017, pp. 311–320 (2017). (in German)

21. Google Inc.: Permissions Overview, May 2018. https://developer.android.com/guide/topics/permissions

22. Grace, M., Zhou, Y., Wang, Z., Jiang, X.: Systematic detection of capability leaks in stock Android Smartphones. In: Proceedings of the 2012 Network and Distributed System Security Symposium, NDSS 2012, pp. 7/5:1–7/5:15 (2012)

23. Guo, H.: Privacy Protector (No root), February 2012. https://play.google.com/store/apps/details?id=net.houzuo.android.privacyprotector

24. Hornyack, P., Han, S., Jung, J., Schechter, S., Wetherall, D.: These aren't the droids you're looking for: retrofitting Android to protect data from imperious applications. In: Proceedings of the 18th ACM Conference on Computer and Communications Security, CCS 2011, pp. 639–652 (2011)

25. Hsu, H.H., Peng, W.J., Shih, T.K., Pai, T.W., Man, K.L.: Smartphone indoor localization with accelerometer and gyroscope. In: Proceedings of the 2014 17th International Conference on Network-Based Information Systems, NBiS 2014, pp. 465–469 (2014)

26. Jeon, J., et al.: Dr. Android and Mr. Hide: fine-grained permissions in Android applications. In: Proceedings of the Second ACM Workshop on Security and Privacy in Smartphones and Mobile Devices, SPSM 2012, pp. 3–14 (2012)

27. Jiang, W., Yin, Z.: Human activity recognition using wearable sensors by deep convolutional neural networks. In: Proceedings of the 23rd ACM International Conference on Multimedia, MM 2015, pp. 1307–1310 (2015)

28. Kang, J., Kim, D., Kim, H., Huh, J.H.: Analyzing unnecessary permissions requested by Android apps based on users' opinions. In: Rhee, K.-H., Yi, J.H. (eds.) WISA 2014. LNCS, vol. 8909, pp. 68–79. Springer, Cham (2015). https://doi.org/10.1007/978-3-319-15087-1_6

29. Khatoon, A., Corcoran, P.: Android permission system and user privacy – a review of concept and approaches. In: Proceedings of the 2017 IEEE 7th International Conference on Consumer Electronics - Berlin, ICCE-Berlin 2017, pp. 153–158 (2017)

30. Khorakhun, C., Bhatti, S.N.: mHealth through quantified-self: a user study. In: Proceedings of the 2015 17th International Conference on E-health Networking, Application & Services, HealthCom 2015, pp. 329–335 (2015)

31. Kitagawa, M., et al.: Market share: final PCs, ultramobiles and mobile phones, all countries, 1Q18 update. Gartner, Inc., Technical report (2018)

32. Knighten, J., McMillan, S., Chambers, T., Payton, J.: Recognizing social gestures with a wrist-worn Smartband. In: Proceedings of the 2015 IEEE International Conference on Pervasive Computing and Communication Workshops, WristSense 2015, pp. 544–549 (2015)

33. Knöll, M.: "On the top of high towers ..." discussing locations in a mobile health game for diabetics. In: Proceedings of the 2010 IADIS International Conference Game and Entertainment Technologies, MCCSIS 2010, pp. 61–68 (2010)

34. Knöll, M., Moar, M.: On the importance of locations in therapeutic serious games: review on current health games and how they make use of the urban landscape. In: Proceedings of the 2011 5th International Conference on Pervasive Computing Technologies for Healthcare and Workshops, PervasiveHealth 2011, pp. 538–545 (2011)

35. Lee, M., Lee, K., Shim, J., Cho, S.j., Choi, J.: Security threat on wearable services: empirical study using a commercial Smartband. In: Proceedings of the IEEE International Conference on Consumer Electronics-Asia, ICCE-Asia 2016, pp. 1–5 (2016)

36. Leontiadis, I., Efstratiou, C., Picone, M., Mascolo, C.: Don't kill my ads!: balancing privacy in an ad-supported mobile application market. In: Proceedings of the Twelfth Workshop on Mobile Computing Systems & Applications, HotMobile 2012, pp. 2:1–2:6 (2012)

37. Martin, D., Vicente, O., Vicente, S., Ballesteros, J., Maynar, M.: I will prescribe you an app. In: Proceedings of the 2014 Summer Simulation Multiconference, SummerSim 2014, pp. 58:1–58:8 (2014)

38. Mayfield, J., Jagielski, K.: FTC report on Internet of Things urges companies to adopt best practices to address consumer privacy and security risks. Technical report, Federal Trade Commission, January 2015. https://www.ftc.gov/news-events/press-releases/2015/01/ftc-report-internet-things-urges-companies-adopt-best-practices

39. Mazzoleni, P., Crispo, B., Sivasubramanian, S., Bertino, E.: XACML policy integration algorithms. ACM Trans. Inform. Syst. Secur. 11(1), 4:1–4:29 (2008)

40. Mohamed, I., Patel, D.: Android vs iOS security: a comparative study. In: Proceedings of the 2015 12th International Conference on Information Technology - New Generations, ITNG 2015, pp. 725–730 (2015)

41. Nauman, M., Khan, S., Zhang, X.: Apex: extending Android permission model and enforcement with user-defined runtime constraints. In: Proceedings of the 5th ACM Symposium on Information, Computer and Communications Security, ASIACCS 2010, pp. 328–332 (2010)

42. Patel, M.: The security and privacy of wearable health and fitness devices. Technical report, IBM Security Intelligence, September 2015. https://securityintelligence.
com/the-security-and-privacy-of-wearable-health-and-fitness-devices/

43. Pombo, N., Garcia, N.M.: ubiSleep: an ubiquitous sensor system for sleep monitoring. In: Proceedings of the 2016 IEEE 12th International Conference on Wireless
and Mobile Computing, Networking and Communications, WiMob 2016, pp. 1–4
(2016)

44. Reeder, B., David, A.: Health at hand: a systematic review of smart watch uses
for health and wellness. J. Biomed. Inform. **63**, 269–276 (2016)

45. Ringer, T., Grossman, D., Roesner, F.: AUDACIOUS: user-driven access control
with unmodified operating systems. In: Proceedings of the 2016 ACM SIGSAC
Conference on Computer and Communications Security, CCS 2016, pp. 204–216
(2016)

46. Russello, G., Crispo, B., Fernandes, E., Zhauniarovich, Y.: YAASE: yet another
Android security extension. In: Proceedings of the 2011 IEEE Third International
Conference on Privacy, Security, Risk and Trust and 2011 IEEE Third International
Conference on Social Computing, PASSAT 2011, pp. 1033–1040 (2011)

47. Saracino, A., Martinelli, F., Alboreto, G., Dini, G.: Data-Sluice: fine-grained traffic
control for Android application. In: Proceedings of the 2016 IEEE Symposium on
Computers and Communication, ISCC 2016, pp. 702–709 (2016)

48. Sbîrlea, D., Burke, M.G., Guarnieri, S., Pistoia, M., Sarkar, V.: Automatic detection of inter-application permission leaks in Android applications. IBM J. Res.
Dev. **57**(6), 10:1–10:12 (2013)

49. Shahmohammadi, F., Hosseini, A., King, C.E., Sarrafzadeh, M.: Smartwatch
based activity recognition using active learning. In: Proceedings of the Second
IEEE/ACM International Conference on Connected Health: Applications, Systems
and Engineering Technologies, CHASE 2017, pp. 321–329 (2017)

50. Siewiorek, D.: Generation Smartphone. IEEE Spectr. **49**(9), 54–58 (2012)

51. Stach, C.: How to assure privacy on Android phones and devices? In: Proceedings
of the 2013 IEEE 14th International Conference on Mobile Data Management,
MDM 2013, pp. 350–352 (2013)

52. Stach, C.: Wie funktioniert Datenschutz auf Mobilplattformen? In: Informatik
2013: Informatik angepasst an Mensch, Organisation und Umwelt, Tagungsband
der 43. Jahrestagung der Gesellschaft für Informatik e.V. (GI), 16.9-20.9.2013,
Koblenz. LNI, vol. 220, pp. 2072–2086 (2013). (in German)

53. Stach, C.: How to deal with third party apps in a privacy system – the PMP
Gatekeeper. In: Proceedings of the 2015 IEEE 16th International Conference on
Mobile Data Management, MDM 2015, pp. 167–172 (2015)

54. Stach, C.: Secure Candy Castle – a prototype for privacy-aware mHealth apps.
In: Proceedings of the 2016 IEEE 17th International Conference on Mobile Data
Management, MDM 2016, pp. 361–364 (2016)

55. Stach, C.: Big brother is smart watching you: privacy concerns about health and
fitness applications. In: Proceedings of the 4th International Conference on Information Systems Security and Privacy, ICISSP 2018, pp. 13–23 (2018)

56. Stach, C., et al.: PATRON – Datenschutz in Datenstromverarbeitungssystemen. In: Informatik 2017: Digitale Kulturen, Tagungsband
der 47. Jahrestagung der Gesellschaft für Informatik e.V. (GI), 25.9-
29.9.2017, Chemnitz. LNI, vol. 275, pp. 1085–1096 (2017). (in German)

57. Stach, C., Dürr, F., Mindermann, K., Palanisamy, S.M., Wagner, S.: How a pattern-based privacy system contributes to improve context recognition. In: Proceedings of the 2018 IEEE International Conference on Pervasive Computing and Communications Workshops, CoMoRea 2018, pp. 238–243 (2018)

58. Stach, C., Mitschang, B.: Privacy management for mobile platforms - a review of concepts and approaches. In: Proceedings of the 2013 IEEE 14th International Conference on Mobile Data Management, MDM 2013, pp. 305–313 (2013)

59. Stach, C., Mitschang, B.: Design and implementation of the Privacy Management Platform. In: Proceedings of the 2014 IEEE 15th International Conference on Mobile Data Management, MDM 2014, pp. 69–72 (2014)

60. Stach, C., Mitschang, B.: ACCESSORS: a data-centric permission model for the Internet of Things. In: Proceedings of the 4th International Conference on Information Systems Security and Privacy, ICISSP 2018, pp. 30–40 (2018)

61. Stach, C., Schlindwein, L.F.M.: Candy Castle – a prototype for pervasive health games. In: Proceedings of the 2012 IEEE International Conference on Pervasive Computing and Communications Workshops, PerCom 2012, pp. 501–503 (2012)

62. Stach, C., Steimle, F., Mitschang, B.: The Privacy Management Platform: an enabler for device interoperability and information security in mHealth applications. In: Proceedings of the 11th International Conference on Health Informatics, HEALTHINF 2018, pp. 27–38 (2018)

63. Stach, C., Steimle, F., Franco da Silva, A.C.: TIROL: the extensible interconnectivity layer for mHealth applications. In: Damaševičius, R., Mikašytė, V. (eds.) ICIST 2017. CCIS, vol. 756, pp. 190–202. Springer, Cham (2017). https://doi.org/10.1007/978-3-319-67642-5_16

64. Steimle, F., Wieland, M., Mitschang, B., Wagner, S., Leymann, F.: Extended provisioning, security and analysis techniques for the ECHO health data management system. Computing **99**(2), 183–201 (2017)

65. Wakabayashi, D.: Freed from the iPhone, the Apple watch finds a medical purpose. The New York Times **12**(27), B1 (2017)

66. Weiser, M.: The computer for the 21st century. Sci. Am. **265**(3), 94–105 (1991)

67. Wijaya, R., Setijadi, A., Mengko, T.L., Mengko, R.K.L.: Heart rate data collecting using smart watch. In: Proceedings of the 2014 IEEE 4th International Conference on System Engineering and Technology, ICSET 2014, pp. 1–3 (2014)

68. Xie, H., Gu, T., Tao, X., Lu, J.: A reliability-augmented particle filter for magnetic fingerprinting based indoor localization on Smartphone. IEEE Trans. Mob. Comput. **15**(8), 1877–1892 (2016)

69. Xu, R., Saïdi, H., Anderson, R.: Aurasium: practical policy enforcement for Android applications. In: Proceedings of the 21st USENIX Security Symposium, pp. 539–552 (2012)

70. Ye, H., Gu, T., Tao, X., Lu, J.: Scalable floor localization using barometer on Smartphone. Wirel. Commun. Mob. Comput. **16**(16), 2557–2571 (2016)

71. Zhang, D., Wang, R., Lin, Z., Guo, D., Cao, X.: IacDroid: preventing inter-app communication capability leaks in Android. In: Proceedings of the 2016 IEEE Symposium on Computers and Communication, ISCC 2016, pp. 443–449 (2016)

All links were last followed on June 1, 2018.

Touch and Move: Incoming Call User Authentication

Aleksandr Eremin[(✉)], Konstantin Kogos[(✉)],
and Yana Valatskayte[(✉)]

Institute of Cyber Intelligence Systems, NRNU MEPhI,
Moscow 115409, Russian Federation
ave_38@mail.ru, kgkogos@mephi.ru,
yana.valatskayte@gmail.com

Abstract. This paper presents two methods of implicit authentication during answering an incoming call based on user behavior biometrics. Such methods allow to increase usability of authentication against common PIN or graphical password. Also, a concept of authentication system based on presented methods is proposed. The paper shows that user's touch dynamics and movement of the hand towards the ear when accepting the call provide all necessary information for authentication and there is no need for user to enter a PIN or graphical password.

Keywords: Implicit authentication · Hand movement · Touch dynamics · Incoming call authentication · Behavioral biometrics

1 Introduction

Nowadays we can't imagine our life without smartphones. These devices have become more than personal assistants. Practically all that a person could ever imagine or wish can be done or taught how to with the help of a smartphone. The data we enter or store there is our digital portrait. A lot of data is sent via smartphones. Even with development of messengers we still make and receive calls and get or transfer sensitive data over it.

If an attacker seizes user's phone, he gets almost full access to all information that is of particular value for the user: personal communication and contacts, accounts on different services, including online banking, data on movements, photos, etc. In addition, an attacker is able to act on your behalf: make and answer calls, conduct correspondence in social networks and e-mail, etc. As Consumer Reports says, smartphone thefts rose from 1.6 to 3.1 million during one year [1]. Therefore it is becoming an increasingly urgent problem to provide mobile phone user authentication.

All authentication methods can be divided into three groups by the authentication factor used during authentication process [2]:

- the knowledge factor – something the user knows;
- the ownership factor – something the user has;
- the inheritance factor – something the user is.

© Springer Nature Switzerland AG 2019
P. Mori et al. (Eds.): ICISSP 2018, CCIS 977, pp. 26–39, 2019.
https://doi.org/10.1007/978-3-030-25109-3_2

The knowledge factor in mobile devices is represented by different passwords, patterns or combinations of points on a photo or a picture. Such methods are rather weak as users usually choose easy-memorized passwords or patterns or associate them with a shape or a letter they form on a screen [3].

Different peripheral devices that the owner uses with his phone introduce the ownership factor. These devices are smart watches, fitness trackers, Bluetooth headphones, etc. The idea of the method is rather obvious: if the phone is connected to the device, there is no reason to worry: the phone is near the owner. However, such method still cannot provide full protection of user's information on the phone.

Methods based on the inheritance factors are now gaining more and more popularity as it's difficult to steal or reproduce a factor that is a part of user's body or character. Yet this methods still requires additional user actions: take a photo, spell a phrase, and place a finger on a fingerprint scanner. Figure 1 [4] shows how these factors correspond with existing methods of mobile phone user authentication.

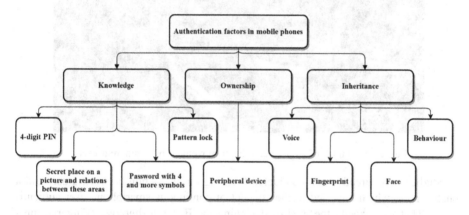

Fig. 1. Authentication factors in mobile phones.

Behavioral biometrics is of a special interest for us for several reasons. Unlike aforesaid factors, behavioral biometrics doesn't require additional actions from the user except his natural movements and actions: gait, keystrokes, and characteristic movements like picking up a phone.

This paper is an extended version of the one published in the Proceedings of 4th International Conference on Information Systems Security and Privacy [4]. In this paper we focused on getting more accurate results due to interval division in hand movement analysis. Also, a new authentication method based on touch dynamics and a concept of an authentication system is proposed for incoming call user authentication.

The main purpose of this research is to suggest new authentication methods based on behavioral biometrics and a concept of an authentication system using this methods.

The remainder of this paper is organized as follows. Section 2 contains an overview of existing approaches to behavioral biometrics and related work. Section 3 presents an incoming call authentication method based on user touch dynamics. Section 4 introduces a method based on hand movement analysis. Section 5 describes an authentication system based on these methods. Conclusions and further research are discussed in Sect. 6.

2 Related Work

Recent researches have already demonstrated that every person has their individual underscore of finger movement over a touch screen – it is called a «swipe». Figure 2 shows individual swipes of 7 users [5].

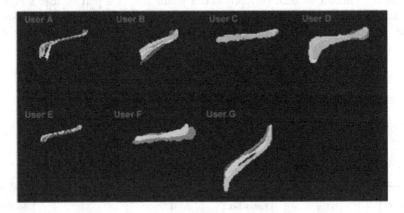

Fig. 2. Examples of over-screen finger movement by 7 different users.

Studies have already been conducted focusing on interaction between a user and a touch screen, which have led to the concept of continuous smartphone user authentication. That was exactly the goal of designing the FAST technology (Fingergestures Authentication System using Touchscreen) [5]. Apart from extracting data from a smartphone touch screen, FAST supplements and checks the data with the digital sensor glove that records phone-holding arm micromovements. The study involved the data collected from 40 users. The type I error corresponded to 0.13%, the type II error – to 4.66%.

There are also studies, the subject of which has been sensor dynamics while entering a password [6]. Main authentication indicators include password entering speed, screen contact points, and touch area. The experiment involved such machine learning methods as naive Bayes classifier, decision tree. 20 users participated. Overall, the error amounted to 3%.

In some cases there is a necessity to authenticate a user answering an incoming call. If a significant owner's loss takes place because of it, there is a need to protect such calls. For example, the bank assistant calls the depositor to check whether a strange transaction made from his account was actually made by depositor, not a thief. If a thief answers such call, he can easily confirm a transaction leaving the depositor and the bank without money.

Such a problem of user authentication can be solved by entering a PIN or a graphical password, but these solutions require additional actions from a user. In [7] it is shown how hand movement analysis can be used in user identification. The data needed for that is collected with built-in sensors of the smartphone. In this case there is no need for a user to enter anything; all necessary authentication information is being collected while user's hand with a phone is moving towards user's ear. That's why an authentication method without any extra user actions can be suggested providing authentication of a person answering an incoming call.

The problem of incoming call authentication was considered in [8]. In this paper, the researchers proposed to replace the input of the password with the characteristics of the hand movement when answering an incoming call. Data, as in previous works, was obtained from built-in sensors (accelerometer and orientation sensor). For user authentication, Dynamic Time Warping Distance and Dynamic Time Warping Similarity algorithms were used. The basic idea of this approach is to obtain the distance between the coordinates of the characteristics vector of the legitimate user and the coordinates of such vectors of the user in relation to which authentication is performed. The closer the vector of the current user to the legal user's vector, the more likely he is a legitimate user. Simplicity of this approach makes it easy to implement. Using the training sample of 10 people's 50 lifts of the phone, the system missed the attacker in 4.4% of cases, and the legal user was blocked in 9.3% of cases. These study shows that the movement of the hand when answering an incoming call is unique for each person.

In [9], "micromovements" of user's hand right after unlocking the smartphone are studied in order to identify a user. To receive data, built-in smartphone sensors (accelerometer, gyroscope, magnetometer, gravity sensor and orientation sensor) are used. In addition, a low-pass filter and a high-pass filter are applied to the data obtained from the accelerometer. Thus, 7 data sources are used. When the system receives USER_-PRESENT event, the data acquisition process starts. The data is obtained at intervals of 2, 4, 6, 8 and 10 s. Then the following features were calculated:

- mean;
- mean absolute deviation;
- median;
- standard error of the mean;
- standard deviation;
- skewness;
- kurtosis.

After this, feature vectors were formed, which were fed to the input of various algorithms of machine learning. As the goal of the research was to check the ability to identify a person, the classification problem was solved using the machine learning algorithm. The authors gained the following results: in 96% of cases the system correctly identified the user using the Random Forest algorithm.

The problem of a mobile phone user authentication when answering an incoming call has several limits and speciality:

- limited time to perform authentication (having no answer, the caller will simply "drop" the call);

- limited operational memory of the device;
- the method used must be simple and user-friendly.

Based on these limits, a method of authentication based on behavioural biometrics was proposed, in which the user would not need to perform any additional actions, except for accepting the call with a touch screen button or placing the phone to his ear, as he usually does answering an incoming call. These actions become a source of the behavioural biometrics data of the user.

We would like to focus your attention on the fact that only standard sensors (gyroscope, accelerometer, touch screen) are needed, and most of modern smartphones are equipped with these sensors.

3   Interaction with Touch Screen

On the ground of the above-mentioned, we can draw a conclusion that there exists a possibility to design a smartphone user authentication method involving characteristic over-screen finger movement based on behavioral biometrics.

Touch dynamics can be described as characteristics of inputs obtained from the touch screen while the user is interacting with the device. Touch dynamics characteristics can be described with a set of functions developed through the analysis of touch screen inputs.

3.1   Gaining and Processing Data

There are several over-screen finger movement parameters which a smartphone touch screen can easily measure:

- X-axis coordinates;
- Y-axis coordinates;
- finger movement time T.

These data allow for calculating values of characteristics which will be unique for every user.

A special application was designed to collect data on interaction between a user and a touch screen. The logic is the user is supposed to swipe in the necessary direction, and the relevant data on the way they touch the screen is sequentially collected.

The application features screens with tasks for the user that enable them to change activities while making the required movements. The tasks include entering of certain sequence of numbers, rotation of the smartphone, connection of screen areas, etc. The aim is to prevent the over-screen movements from being made automatically, which thus allows to collect sample data comprising movements that are closely akin to real ones.

Research conducted to design continuous smartphone user authentication, has outlined several features on the basis of the measured parameters. Those features could later help to draw a conclusion regarding a user's legitimacy.

In their study Mario Frank and his colleagues even evaluate efficiency [10] of the features they have used. Some results are depicted in the Table 1.

Also, a few indicators were added to achieve higher accuracy:

- the maximum speed;
- the X-axis and Y-axis coordinates of the movement vector;
- the X-axis and Y-axis coordinates of the vector that connects the first and the central points of contact;
- the X-axis and Y-axis coordinates of the vector that connects the central and the last points of contact;
- the magnitude of the vector that connects the first and the central points of contact;
- the magnitude of the vector that connects the central and the last points of contact.

Table 1. Features efficiency (example).

Rel. mutual information	Feature description
20.58%	Mid-stroke area covered
19.63%	20%-perc. pairwise velocity
17.28%	Mid-stroke pressure
11.06%	Direction of end-to-end line
10.32%	Stop x
10.15%	Start x
9.45%	Average direction
9.43%	Start y
8.84%	Average velocity
8.61%	Stop y
8.5%	Stroke duration
8.27%	Direct end-to-end distance
8.16%	Length of trajectory

3.2 Implementation

During the work on developing the swipe-based user authentication technique the following machine learning algorithms were involved and evaluated:

- One-Class SVM;
- Isolation Forest;
- Local Outlier Factor.

The training data involved data on 300 movement samples of each of the four types of a user's over-screen movement; the test data involved data on 300 movement samples of each of the four types of the user's over-screen movement as well as 30 movement samples of each of the four types of over-screen movement belonging to ten other users. All the participants touched the same smartphone for data to be collected with the single device. Prior to the beginning of the data collection, the objective of the study was described, and the demonstration of the experiment was held. Afterwards, all the collected data were analyzed, and the selected features were extracted from the input data.

Movements that included few points of contact, particularly less than five, were removed. Most of such movements appeared to be solitary clicks. Users make these movements by accident, and so they can complicate the training algorithm. Figure 3 demonstrates the number of points of interaction in every movement sample in the data set.

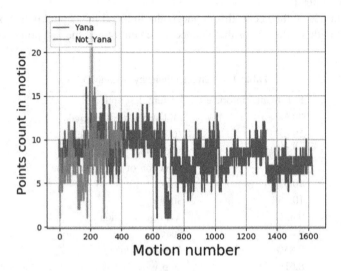

Fig. 3. Number of points of interaction in every data set movement sample.

3.3 Evaluation

The results obtained on the basis of the conducted experiments are shown in Table 2.

Table 2. Number of FRR and FAR errors.

Algorithm	Parameters used in training	Type I error	Type II error
One-Class SVM	nu: 0.155, gamma: 0.005	2%	9%
Isolation Forest	max_samples: 21, n_estimators: 1	2%	2%
Local Outlier Factor	nu: 0.241, gamma: 100	8%	3%

On the grounds of the analysis of the results used while applying the machine learning methods, the conclusion can be drawn that the Isolation Forest method is the most convenient for solving the problem of swipe-based user authentication.

4   Hand Movement

The analysis showed that the movement of the hand when answering an incoming call is unique for each person and the information about this movement can be used for user authentication. To perform it, it is necessary to obtain data from the sensors of the mobile phone, pre-process it and select features for learning the algorithm.

4.1   Sensors Used and Data Obtained

In order to describe the movement of the phone in space, it is necessary to obtain data from the sensors of the phone. An event is generated in the Android OS when a state of any sensor is changed. According to the Android documentation, each sensor generates such an event every 200 ms. This frequency is sufficient to obtain the required amount of data, even about a short movement, such as raising your hand with the phone towards your ear.

The following sensors were used:

- accelerometer (measures the acceleration in m/s^2, with which the phone moves on all three axes, including the force of gravity);
- gyro (measures the rotation rate of the phone in rad/s around each of the axes);
- magnetometer (measures the ambient geomagnetic field for all three axes in µT);
- orientation sensor (measures the degree of rotation around each of the three axes);
- gravity sensor (measures the force of attraction applied to the phone on all three axes).

All sensors generate data about the position of the phone in three axes: X, Y and Z, which are located as shown in Fig. 4 [4].

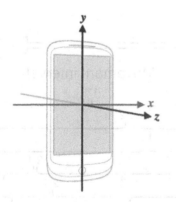

Fig. 4. Sensors' axes.

The received data is saved for further processing into files, one file for each sensor. These files are available only to the developed application.

The process of obtaining data is carried out for two seconds, since this interval is enough to place the phone to your ear.

4.2   Feature Extraction

Previous work [4] showed that the most informative features for the problems connected with phone movement are:

- mean;
- mean absolute deviation;
- median;
- standard error of the mean;
- standard deviation;
- skewness;
- kurtosis;
- the coordinates of the device at the beginning of the movement (when accepting the call);
- the coordinates of the device at the end of the movement (when the device is placed near the ear).

As the result, feature vector has the following structure (a concatenation of the features computed from different axes separately) [4]:

$$v = \left(\left[\bar{x}, \bar{y}, \bar{z}, MAD_x, MAD_y, MAD_z, \ldots \right] \left[\bar{x}, \bar{y}, \bar{z}, MAD_x, MAD_y, MAD_z, \ldots \right] \ldots \right) \quad (1)$$

Square brackets contain the features obtained from one sensor. The length of the vector is 135 (5 sensors, 3 coordinates, 9 features for every sensor).

As an attempt to increase accuracy, interval division was tested. That means that the movement interval was divided in different proportions as shown on Fig. 5 and the features are extracted from every sub-interval separately. This method was proposed in [7].

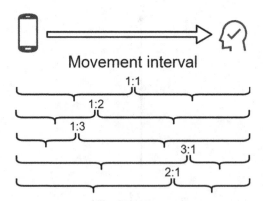

Fig. 5. Movement interval division.

4.3   Implementation

Since there are no data of other classes except the "legitimate user" class in the training sample, the problem being solved is a problem of anomaly detection. That is the reason to implement and evaluate next machine learning algorithms:

- One-Class SVM;
- Isolation Forest;
- One-Class Classifier [11].

During the testing, the above described algorithms of machine learning were compared by several parameters and a suitable algorithm for the proposed authentication method was chosen.

To evaluate the performance of algorithms we use following characteristics:

- FPR – false positive rate:
- FNR – false negative rate;
- ACC – accuracy.

It should be noted that in order to improve the quality of this authentication method, it is necessary to minimize the number of type II errors with a satisfactorily low number of type I errors.

A training set was created containing 50 vectors of features, i.e. 50 hands rising with the phone to the ear were obtained and processed. This size of training set seems to be sufficient, as more movements will negatively affect the usability of this method. In addition, it will be further shown that with the increase in amount of objects in the training set, the quality of the algorithm stops to grow after a certain amount.

A test set contained 50 legitimate user movements (not used in the training set) and 300 movements of 15 other people who pretended to be "intruders".

The appropriate parameters of the algorithms were chosen experimentally to improve the quality of the algorithms.

4.4   Evaluation

There were several algorithms that were tested. Here in this work we show only algorithms with best results we obtained while testing them.

Algorithms performed differently in dependency on size of the training set. Previous work showed that there is no need in large training set, as accuracy stops to grow on training sets larger then 25–30 movements.

Table 3 shows the results of testing without any interval division, as-is. The best results of every algorithm are presented.

This far the best results were obtained with Isolation Forest. The next step was to test whether interval division can improve the results of Isolation Forest. Table 4 shows the results of the test.

Table 3. Evaluation results.

Algorithm	FNR	FPR	ACC
One-Class SVM	0,34	0,18	0,74
One-Class Classifier with Naïve Bayes	0,20	0,02	0,89
Isolation Forest	0,20	0,00	0,93

Table 4. Evaluation results with interval division for Isolation Forest.

Division ratio	FNR	FPR	ACC
1:1	0,30	0,00	0,91
1:2	0,29	0,05	0,88
1:3	0,35	0,02	0,88
3:1	0,12	0,02	0,95
2:1	0,18	0,00	0,95

The best results were performed by Isolation Forest with division ratio 3:1 and 2:1. That is explained by the fact that all the dynamics of the movement is in the first part of the movement. Figure 6 helps to visualize the obtained results.

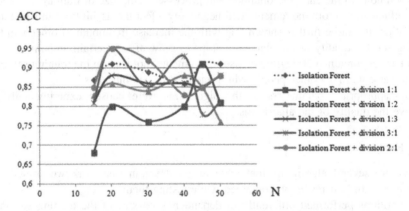

Fig. 6. Isolation Forest results with division dependency on size of training set.

Figure 4 also shows that there is no need in large training set, as it was stated in [4].

5 Authentication System

Along with two methods we propose a system architecture that allows to perform an incoming call user authentication. Such architecture is described in terms of Android OS, but it is also applicable to iOS with some assumptions.

5.1   Service Application

The core of the system is a service application. The main feature of this application is the ability to work in the background and monitor and process events generated by the operating system.

In the Android OS a PHONE_STATE event [12] is generated signaling that the phone state has changed. There are 3 possible states:

- CALL_STATE_IDLE — there is no activity;
- CALL_STATE_OFFHOOK — at least one call is in active state and no incoming calls;
- CALL_STATE_RINGING — a new incoming call is received and is ringing or waiting.

Thus, the service should track the PHONE_STATE event and the appearance of the CALL_STATE_RINGING and CALL_STATE_OFFHOOK states. This means that the incoming call was received and the user transferred it to the active state. As CALL_STATE_RINGING event appears touch screen data should be gathered. After that, appearance of CALL_STATE_OFFHOOK event means that a user has accepted the call and motion data should be gathered. The data obtained from sensors is to be saved in a database for subsequent use.

5.2   Machine Learning Module

This module performs the basic actions for user authentication - training the model and decision-making. This module can be implemented both on the mobile device itself and on a separate computer.

In the learning mode, the machine learning module is started by the service application described above when a sufficient amount of user data has been obtained. These data represent sets of measurements on the X, Y, Z axes received from the sensors when making movements in answering the call. The machine learning module receives this data from the database and performs feature extracting. The resulting vectors are fed into the machine learning algorithm to create and train the model. The trained model is stored for further use in the operating mode.

The operating mode starts when a model is saved and ready for use. In this mode, the machine learning module is also called by the service application every time an incoming call is received. Once the movement has been completed by the user and the data is collected, the module reads this data from the database, extracts the features, forming a feature vector, and feeds it to the input of the trained model.

The model makes a decision about the correspondence of this vector to a legitimate user. If the movement does not correspond to the movements of the user, the call can be rejected, or a user would be asked for a password. In addition, further training of the model can be realized based on the data obtained in the operating mode. Overall operating scheme of suggested system is presented in Fig. 7.

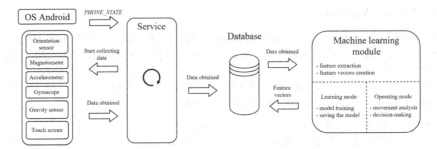

Fig. 7. Operating scheme of authentication system.

6   Conclusions and Further Research

As a result of this research, we propose two methods of user authentication when answering an incoming call that perform pretty accurate. Such results allow drawing a conclusion about the possibility to use these methods to authenticate a user. Also, a concept of an authentication system was presented that makes it possible to use these methods in for real-life authentication.

The purpose of further research is to combine suggested methods and develop a new method that allows to make a decision based on decisions of both methods. This can be solved differently – all the features can be combined in one vector and fed into a machine learning algorithm or these features can be used independently and the results of machine learning algorithms can be combined.

Acknowledgements. This work was supported by Competitiveness Growth Program of the Federal Autonomous Educational Institution of Higher Professional Education National Research Nuclear University MEPhI (Moscow Engineering Physics Institute).

References

1. Consumer Reports. http://www.consumerreports.org/cro/news/2014/04/smart-phone-thefts-rose-to-3-1-million-last-year/index.htm. Accessed 25 Apr 2018
2. Smith, R.E.: Authentication: From Passwords to Public Keys. Williams Publishing House, Moscow (2002)
3. Løge, M.D.: Tell Me Who You Are and I Will Tell You Your Unlock Pattern. Master of Science in Computer Science, Norwegian University of Science and Technology (2015)
4. Eremin, A., Kogos, K.: Incoming call implicit user authentication - user authentication via hand movement pattern. In: Proceedings of 4th International Conference on Information Systems Security and Privacy, pp. 24–29. SCITEPRESS, Portugal (2018)
5. Feng, T., et al.: Continuous mobile authentication using touchscreen gestures. In: Proceedings of IEEE Conference on Technologies for Homeland Security, pp. 12–18. IEEE, USA (2012)
6. Meng, Y., Wong, D.S., Schlegel, R., Kwok, L.: Touch gestures based biometric authentication scheme for touchscreen mobile phones. In: Kutyłowski, M., Yung, M. (eds.) Information Security and Cryptology. Lecture Notes in Computer Science, vol. 7763. Springer, Heidelberg (2013). https://doi.org/10.1007/978-3-642-38519-3_21

7. Maghsoudi, J., Tappert, C.: A behavioral biometrics user authentication study using motion data from android smartphones. In: Proceedings of European Intelligence and Security Informatics Conference, pp. 184–187. IEEE, Sweden (2016)
8. Conti, M., Zachia-Zlatea, I., Crispo, B.: Mind how you answer me! In: Proceedings of the 6th ACM Symposium on Information, Computer and Communications Security, pp. 249–259. ACM, China (2011)
9. Buriro, A., Crispo, B., Zhauniarovich, Y.: Please hold on: unobtrusive user authentication using smartphone's built-in sensors. In: Proceedings of IEEE International Conference on Identity, Security and Behavior Analysis, pp. 1–8. IEEE, India (2017)
10. Frank, M., et al.: Touchalytics: on the applicability of touchscreen input as a behavioral biometric for continuous authentication. Trans. Inf. Forensic. Secur. 8(1), 136–148 (2013)
11. Hempstalk, K., Frank, E., Witten, I.H.: One-class classification by combining density and class probability estimation. In: Daelemans, W., Goethals, B., Morik, K. (eds.) Machine Learning and Knowledge Discovery in Databases. LNCS, vol. 5211. Springer, Heidelberg (2008). https://doi.org/10.1007/978-3-540-87479-9_51
12. Android: Developers Homepage. https://developer.android.com/reference/android/telep-hony/PhoneStateListener.html. Accessed 29 Apr 2018

Elicitation of Privacy Requirements
for the Internet of Things
Using ACCESSORS

Christoph Stach[✉] and Bernhard Mitschang

Institute for Parallel and Distributed Systems, University of Stuttgart,
Universitätsstraße 38, 70569 Stuttgart, Germany
{stachch,mitsch}@ipvs.uni-stuttgart.de

Abstract. Novel *smart* devices are equipped with various sensors to capture context data. The *Internet of Things (IoT)* connects these devices with each other in order to bring together data from various domains. Due to the IoT, new application areas come up continuously. For instance, the quality of life and living can be significantly improved by installing connected and remote-controlled devices in *Smart Homes*. Or the treatment of chronic diseases can be made more convenient for both, patients and physicians, by using *Smart Health* technologies.

For this, however, a large amount of data has to be collected, shared, and combined. This gathered data provides detailed insights into the user of the devices. Therefore, privacy is a key issue for such IoT applications. As current privacy systems for mobile devices focus on a single device only, they cannot be applied to a distributed and highly interconnected environment as the IoT. Therefore, we determine the special requirements towards a permission models for the IoT. Based on this requirements specification, we introduce ACCESSORS, a data-centric permission model for the IoT and describe how to apply such a model to two promising privacy systems for the IoT, namely the *Privacy Management Platform (PMP)* and *PATRON*.

Keywords: Permission model · Data-centric · Derivation transparent · Fine-grained · Context-sensitive · Internet of Things · PMP · PATRON

1 Introduction

Today there is a trend to equip everyday objects, such as wristwatches, with a variety of sensors. Due to new, low-cost and power-saving connection standards, these devices can also be easily interconnected. Due to their versatility and easy handling, these *Things*[1] get into the focus of the general public [4]. As a result, the so-called *Internet of Things (IoT)* is becoming increasingly popular [14]. This opens up a wide range of possible application scenarios for the IoT, including *Smart Homes* [9], *Smart Health* [50], and *Smart Cars* [62].

---

[1] We use the term "Thing" for any device equipped with sensors and Internet access.

© Springer Nature Switzerland AG 2019
P. Mori et al. (Eds.): ICISSP 2018, CCIS 977, pp. 40–65, 2019.
https://doi.org/10.1007/978-3-030-25109-3_3

These versatile fields of application are facilitated by the two key characteristics of the Things: On the one hand, the built-in sensors are able to capture any kind of context information, such as location data, surrounding sounds, or even health data. As these Things are common everyday objects, they are no longer perceived by the user as computers and are always carried along naturally [67]. This makes it possible to capture data about users on a permanent basis.

On the other hand, the Things are interconnected. As a result, they are able to exchange autonomously the captured data with each other [31]. Thus, it is sufficient if only a limited number of sensors are installed in each Thing in order to gain comprehensive contextual knowledge about their users. This knowledge can be used in IoT applications (or *apps*) to adapt their functionalities to their users' private lives. By this, IoT apps are able to predict the most likely user demands in the prevailing situation and provide the currently most beneficial services [36]. So, they contribute to improving the quality of life.

The IoT apps are also not constrained by the usually limited computing power of the Things. By transmitting the data to the *Cloud* (or upstream components, such as *Fog Instances*), IoT apps have access to virtually unlimited resources in terms of computing power, memory, or storage. Studies show that, despite this transmission, data processing can be realized in almost real-time [44].

However, these unlimited processing possibilities result in new threat scenarios [35]. Machine learning techniques can be applied to IoT apps in order to detect connections between existing data sources and derive more knowledge from the available data [29]. Users are extremely worried about the overwhelming potential of these apps [11]. Individuals cannot only be monitored permanently without their knowledge, but also additional information about them can be generated from the collected data. Therefore, privacy has to be a key issue for any IoT app [1].

While there are unambiguous regulations for the processing of personal data from a legal point of view (e.g., the European General Data Protection Regulation [64]), there is a lack of technical approaches for the implementation of comprehensive privacy mechanisms for the IoT [26]. In this respect, it is important that the entire IoT app is taken into account, i.e., effective privacy mechanisms have to be applied to both, the Things as well as their back-ends [53]. Yet, even simple privacy management systems, i.e., systems that restrict access to a certain data processing unit, overwhelm users already [20]. Moreover, users don't know which information can be derived from which data [41] and whether this information poses a privacy threat [19]. For instance, a proximity sensor can disclose the absolute location of a user also, when it gathers the distance to a Thing with a stationary location [24].

For this very reason, we introduce a data-centric and thus comprehensible privacy approach for the IoT, tackling both, Things as well as their back-ends. To that end, we provide the following five contributions in our work:

(1) We deduce requirements towards a permission model for IoT apps from a use case scenario.

(2) We analyze permission models which are applied in existing privacy systems and provide a comprehensive overview of their features and their applicability in the IoT domain.
(3) We construct a data-centric permission model for the Internet of Things, called ACCESSORS.
(4) We apply ACCESSORS to both, mobile devices (*PMP* [56,57]) and distributed stream processing systems (*PATRON* [54,55]), that is, the back-end of IoT apps. However, we could use any of the many similar privacy systems as a foundation for our model without a loss of argument.
(5) We evaluate our model and assess its utility.

This paper is the extended and revised version of the paper entitled "ACCESSORS: A Data-Centric Permission Model for the Internet of Things" [58] presented at the 4th International Conference on Information Systems Security and Privacy (ICISSP) 2018. This extended paper considers all layers of IoT apps, whereas the original paper focuses at the Sensor and Smartphone Layer, only.

The remainder of this paper is as follows: Sect. 2 introduces a real-world use case scenario to illustrate the challenges for a permission model for IoT apps. Then, Sect. 3 postulates five key requirements for such a permission model. Section 4 discusses various existing permission models. Our model—ACCESSORS—is introduced in Sect. 5. Section 6 describes how to apply ACCESSORS to a privacy system. Finally, Sect. 7 assesses our approach before Sect. 8 concludes this work and gives a short outlook on future work.

2   Use Case Scenario

The application of IoT technologies for non-invasive glucose level sensing and diabetes management is described by Istepanian et al. [28]. Figure 1 shows the architecture of such an application. Various sensors (e.g., a glucose meter) initially record a wide range of health data (e.g., blood sugar level) at the *Sensor Layer*. The measurement data of an individual patient is transmitted to his or her Smartphone and consolidated at the *Smartphone Layer* [61]. However, patients do not know exactly what data is being passed on, especially since such a device is capable of collecting different types of data—e.g., some devices add location data to any glucose measurement, as this information might be relevant for later diagnostic analyses [33,52,59].

The *Back-End Layer* accumulates the data of several patients (e.g., grouped by the attending physician) at a central server in order to enable comprehensive analyses [8]. By combining the gathered data, further knowledge can be derived. For instance, a combination of blood sugar values and location data enables to draw inferences about the user's eating behavior as a rising blood sugar level shortly after walking past a candy shop indicates that the user has bought some sweets [32]. The *Presentation Layer* provides tools to present the results to health professionals. However, patients have neither insight into which data is collected at the back-end nor which information can be derived from it via data mining.

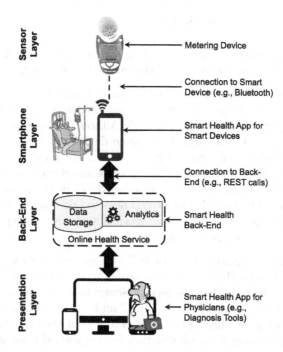

Fig. 1. Architecture of an IoT health application [60].

Despite this insecurity concerning the processing of sensitive data, the number of IoT health devices available is growing significantly. With each generation more sensors and a larger range of features are introduced [65]. The accuracy of the sensors is also improving [34]. But not every IoT app requires this high level of accuracy. This implies that from a privacy perspective, data quality should be downgraded in order to conceal private information which is not required for the app to run. While some of the data provided by such IoT devices is uncritical from a privacy point of view or so vital that the data is required all the time, other sensitive data is required only in case of an emergency. For instance, in case of an insulin shock, health has priority over privacy and thus, any available data should be sent to the physician to provide the best possible medical attendance.

Such a scenario requires a privacy system—or more precisely its permission model—to meet several novel requirements in order to be effective [49]. For instance, focusing on data-centric protection goals is becoming increasingly important [2]. This is further amplified by the fact that IoT apps assemble its data from various sources, some of them even unknown to the user [63]. Moreover, since new devices with all-new sensors are constantly being released, the permission model must adapt to such an evolving environment [1].

3   Requirements Specification

As the scenario given in Sect. 2 shows, the IoT defines some novel requirements towards a permission model, that are detailed in the following.

[R1] Data-Centric Policy Rules. To be understandable and manageable for the user, the permissions have to refer to types of data (e.g., blood sugar level) instead of data providers (e.g., glucometer). Although it is evident that a glucometer measures the blood sugar level, some devices are also able to capture location data. If policy rules are solely based on data providers, a user might allow a health app to use his or her glucometer without knowing that s/he also gave access to non-medical data (e.g., location data) in the process. The same type of data can even be provided by several devices (e.g., the blood sugar level is provided by glucometers and *Apple Watches*). If a user wants to prohibit access to this data, then a respective rule has to be applied to any possible provider.

[R2] Derivation Transparency. An IoT app has access to various types of data via several sensors. However, by combining this data, new information can be derived. Such coherences have to be representable by a permission model. For instance, if A can be derived from B and C and a user prohibits access to A, then an app must not be allowed to access B and C at the same time. This can be archived by describing what information can be derived from which sources. The user can then assign permissions at data level and the privacy system must apply appropriate rules to the respective sources.

[R3] Extendable Permission Model. The IoT is constantly evolving as new sensor technologies or communication standards emerge. A static permission model, that is, a model with a fixed set of protected entities, quickly becomes obsolete. Therefore, the model must be dynamically extendable. In particular, all extensions must be backward compatible, i.e., the extension of the model must not invalidate previous rules.

[R4] Fine-Grained Policy Rules. In order to give a user the opportunity to manage his or her data confidentially, s/he needs full control over the distribution and dissemination of information. This means that the permission model has to support fine-grained policy rules in two respects: On the one hand, the protected entities have to be fine-grained. For instance, Android provides a `Bluetooth` permission which restricts access to any device connected via Bluetooth. Yet, this permission does not address a specific type of data or sensor. As a consequence, users have to permit apps to use a Bluetooth headphone and a Bluetooth medical device at the same time via a single permission. On the other hand, a user has to have several choices how to constrain a certain permission. Most permission models follow a binary logic, only (grant or deny). However, a permission for location data also could restrict the accuracy of the data.

[R5] Context-Sensitive Policy Rules. Since IoT apps are often context-aware, i.e., an app reacts on the situation it is currently used, the policy rules should be context-sensitive as well. For instance, a medical app should have access to any kind of data in case of an emergency. Otherwise, more restrictive policy rules should be applied. Dey defines context as "any information that can be used to characterize the situation of an entity" [17].

4 Related Work

Based on these requirements, we analyze permission models which are currently used in the IoT context. In the following, we differentiate between privacy solutions for the Back-End Layer (Sect. 4.1) and privacy solutions for the Smartphone Layer (Sect. 4.2). The other two layers of an IoT app do not have to be considered specifically, since no data processing is done here, i.e., privacy solutions for the Smartphone and Back-End Layer also cover the privacy issues of these two layers.

4.1 Privacy Solutions for the Back-End Layer

Several methods have been developed to control the information flow in stream processing [68] and event processing systems [25]. These systems can also be applied to analyses performed at the Back-End Layer of an IoT app. Most access control mechanisms currently existing for these systems such as *DEFCON* [37] are attribute-based. That is, these systems ensure that certain attributes (in the stream of events) are only visible to authorized processing operators. However, this is overly restrictive since it implies that operators either always have access to certain attributes or never. In other words, the underlying permission model simply assigns to each attribute either the label "granted" or "denied". Some stream processing systems such as *ACStream* [10] provide context-based access control. That is, they add to each attribute permission pair also information about the context under which the respective privacy rule should be applied. In other words, these triples allow a more fine-grained access control to information. Yet, the access is still controlled at the level of attributes. A different approach towards privacy for the Back-End Layer called PATRON is introduced in Sect. 6.2.

However, all these approaches are not designed for the end user, but for IT specialists. Therefore it is also not possible to enforce individual privacy rules for each user with these approaches, as it is the focus of this paper. Rather, it is intended to provide a simple way to regulate access to vast amounts of data in accordance with a general policy. Therefore, all of the applied simple permission models are not suitable for our purposes.

4.2 Privacy Solutions for the Smartphone Layer

Due to the highly heterogeneous IoT landscape and the various operating systems available for the Things, a lot of different privacy systems and thus permission models are being used at the Smartphone Layer. Yet, there are several efforts to establish Android as the key operating system for the IoT, e.g., *Android*

Things [22] or *RTAndroid*[2] [30]. Although we focus on Android-based privacy systems in our work, the findings can be applied to any mobile platform, as they also use comparable permission-based privacy systems [7].

Android applies a quite simple permission model (see Fig. 2). Each Permission regulates either the usage of a system functions (e.g., adding entries to the calendar) or access to a sensor (e.g., the camera). An app has to request the appropriate permissions before it is able to use such a resource. For *normal* permissions a policy rule is created when an app is installed (i.e., they are automatically granted), while *dangerous* permissions have to be granted at runtime [18].

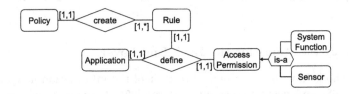

Fig. 2. The permission model applied in android [58].

When new permission types are added or existing permissions are relabeled, app developers have to add these permissions to their already released apps in order to keep them operative [48]. Yet, several system functions and sensors can be controlled by a single permission. This makes it very hard for users to comprehend the permissions [20]. Moreover, there are so many different permissions right now (even for noncritical operations such as the usage of the vibration function) [20] which makes it even harder to grasp the permissions. As a consequence, Google no longer informs about noncritical permissions. However, Google classifies even access to the Internet or the usage of Bluetooth device as noncritical operations (see Fig. 3). Yet, both can have a severe impact on the user's privacy. Thus, such a basic permission model is not applicable for the IoT.

Sekar et al. [47] introduce *Selective Permissions*. This means that every Android permission requested by an app is stored in a *Shadow Manifest* that can be changed at runtime. This allows a user to revoke certain permissions similar to Android runtime permissions. However, Selective Permissions have two advantages. On the one hand, a user can revoke any permission; on the other hand, a missing permission does not lead to a security exception. Instead, a null value is returned to the app. However, this approach does not change the Android permission model and therefore does not meet any of the requirements defined in Sect. 3.

---

[2] A refined version of RTAndroid called *emteria.OS* is available at https://emteria.com.

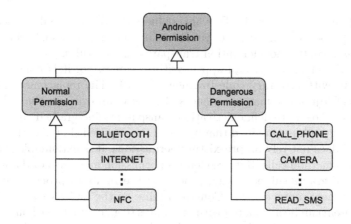

Fig. 3. Classification of android permissions [based on 58, 66]

CRêPE introduces a context-sensitive permission model [12]. Each access to a data source, i.e., each permission request, can be linked to a spatio-temporal context. This context defines a condition under which the permission is granted. However, the rules are mapped to Android permissions and therefore CRêPE has the same shortcomings as the Android permission model.

Apex introduces an XML-based policy language to restrict the use of Android permissions [39]. For instance, the user can define how often a particular permission can be used or in which chronological order permissions can be assigned. Apart from such constraints, the permission model does not allow extensive contextual constraints or fine-grained permission settings. Furthermore, the model is neither data-centric nor derivable and it cannot be extended because it is based on Android permissions.

In *YAASE*, a user defines which operations a particular application may perform on a resource, that is, either a content provider or a service provider [43]. Data from these resources can be tagged, for example, to distinguish between public and private data provided by the same resource. The user defines whether only resources with a certain tag are accessible for an app. S/he can also define operations that must be performed before the data is forwarded to an app, such as a filer operation to remove sensitive data. In this way YAASE is able to define very fine-grained policy rules. However, these rules are not data-centric, transparent or context-sensitive. In addition, the extensibility of the model is limited to specified operations.

Sorbet addresses the unrestricted information flows between apps [21]. Therefore, the underlying permission model allows to specify information-flow constraints to prevent privilege escalation, i.e., the transfer of permissions between apps. This can also be used to introduce a kind of context-sensitivity in Sorbet. Furthermore, the Sorbet is able to protect any kind of component (e.g., services or content providers). So, its permission model is extendable. Moreover, it is possible to define constraints in the model to limit the usage of certain permissions, e.g., by adding a lifespan to it. This also reduces the risk of privilege escalation. Therefore, Sorbet has fine-grained, yet Boolean policy rules. Also, Sorbet neither supports data-centric nor derivation transparent policy rules.

RetroSkeleton introduces an app rewriting system. So, it is able to replace method calls with arbitrary code fragments [15,16]. The replacement rules are specified as Clojure command sequences. The user can draw on the full expression power of Closure to define derivation transparent, fine-grained, and context-sensitive policy rules—provided that s/he has the required skills. As the model is generic and does not rely on preexisting permissions, it is extendable. Yet, as it only replaces method calls, RetroSkeleton's permission model is not data-centric.

Constroid grants subjects (e.g., processes) the rights to process data items (e.g., all business contacts) [45]. Constroid relies on the $UCON_{ABC}$ model [40]. Each data item can be associated with attributes (e.g., contacts without a private phone number) to restrict the access rights. As access rights are linked to data, Constroid considers only create, read, update, and delete operations. Optional conditions specify whether a rule is applicable under a certain context. Yet, the model is not extendable and does not support derivation transparent policy rules.

SPoX is a specification language for security policies [23]. SPoX rules define a state machine that accepts all command sequences that comply with the security policy. Backes et al. [5] use this language in their data protection system *AppGuard*. This enables the user to formulate fine-grained policy rules, e.g., by limiting network access to a specific address. AppGuard's permission model is extensible, because each command can be restricted by policy rules. Thus, new data sources are also supported by AppGuard out of the box. By linking several rules, the user is able to model a kind of derivation transparency. The context in which a particular command is executed can also be restricted [6]. However, these restrictions only apply to the command sequence and not to the context of the user. Furthermore, the data protection model is not data-centric.

Scoccia et al. [46] introduce flexible permissions for Android called *AFP*. In AFP, permissions are assigned to features of an app. This means that an app may only request a permission to perform a specific task. Furthermore, AFP enables the assignment of fine-grained permissions, e.g., by granting access only to selected contacts instead of the entire contact list. Since AFP defines its own permissions, the model is extensible. Nevertheless, the policy rules are neither data-centric nor derivation transparent.

DroidForce introduces data-centric policy rules [42]. *OSL* [27] is used to specify the rules. This enables users to add temporal conditions as well as cardinality constraints and time constraints to each permission. Therefore, both fine-grained and context-sensitive rules are supported. The main feature of DroidForce is its focus on data-centric permissions. This means that the permissions are mapped to data domains (e.g., location data or contact data) and not to sensors or system functions. However, relationships between protected data sources cannot be modeled and the model used cannot be extended.

The *Privacy Management Platform* (*PMP*) [57] introduces the *Privacy Policy Model* (*PPM*) [56] (see Fig. 4). The PPM is extendable and enables fine-grained and context-sensitive policy rules. Therefore, it defines so-called *Service Features*. These are self-contained fragments of an app which can be (de-)activated in order to meet the users' demands. That way, permissions can be directly granted to specific Service Features. Each permission is restricted to a certain purpose to reflect the privacy requirements as good as possible. *Resources* manage the access to data sources or sinks. Related Resources can be pooled in a *Resource Group* (e.g., GPS and WiFi positioning are part of a location Resource Group). So-called *Privacy Settings* can be defined for each Resource (e.g., to reduce the accuracy of location data for a certain Service Feature). The Resources can also be used to define contextual constraints. These constraints specify a scope of application for each privacy rule. Due to these features, the PPM meets most of the requirements towards a permission model for the IoT. However, the missing support of data-centric policy rules overstrains users unjustifiably. The following *Smart Health* example illustrates this issue:

If a user manages his or her electronic health data record on his or her Smartphone, s/he can use a *Smart Health* app. However, s/he only wants this app to gather certain health data, e.g., his or her fitness progress including heart rate (pulse meter), activities (accelerometer and orientation sensor), and training locations (GPS). Additionally, s/he wants to use the camera of the Smartphone for a visual documentation of his or her training progress. S/he could use this electronic health data record to get a special tariff rate from his or her insurance company in which a healthy lifestyle is rewarded.

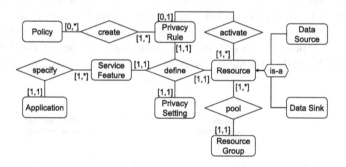

Fig. 4. The Privacy Policy Model (PPM) [based on 56,58].

It is obvious that such a user does not want to share any additional data with his or her insurance company which might indicate an illness (e.g., a high body temperature), as this could lead to a higher insurance rate. The PPM enables to prohibit the *Smart Health* app to access a Bluetooth medical thermometer for the purpose of measuring the body temperature. The thermometer then is represented as a Resource and the measuring is represented as a Service Feature.

However, if we assume that the Smartphone is equipped with a thermographic camera, the user must be familiar with this feature. If s/he does not consider this functionality of his or her device, such a camera can also display the body temperature. To prevent this, s/he must define an additional privacy rule in the PPM for the measuring Service Feature that prohibits access to the camera Resource. For each data source, s/he must reflect what knowledge can be derived from his data.

Although the PPM is able to secure sensitive data in IoT apps, with an increasing number of different sensors, it is almost impossible for a user to keep track of all the possible data leaks due to the Resource-centric Policy Rules of the PPM. Nevertheless, the PPM is a sound foundation for ACCESSORS.

5   The ACCESSORS Model

The study of the related work shows that there is currently no suitable permission model for IoT apps. Exisiting models are too superficial and general-purposed. However, the PPM is well suited for the Smartphone Layer of IoT applications as long as a manageable number of sensors are involved. In an IoT scenario with many different sensors, a different approach is required because humans are used to think data-centric. This means that a user knows what data s/he wants to conceal and s/he does not want to worry about which sensor or data source could disclose this type of data. Current approaches, by contrast, require a separate rule for each data source that contains this information. For this purpose, a permission model must be able to map data producers to the type of data they provide. In this way, the user can select the type of data to be made available to an app (e.g., body temperature) and the model unfolds, which data sources must be considered (e.g., medical thermometer and thermographic camera). Our approach of a **data-centric** permission model for the Internet of Things—ACCESSORS for short—achieves this by introducing six abstraction levels.

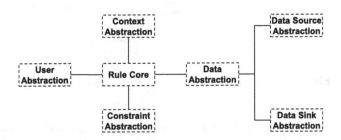

Fig. 5. Basic structure of an ACCESSORS permission.

Figure 5 shows the basic structure of an ACCESSORS permission. In the following, we detail its seven key components (*Rule Core, User Abstraction, Data*

Abstraction, Data Sink Abstraction, Data Source Abstraction, Context Abstraction, and *Constraint Abstraction*) and elaborate on how they contribute to meet the five requirements, specified in Sect. 3.

Rule Core. Similar to the PPM, an ACCESSORS policy rule essentially has three main parts: an *access purpose*, a permission to *access* a data processing unit[3], and a *constraint.* These triplets form the *rule core.* Optionally, each policy rule can be associated with a *context* in which it is activated (see Paragraph Context Abstraction).

User Abstraction. Each *inquiring entity*—i.e., an *app*, a *Smart Thing*, or even a *user*—can specify one or more access purposes that require access to a protected type of data. An access purpose is a code fragment within an app that performs a single task. For example, such an access purpose in the use case scenario described in Sect. 2 could be the graphical representation of all locations on a map where the user measured his or her blood sugar level. In this way, the permissions are not granted to an app in general, but they are valid for a specific access purpose, only. As a consequence, a user can decide which access is justified for a particular type of app and if s/he is willing to grant the specified access rights for the offered service. Similar to PPM, non-essential app features can be skipped to reduce the amount of required private data. *User abstraction* ensures that other types of Smart Things can be added as needed.

Data Abstraction. Data abstraction enables the linking of permissions with both, *data producers* and *data consumers.* However, the focus for both units is on the type of data that is produced or consumed. This means that an inquiring entity must indicate which data it requests access to, e.g., location data or health data, instead of a specific data processing unit such as GPS or a glucometer.

Data Sink Abstraction. Every data consumer is linked to multiple *data sinks* such as *apps* or *services, data stores* or other *Smart Things.* That is, the user can set policy rules on how data can be preprocessed for an app. For example, s/he could allow an app to use a service that stores health data for long-term monitoring of a particular health condition.

Data Source Abstraction. Each data producer is associated with a certain type of *information.* Information is any aspect that can be derived from raw data. This means that it can be the raw data itself (e.g., a single blood glucose level metering) or any other type of higher order data obtained by combining several sources (e.g., a health record with data from different meters). Different *data sources* can be specified for each data type in the ACCESSORS model. A data source does not necessarily have to be a *sensor*, but *apps, data storages*, and *Smart Things* are also qualified as data sources. In this way, complex relationships can be modeled (e.g., the information "activity" can be derived either by

---

[3] A data processing unit is either a *data producer* or a *data consumer* (see Paragraph Data Abstraction).

a combination of data from an accelerometer and a position sensor or directly by readings from a fitness tracker). By *data sink abstraction* and *data sources abstraction*, the policy rules remain completely detached from a specific technology. The rules are automatically adapted to the available data sources and sinks accordingly.

Context Abstraction. An activation context can optionally be assigned to each policy rule. This context describes the conditions under which a rule must be enforced by a privacy system. In accordance with Dey [17], we describe the context as a *spatio-temporal* condition (e.g., a certain rule should only be applied during working hours) or as a higher order *situation* (e.g., a certain rule only applies in the case of a medical emergency). Higher order situations can be modeled as a sequence of values provided by data producers.

Constraint Abstraction. Different constraints can be defined for each rule. The most fundamental constraint is a Boolean constraint to grant or deny access to certain type of data[4]. Depending on the type of data, ACCESSORS supports three additional constraint types. Integer conditions can be used to define an upper or lower limit. For example, maximum accuracy for a particular type of data, such as location data, can be specified in this way. An enumeration constraint defines several valid setting options. For example, for medical records, there may be settings that only allow access to domain-specific data records such as pulmonary data or cardiac data. Finally, string constraints allows to enter textual conditions. For example, a user can specify a MAC address of a Thing with which s/he wants to share his or her data. This ensures that the health data is only sent to the specified destination address.

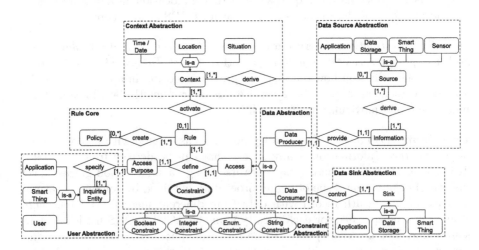

Fig. 6. The data-centric permission model for the Internet of Things [58].

---

[4] If the access permission is denied, the particular code fragment is skipped in the app.

Figure 6 shows the detailed ACCESSORS model with all components of the Rule Core and the six abstraction layers. Overall, ACCESSORS supports data-centric policy rules, since the focus of the permissions is on data types instead of actual data processing units. Since data producers provide higher order information, which can be composed of data from several sources, ACCESSORS is able to model relationships between different types of data and sources. Since the policy rules only link access purposes, access permissions, constraints, and contexts, they are independent of specific inquiring entities or data producers/data consumers. This means that ACCESSORS has two types of extensibility due to its abstraction layers. On the one hand it can be extended (e.g., by adding new Things) and on the other hand it can be advanced (e.g., by adding new relationships between data sources when new methods to derive a certain kind of information from raw data are discovered). Policy rules modeled with ACCESSORS are highly fine-grained. On the one hand, the multi-value constraints enable highly precise fine-tuning of permission rights. On the other hand, since the permissions are bound to a certain access purpose and do not have to be granted to an app in total, the user can tailor the privacy policy precisely to his or her needs. Each policy rule can be enriched by an activation context. This context is generic, as it can be composed of all currently available data sources.

A comparison of the PPM (see Fig. 4) with ACCESSORS (see Fig. 6) shows that the two models have several common components. The rule core of ACCESSORS almost matches the PPM. However, ACCESSORS introduces additional abstraction layers for users, data, data sinks, data sources, contexts, and constraints. Furthermore, ACCESSORS takes a different protection goal into account. While the PPM is designed for Smartphones and therefore only considers apps as potential attackers and sensors or system functions as possible targets (labeled as Resources), ACCESSORS is outright designed for the IoT. For this reason, not only the potential attackers are interpreted in the broader sense (inquiring entities such as apps, Smart Things, or users), but also concerning the protected targets, ACCESSORS has a different focus. The targets are tailored to the types of data instead of data sinks or data sources.

Nevertheless, it appears to be obvious to map the policy rules defined in ACCESSORS to PPM rules due to their great similarities. Moreover, as the PPM is already applied to an existing privacy systems for the Smartphone Layer, the PMP, we can use this infrastructure to enforce the ACCESSORS rules as well. The following section describes how to map ACCESSORS policy rules to PPM rules. Furthermore, we show how ACCESSORS can also be used in a privacy system for the Back-End Layer. To this end, we introduce PATRON, a privacy mechanism for stream processing systems. PATRON focuses at two goals: On the one hand, it hides private information from unauthorized parties and on the other hand, it ensures quality of service of the controlled IoT apps. ACCESSORS is a great support in achieving these goals.

6   Application of ACCESSORS in IoT Privacy Systems

As ACCESSORS is not committed to a certain privacy system, it can be applied to any given privacy system in order to control access to any kind of private data. Due to its similarities to the PPM, the usage of the model in a privacy system for end devices is the most reasonable use case. This case of application is described in Sect. 6.1 using the example of the PMP.

However, ACCESSORS can also be used to identify the privacy demands of users. Due to the systematic yet human comprehensible notation of ACCESSORS, it is also possible to express complex correlations between gathered data and derivable knowledge in an automated processable way. This enables end-users to configure privacy systems for the Back-End Layer of IoT apps. This is described using the example of PATRON in Sect. 6.2.

6.1   Application of ACCESSORS in the PMP

From a modeling point of view, the fine-grained structure of ACCESSORS with its highly branched abstraction layers is necessary in order to gain a high expressiveness of the policy rules. However, from a implementation point of view, the number of utilized components should be kept low in order to reduce complexity. On that account, a mapping of the detailed ACCESSORS policy rules to similar PPM rules, is also recommended.

To that end, it is necessary to convert the access purposes specified by inquiring entities in ACCESSORS to Service Features. However, a Service Feature also defines certain permissions which are required in order to execute a particular code fragment. The focus on a broader range of possible attackers in ACCESSORS is not contradictory to the Service Features and a one-to-one mapping is possible without any further ado.

That is why the transition of data-centric targets modeled in ACCESSORS into PPM Resources poses the biggest problem for the mapping. In particular this implies that all Resources have to be replaced by new data-centric components. Nevertheless, ACCESSORS can be applied to the PMP, due to its modular architecture. In the PMP, each Resource Group is implemented as an independent functional unit which can be installed individually. Moreover, additional Resources can be added to a Resource Group at any point of time [51]. Therefore, existing Resources can be replaced by new data-centric ones in order to apply ACCESSORS to the PMP.

Figure 7 depicts the model of a Resource Group for Smart Watches. The Resource Group defines a common interface for all of its Resources. An arbitrary Resource, which provides the required functionality, can be plugged into the the Resource Group at runtime. That is, the Resources are concrete implementation artifacts of the interface for a given hardware (e.g., an Apple Watch or a Moto 360). The Resource Group also defines feasible Privacy Settings, i.e., how the user is able to restrict access to a particular Resource.

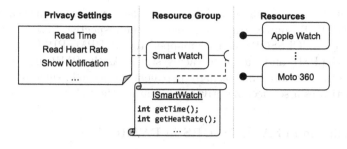

Fig. 7. Model of a PMP resource group [58].

Figure 8 illustrates how this model has to be adapted in order to make the PMP compatible to ACCESSORS privacy rules. In the first instance, the hardware- or service-based focus of the Resource Groups has to be shifted to a data-centric one. The Resource Group given in the example deals with any kind of health-related data. This data can be provided by legit health devices such as a glucometer or by novel Things such as a Smart Watch. Moreover, this Resource Group also deals with data consumers of health data such as analytics libraries. In order to be able to plug in all of these data processing units, the Resource Group's interface has to be broadened accordingly.

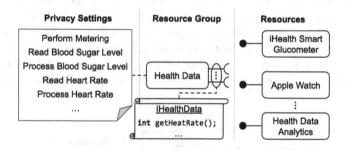

Fig. 8. Application of ACCESSORS in the PMP [58].

The PPM Resource Groups provide only a single plug for one Resource at a time. To support derivation transparency, i.e., to be able to model data which is assembled from various sources, the ACCESSORS Resource Groups need multiple plugs. For instance, it is possible to deduce the blood sugar level considerably accurate by monitoring the activities of a user and his or her eating behavior [69]. So, the Resource Group for health data has to be able to plug in a Resource capturing physical activities and a Resource gathering nutrition data, simultaneously. Furthermore, each Resource can be associated with multiple Resource Groups, e.g., a Smart Watch providing both, location and health data belongs to a location Resource Group as well as a health data Resource Group.

The Privacy Settings for the new data-centric Resource Groups are carried over from the PPM's Resources that are pooled in the respective Resource Group.

That way, ACCESSORS can be mapped to the PPM. PPM rules are executable on the PMP and similar privacy systems. As the PMP runs on Android and Android is becoming increasingly pertinent to the IoT, such an implementation constitutes a serviceable privacy system for the IoT.

6.2   Application of ACCESSORS in PATRON

While the PMP provides access control to private data on Things such as Smartphones, the PATRON research project[5] adopts a different approach. As stream processing systems have proven to be a powerful means to process sensor information [13], they are of major importance for large-scale IoT apps for data processing in the Back-End Layer. For instance, the stream processing system of an IoT Smart Health app could process the users' heart rate, blood pressure, and GPS position to calculate their fitness levels or discover health problems. While many users want to benefit from such apps (e.g., to share their fitness data with their health insurance in order to get a bonus), most users are afraid of the knowledge, which can be gained in addition (e.g., if a disease is discovered and the insurance fee rises). That is, users are not afraid of the data that is processed by an IoT app, but they want to conceal complex *patterns* (e.g., the disease in the example given above) within the data.

The blocking of certain attributes is therefore far too restrictive, as this also prevents the recognition of non-critical patterns (e.g., the fitness level). So, the user defines *private patterns*, i.e., patterns that have to be concealed, and *public patterns*, i.e., patterns that can be used in an IoT app, in PATRON. For the concealing of patterns, several techniques are available. PATRON selects the concealing technique which has the least negative impact on the quality of service.

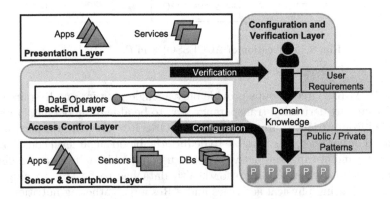

Fig. 9. Simplified PATRON architecture [based on 54,55].

[5] See http://patronresearch.de.

Figure 9 shows the basic architecture of PATRON. In addition to the four layers of an IoT app (Sensor Layer, Smartphone Layer, Back-End Layer, and Presentation Layer), PATRON introduces two novel layers: the *Configuration and Verification Layer* and the *Access Control Layer*.

Configuration and Verification Layer. The Configuration and Verification Layer enables users to specify their requirements concerning privacy. This specification is made in natural language in order to also enable users who are not IT experts to express their requirements. For instance, a user might define the requirement "My insurance company must not be able to detect my unhealthy lifestyle based on the provided data.". Moreover, s/he can also express requirements towards the provided service of an IoT app such as "The insurance company has to be able to detect my fitness level.". It is obvious that users define these requirements, similar to ACCESSORS, based on a certain kind of data instead of sensors which provide this kind of data.

These requirements are transferred by domain experts into public and private patterns—the set of all these patterns is the configuration of PATRON. The assistance of domain experts is essential in this step, because their knowledge about applied analysis techniques and derivable knowledge is required. For instance, only medical experts know, which data sequence indicates a certain health problem. However, a physical attendance of the domain experts in the configuration process is not mandatory. Rather, it is sufficient if their knowledge is available in machine-processable form. Moreover, this accumulated knowledge base has to be expandable, as additional knowledge can be derived from existing data due to the introduction of novel sensors or new analysis techniques.

Besides the configuration of PATRON, the created patterns are also verified in this layer. To this end, all data which is forwarded from the Back-End Layer to the Presentation Layer (e.g., to an insurance company) is analyzed in the Configuration and Verification Layer. This enables to determine whether private patterns have been disclosed due to a misconfiguration or public patterns have been unnecessarily concealed. If this is the case, both, the patterns as well as the domain knowledge base can be adjusted correspondingly. Thus, the user has a confirmation that all of the privacy requirements are considered by PATRON.

Access Control Layer. The actual concealing is done in PATRON's Access Control Layer. The Access Control Layer encapsulate the Back-End-Layer completely, i.e., all incoming data can be analyzed by PATRON before it is shared with the IoT app's back-end and any results of the data operators within this layer can be restrained by PATRON. Various techniques are available for this purpose.

For instance, if the private pattern "eat sweets" (A) followed by "check blood sugar level" (B) followed by "inject insulin" (C) has to be concealed, PATRON could *suppress, obfuscate*, or *reorder* parts of the data. For example, this would have the following effect on the input stream $A \rightarrow B \rightarrow C \rightarrow D$: Suppression could simply drop any of the initial three events (A, B, or C), e.g., B resulting in the input stream $A \rightarrow C \rightarrow D$. Obfuscation modifies an event so that it seems to be a different event, e.g., event A could be disguised as event A' ("eat vegetables"). This leads to the input stream $A' \rightarrow B \rightarrow C \rightarrow D$. Finally, reordering could arrange event D at an earlier stage, e.g., between event A and B. This would also prevent the private pattern $A \rightarrow B \rightarrow C$, as the resulting input stream looks $A \rightarrow D \rightarrow B \rightarrow C$. For more information on the Access Control Layer, please refer to the respective literature [54,55].

Privacy Requirements Elicitation via ACCESSORS. Even though there is system theoretical tool support for the semi-automatical translation of privacy requirements into public and private patterns, the elicitation of these requirements is highly complex [38]. As users should be able to formulate their requirements in natural language, these requirements have to be brought into a formalized, structured form before they can be processed.

The ACCESSORS basic model (see Fig. 5) can be used for this purpose. Guided by the three abstraction classes User Abstraction, Data Abstraction, and Context Abstraction, the user can define who (User Abstraction) should be able to access which patterns (Data Abstraction) in which situation (Context Abstraction). The Constraint Abstraction can be used to define whether it is a public or a private pattern. Moreover, the user can express the weight of each pattern, i.e., how important the respective pattern is for him or her. These weights are then considered by PATRON when selecting the concealing techniques.

Yet, ACCESSORS fulfills in PATRON another substantial purpose. The Data Source Abstraction and Data Sink Abstraction can be used to model PATRON's domain knowledge base. Using these two modules, domain experts are able to specify which data (sources) can be used to derive certain information and how data sinks process data in a specific domain. The domain experts can create ACCESSORS rule fragments in which this expertise is made available. These fragments are then provided to users via the Data Abstraction. From the resulting ACCESSORS rules, the public and private patterns can be derived.

7   Discussion

ACCESSORS is fully **data-centered**, as all its protected entities (data producers as well as data consumers) are connected to a specific type of data (e.g., health data). Apps request access to this data without having to specify which sensor or system function provides this data. ACCESSORS thus also enables **derivation transparency**. Each protected data object can be provided by different sources. In addition, multiple sources can be combined to derive a specific type of data (e.g., the activity of a user can be derived from an accelerometer in combination with a position sensor). ACCESSORS makes it possible to model a single data source as producer of a variety of types of data. For instance, an Apple Watch provides both, location data and health data. The ACCESSORS model is **extendable**. On the one hand, additional data sources and sinks can be added at runtime to react to upcoming hardware. For example, the Apple Watch can measure blood sugar levels after a glucometer upgrade. On the other hand, ACCESSORS supports different types of entities. An app, a Smart Thing, or a user can all be specified as an inquiring entity. In this way, ACCESSORS is not limited to a fixed entity type. In the IoT context, where novel Things are released frequently, such an extensibility is indispensable. Furthermore, ACCESSORS is **fine-grained** and **context-sensitive**. This means that both, multi-valued constraints and spatial-temporal or situational conditions can be added to a policy rule.

Table 1. Comparison of current permission models [based on 58].

Approach	Data-centric	Derivation transparency	Extendable	Fine-grained	Context-sensitive
DEFCON	✓	✗	✗	✗	✗
ACStream	✓	✗	✗	✗	✓
Android	✗	✗	(✓)	✗	✗
Selective Permissions	✗	✗	✗	✗	✗
CRêPE	✗	✗	✗	✗	✓
Apex	✗	✗	✗	(✓)	(✓)
YAASE	✗	✗	(✓)	✓	✗
Sorbet	✗	✗	✓	(✓)	(✓)
Retro-skeleton	✗	(✓)	✓	(✓)	(✓)
Constroid	✓	✗	✗	(✓)	✓
AppGuard	✗	(✓)	✓	✓	(✓)
AFP	✗	✗	✓	✓	✓
DroidForce	✓	✗	✗	✓	✓
PMP	✗	✓	✓	✓	✓
ACCESSORS	✓	✓	✓	✓	✓

Table 1 compares ACCESSORS with the permission models applied in the analyzed related work (see Sect. 4). In particular, the five key requirements towards a permission model for the IoT (see Sect. 3) are taken into account, which are [**R1**] data-centric policy rules, [**R2**] derivation transparency, [**R3**] extendable permission model, [**R4**] fine-grained policy rules, and [**R5**] context-sensitive policy rules. Due to the comprehensive abstraction approach covering users, data, data sinks, data sources, contexts, and constraints ACCESSORS is able to meet all requirements towards a permission model for the IoT.

8 Conclusion and Future Work

With the rise of the IoT, there constantly arise novel application fields for this technology. The IoT can improve the quality of life and living (Smart Homes), facilitate the treatment of chronic diseases (Smart Health), and make road traffic safer and more comfortable (Smart Cars), just to name a few of such application fields. For this purpose, however, a great amount of private data about the user has to be collected. Therefore, such applications not only improve the quality of life, but also pose a threat towards privacy. Thus, users need powerful, yet easy to manage mechanisms to control the access to their data.

In this paper we examine whether the currently existing privacy systems for Things are also suitable for the IoT. Since the analysis of these systems shows that the permission models applied by them do not meet all the requirements towards a privacy system for the IoT—namely, data-centric policy rules, derivation transparency, extendable permission model, fine-grained policy rules, and context-sensitive policy rules—we come up with a novel permission model called ACCESSORS. We show that this model not only meets all requirements towards a permission model for the IoT, but that it can also be easily integrated into existing privacy systems for the IoT. We illustrate this exemplarily for the PMP, a privacy system for the Smartphone Layer, and for PATRON, aprivacy systems for the Back-End Layer.

As shown in Sect. 6, ACCESSORS can be used in both, privacy systems for the Smartphone Layer and privacy systems for the Back-End Layer. The aim of future work therefore is to combine these two types of privacy system via ACCESSORS. Since both types can be configured by using ACCESSORS, users would be able to make their privacy requirements elicitation once and then transfer it to all of their Things as well as the back-end. Synergy effects can be achieved by this combination. On the one hand, particularly confidential data can be blocked at an early stage in the Smartphone Layer which increases data security, as this data thereby never leaves the user's Thing. On the other hand, a pattern-based privacy solution in the back-end enables the highest possible quality of service, since certain attributes are not systematically filtered out. Instead, only complex sequences of attributes declared as private patterns are concealed, while public attribute sequences remain unaffected.

Alpers et al. [3] describe an approach how privacy rules can be defined and managed at a central site once and then transferred and applied to any end device of a user. Future work will have to consider how this approach can be applied to ACCESSORS. In addition, it has to be assessed to what extent the approach can be extended so that it can also be embedded in the Configuration and Verification Layer of PATRON.

Acknowledgments. This paper is part of the PATRON research project which is commissioned by the Baden-Württemberg Stiftung gGmbH. The authors would like to thank the BW-Stiftung for the funding of this research.

References

1. Aggarwal, C.C., Ashish, N., Sheth, A.: The Internet of Things: a survey from the data-centric perspective. In: Aggarwal, C. (ed.) Managing and Mining Sensor Data, pp. 383–428. Springer, Boston (2013). https://doi.org/10.1007/978-1-4614-6309-2_12

2. Agrawal, D., El Abbadi, A., Wang, S.: Secure and privacy-preserving data services in the cloud: a data centric view. Proc. VLDB Endow. **5**(12), 2028–2029 (2012)
3. Alpers, S., et al.: PRIVACY-AVARE: an approach to manage and distribute privacy settings. In: Proceedings of the 2017 3rd IEEE International Conference on Computer and Communications, ICCC 2017, pp. 1460–1468 (2017)
4. Aman, M.N., Chua, K.C., Sikdar, B.: Secure data provenance for the Internet of Things. In: Proceedings of the 3rd ACM International Workshop on IoT Privacy, Trust, and Security, IoTPTS 2017, pp. 11–14 (2017)
5. Backes, M., Gerling, S., Hammer, C., Maffei, M., von Styp-Rekowsky, P.: App-Guard – enforcing user requirements on Android apps. In: Piterman, N., Smolka, S.A. (eds.) TACAS 2013. LNCS, vol. 7795, pp. 543–548. Springer, Heidelberg (2013). https://doi.org/10.1007/978-3-642-36742-7_39
6. Backes, M., Gerling, S., Hammer, C., Maffei, M., von Styp-Rekowsky, P.: App-Guard – fine-grained policy enforcement for untrusted Android applications. In: Garcia-Alfaro, J., Lioudakis, G., Cuppens-Boulahia, N., Foley, S., Fitzgerald, W.M. (eds.) DPM/SETOP -2013. LNCS, vol. 8247, pp. 213–231. Springer, Heidelberg (2014). https://doi.org/10.1007/978-3-642-54568-9_14
7. Barrera, D., Kayacik, H.G., van Oorschot, P.C., Somayaji, A.: A methodology for empirical analysis of permission-based security models and its application to Android. In: Proceedings of the 17th ACM Conference on Computer and Communications Security, CCS 2010, pp. 73–84 (2010)
8. Bitsaki, M., et al.: An integrated mHealth solution for enhancing patients' health online. In: Lacković, I., Vasic, D. (eds.) 6th European Conference of the International Federation for Medical and Biological Engineering. IP, vol. 45, pp. 695–698. Springer, Cham (2015). https://doi.org/10.1007/978-3-319-11128-5_173
9. Brush, A.B., Lee, B., Mahajan, R., Agarwal, S., Saroiu, S., Dixon, C.: Home automation in the wild: challenges and opportunities. In: Proceedings of the SIGCHI Conference on Human Factors in Computing Systems, CHI 2011, pp. 2115–2124 (2011)
10. Cao, J., Carminati, B., Ferrari, E., Tan, K.L.: ACStream: enforcing access control over data streams. In: Proceedings of the 2009 IEEE 25th International Conference on Data Engineering, ICDE 2009, pp. 1495–1498 (2009)
11. Chin, E., Felt, A.P., Sekar, V., Wagner, D.: Measuring user confidence in smartphone security and privacy. In: Proceedings of the Eighth Symposium on Usable Privacy and Security, SOUPS 2012, pp. 1:1–1:16 (2012)
12. Conti, M., Nguyen, V.T.N., Crispo, B.: CRePE: context-related policy enforcement for Android. In: Burmester, M., Tsudik, G., Magliveras, S., Ilić, I. (eds.) ISC 2010. LNCS, vol. 6531, pp. 331–345. Springer, Heidelberg (2011). https://doi.org/10.1007/978-3-642-18178-8_29
13. Cugola, G., Margara, A.: Processing flows of information: from data stream to complex event processing. ACM Comput. Surv. **44**(3), 15:1–15:62 (2012)
14. Davies, N., Taft, N., Satyanarayanan, M., Clinch, S., Amos, B.: Privacy mediators: helping IoT cross the chasm. In: Proceedings of the 17th International Workshop on Mobile Computing Systems and Applications, HotMobile 2016, pp. 39–44 (2016)
15. Davis, B., Chen, H.: RetroSkeleton: retrofitting Android apps. In: Proceeding of the 11th Annual International Conference on Mobile Systems, Applications, and Services, MobiSys 2013, pp. 181–192 (2013)
16. Davis, B., Sanders, B., Khodaverdian, A., Chen, H.: I-ARM-Droid: a rewriting framework for in-app reference monitors for Android applications. In: Proceedings of the 2012 IEEE Conference on Mobile Security Technologies, MoST 2012, pp. 28:1–28:9 (2012)

17. Dey, A.K.: Understanding and using context. Pers. Ubiquitous Comput. **5**(1), 4–7 (2001)
18. Enck, W., Ongtang, M., McDaniel, P.: Understanding Android security. IEEE Secur. Priv. **7**(1), 50–57 (2009)
19. Felt, A.P., Egelman, S., Wagner, D.: I've got 99 problems, but vibration ain't one: a survey of smartphone users' concerns. In: Proceedings of the Second ACM Workshop on Security and Privacy in Smartphones and Mobile Devices, SPSM 2012, pp. 33–44 (2012)
20. Felt, A.P., Ha, E., Egelman, S., Haney, A., Chin, E., Wagner, D.: Android permissions: user attention, comprehension, and behavior. In: Proceedings of the Eighth Symposium on Usable Privacy and Security, SOUPS 2012, pp. 3:1–3:14 (2012)
21. Fragkaki, E., Bauer, L., Jia, L., Swasey, D.: Modeling and enhancing Android's permission system. In: Foresti, S., Yung, M., Martinelli, F. (eds.) ESORICS 2012. LNCS, vol. 7459, pp. 1–18. Springer, Heidelberg (2012). https://doi.org/10.1007/978-3-642-33167-1_1
22. Google Inc.: Android Things, May 2018. https://developer.android.com/things
23. Hamlen, K.W., Jones, M.: Aspect-oriented in-lined reference monitors. In: Proceedings of the Third ACM SIGPLAN Workshop on Programming Languages and Analysis for Security, PLAS 2008, pp. 11–20(2008)
24. Harle, R.K., Tailor, S., Zidek, A.: Bellrock - anonymous proximity beacons from personal devices. In: Proceedings of the 2018 IEEE International Conference on Pervasive Computing and Communications, PerCom 2018, pp. 284–293 (2018)
25. He, Y., Barman, S., Wang, D., Naughton, J.F.: On the complexity of privacy-preserving complex event processing. In: Proceedings of the Thirtieth ACM SIGMOD-SIGACT-SIGART Symposium on Principles of Database Systems, PODS 2011, pp. 165–174(2011)
26. Henrik, Z.J., Garcia, M.O., Klaus, W.: Privacy in the Internet of Things: threats and challenges. Secur. Commun. Netw. **7**(12), 2728–2742 (2014)
27. Hilty, M., Pretschner, A., Basin, D., Schaefer, C., Walter, T.: A policy language for distributed usage control. In: Biskup, J., López, J. (eds.) ESORICS 2007. LNCS, vol. 4734, pp. 531–546. Springer, Heidelberg (2007). https://doi.org/10.1007/978-3-540-74835-9_35
28. Istepanian, R.S.H., Hu, S., Philip, N., Sungoor, A.: The potential of internet of m-health things "m-IoT" for non-invasive glucose level sensing. In: Proceedings of the 2011 Annual International Conference of the IEEE Engineering in Medicine and Biology Society, EMBS 2011, pp. 5264–5266 (2011)
29. Jordan, M., Mitchell, T.: Machine learning: trends, perspectives, and prospects. Science **349**(6245), 255–260 (2015)
30. Kalkov, I., Franke, D., Schommer, J.F., Kowalewski, S.: A real-time extension to the Android platform. In: Proceedings of the 10th International Workshop on Java Technologies for Real-time and Embedded Systems, JTRES 2012, pp. 105–114(2012)
31. Khan, R., Khan, S.U., Zaheer, R., Khan, S.: Future internet: the Internet of Things architecture, possible applications and key challenges. In: Proceedings of the 2012 10th International Conference on Frontiers of Information Technology, FIT 2012, pp. 257–260 (2012)
32. Knöll, M.: Diabetes City: how urban game design strategies can help diabetics. In: Weerasinghe, D. (ed.) eHealth 2008. LNICST, vol. 0001, pp. 200–204. Springer, Heidelberg (2009). https://doi.org/10.1007/978-3-642-00413-1_28

33. Knöll, M.: "On the top of high towers ..." discussing locations in a mobile health game for diabetics. In: Proceedings of the 2010 IADIS International Conference Game and Entertainment Technologies, MCCSIS 2010, pp. 61–68 (2010)
34. Kovatchev, B.P., Gonder-Frederick, L.A., Cox, D.J., Clarke, W.L.: Evaluating the accuracy of continuous glucose-monitoring sensors. Diabetes Care **27**(8), 1922–1928 (2004)
35. Kozlov, D., Veijalainen, J., Ali, Y.: Security and privacy threats in IoT architectures. In: Proceedings of the 7th International Conference on Body Area Networks, BodyNets 2012, pp. 256–262 (2012)
36. Metzger, A., Cassales Marquezan, C.: Future internet apps: the next wave of adaptive service-oriented systems? In: Abramowicz, W., Llorente, I.M., Surridge, M., Zisman, A., Vayssière, J. (eds.) ServiceWave 2011. LNCS, vol. 6994, pp. 230–241. Springer, Heidelberg (2011). https://doi.org/10.1007/978-3-642-24755-2_22
37. Migliavacca, M., Papagiannis, I., Eyers, D.M., Shand, B., Bacon, J., Pietzuch, P.: DEFCON: high-performance event processing with information security. In: Proceedings of the 2010 USENIX Conference on USENIX Annual Technical Conference, USENIXATC 2010, pp. 1–15 (2010)
38. Mindermann, K., Riedel, F., Abdulkhaleq, A., Stach, C., Wagner, S.: Exploratory study of the privacy extension for system theoretic process analysis (STPA-Priv) to elicit privacy risks in eHealth. In: Proceedings of the 2017 IEEE 25th International Requirements Engineering Conference Workshops, REW 2017, pp. 90–96 (2017)
39. Nauman, M., Khan, S., Zhang, X.: Apex: extending Android permission model and enforcement with user-defined runtime constraints. In: Proceedings of the 5th ACM Symposium on Information, Computer and Communications Security, ASIACCS 2010, pp. 328–332 (2010)
40. Park, J., Sandhu, R.: The UCON$_{ABC}$ usage control model. ACM Trans. Inf. Syst. Secur. **7**(1), 128–174 (2004)
41. Perera, C., Zaslavsky, A., Christen, P.: Context aware computing for the Internet of Things: a survey. IEEE Commun. Surv. Tutor. **16**(1), 414–454 (2014)
42. Rasthofer, S., Arzt, S., Lovat, E., Bodden, E.: DroidForce: enforcing complex, data-centric, system-wide policies in Android. In: Proceedings of the 2014 Ninth International Conference on Availability, Reliability and Security, ARES 2014, pp. 40–49 (2014)
43. Russello, G., Crispo, B., Fernandes, E., Zhauniarovich, Y.: YAASE: yet another Android security extension. In: Proceeding of the 2011 IEEE Third International Conference on Privacy, Security, Risk and Trust and 2011 IEEE Third International Conference on Social Computing, PASSAT 2011, pp. 1033–1040 (2011)
44. Sarkar, S., Misra, S.: Theoretical modelling of fog computing: a green computing paradigm to support IoT applications. IET Netw. **5**(2), 23–29 (2016)
45. Schreckling, D., Posegga, J., Hausknecht, D.: Constroid: data-centric access control for Android. In: Proceedings of the 27th Annual ACM Symposium on Applied Computing, SAC 2012, pp. 1478–1485 (2012)
46. Scoccia, G.L., Malavolta, I., Autili, M., Di Salle, A., Inverardi, P.: User-centric Android flexible permissions. In: Proceedings of the 2017 IEEE/ACM 39th International Conference on Software Engineering Companion, ICSE-C 2017, pp. 365–367 (2017)
47. Sekar, L.P., Gankidi, V.R., Subramanian, S.: Avoidance of security breach through selective permissions in Android operating system. ACM SIGSOFT Softw. Eng. Notes **5**(37), 1–9 (2012)

48. Sellwood, J., Crampton, J.: Sleeping Android: the danger of dormant permissions. In: Proceedings of the Third ACM Workshop on Security and Privacy in Smartphones & Mobile Devices, SPSM 2013, pp. 55–66 (2013)
49. Sicari, S., Rizzardi, A., Grieco, L.A., Coen-Porisini, A.: Security, privacy and trust in Internet of Things: the road ahead. Comput. Netw. **76**(C), 146–164 (2015)
50. Siewiorek, D.: Generation smartphone. IEEE Spectr. **49**(9), 54–58 (2012)
51. Stach, C.: How to assure privacy on Android phones and devices? In: Proceedings of the 2013 IEEE 14th International Conference on Mobile Data Management, MDM 2013, pp. 350–352 (2013)
52. Stach, C.: Secure Candy Castle – a prototype for privacy-aware mHealth apps. In: Proceedings of the 2016 IEEE 17th International Conference on Mobile Data Management, MDM 2016, pp. 361–364 (2016)
53. Stach, C., et al.: The AVARE PATRON: a holistic privacy approach for the Internet of Things. In: Proceedings of the 15th International Conference on Security and Cryptography, SECRYPT 2018, pp. 372–379 (2018)
54. Stach, C., et al.: PATRON – Datenschutz in Datenstromverarbeitungssystemen. In: Informatik 2017: Digitale Kulturen, Tagungsband der 47. Jahrestagung der Gesellschaft für Informatik e.V. (GI), 25 September–29 September 2017, Chemnitz. LNI, vol. 275, pp. 1085–1096 (2017, in German)
55. Stach, C., Dürr, F., Mindermann, K., Palanisamy, S.M., Wagner, S.: How a pattern-based privacy system contributes to improve context recognition. In: Proceedings of the 2018 IEEE International Conference on Pervasive Computing and Communications Workshops, CoMoRea 2018, pp. 238–243 (2018)
56. Stach, C., Mitschang, B.: Privacy management for mobile platforms - a review of concepts and approaches. In: Proceedings of the 2013 IEEE 14th International Conference on Mobile Data Management, MDM 2013, pp. 305–313 (2013)
57. Stach, C., Mitschang, B.: Design and implementation of the Privacy Management Platform. In: Proceedings of the 2014 IEEE 15th International Conference on Mobile Data Management, MDM 2014, pp. 69–72 (2014)
58. Stach, C., Mitschang, B.: ACCESSORS: a data-centric permission model for the Internet of Things. In: Proceedings of the 4th International Conference on Information Systems Security and Privacy, ICISSP 2018, pp. 30–40 (2018)
59. Stach, C., Schlindwein, L.F.M.: Candy Castle – a prototype for pervasive health games. In: Proceedings of the 2012 IEEE International Conference on Pervasive Computing and Communications Workshops, PerCom 2012, pp. 501–503 (2012)
60. Stach, C., Steimle, F., Mitschang, B.: The Privacy Management Platform: an enabler for device interoperability and information security in mHealth applications. In: Proceedings of the 11th International Conference on Health Informatics, HEALTHINF 2018, pp. 27–38 (2018)
61. Stach, C., Steimle, F., Franco da Silva, A.C.: TIROL: the extensible interconnectivity layer for mHealth applications. In: Damaševičius, R., Mikašytė, V. (eds.) ICIST 2017. CCIS, vol. 756, pp. 190–202. Springer, Cham (2017). https://doi.org/10.1007/978-3-319-67642-5_16
62. Svangren, M.K., Skov, M.B., Kjeldskov, J.: The connected car: an empirical study of electric cars as mobile digital devices. In: Proceedings of the 19th International Conference on Human-Computer Interaction with Mobile Devices and Services, MobileHCI 2017, pp. 6:1–6:12 (2017)
63. Takabi, H., Joshi, J.B.D., Ahn, G.J.: Security and privacy challenges in cloud computing environments. IEEE Secur. Priv. **8**(6), 24–31 (2010)

64. The European Parliament and the Council of the European Union: Regulation (EU) 2016/679 of the European Parliament and of the Council of 27 April 2016 on the protection of natural persons with regard to the processing of personal data and on the free movement of such data, and repealing Directive 95/46/EC (General Data Protection Regulation). Official journal of the european union, European Union (2016)

65. Vashist, S.K., Schneider, E.M., Luong, J.H.: Commercial smartphone-based devices and smart applications for personalized healthcare monitoring and management. Diagnostics 4(3), 104–128 (2014)

66. Wei, X., Gomez, L., Neamtiu, I., Faloutsos, M.: Permission evolution in the Android ecosystem. In: Proceedings of the 28th Annual Computer Security Applications Conference, ACSAC 2012, pp. 31–40 (2012)

67. Weiser, M.: The computer for the 21st century. Sci. Am. **265**(3), 94–105 (1991)

68. Xie, X., Ray, I., Adaikkalavan, R., Gamble, R.: Information flow control for stream processing in clouds. In: Proceedings of the 18th ACM Symposium on Access Control Models and Technologies, SACMAT 2013, pp. 89–100 (2013)

69. Zeevi, D., et al.: Personalized nutrition by prediction of glycemic responses. Cell **163**(5), 1079–1094 (2015)

All links were last followed on June 1, 2018.

A Simple Attack on CaptchaStar

Thomas Gougeon[(✉)] and Patrick Lacharme[(✉)]

Normandie Univ., UNICAEN, ENSICAEN, CNRS, GREYC, 14000 Caen, France
thomas.gougeon@laposte.net, patrick.lacharme@ensicaen.fr

Abstract. CaptchaStar is a new type of Captcha, proposed in 2016, based on shape recovery. This paper shows that the security of this Captcha is not as good as intended. More precisely, we present and implement an efficient attack on CaptchaStar with a success rate of 96%. The impact of this attack is also investigated in other scenarios as noise addition, and it continues to be very efficient. This paper is a revised version of the paper entitled *How to break CaptchaStar*, presented at the conference ICISSP 2018 [29].

Keywords: Security · Captcha

1 Introduction

CAPTCHA[1] is an acronym meaning Completely Automated Public Turing test to tell Computers and Humans Aparts. Historically, Turing tests were defined by Turing in [52], but the concept of Captchas has been revisited in 1996 by Naor [40] and by von Ahn et al. in 2003 [1]. A Captcha is trying to find out if an entity is a real live human or a computer program. They are used by many Internet giants as protection against spams or various bots, but other usecases have been also investigated as passwords security [44]. These tests should be easy to solve by a human and hard for a program, involving success rates for both human and program. Thus, a Captcha is a program that can paradoxically generate Turing tests that it itself cannot solve [2]. Moreover the letter P in Captcha means Public, in the sense that the security of the scheme should not be based on *obscurity*, as for cryptographic algorithms. Captchas have been implemented by using various techniques, as text distortion, image recognition or audio tests. While the early Captchas were not always user-friendly, new generations of Captchas have been designed as real games. Typically, the importance of user-friendly Captchas has been underlined by Chellapilla et al. [15] and later by Fidas et al. [23] and Yan and El Ahmad [57]. Sometimes, modern Captchas also use a behaviour analysis system in combination with other challenges.

Nevertheless, progress realised in machine learning and image recognition have produced multiple attacks on these systems. For example, Chinese Captchas have been recently solved with deep learning techniques [6]. History of Captchas

---

[1] Captcha will be now written in lower-case for a better readability of the paper.

© Springer Nature Switzerland AG 2019
P. Mori et al. (Eds.): ICISSP 2018, CCIS 977, pp. 66–85, 2019.
https://doi.org/10.1007/978-3-030-25109-3_4

is a long sequence of new designs and new attacks on all these systems. Even the most sophisticated Captchas are generally broken with high success rates. Moreover, another type of attack, called relay attacks, is a significant problem. In these attacks the challenge is simply relayed to a human solver and it is known that several service providers propose to solve a large number of Captcha for very low price [39]. Actually, the design of secure Captchas in the cryptographic meaning is probably impossible. However, these systems are still considered to be relevant, useful and continue to be used in practice, as presented by Thomas et al. in [50]. In particular, authors outline that Captcha solving are not free and, consequently, it increases the cost of creating fraudulent accounts. In their experiments, they conclude that Captchas are able to prevent 92 % of fraudulent accounts. In other terms, Captchas are not designed to avoid all automatic attacks, but are rather intended to minimize their effects.

CaptchaStar is a new concept of Captcha proposed at ACNS 2016 by Conti, Guarisco and Spolaor in [18]. The system proposes to the user an interactive image recognition challenge, different to other image-based Captchas. The proposed challenge is composed of white pixels (called stars), randomly mixed during the generation of the challenge. These stars move in the same time than the cursor of the mouse, inside a square grid, and if the cursor is near to a given place, a shape appears on the grid. If so, the user shall click and the coordinates of the cursor are sent to the server. If the position is close to the correct place, the user is considered as human. A demo is available on the website of CaptchaStar [19]. This Captcha is rather user-friendly and suitable for mobile applications, because it does not requires a keyboard. CaptchaStar proposes several parameters for the challenge generation, the proposed combination of parameters achieves a success rate of 90% for a human in less than 30 s on average. Authors of CaptchaStar investigated the resiliency of their system against several traditional and automatic attacks, or relay attacks, without having identified any vulnerabilities.

Nevertheless, we consider in this paper an heuristic, able to solve the challenge in an efficient way. More precisely, we propose an attack, based on the concentration of pixels, with a success rate of 96%, in less than 12 s, on the implementation proposed on the website of CaptchaStar. We also investigate the success rate of our attack on challenges generated with modified parameters, as with a larger amount of noise. Experiments show that it does not prevent this attack. This paper is a revised version of the paper entitled *How to break CaptchaStar*, presented at the conference ICISSP 2018 [29]. It includes more details and examples on the proposed attack, with a description of heuristic attacks examined in the original paper of CaptchaStar for comparison.

Organisation. The state-of-the-art of attacks on Captchas is described in Sect. 2, both on text-based Captchas (Sect. 2.1) and on image-based Captchas (Sect. 2.2). CaptchaStar is presented in Sect. 3. We describe our attack in Sect. 4, including a presentation of our heuristic (Sect. 4.1), the attack itself (Sect. 4.2) and the implementation (Sect. 4.3). Finally we propose a discussion on the security of CaptchaStar in Sect. 5, by investigating the noise addition or the possibility to hide several figure during the challenge generation (Sect. 5.1) and other countermeasures (Sect. 5.2).

2   Attacks on Captchas: A State-of-the-Art

Text-based Captchas have been widely deployed on the Internet since fifteen years, because they are simple to understand for a large public. This type of Captcha asks the user to read a distorted word (or a random sequence of characters). Nevertheless, important attacks on these Captchas were quickly published. Variants using 3D-text or video have been proposed but have been also broken.

Thus, the failure of this Captchas encouraged the design of other types of Captcha. Shortly after, image-based Captchas, audio Captchas or game-based Captchas have emerged. However, they were not really stronger in term of security. Thus, the recent Captcha of Google, called NoCaptcha, based on a Behaviour Analysis System, is also analysed and partially broken in [48].

The design of Captcha systems should take into account several parameters, particularly the success rate and the usability. Typically, a success rate of 0.01% for the attacker is suggested as acceptable in [14,56], but an higher rate between 0.6% and 1% is considered as more realistic in [12,59].

The success rate for the attacker is obviously a trade-off because it is linked to the success rate of a genuine human, proposed at 90% in [14,56]. Nevertheless, in most case this last rate is often hard to reach, particularly in the case of audio Captcha [11]. Finally, a second parameter is the time to solve the Captcha: the attack should not be slower than a human response. For example, in [12,45], it is suggested that human should be able to sent the response within 30 s.

2.1   Text-Based Captchas

First text-based Captchas were composed of one or several distorted words in an image, as for example, the test of Baird et al. in 2002 [7] or the old Yahoo's Captchas Gimpy and Ez-Gimpy. Another example, called reCaptcha, was proposed in 2008 by von Ahn et al. in [5], and later acquired by Google. ReCaptcha combined two words, where the first one was only distorted and the second one was scanned from various books. Challenges proposed by this type of Captcha are not necessary composed of existing words, as the MSN Captcha (2009), which is constituted by four random words of eight characters with digits and upper-case letters. Numerous text-based Captchas have been implemented. Burztein et al. [13] identify three categories of features for a text-based Captcha:

- visual features;
- anti-segmentation features;
- anti-recognition features.

More sophisticated text-based Captchas have also been proposed, as hollow Captchas, 3D text-based Captchas or animated text-based Captchas, as proposed in [20,35]. For example, NuCaptcha was one of the first deployed video Captcha scheme, combined with a Behaviour Analysis System.

One of the first attack on these Captchas was proposed by Mori and Malik on Gimpy and Ez-Gimpy in [38], with a success rate of 92% for the first one and

33% for the second one. They propose two approaches: a part-based approach, consisting in a character recognition combined with lexical information, and a holistic approach, consisting in finding words immediately. The following year, six other text-based Captchas are broken by Chellapilla and Simard in [16]. They use segmentation and machine learning techniques to attack these Captchas, with various success rates, as 45.7% for the Yahoo Captcha and 4.9% for the Google/Gmail Captcha. Between 2007 and 2011, Yan and El Ahmad broke a large set of text-based Captchas using very simple techniques (as the pixel count by letters), or more evaluated techniques in several papers [55,56,58], including the MSN Captcha. For example, success rates on (old) Microsoft Captcha, Megaupload or reCaptcha are between 33% and 90%. This last work improves the success rate of previous attacks on reCaptcha, where the success rate was between 10% and 31% [53] and will be again improved in 2013 by Goodfellow et al. in [27]. Real-world Captchas are also solved by Hindle et al. using simple techniques, as the PirateBay Captca with a success rate of 61% [32].

More recent contributions on text-based Captchas attacks include the attack of Bursztein et al. on several Captcha systems in [8]. These attacks are based on SVM and KNN classifiers and achieve variable success rates (from 0% to 93%). Hollow Captchas are attacked by Gao et al. with success rates between 36% and 89% [24]. Another attack on many text-based Captchas has been presented by Gao et al. in [25]. It uses Gabor filters, with a success rate between 5% and 77% on various Captchas as the new version of reCaptcha. 3D text-based Captchas are also attacked in [42], with success rate between 27% and 76%, whereas animated text-based Captchas are attacked in [54], with 77% of reconstruction accuracy for the enhanced attack strategy. As we can see, the success rate of all these attacks is clearly higher than 0.01% or even 1%, as proposed above. Moreover the strategies used in these attacks are variable, from very simple techniques to advanced machine learning-based techniques.

2.2   Image-Based Captchas and Variants

In traditional image-based Captchas, the user is asked to link one or several words with one or several images [17]. Nevertheless, most of the first generation of image-based Captchas were simply vulnerable to random guessing attacks, because there was only a limited number of possible response to the challenge. In 2007, the Captcha Asirra (Animal Species Image Recognition for Restricting Access), proposed by Microsoft and described in [22], asks the user to identify dogs and cats in a large set of random images. This Captcha can be solved by humans with a rate of 99.6% in less than 30 s and was considered as more user-friendly than traditional Captchas. Others image-based Captchas include ARTiFACIAL [45] and Imagination [21]. The first one is composed of two tests, whereas the second one exploits the capacity of a human to recognise human faces from images. Other image-based Captchas have been proposed, with a design based on image-orientation [28], polygonal sub-images orientation [34], gender identification [33] or combination of these techniques [30].

Most of these image-based Captchas were no more secure than text-based schemes For example, Golle proposed an attack in 2008 on Asirra, using a machine learning technique (more precisely a SVM classification) with a success rate of 10% [26]. Zhu et al. have presented in 2010 an attack on ARTiFACIAL Imagination with a success rate of 75% and 18% respectively. Sivakorn et al. presented recently an attack on several image-based Captcha in [48], using deep learning approaches.

Audio Captchas have also been proposed, as [46], because they are useful for people visually impaired, even if they are difficult for a non-English speaker. Attacks on audio Captcha can be found in [9,10,49], where the conclusion is a total failure of these systems. The objectives of game-based Captchas is to make fun (for the user) a Captcha solver. These Captchas are also called Games with a purpose in [4]. One of the game-based Captcha was propsoed by van Ahn and Dabbish in 2004 [3]. Four game-based Captchas are analysed in depth by Mohamed et al. in [37], in terms of resistance to automated attacks, relay attacks and usability. MathCaptchas have also been solved [31]. Finally, two new (and independent) schemes, both called DeepCaptcha, are proposed in [41,43] using deep learning. To the best of our knowledge, there are no attacks against these last two schemes.

Relay attacks are possible on text-based Captcha, image-based Captcha or video Captcha. They are more difficult in the case of game-based Captcha, due to the dynamic nature of these Captcha. The resistance depends obviously of the game and is analysed in [37] on several examples of Captchas. The mitigation against relay attacks has been taken into account by some Captcha. For example, a text-based Captcha, called iCaptcha [51], was also designed to avoid relay attacks with a timing analysis between interactions, based on a sequence of mouse clicks. The objective of interactive Captcha is also the mitigation of these attacks, as presented in [36]. As presented below, CaptchaStar also uses an interactive system in order to mitigate these attacks.

3   Presentation of CaptchaStar

3.1   System Description

CaptchaStar proposes to the user a grid with a black background, where white stars are randomly disposed in the grid. More precisely, a star is a square of 5×5 pixels, whereas the grid is formed by a square of 300×300 pixels. When the user moves the mouse cursor, the stars move in a pseudo-random way in interaction with the user. The objective for the user is to move the cursor until he is able to recognise a shape (the shape is different for each challenge). There is only one position of the cursor in the grid, that gives the original shape and this position is the correct solution of the challenge. When the cursor is far away from the solution, the stars form a random scatter plots, but approaching the solution, the stars aggregate. Once the user is confident that its cursor is correctly positioned, he clicks to submit its answer to the server (the coordinates of the cursor). Then, the server compares the submitted cursor position to the solution, and if the coordinates of this position are close enough, the user is considered as a human. In practice, the server computes the distance between the coordinates and this distance should be lower than a given threshold. Figure 1 illustrates the process of solving a CaptchaStar challenge on the website of CaptchaStar [19].

More precisely, the challenge is created as follows. The server accesses to a large image database and selects randomly one image. CaptchaStar uses currently a base of 5,000 images with two colors, but the size of this base can be easily increased. This image is decomposed into stars using a sampling algorithm and these stars are randomly mixed and positioned on the grid. In addition, some noisy stars are randomly inserted on the grid. The number of these noisy stars is customisable, as detailed below. The exact sampling algorithm is not described in this paper because we don't use it in the attack presented in this paper.

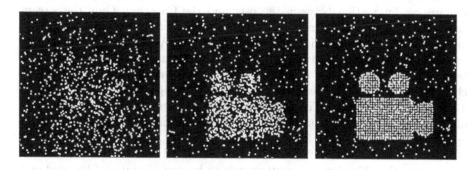

Fig. 1. Solving a CaptchaStar challenge on [19].

As for any Captcha, the usability and the complexity of the proposed challenge is a tradeoff that depends on several parameters values:

- the noise (ψ) defining the percentage of added stars;
- the sensitivity (δ) representing the relationship between the cursor movement and the movement of each star;
- the number of possible solutions ($NSol$) representing the number of shapes hidden in the Captcha;
- the rotation indicates whether the picture is rotated by a random degree or not;
- the threshold (α) corresponds to the maximum distance between the answer and the solution to be considered as a human.

More formally, after the random selection of the picture, the sampling algorithm generates a set of n stars from it, denoted by the set $\mathbf{S} = \{s^i, 1 \leq i \leq n\}$. Actually, each star s^i is defined by two coordinates, denoted by (s_x^i, s_y^i), in the grid. The original coordinates of each stars are saved and are denoted by $P^i = (P_x^i, P_y^i)$ for each star s^i. In addition to these stars, there are $\psi \times n$ noisy stars that are generated with random coordinates. Recalling that ψ is a percentage, typically between 70% and 200%. Thus, the number of noisy stars can be greater than the number of stars derived from the figure.

The exact solution of the challenge is a pair of coordinates $sol = (sol_x, sol_y)$ where each coordinate is picked randomly in the range $[5, 295]$. Thus, the solution is never too close of the edges of the grid. This solution has been randomly generated by the sampling algorithm, independently to the original figure. Thus, two challenges generated from the same picture, have a different solution in order to avoid replay attacks.

3.2 Security

CaptchaStar is protected against traditional attacks on Captchas, as indirect attacks, database exhaustion (due to a small number of image in the database) or leak of database (because the solution of the challenge is independent to the image), random choice, and pure relay attacks [18] (resolving the scheme requires an interaction between the user and the Captcha). Only the stream relay attacks that is the more powerful one, is a real threat to this Captcha, but, as for almost Captcha schemes, it is difficult to set up. As claimed above, machine learning techniques are one of the most powerful attacks against Captchas. A technique similar to [26] is used in [18] in order to extract the features of the challenges. Then they trained Random Forest and Support Vector Machine with $4,000$ random challenges. The best choice of parameters provided a success rate of 78.1% with a computation time of 421 s (and a parameter $\psi = 70\%$ for noise addition during the generation of the challenges).

Automatic attacks using ad-hoc heuristics have been also examinated. In these cases, the objective for an attacker is to browse all states of the grid and identify a specific state that corresponds to the solution. It should require an heuristic that recognize the presence of a shape, e.g. looking at the dispersion of the stars or the distance between the most distant stars. At high level, the fastest heuristic leads to less than 1% of success rate with a computing time greater than 60 s, whereas the best heuristic in term of success rate is 1.92% with a computing time of 1,500 s [18]. For comparison, a human is able to solve a CaptchaStar challenge proposed in an average time of 23.1 s with a success rate of 91.0% with the parameters used in the demo site (described in the next section).

More precisely, 3 different heuristics, that are described in the following together with their success rate and computation time, have been investigated. For each heuristic, the state leading to the minimum score is the solution submitted by the automated attack. They decided to compute a score for all the $84,100$ states.

Let S^k be the challenge state generated when the cursor is in position k, in coordinates (cur_x^k, cur_y^k), with $1 \leq k \leq 84,100$. The pair (s_x^i, s_y^i) denotes the coordinates of each star s^i belonging to S_k. Let $M_{i,j}^k$ be the grid of pixels of the challenge with $1 \leq k \leq 84,100$ and $1 \leq i,j \leq 300$. Each cell of the grid is defined as follows:

$$M_{i,j}^k = \begin{cases} 0, & \text{if pixel}(i,j) \text{ is white} \\ 1, & \text{otherwise.} \end{cases}$$

This grid M^k can be decomposed into squared tiles t of $\ell \times \ell$ pixels. In this case, the pixels of each tile are defined by $t_{i,j}$ with $1 \leq i, j \leq \ell$.

MinGap: This heuristic aims to evaluate the distance between the most distant stars. The computed score represents the sum of two values. The first value represents the gap between the x component of the leftmost star and the x component of the rightmost star. The second value is computed in the same way for the y axis. For each state S^k, the score is computed as follows:

$$MinGap(k) = \left(\max_{s^i \in S^k} s^i_x - \min_{s^i \in S^k} s^i_x \right) + \left(\max_{s^i \in S^k} s^i_y - \min_{s^i \in S^k} s^i_y \right).$$

MinDist: This heuristic aims to evaluate the dispersion of the stars in the grid. It splits the grid in a set T^k of 144 squared tiles of 25×25 and evaluates the stars dispersion in each tile. For each tile t belonging to T^k, a score is computed as follows: $\text{score}(t) = |2 \times \sum_{i=1}^{25} \sum_{j=1}^{25} t_{i,j} - 25^2|$, where $t_{i,j}$ is the pixel in the tile t, defined for $1 \leq i, j \leq \ell$. The returned score of a state S^k is the sum of the scores of all the tiles:

$$MinDis(k) = \sum_{t \in T^k} \text{score}(t).$$

Table 1. Execution time and success rate of ad-hoc attacks on CaptchaStar using T_2 parameters (from [18]).

Heuristic	MinDist	MinSumDist	AllSumDist
Time (s)	65	765	1500
Success rate	0.07%	0.50%	1.92%

MinSumDist: This heuristic aims to detect when stars are clustered together, even in different groups. It sums, for each star, the minimum euclidean distance from another star. $d(x, y)$ represents the euclidean distance between x and y. For each state S^k, the score is computed as follows:

$$MinSumDist(k) = \sum_{s^i \in S^k} \min_{s^j \in S^k} d(s^i, s^j).$$

AllSumDist: This heuristic is almost the same of the previously considered, but it sums all the euclidean distance, not only the minimum. For each state S^k, the score is computed as follows:

$$AllSumDist(k) = \sum_{s^i \in S^k} \sum_{s^j \in S^k} d(s^i, s^j).$$

Table 1 presents the execution time and the success rates of the 3 heuristics considered by the CaptchaStar authors. The best one reaches a success rate lower than 2% with an extremely high execution time. All these ad-hoc attacks are therefore totally inefficient against CaptchaStar.

The principles of these three heuristics (dispersion and cluster of stars) are good ones, because our attack is precisely based on aggregation of stars when a shape appears in the grid. Nevertheless, They have not been sufficiently adapted to attack the system.

4   Attack on CaptchaStar

4.1   Heuristic

The choice of our heuristic comes from the observation that the more the cursor is close to the solution of the challenge, the more the stars are aggregated (excepted to the noisy stars). For example, we see on the Fig. 1 that the aggregation is particularly noticeable when the cursor is at the coordinates of the solution (note that $NSol = 1$ in this figure). The attack estimates the stars concentration in the grid for all cursor positions, independently to the shape. Thus, the proposed heuristic is not directly related to shape recovery, but it aims to maximise the concentration of the stars into a part of the grid. The state of the grid maximising this concentration is considered as the solution of the challenge. The concentration of the stars is computed as follows.

The grid, corresponding to the state S^k, is separated in a set, denoted T^k, of squared tiles, each of $\ell \times \ell$ pixels. A given tile t countains ℓ^2 pixels $t_{i,j}$, with $1 \leq i, j \leq \ell$. We consider that $t_{i,j} = 0$ if this pixel is black and $t_{i,j} = 1$ otherwise. The concentration of pixels is computed for each tile $t^k \in T^k$, providing a score for each tile. More precisely, this score is the number of white pixels in the tile:

$$\text{score}(t^k) = \sum_{i=1}^{\ell} \sum_{j=1}^{\ell} t_{i,j}^k$$

[29]. For a given state S^k, the set P^k of each score score(t^k) (with $t^k \in T^k$) is stored. Finally, the final score of the state S^k is computed by summing up the n_{max} first values of P^k, as follows:

$$\text{maxConcentration}(k) = \sum_{i=0}^{n_{max}} P_i^k$$

[29]. For example, with parameters $\ell = 10$ and $n_{max} = 20$, the heuristic computes the number of white pixels in each 10×10 tiles of the grid, and the heuristic adds the 20 largest scores for the computation of maxConcentration. The exact choice of these values, used in our experiment, is discussed in Sect. 4.3. These values are chosen as a tradeoff between computational time and success rate.

4.2   Description of the Attack

At high level, the proposed attack computes for each state (obtained by moving the cursor position) the score maxConcentration, according the previous heuristic. The position corresponding to the state with the highest score is considered as the solution of the challenge. It is this position that is sent to the server. Actually, the attack is composed of two steps in order to be more efficient in term of execution time. More precisely, the first step determines an approximate position for the solution by looking at a sub-part of the possible states. The second step, examining at all the states around the approximate solution, aims to determine the exact position of the solution. There are $290 \times 290 = 84,100$ possible solutions to a given challenge and a score should be computed for all these states. During the first phase, the scores are only computed for n_s of these states, where n_s is an integer lower then $84,100$. In this case, the grid is split in a set of n_s squared tiles and each tile center is used as coordinates k to generate the n_s states S^k, for which a score is computed. The first part of the attack returns the coordinates c_k of the state S^k leading to the maximum score among the n_s states (it means that only n_s scores are computed). This score is supposed an approximate solution of the challenge. Then, the second phase considers the coordinates c_k, provided by the first step, as the center of a tile of size $\ell_2 \times \ell_2$. A score is computed using the same heuristic $maxConcentration$ for all the states generated by the $\ell_2 \times \ell_2$ coordinates of the tile (consequently ℓ_2^2 scores are computed in this second step). Table 2 gives the values used in the attack. Their choice is discussed in the next section.

Table 2. Parameters value used for the attack [29].

Parameters	ℓ	n_{max}	n_s	ℓ_2
Value	10	20	2, 500	20

Figure 2 illustrates the result of the attack, after the first phase with an approximate solution, and after the second phase, on one example. The choice to split the attack into two phases reproduces actually the human behaviour. When a human tries to solve this type of challenge, it begins with random movements of the mouse until the formation of a shape for a given position of the cursor. At this moment, the user will move slowly the mouse around the previous position.

4.3   Experiments

CaptchaStar proposes 6 sets of parameters (from T_1 to T_6), as presented in Table 3, where Rate corresponds to the success rate of a human, Time corresponds to the time to solve the challenge by a human (on average), and the other parameters as presented in Subsect. 3.1.

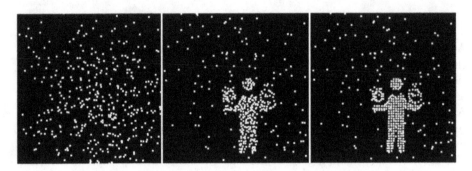

Fig. 2. The two phases of the attack realised on the website [19].

Table 3. Parameters proposed by CaptchaStar [18].

Test	T_1	T_2	T_3	T_4	T_5	T_6
ψ	0%	70%	70%	10%	0%	250%
δ	5	7	7	7	10	5
$NSol$	1	1	1	2	3	1
Rate (%)	77.0	87.1	91.0	46.4	82.7	75.5
Time (s)	15.0	18.8	23.1	59.5	32.8	31.1

The set of parameters T_3 provides the best success rate for a human. The parameters, used in the web site of CaptchaStar, are not detailed, but it seems that the rotation is not implemented. In other side, the noise, the sensitivity, the number of possible solutions seems to be parameters of T_2 and T_3. As a consequence, we suppose that on the demo version the parameters used are T_2 (the only difference between T_2 and T_3 is the rotation).

Our attack is implemented in Javascript with Chromium 51.0.2704.79 on Ubuntu 14.04 (64-bit). The Javascript code is directly executed in the console of the browser after connection on the CaptchaStar demo website. The verification of each server is realized on the server side. The grid uses a Canvas, an HTML5 object, from this object it is easy to extract the RGBA values for each pixel using JavaScript. Pixels are black or white, so using the RGBA values, the entire grid is designed by a binary matrix. When the cursor moves, the stars positions (i.e. the binary matrix) are updated on the client side, with a JavaScript code. Therefore, it is possible to move the stars with a program using JavaScript calls. The challenge generation and verification are done with a PHP script on the server side.

The attack was executed on $1,000$ challenge, with a success rate of 96% and an execution time lower than 12 s per Captcha. Recalling that, a success rate of 1% for an attacker is considered as a success, even if most of Captchas have been attacked with an higher success rate. One can note that, the obtained success rate by the automated attack is greater than the one obtained by the user study

(87.1%), and the execution time of the attack is lower than the solving time of a human (18.8 s) for the set of parameter values T_2 (see Table 3).

The challenges that are not successfully solved by this attack, come generally from images having a large blank zone that interferes with our heuristic. Nevertheless, only some cases of this type of figures are not recognized. Figure 3 shows two examples having resisted to the proposed attack. Moreover the solution found by the attack is not so far to the exact solution, and the attack could be successful with optimised parameters.

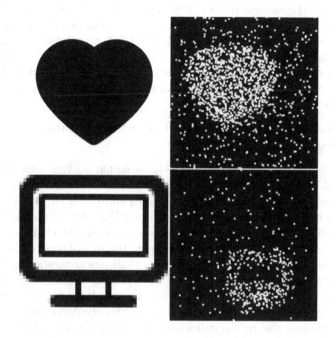

Fig. 3. Two examples, not recognised by the attack, presented in [29].

The set of parameters (ℓ, n_{max}, n_s, and ℓ_2) used in the attack has been chosen experimentally, without garantee on their optimality. The reason is twofold. The first one is about the programming language. We have run our experiments using JavaScript for simplicity but the execution time is clearly not optimal with this language. The more the values of ℓ_2 and n_s are increased, the more the accuracy of the attack is high. The division of the attack into two steps was only proposed for a lower execution time, not for the success rate. Using another programming language, as the C language, and make the computation of the scores in parallel, can strongly reduce the execution time, and consequently the success rate. For example, there exists, some solution as Selenium driver, to interact between JavaScript and other languages. The second reason comes from CaptchaStar itself. An exhaustive research on the parameters ℓ, n_{max}, n_s, and ℓ_2 would give only the best success rate for a given implementation of

CaptchaStar. Optimal parameters of the attack depend on parameters used in the CaptchaStar implementation. Finally, in an optimal version of the attack, the parameters could be chosen dynamically depending, for example, on the number of stars of the challenge.

5   Discussions

5.1   Challenges Generation

The attack and the success rate of 96%, described in the previous section, has been achieved on the website of CaptchaStar [18]. Thus, this rate corresponds to the set of parameters T_2 ($\psi = 70\%$, $\delta = 7$, $NSol = 1$, no rotation). If another set of these parameters was used, the success rate of the attack would be different. In this section we investigate the success rate of the attack under different parameters, independently to the implementation. Experiments on two parameters have been executed:

1. The number of noisy stars added by the sampling algorithm.
2. The number of solutions of the challenge.

In the Table 3, tests T_2 and T_6 have the same parameters, excepted a noise percentage of 70% against 250% and a lower sensitivity. We can see on this table that the success rate for a human is 87.1% for T_2 and 75.5% for T_6. Similarly, the time to solve the Captcha for a human is around 18.8 s for T_2 and 31.1 s for T_6. We conducted our experiment by adding noisy stars in the challenge after the sampling algorithm (consequently, in addition to the 70% of noisy stars generated by the PHP script of the server). Indeed, the challenge generation is realized in the server side. The attack is realized on 100 samples, adding noisy stars up to 200% to each challenge. The success rate of the attack fell to 91%. This rate is lower than the attack of the previous section (with only 70% of additional noisy stars). Nevertheless, this rate is still a high success rate and it is higher than the success rate for a human (75.5%) with the set of parameters T_6. The left part of Fig. 4 illustrates the recovered challenge, with an additional noise of 200%. In this figure, noisy stars seems significantly lower than anticipated. In fact, stars representing the noise are not always displayed on the grid when moving the cursor. The reason comes from CaptchaStar implementation: coordinates of stars can be moved out of the grid.

The sensitivity corresponds to the movement amplitude of the stars when moving the mouse cursor. The more the sensitivity is high, the more the movement amplitude is important. Details on this movement are ommited because they are not useful in our attack (they can be found in [18]). It seems that this parameter does not really influence our heuristic. In particular, it is independent to the number of stars displayed on the grid. The sensitivity can slightly modify the concentration of pixels in states generated by a cursor position close to the exact solution (the stars will aggregate faster or slower depending the value of the sensitivity). Nevertheless, if parameters ℓ_2 and n_s are not too small, the influence of sensitivity becomes negligible. Thus, we think that by optimising the parameter values of the attack, the sensitivity is not important for this attack.

Even if there is only one figure hidden in the implementation of CaptchaStar, the parameter $NSol$ gives the possibility to hide several figure into the Captcha. In this case, if one figure is correctly retrieved, then the user is considered as human. Roughly speaking, this case is close to the first parameter on noise addition, because if there are two figures, each figure becomes noise for the other figure. Experiments are realized, by hiding a second figure in each challenge sent by the website (in addition to the other stars of the grid). The attack is realized on 100 samples with a success rate of 94%. Consequently, this rate is only 2% lower than the success rate with one figure. For comparison, the success rate of a genuine user falls from 90% to 50% between tests T_3 and T_4 with the same parameters excepted a lower noise and a second image hidden in T_4 (see Table 3). The right part of Fig. 4 illustrates the attack result on a challenge containing 2 hidden figures (with the noise addition $\psi = 70\%$).

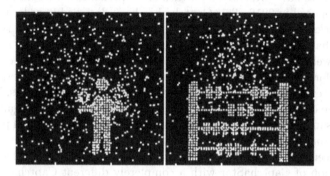

Fig. 4. Executing CaptchaStar attack with other parameters (from [29]).

5.2 Other Countermeasures

Several additional countermeasures have been considered for CaptchaStar [18]. For example, the possibility to detect an attack by analysing the movement of the mouse cursor is mentioned. We think that it could be a hard task because human solve the Captcha in the same way. As mentioned above, the attack reproduces actually the human behaviour by decomposing it into two phases. Moreover, during the first phase where only n_s scores are computed, we can simulate the mouse cursor movements of a human (if exists) on the whole grid and capturing only the states that are needed for the attack. Indeed, execution time only increases when a score is computed for a state, not when the cursor moves. Randomization cursor movement is also possible for the same reason. Using the same strategy during the second phase, we can simulate random movements around the approximate solution produced by the first phase. There are only $\ell_2 \times \ell_2$ scores to compute, so it is easy to propose a random trail which visits each state. We think that these behaviours are not far away from a human behaviour when a genuine user is near the solution.

Another countermeasure consists in hiding several figures in the challenge, as considered in the previous section. Nevertheless, the Captcha can force the user to send the cursor position only if one fixed figure is appearing. For example, a figure of a cat and a figure of a dog are hidden in the challenge, and the user is asked to recover the cat and not the dog. Clearly, the proposed attack is not able to detect if the shape is a dog or a cat, then it will submit the shape with the best score. Nevertheless, this countermeasure leads to a success rate close to 50%. Moreover, it is hard to hide several figure, even in a limited number, because it would provide too much noise for a real human. Finally, machine learning techniques, as presented in [47], could be combined with our attack.

6   Conclusion

In this paper we have presented an attack on CaptchaStar, a recent image-based Captcha proposed in 2016. This Captcha has been designed in order to mitigate several attacks, but it has an important vulnerability, exploited by this attack. Our attack has a success rate of 96% and the challenge is recovered in less than 12 s on the website of CaptchaStar. Thus, the success rate and time of solving is lower than for a human. Different parameters in the challenge generation have also been investigated, in order to consider possible countermeasures. Typically, the challenge can be made more noisy. Nevertheless, the attack is again effective and, in the same time, the success rate for a human with these sets of parameters decreases strongly.

Thus, it seems difficult to establish efficient countermeasures for this Captcha. A combination of CaptchaStar with a completely different Captcha could be a solution. In this case, CaptchaStar would provide some resistance to classical attacks as relay attacks, and the second Captcha would reduce the success rate of this attack. Nevertheless, the proposed attack could be also combined with other techniques, such as machine learning.

A   Appendix

Figure 5 describes the first part of the attack on a toy example with $n_{max} = 2$, $\ell = 4$, $n_s = 4$. First, the grid is split in 4 tiles. Each tile center represents the coordinates c_k, generating a state S^k. Then, a score is computed with the *maxConcentration* heuristic. It splits the grid in 9 tiles of 4×4 pixels. To compute the score, the number of pixels of the two tiles containing the largest numbers of pixels are added. For the state S^3, the tiles containing the largest number of pixels are the center tile, and the one at the top center. They both contain 2 stars, and each star contains 4 pixels, therefore the obtained score for S^3 is 16. This is the maximum score among the generated states, therefore c_3 represents the coordinates of the approximate solution.

Figure 6 describes the second part of the attack with $\ell_2 = 2$. A tile of size 2×2 pixels is drawn using c_3 as its center. A state is generated for each point of the tile and a score is computed using the *maxConcentration* heuristic. The points are represented by the coordinates $\{c_3, c_5, c_6, \ldots, c_{12}\}$. S^8 is the state leading to the largest score, and it is the solution of the challenge.

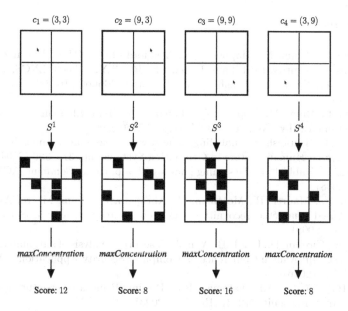

Fig. 5. First phase of the attack on a toy example with a grid 12×12 pixels where stars are represented by black squares of 2×2 pixels. Attack parameters are $n_s = 4$, $\ell = 4$, and $n_{max} = 2$.

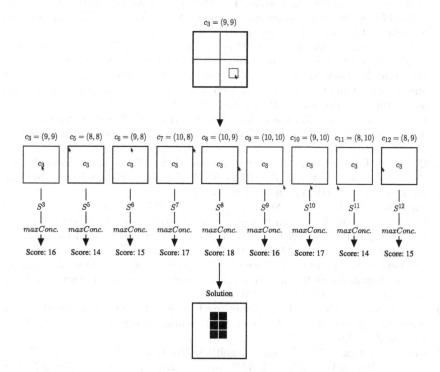

Fig. 6. Second phase of the attack on the same toy example. Attack parameters are $\ell = 4$, $n_{max} = 2$, and $\ell_2 = 2$. Coordinates of the extracted solution are c^8.

References

1. von Ahn, L., Blum, M., Hopper, N.J., Langford, J.: CAPTCHA: using hard AI problems for security. In: Biham, E. (ed.) EUROCRYPT 2003. LNCS, vol. 2656, pp. 294–311. Springer, Heidelberg (2003). https://doi.org/10.1007/3-540-39200-9_18
2. von Ahn, L., Blum, M., Hopper, N.J., Langford, J.: Telling humans and computers apart automatically. Commun. ACM **47**(2), 57–60 (2004)
3. von Ahn, L., Dabbish, L.: Labeling images with a computer game. In: SIGCHI Conference on Human Factors in Computing Systems, pp. 319–326 (2004)
4. von Ahn, L., Dabbish, L.: Designing games with a purpose. Commun. ACM **51**(8), 58–67 (2008)
5. von Ahn, L., Maurer, B., McMillen, C., Abraham, D., Blum, M.: reCAPTCHA: human-based character recognition via web security measures. Science **321**, 1465–1468 (2008)
6. Algwil, A., Ciresan, D., Liu, B.B., Yan, J.: A security analysis of automated Chinese turing tests. In: Annual Conference on Computer Security Applications (ACSAC), pp. 520–532 (2016)
7. Baird, H.S., Coates, A.L., Fateman, R.J.: PessimalPrint: a reverse turing test. Int. J. Doc. Anal. Recognit. **5**(2–3), 158–163 (2003)
8. Bursztein, E., Aigrain, J., Moscicki, A., Mitchell, J.C.: The end is nigh: generic solving of text-based CAPTCHAs. In: USENIX Workshop on Offensive Technologies (WOOT) (2014)
9. Bursztein, E., Beauxis, R., Paskov, H.S., Perito, D., Fabry, C., Mitchell, J.C.: The failure of noise-based non-continuous audio CAPTCHAs. In: IEEE Symposium on Security and Privacy (S&P), pp. 19–31 (2011)
10. Bursztein, E., Bethard, S.: DeCAPTCHA: breaking 75% of ebay audio CAPTCHAs. In: USENIX Coference on Offensive Technologies (2009)
11. Bursztein, E., Bethard, S., Fabry, C., Mitchell, J.C., Jurafsky, D.: How good are humans at solving CAPTCHAs? A large scale evaluation. In: IEEE Symposium on Security and Privacy (S&P), pp. 399–413 (2010)
12. Bursztein, E., Martin, M., Mitchell, J.: Text-based CAPTCHA strengths and weaknesses. In: ACM Conference on Computer and Communications Security (CCS), pp. 125–138 (2011)
13. Bursztein, E., Moscicki, A., Fabry, C., Bethard, S., Mitchell, J.C., Jurafsky, D.: Easy does it: more usable CAPTCHAs. In: Conference on Human Factors in Computing Systems (CHI), pp. 2637–2646 (2014)
14. Chellapilla, K., Larson, K., Simard, P.Y., Czerwinski, M.: Building segmentation based human-friendly human interaction proofs (HIPs). In: Baird, H.S., Lopresti, D.P. (eds.) HIP 2005. LNCS, vol. 3517, pp. 1–26. Springer, Heidelberg (2005). https://doi.org/10.1007/11427896_1
15. Chellapilla, K., Larson, K., Simard, P.Y., Czerwinski, M.: Designing human friendly human interaction proofs. In: ACM Conference on Human Factors in Computing Systems (CHI), pp. 711–720 (2005)
16. Chellapilla, K., Simard, P.Y.: Using machine learning to break visual human interaction proofs (HIPs). In: Neural Information Processing Systems (NIPS), pp. 265–272 (2004)
17. Chew, M., Tygar, J.D.: Image recognition CAPTCHAs. In: Zhang, K., Zheng, Y. (eds.) ISC 2004. LNCS, vol. 3225, pp. 268–279. Springer, Heidelberg (2004). https://doi.org/10.1007/978-3-540-30144-8_23

18. Conti, M., Guarisco, C., Spolaor, R.: CAPTCHaStar! A novel CAPTCHA based on interactive shape discovery. In: Manulis, M., Sadeghi, A.-R., Schneider, S. (eds.) ACNS 2016. LNCS, vol. 9696, pp. 611–628. Springer, Cham (2016). https://doi.org/10.1007/978-3-319-39555-5_33

19. Conti, M., Guarisco, C., Spolaor, R.: CAPTCHaStar demo (2016). http://captchastar.math.unipd.it/demo.php

20. Cui, J.S., Mei, J.T., Zhang, W.Z., Wang, X., Zhang, D.: A CAPTCHA implementation based on moving objects recognition problem. In: IEEE International Conference on E-Business and E-Government (ICEE), pp. 1277–1280 (2010)

21. Datta, R., Li, J., Wang, J.Z.: Imagination: a robust image-based CAPTCHA generation system. In: ACM International Conference on Multimedia, pp. 331–334 (2005)

22. Elson, J., Douceur, J.R., Howell, J., Saul, J.: Asirra: a CAPTCHA that exploits interest-aligned manual image categorization. In: ACM Conference on Computer and Communications Security (CCS), pp. 366–374 (2007)

23. Fidas, C., Voyiatzis, A., Avouris, N.: On the necessity of user-friendly CAPTCHA. In: SIGCHI Conference on Human Factors in Computing Systems (CHI), pp. 2623–2626 (2011)

24. Gao, H., Wang, W., Qi, J., Wang, X., Liu, X., Yan, J.: The robustness of hollow CAPTCHAs. In: ACM Conference on Computer and Communications Security (CCS), pp. 1075–1086 (2013)

25. Gao, H., et al.: A simple generic attack on text CAPTCHAs. In: Network and Distributed System Security Symposium (NDSS) (2016)

26. Golle, P.: Machine learning attacks against the asirra CAPTCHA. In: ACM Conference on Computer and Communications Security (CCS), pp. 535–542 (2008)

27. Goodfellow, I.J., Bulatov, Y., Ibarz, J., Arnoud, S., Shet, V.D.: Multi-digit number recognition from street view imagery using deep convolutional neural networks. coRR abs/1312.6082 (2013)

28. Gossweiler, R., Kamvar, M., Baluja, S.: What's up CAPTCHA? A CAPTCHA based on image orientation. In: 18th International Conference on World Wide Web (WWW), pp. 841–850 (2008)

29. Gougeon, T., Lacharme, P.: How to break CAPTCHaStar. In: 4th International Conference on Information Systems Security and Privacy (ICISSP), pp. 41–51 (2018)

30. Hernández-Castro, C.J., R-Moreno, M.D., Barrero, D.F., Gibson, S.: Using machine learning to identify common flaws in CAPTCHA design: FunCAPTCHA case analysis. Comput. Secur. **70**, 744–756 (2017)

31. Hernández-Castro, C.J., Ribagorda, A.: Pitfalls in CAPTCHA design and implementation: the math CAPTCHA, a case study. Comput. Secur. **29**, 141–157 (2010)

32. Hindle, A., Godfreya, M.W., Holt, R.C.: Reverse engineering CAPTCHAs (2008)

33. Kim, J., Kim, S., Yang, J., Ryu, J., Wohn, K.: FaceCAPTCHA: a CAPTCHA that identifies the gender of face images unrecognized by existing gender classifiers. Multimed. Tools Appl. **72**(2), 1215–1237 (2014)

34. Kim, J., Chung, W., Cho, H.: A new image-based CAPTCHA using the orientation of the polygonally cropped sub-images. Vis. Comput. **26**, 1135–1143 (2010)

35. Kluever, K.A., Zanibbi, R.: Balancing usability and security in a video CAPTCHA. In: ACM Symposium on Usable Privacy and Security (SOUPS) (2009)

36. Mohamed, M., Gao, S., Saxena, N., Zhang, C.: Dynamic cognitive game CAPTCHA usability and detection of streaming-based farming. In: Workshop NDSS on Usable Security (USEC) (2014)

37. Mohamed, M., et al.: A three-way investigation of a game-CAPTCHA: automated attacks, relay attacks and usability. In: ACM Symposium on Information, Computer and Communications Security (ASIACCS), pp. 195–206 (2014)

38. Mori, G., Malik, J.: Recognizing objects in adversarial clutter: breaking a visual CAPTCHA. In: Conference on Computer Vision and Pattern Recognition (CVPR), pp. 133–144 (2003)

39. Motoyama, M., Levchenko, K., Kanich, C., McCoy, D., Voelker, G.M., Savage, S.: Re: CAPTCHAs-understanding CAPTCHA-solving services in an economic context. In: USENIX Security Symposium, vol. 10, pp. 435–462 (2010)

40. Naor, M.: Verification of a human in the loop or identification via the turing test (1996)

41. Nejati, H., Cheung, N.M., Sosa, R., Koh, D.C.I.: DeepCAPTCHA: an image CAPTCHA based on depth perception. In: ACM Multimedia Systems Conference (MMSys), pp. 81–90 (2014)

42. Nguyen, V.D., Chow, Y.W., Susilo, W.: On the security of text-based 3D CAPTCHAs. Comput. Secur. **45**, 84–99 (2014)

43. Osadchy, M., Hernandez-Castro, J., Gibson, S., Dunkelman, O., Perez-Cabo, D.: No bot expects the deepCAPTCHA! Introducing immutable adversarial examples with applications to CAPTCHA. iACR Cryptology ePrint Archive (2016)

44. Pinkas, B., Sander, T.: Securing passwords against dictionary attacks. In: ACM Computer and Security Conference (CCS), pp. 161–170 (2002)

45. Rui, Y., Liu, Z.: Artifacial: automated reverse turing test using facial features. Multimed. Syst. **9**(6), 493–502 (2004)

46. Shirali-Shahreza, S., Shirali-Shahreza, M.: CAPTCHA for children. In: IEEE International Conference on System of Systems Engineering (SoSE), pp. 1–6 (2008)

47. Simonyan, K., Zisserman, A.: Very deep convolutional networks for large-scale image recognition. arXiv preprint arXiv:1409.1556 (2014)

48. Sivakorn, S., Polakis, I., Keromytis, A.D.: I am robot: (deep) learning to break semantic image CAPTCHAs. In: IEEE European Symposium on Security and Privacy (EuroS&P), pp. 388–403 (2016)

49. Tam, J., Simsa, J., Hyde, S., von Ahn, L.: Breaking audio CAPTCHAs. In: Advances in Neural Information Processing Systems (NIPS), pp. 1625–1632 (2008)

50. Thomas, K., McCoy, D., Grier, C., Kolcz, A., Paxson, V.: Trafficking fraudulent accounts: the role of the underground market in Twitter spam and abuse. In: USENIX Security Symposium. pp. 195–210 (2013)

51. Truong, H.D., Turner, C.F., Zou, C.C.: iCAPTCHA: the next generation of CAPTCHA designed to defend against 3rd party human attacks. In: IEEE International Conference on Communications (ICC), pp. 1–6 (2011)

52. Turing, A.M.: Computing machinery and intelligence. Mind **59**(236), 433–460 (1950)

53. Wilkins, J.: Strong CAPTCHA guidelines. Technical Report (v1.2) (2009)

54. Xu, Y., Reynaga, G., Chiasson, S., Frahm, J.M., Monrose, F., van Oorschot, P.C.: Security and usability challenges of moving-object CAPTCHAs: decoding codewords in motion. In: USENIX Security Symposium, pp. 49–64 (2012)

55. Yan, J., Ahmad, A.S.E.: Breaking visual CAPTCHAs with naive pattern recognition algorithms. In: Annual Computer Security Applications Conference (ACSAC), pp. 279–291 (2007)

56. Yan, J., Ahmad, A.S.E.: A low-cost attack on a Microsoft CAPTCHA. In: ACM Conference on Computer and communications security (CCS), pp. 543–554 (2007)

57. Yan, J., Ahmad, A.S.E.: Usability of CAPTCHAs or usability issues in CAPTCHA design. In: 4th Symposium on Usable Privacy and Security (SOUPS), pp. 44–52 (2008)
58. Yan, J., Ahmad, A.S.E.: CAPTCHA security: a case study. IEEE Secur. Priv. **7**(4), 22–28 (2009)
59. Zhu, B.B., et al.: Attacks and design of image recognition CAPTCHAs. In: ACM Conference on Computer and Communications Security (CCS), pp. 187–200 (2010)

Notify This: Exploiting Android Notifications for Fun and Profit

Efthimios Alepis[(✉)]

Department of Informatics, University of Piraeus,
80, Karaoli & Dimitriou, 18534 Piraeus, Greece
`talepis@unipi.gr`

Abstract. In the era of telecommunications, where mobile phones are becoming continuously smarter, how users interact with smartphones plays a very essential role, magnified by statistics that reveal great increase in human time spent in human-smartphone interaction. Some of the basic reasons for users to use their smartphones include notifications, whose functionality has been investigated and improved over the last decade. As a result, this mechanism, namely smartphone notifications, is not only well-rounded by both OS vendors and app developers, but is also inextricably accompanying vital parts of the majority of modern mobile applications. This paper analyzes flaws in this fundamental mechanism, as found in the most widespread mobile OS to date, namely Android. After presenting forging smartphone application notifications and Denial of Service attacks to the users' device, accomplished both locally and remotely, we conclude by proposing generic countermeasures for the security threats in question.

Keywords: Android · Notifications · Phishing · Local DoS

1 Introduction

Modern mobile devices have penetrated in every aspect of users' daily routines, making them an indispensable part of their daily lives. Initially, their goal was to provide communication to users via various means e.g. calls, short messages, video conference and chatting. Nevertheless, currently, they have stormed other activities such as infotainment, Internet browsing, fitness monitoring, mobile health, or even finance. The fact that these devices are small enough to be seamlessly carried on daily basis and the fact that they are able to perform multiple tasks and process data from a plethora of embedded sensors has enabled developers to create numerous applications and a new niche market.

Smartphones are firstly "mobile phones", by definition devices that offer mobility. As a result, smartphones offer both time and place independence to their users. These two "characteristics" can be considered as of great importance to human-computer interaction and subsequently to user profiling. Time and place independence is two-fold both for users and for their smartphones. Users

© Springer Nature Switzerland AG 2019
P. Mori et al. (Eds.): ICISSP 2018, CCIS 977, pp. 86–108, 2019.
https://doi.org/10.1007/978-3-030-25109-3_5

are always and everywhere able to use their smartphones for a countless number of reasons, establishing direct and explicit interaction with them. On the other hand, smartphones, even when they are not directly used by their users and remain idle, are able to exchange data with their environment, which is actually their users' environment too.

The aforementioned reasons of time and place independence have made smartphones popular to people all around the globe. As a result, we are witnessing an era where users have powerful ultramobile devices in their pockets, in a sense accompanying them during their everyday life, while in most cases an Internet wireless connection is also present, connecting them with the entire digital world, as well as with other mobile users. To this end, services such as instant messaging, on-line gaming and real time voip calls, have forced the need of almost always having smartphones powered on. Being functional everywhere and at any time, also forced smartphone manufacturers to enable them to be context aware. The latter is greatly utilized by myriads of applications for reasons such as adaptation, user experience, recommendations, advertising and data mining. Consequently, as not only users are better "served" by their smartphones and their software services, but also large profits are gained, the need of context awareness in smartphones is there to stay and presumably go larger and more precise.

The interaction between users and mobile devices has increased significantly over the years and as a result the means of realizing this bi-directional communication has also evolved. Back in 2014 a comprehensive study on mobile phone notifications [1] regarding user-smartphone engagement, revealed that users had to deal with 63.5 notifications on average per day, mostly from messenger and email applications. Obviously, this number has been further increased significantly over the last years with the rise of apps such as WhatsApp and Facebook messenger, with notification messages overpassing billions in numbers in daily basis [2].

At the same time other recent studies reveal that push notifications draw users' attention, with user average opening notification rates being over 90% [3]. Notifications also allow developers to increase user engagement with their app and improve user retention rates [3]. Mobile notifications seem to clearly influence user engagement positively and also improve user conversion rates. As stated in [4]:

> "*In 2015, users who enabled push notifications launched an app an average of 14.7 times per month, whereas users who did not only launched an app 5.4 times per month. In other words, users who opted in to push messages averaged 3x more app launches than those who opted out.*"

Equivalent findings are also reported in [5]:

> "Analysis of 63 million app users' first 90-days reveals more frequent messaging increases mobile app retention rates by 3× to 10×".

As a result, smartphone notification services are incorporated in the majority of modern mobile apps and in numerous market categories, ranging from mobile health applications [6] and adaptive mobile smart applications [7], to intelligent mobile systems that utilize this mechanism using machine learning approaches [8]. The "penetration" of notifications in human-mobile interaction is so high that there is already research conducted regarding their applications also to wearable and vibrotactile mobile technologies [9].

In view of the above this paper investigates the means of establishing user-smartphone interaction and highlights the necessity of providing mobile users with secured and trusted mechanisms for their interaction with mobile devices. Towards this direction, this paper examines in depth the basic interaction mechanisms available in the Android Operating System, the worlds' most popular mobile platform to date, in terms of market-share. Our research illustrates flaws in the Android's notification native mechanisms which can be exploited and lead to a number of attacks, presented in this work. Subsequently, this paper also discusses about countermeasures in order to provide defense solutions to the attacks. This paper is an extended version of our previous work, illustrated in [10]. More specifically this paper investigates in greater depth the concept of human-smartphone interaction, namely by examining the possible ways of how this bi-directional communication can be realized. Consequently, this paper also discusses extensively about the problems that emerge for the companies involved in the mobile app "world", in regard to the disclosed security issues that arise from the Android notifications mechanism, while at the same time provides a wider view in the related scientific literature. Finally, this paper also explores proposed countermeasures that could be applied in order to either minimize, or even, in some cases, eliminate the described threats.

Main Contributions: The main contribution of this work is to illustrate how the most used smartphone OS to date incorporates flaws in one of the most basic and fundamental user-smartphone interaction mechanisms. Towards this end, successful attacks in the most recent versions of Android, using AOSP as a reference, are presented. These attacks can affect additively the majority of Android users to date. More specifically, this paper presents forging notification attacks that include home-screen shortcuts, attacks in notifications that result in DOS attacks and also attacks concerning web push notifications. To the best of our knowledge, and according to the malware samples of [11], notifications are used for aggressive advertisement via the malware families of Airpush and Kuguo. Overall, we aim in providing a thorough analysis in the core means of realizing Human-Smartphone interaction, both for providing a way to detect flaws and also for better locating their corresponding working solutions.

Organization of This Work: The rest of this work is organized as follows. In the next section we present the related work. Section 3 provides the background and the basis for the problem setting. Then, Sect. 4 presents two distinct categories of attacks through Android Notifications. Consequently, Sect. 5 analyzes the problems that may arise by the exploitation of the security issues in question. Finally, the article concludes discussing possible countermeasures for the illustrated attacks on Android notifications.

2   Related Work

Android has been designed in order to run in mobile devices with constrained capabilities in terms of both computation or size. The size of the device, as Android mainly targets handheld devices, implies many restrictions in the resulting User Interface (UI). As a result, from a point of view the UI can be considered as a set of layers which are stacked one on top of the other. However, as demonstrated in [12]: *"Phishing attacks can be mounted convincingly because the Android UI does not identify the currently running application"*. This was exploited by Niemietz and Schwenk [13] who managed to create the first UI redressing attack for Android. While positioning other UI elements, namely "drawing", on top of other activities and partially covering them has been recently restricted by the OS and requires a high level of permissions to be accomplished, researchers have recently started to find novel ways to do it. There is a bulk of the attacks that exploit a recently introduced Android permission, the `System_Alert_Window` [14,15]. According to Google Developer resources [16]: *"Very few apps should use this permission; these windows are intended for system-level interaction with the user"*. Nevertheless, due to backward compatibility issues, an adversary may easily use this permission without the user's knowledge or consent by targeting lower API levels during app installation. While these attacks have provenly severe impact, the apps that can exploit this feature are rather limited and can be easily "uncovered" by simply scanning the app manifest for the corresponding permissions. On the contrary, an even more stealth attack allows an adversary to overlay activities without requesting any permission from the user [17].

However, in order to timely present the user a screen which requires him to provide his credentials, one needs to be aware of which is the foreground activity. Methods to do this are discussed in [17,18], however, they are rendered useless as of Android Nougat, since access to `/proc` file system has been significantly restricted. To counter this lack of knowledge, an adversary may resort to other means, e.g. masquerade as a legitimate app and convince the user to interact with. Note that by design, in Android all apps are aware of which apps are already installed in the device, so the adversary can easily find a target one. In this regard, in [19]; a closely related work to ours, a set of attacks which exploit notifications was proposed. This work's concept is that the user has been tricked into installing a malicious app named "Notish" which issues notifications that look like ones from other legitimate apps luring them to disclose sensitive information e.g. credentials. The attacks that the authors demonstrate apply not only to Android, but iOS and Blackberry, while a spam scenario also exists.

Perhaps the most relevant to ours can be considered the work of [19], for this reason it is further analyzed. Back in 2012 the authors where supporting that they first presented a paper regarding the security of notifications in mobile phones. Specifically examining the Android OS, they covered platforms 2.3 and 4.0 (API level 14). Nevertheless, since then many years have passed and considering the small mobile OS lifetime, this period was quite significant for many reasons. Most importantly, Android has changed a lot since 2012, providing 12 newer API levels to date, with the introduction of Android Oreo and the "runtime" permission offered by Android Marshmallow, always hardening the OSes security. To this end, notification services can be considered as much different compared with the situation in 2012. More specifically, not only are their security mechanisms more improved, but also the attacks described in [19] do not actually apply in the settings of Android in its latest versions. The most basic reason is that these attacks depended on hard-coded resource graphics, which, after being submitted for publication to Google Play Store, they would immediately be discarded by the Google Bouncer as it would find them fraudulent. Moreover, most of the notifications' functionalities that are exploited in this paper, such as replacing the notifications' icon, where introduced very recently. e.g. the `Notification.Builder setSmallIcon (Icon icon)` function was added in API level 23. Furthermore, in the last versions of Android, the app name has been supplementarily added in notifications, enhancing their security even more, once again rendering these past attacks ineffective.

The interested reader may refer to [20,21] for more on phishing attacks on Android.

3   Human-Smartphone Interaction

Smartphones are the evolution of feature-phones. Mobile phones, are by definition devices that offer mobility. As a result, smartphones offer both time and place independence to humans. These two characteristics are very important to human-computer interaction and subsequently to a large number of research areas, such as user modeling, user profiling, adaptive systems and recommendation systems. Time and place independence is two-fold both for users and for their smartphones. Users are always and everywhere able to use their smartphone for a countless number of reasons, establishing direct and explicit interaction with them. On the other hand, smartphones, even when they are not used by their users and remain idle, are able to exchange data with their environment, which is actually their users' environment too, realizing context awareness.

Mobility anytime and anywhere is also interconnected to new digital oriented capabilities for humans, varying from education and entertainment, to health apps and even lifesaving services. The rise of smartphones located users on the map, providing location aware services, such as navigation, real time shopping suggestions and social media to name some. Time and place independence of smartphones also enabled mobile learning [22], mobile entertainment and gaming, mobile government, mobile health [23] and also a number of services which towards smart health and smart cities [24].

Further investigating the interaction between humans and smartphones, we may come up in itemizing the most profound and basic reasons for humans using this "special" computing device, namely the smartphone, that has drown much of the users' interest over the last decade. The categorization of these actions could inarguably differ, facilitating other points of view, however, for the purposes of this study we split them in the following four categories:

(a) Communicating with others (calling, texting etc.) (b) Internet browsing, (c) Using 3rd party applications (m-banking, infotainment etc.), (d) Responding to notifications Having these four basic categories of actions i mind in using a mobile device, we investigated why, how, when and under what conditions an average user might be using a smartphone. While there might be overlaps in these categories, discussed in the following paragraphs, we consider these reasons of realizing human-smartphone interaction as distinct.

Communicating between people via calling, texting etc. are basic and fundamental actions performed in mobile devices even before the existence of smartphones, namely since the appearance of feature phones. This kind of interaction is accomplished through applications that accompany the OS and are developed by the OS vendor. Certainly, both phone calling and text messaging can be also realized by third party applications, while VoIP solutions are also rapidly appearing. Nevertheless, this can be considered as a fundamental reason for using a mobile device, since its very existence and before having these devices being able to connect to the Internet.

Using the well-known mobile browsers for visiting and interacting with web pages through mobile devices is also considered as a very important reason of human-smartphone interaction. Notably, in 2016 mobile phone users who visit the web overpassed the corresponding number of personal computer users [25]. The latter not only highlights the importance of such an interaction, but it also indicates the closer connection to humans' lives that smartphones have managed to acquire.

Using third party applications in a smartphone can be considered as one of the most important and basic reasons of interaction between users and mobiles. The incorporation of all kinds of applications that are of the users' interests has been perhaps the basic reason for smartphones having operating systems that support this kind of functionality and thus make them considerably distinguishable to "ordinary" feature phones. The extraordinary adoption of app stores where users can browse and install applications of numerous categories supports the aforementioned argument. Additionally, recent studies [26] between smartphones provide strong indications that mobile applications are the users' preferred way of interaction when using their smartphone for some reason (e.g. play a game, buy tickets, check a personal bank account balance), compared with the corresponding services relying in web pages. The usage of third party applications of course implies the existence of notifications in a high percentage of use cases, such as receiving and consequently responding to instant messages. This part of interaction, however, is covered separately in the following paragraphs.

Finally, as already mentioned, we consider that users responding to smartphone notifications is a special interaction between humans and smartphones. By using the term "responding", we consider both the cases when users actually respond to received notifications by "opening" them, as well as the cases of even more basic actions, such as using the smartphones' built-in notification drawer to see and/or read the messages of the notifications, even if the users, in some cases, decide not to "open" a notification and just "clear" it after reading its message.

This kind of interaction can be considered of great importance as it forms a very common reason of using the smartphone in modern human-smartphone interaction and because it is expected to grow even more and become more important in the years to come. Conclusively, a smartphone can receive notifications for a large number of reasons that include, yet are not limited to, the following:

- Having missed a phone call
- A newly received text message
- System automatically updated applications
- System automatically updated applications
- Results from periodically scheduled jobs such as software update checking and virus scanning
- Messages from carriers
- Push notifications coming from external resources, corresponding to installed applications. Perhaps the most notable ones in this category are instant messaging applications such as WhatsApp, Viber and Facebook messenger
- Web push notifications that constitute a quite "recent" addition in most mobile browsers' capabilities, where even not used web pages are able to transmit their notifications to targeted mobile devices
- Local app notifications, where third party apps create and issue a notification in order to be read by the user, or require an action taken by the user

These categories of actions involving notifications directly, or indirectly can be considered as both significant and basic, however for the purposes of this study one should investigate the underlying reasons why this "kind" of interaction is important more thoroughly. Thus the reader may have both a rational explanation and also the evidence deriving from the users' experience about the authors' claims. Notifying in terms of mobile computing means, at its fundamental definition, implies finding a way to reach the user, gain his/her attention. This can be variously achieved, aligned with the Operating System's supported corresponding functionalities. A foreground application being used by a smartphone user can change/update its Graphical User Interface (GUI) to provide new information to the user. The same use-case may occur in a web environment, where a web page may dynamically adjust its content. When considering applications that are not currently active, or are running in the background, or are even closed since the mobile device is switched off, the ways to accomplish user notification changes significantly, since additional parameters have to be taken into account. Notably, new information that would change the contents of an Android activity but would not be launched until a user actually opened the corresponding application cannot be considered as a timely, nor an acceptable way to realize user attention. On the contrary, modern mobile notifications try to "force" user interaction and do not rely on waiting when or whether the user decides to check their corresponding app.

In this regard, smartphone app developers and consequently their produced native mobile applications have the ability to choose among a variety of programmatically feasible solutions in order to draw users' attention, such as newly launched activities, opened web pages through browsers, dialog messages, toast messages and of course native Android notifications. The latter, however, has some considerable advantages to count, as it will be further explained, thus may be chosen as the prevailing solution in a majority of use cases where an application is not being used, or when a device is switched off.

Essentially, all the aforementioned ways of interaction can actually "work" towards the direction of informing the user about something, depending on specific circumstances. Nevertheless, as it will be further discussed, in the cases where users are either not using their mobile device, or a specific app, developers may opt in favor of the native Android notifications to accomplish user-app interaction. Toast messages involve two basic drawbacks in these cases. First, they are useless when a mobile device is switched off or locked, since they will not appear. In the case where the mobile device is unlocked and awaken, a displayed toast message can only provide short information to a user, for a maximum time period of 5 s, without necessarily providing the identity of the message issuer. Newly launched activities, or launched mobile pages through mobile browsers are definitely more "permanent" than toast messaging solutions, since they do not disappear after a specific period of time, nor get affected by the state of the mobile device, namely when they are closed and/or locked. However, both are invasive in terms of user-mobile interaction since they impose their presence as the foreground app in the mobile device's main User Interface (UI). Moreover, there is no guarantee that they are going to be the foreground app when the user unlocks the phone, since other, newer, activities might have been launched, putting them in the background. Android dialog messages suffer the same disadvantages too. Additionally, dialog messages are required to hold the quite "dangerous" system permission that allows them to draw over other screens to accomplish the desirable result, namely the SYSTEM_ALERT_WINDOW permission, that can be maliciously used [15].

As a result, deductively, we lead to reason about why the Android notifications seem to be the preferred by developers and users, and also the suggested by Google, way of realizing the communication between a user and an unused app, or even more precisely, between a user and an application that is not in the smartphone's foreground. In addition, the internal design of Android notifications provides them with some valuable assets in terms of establishing an effective and accepted solution for asynchronous or semi-synchronous background initiated communication between users and apps. These assets include great levels of effectiveness in terms of OSes resources usage, permanence and user friendliness in terms of providing a noninvasive way of notifying users.

Nevertheless, there are two points that require significant attention. All kinds of notifications issued from a "background", invisible to the user, process when either a device is locked or when a user is using an irrelevant application also means that having knowledge about the identity of the notification issuer is also very critical for the user. When a user is actually using an application and the application's content changes, users can feel quite sure, presumably, that the changed content originates from the application they use. On the contrary, when users receive incoming information from an application they are not actively using, they rationally need to be able to verify its actual source. This is the reason why, when receiving an email from an unknown source requesting the bank credentials to proceed to an action issued by a well-known bank, most users, hopefully, consider this email as fake and subsequently delete it. Accordingly, a mobile phone user is expecting to be able to confirm a notifications' issuer actual identity before proceeding to an action that could range from posting an unwanted message to a social network, to exposing the user's login credentials for his/her bank account, or a company's server login. To this end, the notifications' nature can be considered as even more deceptive when they are asynchronous to the users' current interaction, since by definition are not expected to appear when users are using the issuing applications and respectively know their origin. In these cases, when a user is interacting with a specific application and a notification message needs to be communicated with him/her by this application, then this is usually realized either through the application's GUI, or through a corresponding dialog message.

Concluding from the above, Android notifications are the profound, preferred and statistically the most used way of informing users about applications' messages. As a result, it is crucial for the users' safety and also for consistency reasons to have proofs about their secure use. It should be also noted that due to the "nature" of the notification underlying mechanisms, the users consider that notifications are send from the OS itself as a mediate and as a result they blindly trust them. Notably, this paper's claims come in compliance with a recent and quite thorough study regarding the trends of the new "generation Z" [27]. This study's findings reveal that a surprising 50% of modern smartphone users "check" their smartphones more than 15 times per hour, while a quarter of all users check their smartphone on an average of more than 30 times per hour.

As already mentioned, the aim of this paper is twofold. On the one hand, it provides evidence, regrettably, that Android notifications, can be provably be insecure as of the time of writing this paper, namely in 2018, in contrast to their wide adoption and increased interest by both developers and users. On the other hand, after analyzing the potential threats, the authors also suggest solutions that may address the arising security issues. Towards this direction, even though applying the countermeasures will not provide ground proof that Android notifications will subsequently become secure, closing security holes still improves them and also helps towards the direction of maturing an ever developing and constantly evolving mobile operating system. For these reasons, the analyzed underlying security issues and not only statically illustrated, rather than the causes of their origin are investigated and generic solutions as countermeasures are proposed. Leaving the programming level and anatomizing the more abstract level of the Android Notifications' infrastructure in terms of Human-Smartphone interaction not only reveals this "mechanism's" profound architecture, but also projects both its strengths and weaknesses.

4   Attacks Through Android Notifications

In this section we discuss about attacks through the exploitation of the native Android Notifications mechanism. More specifically, our main focus will be to illustrate the feasibility of forging application notifications, which expose the users' privacy and security. Secondly, we present how Android's notifications can be exploited to launch Denial of Service (DoS) attacks, both locally and remotely.

4.1   Forging App Notifications

As already analyzed in the previous section, the interaction between smartphone apps and users is bidirectional. In the case of users' initiated interaction, namely user-to-app, users are having knowledge about the applications that they launch and use. In this paper we are going to provide evidence that by designing a fine-tuned, yet realistic, attack to Android users, the app-to-user interaction can be exploited. In particular, the attack that is illustrated in this section involves a number of steps from the attacker's side, involving fundamental Android compo-nents and services. The impact of forging notifications can be considered rather high, as it can be used to deceive them to collect user credentials, perform user profiling, or even blackmailing. The steps of the attack are illustrated in detail in Fig. 2. Following, a use case is also presented and analyzed. For the purposes of highlighting the dangers that accompany this attack, in our step-by-step use case scenario we have randomly chosen "PayPal" as the "target" app. The steps are the following:

- A user installs a zero-permission app through Google Play. The apps name is BobApp and requires only Internet access (even this permission can by bypassed if necessary).
- The installed app retrieves the list of installed applications in the victim's device. The list is communicated to a service owned by the attacker.
- The attacker determines whether an app that he would like to make an attack to is available in victims' devices. In this scenario it is "PayPal".
- The attacker issues an update for the app, through Google Play, where the app's name is replaced, namely "BobApp" becomes "PayPal". The update is expected to be launched automatically, usually by night, when the device is unattended (e.g. probably left charging and connected to a Wifi).
- After a successful application update, the malicious app's name has been changed, while the user (owner) has no way to know about it.
- To build a complete notification, the malicious app requires a title, a text and also the target app's icon. This is accomplished by utilizing the actual genuine target app's resources. More specifically, the target app's package is located and the app's graphics are retrieved through the application's resources and the application's metadata. As a result, a new notification is triggered, with an identical to the genuine app interface.

- After triggering the malicious notification, the user is expected to select it and subsequently launch a malicious activity. The malicious activity can further utilize the genuine app's resources in order to provide a UI that will lure the user.
- Finally, the user is asked to provide private information e.g. credentials that are communicated to the attacker who compromises the victim's account.

The above scenario has been tested both locally and also through Google Play. A forged notification for PayPal on Nougat OS version is illustrated in Fig. 1. More interestingly, since the actual identifier for an app that is located in Google Play consists only of its package name, namely, the app name is not required to be unique regarding the app store, one can very easily, conducting a simple search with "common" keywords such as, e.g. "Calculator", or "Dictionary", find numerous apps in Google Play sharing the same name, thus proving this paper's claims. Moreover, after a thorough research we have come up with the conclusion that bypassing a notification's actual app name is almost impossible by other means in AOSP. Analyzing the AOSP source code, we deducted that achieving this programmatically requires the "substitute_notification_app_name" signature level permission, which only 3 system apps actively have. Indeed, our independent research revealed that these apps are "Easter Eggs", "Google Play" and "Shell".

The combination of using other apps' resources and changing the app name arbitrarily through background "silent" updates, makes the described attack scenario both effective and real. Indeed, the described attack proves to the readers that Android users can be led to a situation where they would not be able to reason about the origin of their smartphones' notifications, hence left unprotected to potential malware apps.

Finally, another part of the Android's user interaction mechanism that has been found to have flaws is the home-screen application shortcuts. Home-screen shortcuts are coupled to notifications in many cases since once one or more notifications have been issued by an application, an indicative change appears in the corresponding app's shortcut (e.g. an indicating number of unread notifications). Nonetheless, home-screen shortcuts are also being frequently used by users to initiate an interaction with an app. Our independent research has revealed that Android home-screen app shortcuts can also be easily forged and a malicious application can appear on a device's home-screen as if it was another application, with identical icon and name. Both the home-screen icon and also the name of the shortcut are not hard-coded and do not originate from the app's resources. Deductively, every application is able to create a home-screen shortcut as being another app installed in the mobile device in question. In this sense, forged app notifications can additionally "cooperate" with forged app home-screen shortcuts to further deceive the users. Even without having notifications issued, home-screen shortcuts provide attackers with another attack-vector in the human-smartphone interaction.

Once again, it should be highlighted that both the issuing of notifications, as well as the creation of home-screen shortcuts is accomplished through app

(a) A forged Paypal notification.   (b) System info.

Fig. 1. A forged notification on a fully updated Android installation, source: [10].

service calls to the underlying mobile OS and subsequently the OS is responsible for the integration of these functions. As a result, users are familiar with the "idea" that they are "secured" and protected, namely, that both home-screen shortcuts represent the genuine apps and also the notifications originate from legitimate sources. As a result, "breaking" this fundamental trust does not only affect the involved apps, but also the mobile OS.

Both the aforementioned security issues, regarding forged notifications and forged home-screen shortcuts, have been responsibly disclosed to Google's Android Security Team which has been given the appropriate time in order to issue the corresponding software bug fixes.

4.2   DoS Through Notifications

From a different point of view and exploiting another flaw of Android notification mechanism, notifications can be used to launch a denial of service both locally and remotely. More specifically, this attack exploits a bug in Android's NotificationManager service, during the process of memory allocation for the

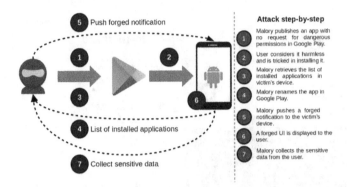

Fig. 2. Attack overview, source: [10]

creation of a Notification. In particular, the notification's builder object expects an icon object of an arbitrary size, yet allocates memory for any given image graphic. Potentially, this bug may allow arbitrary code execution, however, to this point, we were not able to practice that. As a result, the attack; currently being in the process of being patched by the Android Security Team, is launched when a properly crafted notification is sent to the NotificationManger object. After launching the attack, the System UI process repeatedly keeps crashing, blocking the user from making any other interaction apart from answering a call and rebooting. Notably, while answering calls is theoretically allowed, the UI does not revert to the original state. Furthermore, by registering a broadcast receiver Android object awaiting for the "BOOT_COMPLETED" event acton and re-issuing the maliciously crafted notification makes the device unusable, since the device will immediately fall to the previous looping state. At this point it is worth mentioning that a possible countermeasure, while awaiting for a patch applied by Google, is to uninstall the malicious application through a possible "safe mode" device state, or re-flashing the whole device.

To launch this attack, actually almost no code is required, since only a "big" image of high resolution is needed to be sent to NotificationManager service for rendering. In our tests we used a high resolution (4096 × 4096) PNG file, of rather low file size (2.79 KB), however larger graphics have been found to achieve the same effect. Such a "malicious" image can either be stored in the application's resources, or be loaded dynamically from remote resources. Nevertheless, some critical issues also arise by this actual "capability" to be able to be loaded dynamically, from other resources than the actual application that is firing the notification.

Clearly, the above described scenario is triggered locally, by a malicious installed app. Nonetheless, this can also be triggered remotely. As of API level 23, the Notification.Builder class includes a new method, namely "Notification.Builder setSmallIcon (Icon icon)", which accepts an icon rather that a resource. This way, many apps (e.g. Youtube), use Internet resources to download their graphics. Since this information is not private and servers want to take advantage of caching, such graphics are mostly transmitted via plain HTTP. Using a simple man-in-the-middle attack, an adversary can replace the requested graphic with a high resolution graphic and brick the devices remotely.

Even when examining the case where a device is targeted in API levels less than 23, where the new "setSmallIcon" function was not available and even if there was the possibility of pre-checking the resources of each app that could be used as icons, the problem still exists. Namely, since apps' resources are "public" to other installed apps, a malicious application could very easily scan the device for all installed apps' resources and select a high resolution image and use it for the attack.

4.3   Web Push Notifications

Quite recently, the ability to fire notifications has been also given to web pages, with a big number of modern and popular mobile browsers already supporting this feature. In our tests we have successfully tested web push notifications on Android devices running Chrome version ≥ 42, Mozilla version ≥ 44 and Samsung Internet browser version ≥ 4.0. Having the ability to notify a user asynchronously was one of the very basic advantages that native mobile applications had in the past, in contrast to web pages, whose lifetime of interaction with the user was bounded to the time the user spent in browsing on a specific web page.

Web push notifications were introduced to fill this gap. This functionality is established through a "bridge" between the native app world and the web pages ecosystem, provided by the mobile browser. A mobile browser is a "special" kind of software entity. Since it operates in both of these "worlds", it is actually a native mobile application installed in a smartphone, while simultaneously its basic purpose is to serve web pages. As a result, having some special permissions given by the user explicitly, a web page is able to send a push notification asynchronously to the browser and consequently, the browser is responsible for "communicating" this notification to the user's device, utilizing the OSes native mechanisms.

However, the latter introduces another attack vector for phishing attacks. Assuming the case of a user accepting notifications from a malicious web page from his mobile browser, the web page is able to push an arbitrary notification to the device at any given point. Practically, in our phishing scenario, the malicious web page pushes a notification with the icon of an app with millions of downloads, expecting users to respond. The notification redirects the user to a webpage which replicates the UI of the targeted app requesting for sensitive information, e.g. credentials. While the notification may verbally state that the notification originates from the browser, yet the visual identity, the displayed icon and the notification text, may lure many users.

Under the precondition that a web page is able to determine which applications a user has installed in her/his device, recently published in [28], a forging app notification use case could be able to appear in the scenario of web push notifications too. Both text and graphics can be easily arbitrarily loaded through web resources. However, the actual notifications "issuer" in these cases is always the name of the browser (e.g. Chrome), accompanied by the notification's title. In this sense, a user may be lured and open a malicious notification believing that one of her/his installed mobile apps has fired it by seeing the graphic and the text involved. However, as already mentioned, a more attentive examination by the user could reveal that the notification was fired by the browser and not by the actual installed app. Nonetheless, since a web notification containing information about an installed app is not very common, users may more easily be deceived in such a scenario.

The case of issuing a DoS attack to a device through web push notifications has been also investigated. Nevertheless, in our experiments, this kind of attack has been proven to be unsuccessful. The maliciously crafter graphic that we uses in our experiments is presumably firstly "rendered" by the browser to meet the proper size, thus blocking the attack. Processing a very high definition graphic by a mobile app would require processing time, which could eventually lead to an Application not Responding (ANR) situation. The browsers in our tests seem to properly handle such situations and result in either firing the notification with its graphic scaled, or providing a "default", "harmless" icon for the notification to be issued.

5   Emerging Problems for the Involved Companies

Evidently, exploiting the OSes underlying notification mechanisms results in numerous problems for all involved parties and users. In the previous sections regarding the attacks through the notification services, the users' exposure is evident. This section focuses on describing the emerging problems from the perspective of the involved companies. To this end, three major categorizations can be made. Firstly, regarding the unauthorized access and consequently usage of other companies' resources and trademarks. Secondly, regarding problems that may drive users to uninstall an application and finally, regarding breaking the users' trust on both applications and the companies that develop them.

5.1   Unauthorized Usage of Companies' Trademarks

As described in Sect. 4.1, in order to forge a notification, a malicious application accesses application resources within the target mobile device. More specifically, each installed application in a mobile device, even though it "lives" inside its sandbox, is able to reach all the installed applications' resources, residing in their own sandboxes. These resources include strings, such as application names and also graphics, such as companies' logos and trademarks. This "behavior" can by no means be considered intended. In fact, every developer uploading an application with an un-licensed graphic (e.g. an icon or graphic from another company) in Google Play cannot publish the application unless the graphic is removed or replaced. Nevertheless, an application installed in an Android device may declare no "violating" graphics when published, passing through all checks made by Google Play and afterwards, without any legal permission, use arbitrarily other companies resources. This realization leads potentially not only in the creation of forged notifications, but also and even more alarmingly, to the creation of forged user interfaces, identical to the genuine applications', that can be used subsequently along with the forged notifications for even more successful phishing attacks. As an example a malicious application may utilized a bank's application resources, both graphics and names in order to push a forged notification to a user which will, in turn, open a forged activity requesting user bank credentials with all the legitimate UI elements. At this point, it should be highlighted that using intellectual properties and/or trademarks without legal permission, is anywise prohibited for a number of legal reasons.

5.2 Users Drop Off

Reaching users is perhaps one of the most important objectives of companies, while loosing them can be considered as a basic loss. Evidently, nearly one out of four users abandons mobile apps after only one use, while it is estimated that 62% of users use an app less than eleven times before uninstalling the app [29]. As stated in [30], mobile app marketers focus on attracting as many new users to the app as possible, touting the number of users as the strongest pillar of their app success. In the aforementioned article it is also stated that across all industries, 71% of all app users churn within 90 days of first app installation.

Both the factors that influence customer retention in the mobile sector, as well as the effectiveness of mobile phone customer retention strategies, have already been investigated in a small yet significant number of scientific papers, such as [31,32]. The authors of [33] take research in mobile user retention a step further, by modeling user retention rates in mobile games using stochastic processes and conclude in obtaining analytical insight into frequency and longevity of product use.

Considering these facts, users' drop off affects dramatically companies. Malicious apps, exploiting the attacks described in the previous section are able to initiate a countless number of actions within a mobile device, mimicking legitimate apps. Such actions, that negatively affect the user and also the operating system may vary from annoying the users, trying to steal important credentials from them, to causing "troubles" to the mobile device (e.g. battery draining, restarts through DoS attacks) and to the OS, and even inciting the OS to inform the users that a legitimate app should be uninstalled since it is causing inconsistency to the system.

5.3 Breaking Users' Trust

Foremost, regardless of whether a company has a mobile app with millions of users, or less, all companies around the globe that deal with users should definitely protect their users' trust. No matter whether a user has experienced a problem with a specific mobile app in his device, the time that he "feels" that he cannot trust an app there is a high possibility that he will uninstall the app and that he will also spread the negative word. During the last decade, we are all witnesses of the great importance of public opinion in the era of information, social media and big data.

Trust and expectation on privacy settings of smartphone users in analyzed and discussed in [34]. A relevant study is presented in [35], where the authors focus on the understanding of the users' trust models on smartphone applications. Interestingly, even back in 2013, the authors of [36] conducted another study that illustrates statistical analysis results which indicate that the users' security background has slight impact on their security awareness in the smartphone ecosystem.

To this end, possessing ground evidence that a malicious app, spread through the legitimate app markets, is able to forge notifications of other apps and successfully lure the users in order to steal their credentials from e.g. banking apps, or even be able to break Two factor Authentication (2FA), by exploiting the aforementioned security bugs, would arguably break user trust both for the affected app companies and also indirectly for the OS vendors.

6   Countermeasures and Conclusions

Unsurprisingly, mobile devices and their accompanied Operating Systems cannot surpass their size and screen constraints, since for the same reasons they have been so popular and widespread compared to personal computers. Nevertheless, by cause of these size constraints, the Android UI lacks in verifying the source of graphic UI components, leading in exposing the users to many risks. In the related scientific literature, several approaches have been proposed to counter such issues. For instance, a third party framework named "SecureView" was proposed in [19]. SecureView allows the user to choose a security image as well as writing a text-based security greeting after installing an application in her/his device. This way, whenever a sensitive view is displayed, the application can show the security image and greeting on the sensitive view to provide view authentication to the user. These kinds of countermeasures can also be found to have drawbacks. One the one hand, using such a framework from applications implicitly means trusting a third party company. On the other, having users supply both different security images and greetings for a number of their installed applications might not work for obvious reasons, including user frustration and negative user experience.

The researchers in [37] propose the introduction of a visual identity to facilitate the user identify which app he is actually interacting with. Their proposed solution tracks the origin of the app that created the displayed dialog and presents it in the notification bar. Wu et al. monitor the WindowManagerService to determine the presence of a floating window by re-calculating the Z-order of all windows and hooking all the calls which are triggered when creating and clicking on a window [38]. This approach may not counter UI replication attacks, but it defends many overlay attacks. Ying et al. propose a similar visual identity to Bianchi et al. for identifying the source of a UI element also tweaking Window

Manager [39]. WindowGuard hooks the Activity Manager, the Window Manager and Package Manager services to monitor overlaying UI elements and activity transition in order to detect possible attacks [40].

A different approach is the automated screenshot mechanism is proposed in both [41,42] to find similarities between apps and determine whether a UI attack is being made by an app.

Other solutions to UI attacks are presented in [43–45]. For more on phishing attacks and countermeasures the interested reader may refer to [46,47].

From the aforementioned defense mechanisms it is clear that the proposed mechanisms can provide only partial measures against our attacks, while in many cases these measures cannot be applied. The main reasons about that are both the context awareness of our app and also the "renaming attack" illustrated in this paper. In this regard, the displayed UI is rendered according to the targeted applications that are already installed in the device, so screenshot mechanisms are rendered useless. A very important aspect that needs to be taken into consideration is that these attacks are actually triggered by the user. Consequently, there are no overlays to be detected by the system and due to the renaming, all the appropriate visual signatures can be easily circumvented.

Therefore, when the interaction between human and smartphone is initiated by the user, it is of utmost importance to ensure that the user is actually launching the application s/he intended to launch. While using the applications' basic shortcuts it seems that s/he is protected, since an application using another apps graphic as a the app's launcher icon requires it being placed in the apps resources, which consequently would give Google Bouncer the ability to "intercede" when another apps graphic has been detected in Google Play. Unfortunately, this is not the case with home-screen app shortcuts. As already discussed, home-screen app shortcuts can be easily arbitrarily created by other apps, producing "identical" forged app shortcuts. In this case, the OS must provide some new rules and/or checks to overpass this problem e.g. test whether a specific icon matches the resources of another app.

In the cases where the interaction between human and smartphone is implicitly initiated by applications, the problem seems a little more complicated. As it is already mentioned, some "ways" that evolve in user notification, such as activity launches, dialogs and toasts, have clear disadvantages and are rejected by developers in most cases. The major contribution of this work is the investigation of the Android Notifications' mechanism from its security perspective. Generically, notifications are not tightly coupled to their issuer, since they refer to a way of "leaving a notice" for the user through the OSes features, both enhancing user experience and also preserving the valuable smartphone resources. Consequently, this notice is left to be opened by the user end navigate her/him to another UI to continue her/his interaction, presumably a native mobile app, or even a web page. It may be considered as "common sense" that anyone who "picks up" a notice in either her/his mailbox or her/his mobile navigation drawer, should be able to identify the sender. As a result, all involved parties in software development should work towards this direction, safeguarding the users, as their ultimate aim.

Having these in mind, regarding the notifications' issues, there are several solutions that could be proposed for the OS vendor. Being able to prove the notification's issuer ID, would involve an ID to be passed either to the notifications current app name, or the required graphic or even to both. As we have proven both the name of the notification and also the graphics could be easily being forged. The apps' package name can be considered as a candidate that identifies each app, which also cannot exist as duplicate in Google Play. Nevertheless, it has some drawbacks, since while enhancing users' security, it negatively affects user experience. Forcing the icons/graphics of notifications originating only from local resources is another option, which would nevertheless require the OS to rollback to a previous solution, with clear negative results in the market. Other kinds of side-countermeasures could include removing the potential from apps to being able to determine which apps are installed in users' devices, or making a special check for Google Play apps who are making a change in their app name and consequently removing them for the automated updated app list.

After conducting our independent research, to improve the security of the users against similar attacks, we propose several countermeasures. First, the OS should request the users direct consent before updating distinctive characteristics of the installed apps like names, logos etc. This measure can easily be applied by the Android and does not hinder usability nor user experience but protects users from transformation attacks providing timely alerts. To further improve transparency of the updates, we also argue that the users should be able to have an auditable trace of the updates. Certainly, users are not expected to go through code changes, nevertheless, they should be able to see how the installed apps evolve through time. Currently, the users are able to go through only the lists of changes that developers push in Google Play. Nevertheless, users would like to keep track whether the app logos changed through time, the app developer/company, the terms of service and the requested permissions as either of these changes may imply further risk exposure for the user and may not be in accordance with the initial Terms of Service he granted his consent. Special care should be made for homoglyphs to counter cases where character encoding is exploited to present names that are visually similar on specific fonts e.g. "Facebook", "Faceb00k" and "Facebook", a widely used technique in email phishing attacks [48,49].

Furthermore, for the case of notifications, we argue that users should be able to trace their origin. In order to achieve this we believe that Android should enable users to see the name of the app and its developer when deemed necessary. Of course, this feature is not always needed, therefore we propose a mechanism as the one illustrated in Fig. 3. Obviously, parts Fig. 3a and b are the current functionality, so Fig. 3c is the added functionality that we propose. In this regard, when users receive a notification that they may consider suspicious or want to verify that it belongs to a sensitive app (e.g. a banking app) they only have to swipe a bit more and check its origin.

(a) A standard notification in (b) Swiping left one may (c) Swiping left again one may
Android.   change the notification settings. see the origin of the notification.

Fig. 3. Swiping left again one may see the origin of the notification.

Finally, we believe that apps should further exploit 2FA methods to authenticate users. Constantly requesting user credentials, after user authentication is exploited by malware to harvest user credentials. Alternative methods like Google's authenticator or even biometrics should be considered as in these cases the user credentials are not revealed. While face authentication in mobile devices cannot be considered successful, and other means e.g. fingerprint may imply limited user adoption (not all devices are equipped with fingerprint readers), developers may explore the usage of PIN/pattern in addition to motion patterns to authenticate the user of their apps. The latter may prevent unauthorised usage even in the case of shoulder surfing or temporarily sharing the device with another person.

Acknowledgments. This work was supported by the European Commission under the Horizon 2020 Programme (H2020), as part of the *OPERANDO* project (Grant Agreement no. 653704) and is based upon work from COST Action *CRYPTACUS*, supported by COST (European Cooperation in Science and Technology). The authors would like to thank *ElevenPaths* for their valuable feedback and granting them access to Tacyt.

References

1. Pielot, M., Church, K., de Oliveira, R.: An in-situ study of mobile phone notifications. In: Proceedings of the 16th International Conference on Human-computer Interaction with Mobile Devices & #38; Services, MobileHCI 2014, New York, NY, USA, pp. 233–242. ACM (2014)

2. ZDNet: Whatsapp: Now one billion people send 55 billion messages per day. http://www.zdnet.com/article/whatsapp-now-one-billion-people-send-55-billion-messages-per-day/. Accessed 27 July 2017
3. Biznessapps: What is a push notification? And why should you care? https://www.biznessapps.com/blog/what-is-a-push-notification/. Accessed 27 July 2017
4. O'Connell, C.: The year that push notifications grew up (2015). http://info.localytics.com/blog/2015-the-year-that-push-notifications-grew-up. Accessed 01 Sept 2017
5. Urban Airship: New urban airship study reveals app publishers that don't message users waste 95 percent of their acquisition spend. https://www.urbanairship.com/company/press-releases/new-urban-airship-mobile-app-retention-study. Accessed 01 Sept 2017
6. Freyne, J., Yin, J., Brindal, E., Hendrie, G., Berkovsky, S., Noakes, M.: Push notifications in diet apps: influencing engagement times and tasks. Int. J. Hum. Comput. Interact. **33**, 833–845 (2017)
7. Kerber, F., Gehring, S., Krüger, A., Löchtefeld, M.: Adding expressiveness to smartwatch notifications through ambient illumination. IJMHCI **9**, 1–14 (2017)
8. Mahmud, M.S., Islam, M.S., Rahman, M.A.: Smart fire detection system with early notifications using machine learning. Int. J. Comput. Intell. Appl. **16**, 1–17 (2017)
9. Wang, Y., Millet, B., Smith, J.L.: Designing wearable vibrotactile notifications for information communication. Int. J. Hum. Comput. Stud. **89**, 24–34 (2016)
10. Patsakis, C., Alepis, E.: Knock-knock: the unbearable lightness of Android notifications. In: Mori, P., Furnell, S., Camp, O. (eds.) Proceedings of the 4th International Conference on Information Systems Security and Privacy, ICISSP 2018, Funchal, Madeira - Portugal, 22–24 January 2018, pp. 52–61. SciTePress (2018)
11. Wei, F., Li, Y., Roy, S., Ou, X., Zhou, W.: Deep ground truth analysis of current Android malware. In: Polychronakis, M., Meier, M. (eds.) DIMVA 2017. LNCS, vol. 10327, pp. 252–276. Springer, Cham (2017). https://doi.org/10.1007/978-3-319-60876-1_12
12. Chin, E., Felt, A.P., Greenwood, K., Wagner, D.: Analyzing inter-application communication in Android. In: Proceedings of the 9th International Conference on Mobile Systems, Applications, and Services, pp. 239–252. ACM (2011)
13. Niemietz, M., Schwenk, J.: UI redressing attacks on Android devices. Black Hat Abu Dhabi (2012)
14. Ying, L., Cheng, Y., Lu, Y., Gu, Y., Su, P., Feng, D.: Attacks and defence on Android free floating windows. In: Proceedings of the 11th ACM on Asia Conference on Computer and Communications Security, ASIA CCS 2016, New York, NY, USA, pp. 759–770. ACM (2016)
15. Fratantonio, Y., Qian, C., Chung, S., Lee, W.: Cloak and dagger: from two permissions to complete control of the UI feedback loop. In: Proceedings of the IEEE Symposium on Security and Privacy (Oakland), San Jose, CA (2017)
16. Android Developer: Manifest.permission - SYSTEM_ALERT_WINDOW. https://developer.android.com/reference/android/Manifest.permission.html#SYSTEM_ALERT_WINDOW. Accessed 28 Mar 2017
17. Alepis, E., Patsakis, C.: Trapped by the UI: the Android case. In: Dacier, M., Bailey, M., Polychronakis, M., Antonakakis, M. (eds.) RAID 2017. LNCS, vol. 10453, pp. 334–354. Springer, Cham (2017). https://doi.org/10.1007/978-3-319-66332-6_15
18. Chen, Q.A., Qian, Z., Mao, Z.M.: Peeking into your app without actually seeing it: UI state inference and novel android attacks. In: USENIX Security Symposium, pp. 1037–1052 (2014)

19. Xu, Z., Zhu, S.: Abusing notification services on smartphones for phishing and spamming. In: Proceedings of the 6th USENIX Conference on Offensive Technologies, USENIX Association, p. 1 (2012)
20. Felt, A.P., Wagner, D.: Phishing on mobile devices. In: Proceedings of the Web 2.0 Security and Privacy 2011 Workshop (2011)
21. Virvilis, N., Tsalis, N., Mylonas, A., Gritzalis, D.: Mobile devices: a phisher's paradise. In: 2014 11th International Conference on Security and Cryptography (SECRYPT), pp. 1–9. IEEE (2014)
22. Virvou, M., Alepis, E.: Mobile educational features in authoring tools for personalised tutoring. Comput. Educ. **44**, 53–68 (2005)
23. Papageorgiou, A., Strigkos, M., Politou, E.A., Alepis, E., Solanas, A., Patsakis, C.: Security and privacy analysis of mobile health applications: the alarming state of practice. IEEE Access **6**, 9390–9403 (2018)
24. Casino, F., Patsakis, C., Batista, E., Borras, F., Martínez-Ballesté, A.: Healthy routes in the smart city: a context-aware mobile recommender. IEEE Softw. **34**, 42–47 (2017)
25. StatCounter GlobalStats: Mobile and tablet internet usage exceeds desktop for first time worldwide. http://gs.statcounter.com/press/mobile-and-tablet-internet-usage-exceeds-desktop-for-first-time-worldwide. Accessed 01 Sept 2017
26. Flurry Analytics: U.s. consumers time-spent on mobile crosses 5 hours a day. http://flurrymobile.tumblr.com/post/157921590345/us-consumers-time-spent-on-mobile-crosses-5. Accessed 01 Sept 2017
27. Commscope: The generation z study of tech intimates (2017). https://commscope.com/insights/uploads/2017/09/Generation-Z-Report.pdf
28. Alepis, E., Patsakis, C.: The all seeing eye: web to app intercommunication for session fingerprinting in Android. In: Wang, G., Atiquzzaman, M., Yan, Z., Choo, K.-K.R. (eds.) SpaCCS 2017. LNCS, vol. 10656, pp. 93–107. Springer, Cham (2017). https://doi.org/10.1007/978-3-319-72389-1_9
29. Perez, S.: Nearly 1 in 4 people abandon mobile apps after only one use (2016). https://techcrunch.com/2016/05/31/nearly-1-in-4-people-abandon-mobile-apps-after-only-one-use/
30. Perro, J.: Mobile apps: What's a good retention rate? (2018). http://info.localytics.com/blog/mobile-apps-whats-a-good-retention-rate
31. Samanta, I.: Exploring the factors of customer retention in mobile sector. IJSITA **3**, 36–46 (2012)
32. Peng, J., Zhang, S., Quan, J., Wei, Z.: Effectiveness of mobile phone customer retention strategies. In: 11th Wuhan International Conference on E-Business, WHICEB 2012, Wuhan, China, 26–27 May 2012, vol. 63. Association for Information Systems (2012)
33. Viljanen, M., Airola, A., Pahikkala, T., Heikkonen, J.: Modelling user retention in mobile games. In: IEEE Conference on Computational Intelligence and Games, CIG 2016, Santorini, Greece, 20–23 September 2016, pp. 1–8. IEEE (2016)
34. Zhou, Y., Raake, A., Xu, T., Zhang, X.: Users' perceived control, trust and expectation on privacy settings of smartphone. In: Wen, S., Wu, W., Castiglione, A. (eds.) CSS 2017. LNCS, vol. 10581, pp. 427–441. Springer, Cham (2017). https://doi.org/10.1007/978-3-319-69471-9_31
35. Choi, H., Choi, Y.-J., Kim, K.-M.: The understanding of building trust model on smartphone application: focusing on users' motivation. In: Kim, K.J., Ahn, S.J. (eds.) Proceedings of the International Conference on IT Convergence and Security 2011. LNEE, vol. 120, pp. 13–20. Springer, Dordrecht (2012). https://doi.org/10.1007/978-94-007-2911-7_2

36. Mylonas, A., Gritzalis, D., Tsoumas, B., Apostolopoulos, T.: A qualitative metrics vector for the awareness of smartphone security users. In: Furnell, S., Lambrinoudakis, C., Lopez, J. (eds.) TrustBus 2013. LNCS, vol. 8058, pp. 173–184. Springer, Heidelberg (2013). https://doi.org/10.1007/978-3-642-40343-9_15

37. Bianchi, A., Corbetta, J., Invernizzi, L., Fratantonio, Y., Kruegel, C., Vigna, G.: What the app is that? deception and countermeasures in the Android user interface. In: 2015 IEEE Symposium on Security and Privacy (SP), pp. 931–948. IEEE (2015)

38. Wu, L., Brandt, B., Du, X., Ji, B.: Analysis of clickjacking attacks and an effective defense scheme for Android devices. In: 2016 IEEE Conference on Communications and Network Security (CNS), pp. 55–63. IEEE (2016)

39. Ying, L., Cheng, Y., Lu, Y., Gu, Y., Su, P., Feng, D.: Attacks and defence on Android free floating windows. In: Proceedings of the 11th ACM on Asia Conference on Computer and Communications Security, pp. 759–770. ACM (2016)

40. Ren, C., Liu, P., Zhu, S.: Windowguard: Systematic protection of GUI security in Android. In: Network and Distributed System Security Symposium (2017)

41. Malisa, L., Kostiainen, K., Och, M., Capkun, S.: Mobile application impersonation detection using dynamic user interface extraction. In: Askoxylakis, I., Ioannidis, S., Katsikas, S., Meadows, C. (eds.) ESORICS 2016. LNCS, vol. 9878, pp. 217–237. Springer, Cham (2016). https://doi.org/10.1007/978-3-319-45744-4_11

42. Malisa, L., Kostiainen, K., Capkun, S.: Detecting mobile application spoofing attacks by leveraging user visual similarity perception. In: Proceedings of the Seventh ACM on Conference on Data and Application Security and Privacy, pp. 289–300. ACM (2017)

43. Fernandes, E., Chen, Q.A., Paupore, J., Essl, G., Halderman, J.A., Mao, Z.M., Prakash, A.: Android UI deception revisited: attacks and defenses. In: Gros.sklags, J., Preneel, B. (eds.) FC 2016. LNCS, vol. 9603, pp. 41–59. Springer, Heidelberg (2017). https://doi.org/10.1007/978-3-662-54970-4_3

44. Marforio, C., Jayaram Masti, R., Soriente, C., Kostiainen, K., Čapkun, S.: Evaluation of personalized security indicators as an anti-phishing mechanism for smartphone applications. In: Proceedings of the 2016 CHI Conference on Human Factors in Computing Systems, pp. 540–551. ACM (2016)

45. Wu, L., Du, X., Wu, J.: Effective defense schemes for phishing attacks on mobile computing platforms. IEEE Trans. Veh. Technol. **65**, 6678–6691 (2016)

46. Heartfield, R., Loukas, G.: A taxonomy of attacks and a survey of defence mechanisms for semantic social engineering attacks. ACM Comput. Surv. (CSUR) **48**, 37 (2016)

47. Aleroud, A., Zhou, L.: Phishing environments, techniques, and countermeasures: a survey. Comput. Secur. **68**, 160–196 (2017)

48. Holgers, T., Watson, D.E., Gribble, S.D.: Cutting through the confusion: a measurement study of homograph attacks. In: USENIX Annual Technical Conference, General Track, pp. 261–266 (2006)

49. Liu, C., Stamm, S.: Fighting unicode-obfuscated spam. In: Proceedings of the Anti-Phishing Working Groups 2nd Annual eCrime Researchers Summit, pp. 45–59. ACM (2007)

The Current State of the Holistic Privacy and Security Modelling Approach in Business Process and Software Architecture Modelling

Sascha Alpers[(⊠)], Roman Pilipchuk, Andreas Oberweis,
and Ralf Reussner

FZI Forschungszentrum Informatik, Haid-und Neustraße 10-14,
76131 Karlsruhe, Germany
{alpers,pilipchuk,oberweis,reussner}@fzi.de

Abstract. Modelling is central for business process and software architecture documentation and analysis. However, business processes and software architectures are specified with their own highly developed languages, methods and tools. There are approaches in the literature for modelling privacy and security issues using existing business process or architecture modelling languages to express different requirements by enriching these languages with annotations. Nevertheless, there is a lack of formalization and therefore the potential use for tool-based analyses are limited. In addition, the continuity between business and software models is not granted, but when modelling compliance requirements like privacy, traceability is very important, e.g. for compliance checks. In this contribution, approaches for modelling security and privacy in business and software models are examined. One key finding is that there is currently no comprehensive modelling approach which covers the necessary aspects and perspectives. This could include processes as well as, for example, organizational and data structure questions. In conclusion, we suggest developing a new holistic modelling approach which includes the needed aspects and with a concept for the traceability of the requirements from business models to software architecture models.

Keywords: Business architecture · Software architecture · Modelling · Privacy

1 Introduction

Many companies, especially large companies, model their organizational processes and software systems. This is to define and improve them, identify and reduce flaws. Explicit models of processes and software architectures not only enable their analysis and optimisation, these models also save costs during the evolution of processes and software architectures. However, business and software system experts typically use different modelling languages. There exist many languages for modelling business processes. BPMN, a semi-formal notation, is the most prominent one. Petri nets provide a formalized view of processes. Transformations which establish mappings between BPMN and Petri nets exist. In the following, we focus primarily on Petri net [1] models and consider BPMN only marginally. The state-of-the-art modelling

© Springer Nature Switzerland AG 2019
P. Mori et al. (Eds.): ICISSP 2018, CCIS 977, pp. 109–124, 2019.
https://doi.org/10.1007/978-3-030-25109-3_6

language for software systems is UML [2]. As neither business process modelling languages nor UML have elements capable for modelling privacy, extension mechanisms exist for introducing additional symbols to model various aspects of privacy. Additionally, security is also relevant because privacy is related to some security goals such as confidentiality or integrity. Both security and privacy are becoming increasingly important, for example due to the upcoming General Data Protection Regulation (GDPR) [3].

Although there are many approaches to extending business process modelling notations and UML to cover security and other aspects, there is no common and generally accepted approach for modelling privacy. A broad variety of approaches exists for introducing additional symbols to model privacy directly or indirectly, through security elements. However, the extent to which privacy can be modelled depends on the proposal. Additionally, modelling approaches which support transformations from business process models to software design to keep business process models like Petri nets and software models like UML consistent with each other are missing. Due to these reasons, we analysed the capabilities of existing software architecture-oriented and business process-oriented modelling approaches to model privacy aspects. We analysed, how privacy can be modelled and investigated the possibility of and need for a comprehensive modelling language in the field of privacy to cover business processes and software systems. We selected these approaches according to their abilities to model privacy aspects directly or indirectly, through security aspects. The selected approaches were analysed and compared with each other to identify their similarities and differences. This was done to understand the need for a comprehensive model of privacy aspects and to explore how it could be realized, beginning from a business process model and then leading to a software architecture model. For this, we categorized the approaches and identified two criteria, namely "security mechanisms" and "different views". "Security mechanisms" describes the elements and mechanisms by which the approach supports privacy modelling. The second criterion, "different views", groups approaches according to the view of the stakeholder for whom the approach is intended. Our results show that only a few approaches actually introduce elements to model privacy principles. In the following Sect. 2, we describe why the needs for a holistic modelling approach is increasing. Section 3 presents the business process-based approaches. Software architecture-based approaches are presented in Sect. 4. Section 5 discusses similarities and differences between both approaches. The contribution ends with some concluding remarks in Sect. 6.

This paper is an extended version of a paper presented at the 4th International Conference on Information Systems Security and Privacy in 2018 on Madeira Island, Portugal [4]. The expansion consists in particular of the new Sect. 2 (Increasing Need for Holistic Modelling) and a further developed and more detailed conclusion.

2   Increasing Need for Holistic Modelling

In the past few years, companies have faced the increasing problem of cybercrime [5]. Cybercriminals are becoming more organized and cooperating in larger groups, allowing them to undertake more and more complex attacks. Companies also face a growing number of security laws with which governments require them to comply. Especially companies that operate globally have to comply with the laws of different countries. To state some of them, the Basel Accords and Minimum Requirements for Risk Management (MaRisk) [6] regulate the risk management for the finance sector; the IT Security Act [7] regulates the security of IT systems for critical infrastructures; and the General Data Protection Regulation (GDPR) [3] governs data collection, processing and the use of personal data in the European Union. However, privacy regulation is not new. In 1970 the first formal worldwide data protection law came into force in the German federal state of Hesse [8], in 1984 the *Bundesverfassungsgericht* (Federal Constitutional Court) created the basic right of informational self-determination based on the general right of personality (Art. 1(1) and Art. 2(1) German *Grundgesetz* [Basic Law]) [9] and in the European Union, a 1995 European directive set the framework conditions for the processing of personal data [10]. But the GDPR imposes financial penalties of up to 20.000.000 Euro or if higher four percent of an organization's worldwide turnover, which is similar to other regulations.

The business of companies is becoming more complex every year. Supply chains and manufacturing are increasingly distributed all other the world and operate in complex ecosystems. Thus, companies face the complicated task of developing rules and standards in order to protect their sensitive personal data and business secrets according to their needs. They are of the utmost importance, as only the business level of a company knows which data are critical and their required level of protection. Altogether, we see that IT security is becoming more and more crucial for companies of all kinds. That is why the business level is charged with several additional goals pertaining to IT security. Firstly, to prevent cybercriminal attacks, reputational damage and consequently the loss of monetary income, they have to establish organization-wide IT security. There are various guidelines like the ISO/IEC 27000-series [11] or the IT Baseline Protection [12] which describe how to establish, manage and maintain information security effectively in organizations. Access control requirements from the business level perspective are described there too. Guidelines like ITIL [13] or COBIT [14], which comprise sets of practices for IT service management, introduce dedicated business processes for IT security and access control. Therefore, establishing organization-wide IT security is a complicated task involving different departments and various models. Secondly, during the establishment of organization-wide IT security, companies have to comply with an increasing number of security laws. This means that the compliance department is a fundamental part in the whole process. Thirdly, as only the business level knows which assets need to be protected, they have to define the rules and standards on how to interact with these assets. To sum up, the business level in a company becomes a key point in establishing security and privacy and therefore has to work closely with many different departments like IT and compliance departments, resulting in diverse models relevant for IT security and privacy. Thus, there is a need for a systematic transformation between these models to keep them consistent with one another. Only in this way can a good alignment can be realized.

IT security and privacy has become crucial for all kind of companies. One thing IT security and privacy have in common is the need for access control requirements. Both IT security and privacy impose access restrictions on certain data. While IT security describes principles, algorithms and protocols on how to restrict access, privacy describes who should have access to which personal data and how to handle it. These access control requirements come partially from security laws and security guidelines. The business level establishes the other part in terms of rules and standards, as described above. They are both modelled increasingly in business processes, due to the obligation or decision of companies to implement IT service management guidelines like ITIL or COBIT. IT departments must adapt these access control requirements such as enterprise architectures, system architectures and so on in their own models. A typical modelling language here is UML [2, 15]. Different knowledge about terminology is a problem and creates a communication gap that opens up the potential for errors. This poses a severe problem, because any error can undermine security. Thus, both the IT department and the business level have an interest in keeping their numerous models consistent, so that access control requirements are implemented correctly and consistently.

Often, the fact that companies are evolving is neglected. This means that systems, requirements, business processes, enterprise architecture and other models steadily evolve. They all have a lifecycle and affect each other in non-trivial ways [16]. Their complex interrelations are not understood well and have not yet been adequately researched [16]. As stated above, problems here may lead to security breaches. Hence, there is the need for a fast and automatic transformation between the models to keep IT security and privacy information correct and consistent. Additionally, it is important to understand the mutual dependencies so that the various departments can react to changes. Traceability between the models can help, since it allows tracing and understanding design decisions. Both traceability between business and IT models and their mutual interdependence are not yet well researched.

Access control requirements formulated in law and in guidelines must be incorporated and extended by the business level and then implemented by the IT department. There is a need for a transformation between all models of the involved parties. Considering the increasing number of companies implementing guidelines like ITIL and COBIT, as well as the close collaboration between the business level and the compliance department, business processes today comprise many access control requirements. These business level access control requirements represent the demands of law. A promising way to close the gaps described above would be to extract the access control requirements from business processes and transform them to the various models of the IT. Enterprise architectures offer the right granularity and could be analysed as to whether they comply with the extracted access control requirements by using a data flow analysis. Another possibility is to transform the access control requirements directly into permissions for an access control system. Clearly, the increasing need opens a large and promising field of research for transformation and consistency problems between models of different areas.

3 Software Architecture-Oriented Approaches

This chapter introduces the software architecture-oriented approaches for modelling privacy. The first section gives a brief introduction to the de facto standard modelling language in the field of software engineering and the second section is an inspection of the architecture-based approaches in the context of privacy and confidentiality.

3.1 Modelling

The Unified Modelling Language (UML) is the current standard for modelling architecture in software engineering. De facto UML is a general-purpose language which is
standardized by the Object Management Group (OMG). It comprises 14 diagrams
divided in two major diagram types: structure diagrams and behaviour diagrams [2].
While structure diagrams mainly focus on illustrating the static structure of a system,
behaviour diagrams point out its dynamic part. The sequence diagram shows the
chronological flow of messages between objects. It brings an additional technical
dimension to the practice and is an integral part of the described static structure. The
use case diagram visualizes functional requirements, including the different actor
groups and their suitable participatory methods or relationships. Class diagrams
describe classes, associations, methods and their attributes. This is a short overview of
the modelling diagrams in UML. A detailed explanation can be found in the UML
specification [2].

3.2 Analysis of Software Architecture-Oriented Approaches

This section surveys the software architecture-based approaches. Table 1 summarizes
all analysed papers, the types of UML diagrams used, whether they extend through
UML profile or not, and what the extension allows to be modelled.

[17] propose an extension to the UML use case diagram for representing privacy
specifications like pseudonymization, anonymization and consent in an easily understandable way (see Table 1 no. 1). The extension is not based on the UML profile
extension mechanism. Instead, a Microsoft Visio extension ribbon is created that offers
the required elements. All possible privacy requirements and specifications can be
expressed due to the use of free text fields. Furthermore, in use case diagrams the
extension works by introducing a 'super container' in-between actors and use cases.
Privacy control classes and obligations are stated inside the super container. This
extension enables it to express all kinds of privacy principles and allows a technical
specification of other security principles like confidentiality. [18] introduced a UML
profile which is capable of expressing different privacy concepts through privacy
policies incorporated in various UML diagrams (see Table 1 no. 2). Privacy policies
are composed of one or more statements which describe the rules specified in the
privacy policy. Besides that, they also specify the purpose of data collection, its
management, and the prerequisites that need to be met. Private data and actions performed on it can be aggregated and translated into standardized stereotypes to, for
example, identify to whom the access to private data is granted, the period, and the
usage behaviour of the target groups. Several other stereotypes describe how the data
are provided and managed, either by a user or by a system. In both cases, the UML
profile allows the design of privacy-aware applications by modelling the application's
privacy policy and keeping track of the elements responsible for enforcing it. The
profile not only allows modelling of access control on private data, but also of privacy
principles like consent, data security and purpose limitation.

[19] proposed a UML profile, called UMLSec, which is shown in Table 1 no 3. It is
specifically constructed to express security-relevant information within various UML

Table 1. Overview of software architecture-oriented approaches [4].

No.	Paper	Diag. type	Ext. through	To model
1	Engineering Privacy for Big Data Apps with the Unified Modelling Language	Use Case	Super container	Privacy specifications
2	Towards a UML Profile for Privacy-Aware Applications	Various	UML profile	Privacy policies
3	UMLsec: Extending UML for Secure Systems Development (+2)	Various	UML profile	Security requirements/primitives/management and threat scenarios
4	Supporting Confidentiality in UML: A Profile for the Decentralized Label Model	Class	UML profile	Decentralized label model
5	Towards the Engineering of Security of Information Systems (ESIS): UML and the IS Confidentiality	Sequence	UML profile	Access control and information flow control
6	A UML Profile for Requirements Analysis of Dependable Software	Class	UML profile	Problem frames (e.g., confidentiality, integrity)
7	Extending UML for Designing Secure Data Warehouses (+2)	Class	UML profile	Security classes and separation of duty
8	Weaving Security Aspects into UML 2.0 Design Models	Class and Sequence	UML profile	Security requirements and aspect-oriented solutions
9	CMP: A UML Context Modelling Profile for Mobile Distributed Systems	Class	UML profile	Privacy restrictions

diagrams. In particular, it enables non-experts in the area of security to express their security needs easily. UMLSec enables software engineers to express basic security requirements including security concepts, security primitives, security management and threat scenarios. This allows modelling of confidentiality of information and information flows. Furthermore, it is possible to check whether the constraints associated with the stereotypes are fulfilled by a given specification and, by this, indicate possible vulnerabilities [20].

[21] present a UML profile with a decentralized label model incorporated into UML class diagrams (see Table 1 no. 4). This allows the modelling of confidentiality at design time. The so-called UMLs profile allows the specification of confidential information flow in a fine-grained manner. Different stereotypes defining owners and

users are used to annotate classes, attributes, operations, parameters, errors, and return types. These labels are used to decide whether the information flow is permitted or not. Declassification of information is realized with the authorityConstraint. It models the weakening of the confidentiality of information coming from more confidential sources. This is necessary for operations processing confidential data but providing less confidential results. The approach is presented for class diagrams, but it is extendable to other diagram types such as interaction, use case and activity diagrams.

The work of Goudalo et al. [22] elaborates on modelling security aspects of information systems (see Table 1 no. 5). They propose a UML profile on how to properly encapsulate security knowledge during design time. An example is shown in the context of confidentiality. Confidentiality of information and information flow is modelled in sequence diagrams by defining stereotypes modelling the confidentiality levels of resources, subjects, and subsystems. In essence, software engineers are able to model confidentiality in diverse ways by using this UML profile.

Table 1 no. 6 shows the work of Hatebur et al. [23]. They build upon a UML profile for expressing problem frames in UML class diagrams. Problem frames are patterns are used to define problem classes by their contexts and characteristics. The extended UML profile expresses dependability requirements. In the case of security, the traditional goals of confidentiality, availability and integrity can be expressed. These goals are modelled with stereotypes and include specifications like the data to be secured, the attacker and the stakeholder of data. Additionally, problem frames allow the expression of arbitrary confidentiality requirements. The authors mention that the main advantage of their approach is the ability to express dependability requirements without the anticipation of a solution. This clearly separates the problem space from the solution space. Furthermore, it is easy to visually distinguish between different security requirement classes.

The approach of [24], SECDW allows the modelling of confidentiality aspects in UML class diagrams (see Table 1 no. 7). SECDW is an extension intended for the domain of data warehouses. The approach introduces a UML profile that enables the specification of security classes for information and users. Tuples composed of security classifications, sets of user compartments (classification of users in department like structures), and user roles allows the specification of constraints about which users are allowed to read certain information. Triki et al. [25] proposes an extension (SECDQ+) with the ability to model leaks of confidential information. Examples are health information or company turnover which, if accessed in combinations of datasets, leak additional undesired information. This problem is known as conflict of interest [25].

The UML profile of [26] is capable of both capturing security requirements and specifying security solutions (see Table 1 no. 8). This is achieved by placing security aspects into UML class and sequence diagrams in an aspect-oriented modelling manner. Besides that, the approach allows the expression of the separation of security concerns for software functionalities. Security experts can specify security solutions as aspects in the UML model and model their points (where the security solutions are implemented) in UML sequence diagrams. In consequence, the solution is easily understandable even for non-security experts.

The UML profile of [27] models privacy restrictions in UML class diagrams (see Table 1 no. 9). The target field is in the context of mobile distributed systems, but the approach can be used in other contexts as well. The main idea is to bind access rights to context information. This is done by formulating privacy restrictions on context information. Privacy restrictions are composed of the source and validity of the context information, as well as the access rights in the form of confidentiality levels. In Simons' UML profile, constraints are used to validate the model. This is accomplished by imposing restrictions on the defined stereotypes to enforce the correct use of the profile.

4   Business Process-Oriented Approaches

Privacy and security are business requirements, and therefore privacy as well as security requirements are increasingly included in enterprise modelling [28]. This can be achieved in different ways:

- via models of privacy and security aspects using normal enterprise modelling languages
- in the form of annotations
- with the help of more-or-less formalized privacy/security notation add-ons for existing modelling languages

For business processes as one component of enterprise modelling, we analysed 'Petri nets' and 'Business Process Model and Notation (BPMN)'.

4.1   Analysis of Petri Net-Based Approaches

There are plenty of approaches to using Petri nets for modelling information security aspects, particularly information confidentiality. They can be used to model privacy requirements as well, but special privacy model extensions are not common today. The problem is that some of the approaches only focus on the technical level, which generally means that they are discussing problems like algorithms, protocols or technical architecture, using Petri nets for visualisation, but omit the business process perspective.

Huang and Kirchner have introduced a formal method to verify whether the compositions of sub-policies fulfil the required general policies of a company [29]. They used coloured Petri nets and Petri net-based properties like completeness, termination, consistency and confluence. One use case is the verification as to whether a set of policies fulfils a general policy like GDPR. Therefore, the requirements of the GDPR must be transformed into a model.

[30] extended object Petri nets by using modules to define security services like the decryption and encryption of data. This could be interesting for data protection because encrypted data need not be protected itself as long as the key is strong and kept secret. [31] defined a framework for the assessment of security protocols. They used coloured stochastic activity nets and implemented probabilistic model checking. In addition, [32] analysed security protocols and a Petri net extension called S-net, which is designed such that the terms of the Security Protocol Language [33] can be used. Other Petri net-based approaches aim at building models for special concepts. For example, [34] modelled the Chinese wall policy with coloured Petri nets; afterwards, they used a

coverability graph to analyse the guarantees of the Chinese wall policy. [35] used coupled Petri nets for the risk analysis of computer networks. Sun et al. published a 'Verification Mechanism for Secured Message Processing in Business Collaboration' [36]. They used the role-based access control (RBAC) mechanism and hierarchical coloured Petri nets to detect conflicts in message access within collaboration process instances to the role-based policy. A similar approach from [37] focused on the confidentiality of information exchanges between organizations and therefore has special places in coloured activity nets for incoming and outgoing information. Chinese wall and interorganizational information exchange are also relevant for privacy protection questions. As shown, many approaches use Petri nets for modelling security aspects, but focus on a technical level or only cover one single aspect. Therefore, these approaches are not suitable for use by business process experts to model their security requirements and discuss them with technical experts.

In addition, some approaches use Petri nets for modelling or analysing security aspects of business processes. Accorsi and Wonnemann developed InDico [38], an information-flow analysis method for labelling Petri net-based business process models. InDico focuses on 'information propagation throughout the systems (end-to-end) rather than mere data access (point to point)' [38]. Accorsi et al. [39] published an extension of InDico for analysing information-flow effects during process execution. They used security levels (called 'levels of confidentiality') but reduced them to two, and analysed the structural interferences between them. It is impossible to express different levels of confidentiality for the same place in one business process scheme, e.g., different information, or more than two levels of confidentiality for the whole business process scheme. Li et al. [40] described a coloured Petri net extension for detecting confidentiality problems in information-flow models. They use security levels and add the concrete security levels as attributes of the tokens. Li et al. did not focus on the resources handling the information. Knorr [41], who also used security levels, presented a method to verify multilevel security policies in workflow models, but he modelled control and information flow as different arcs in his workflow Petri nets. Atluri and Huang [42], who have also used Petri nets, presented a multilevel security approach with security levels for places and tokens. They later extended their approach with more concepts, like separation of duty and role-based access, using a coloured, timed Petri net [43]. They did not consider resources or the possibility of reducing the security level of a token, e.g., when information is truncated.

The large number of approaches for modelling security aspects using (high-level) Petri nets shows that the integration and processing of confidential information in Petri net-based business process models is currently a major challenge. This is one reason why we think Petri nets are also suitable for privacy questions. Other reasons in favour of Petri nets are their mathematical foundation and the availability of a broad range of analysis methods. Especially for analysis functionality, formal Petri nets are necessary.

4.2   Analysis of BPMN-Based Approaches

Extensions of the Business Process Model and Notation for modelling security requirements exist for each of the three classic security objectives: confidentiality, integrity and availability. Leitner et al. [44] have published a systematic literature review on 'Security Aspects in the Business Process Model and Notation'. Therefore, we do not provide a detailed overview here. In summary, some publications use BPMN for security questions without new extensions. In [45], Meland and Gjaere argue that there is no need for new BPMN extensions for many questions. Several other approaches extend the BPMN notation, e.g., with new symbols to create a faster overview of security issues for the model users [46]. Focusing on privacy as part of security, [47] used BPMN to introduce privacy in business process models, while Labda et al. [48] extended BPMN to privacy-aware BPMN. They focused not only on modelling privacy aspects, but also proposed a methodology for transferring them into the implementation.

5   Comparing Approaches

We have identified two criteria through which the software architecture-oriented and business process-oriented approaches can be conceptionally compared. In summary, only a few approaches we reviewed introduced elements to model actual privacy principles [17, 18, 43]. Most of them introduce privacy as a way of establishing confidentiality and restricting access to information.

5.1   Security Mechanisms

This criterion describes the expression of privacy in models in terms of how it is expressed, and through which security and privacy mechanisms it is represented. We recommend the following two characteristics for an analysis:

- Information flow and access control: this characteristic establishes privacy by introducing concepts that restrict the information flow or the access to information, functions or system parts by imposing rights. Approaches with this characteristic introduce concepts of confidentiality in various ways as well as in different degrees. These concepts are used either directly or can be used to express privacy in a certain way. Examples are Chinese wall policy and confidentiality levels. The following approaches fulfil this characteristic [19, 21, 22, 24, 27, 34, 36–41, 43, 47].
- General structures: approaches with these characteristics use abstract structures to express either several or a particular security and privacy principle. An example is the problem frames of [23] which provide the ability to express a problem and, through this, express an actual security principle. Another example, common in the security area, is policies. We identified the following approaches fulfilling this characteristic [17, 18, 23, 26, 29–32, 35, 43].

Each approach is assigned to one of the above characteristics. The approaches we reviewed focus either on the key feature of confidentiality to express privacy, or on introducing various other structures through which privacy is expressible. The first are grouped under the characteristic 'information flow and access control' and the latter ones under the characteristic 'general structures'. Our analysis shows that nearly half of the reviewed software architecture-oriented and business process-oriented approaches fulfil the first characteristic. They all introduce elements to model confidentiality. Some of them additionally use confidentiality mechanisms to establish privacy in a specific way [24, 34, 36–41]. The other approaches of the first group only introduce modelling elements for confidentiality. These modelling elements are not directly for the purpose of expressing privacy [19, 21, 22, 27, 47]. The other half of the reviewed approaches utilize various other mechanisms to model privacy. The approach [17], for example, introduces new structures like super containers and problem frames to express privacy. Some others use policies [18, 19].

5.2 Different Views

This criterion distinguishes the approaches according to their view on the model. As there are various stakeholders with different concerns to express, different views arise that fulfil the needs of a specific stakeholder. Typical examples from the field of security are the attacker view and security specialist view. The attacker view introduces model elements showing how the attacker could break into the system. The opposite side highlights the security measures in place, namely the security specialist view.

The criterion 'different views' divides the approaches according to the needs of their stakeholders. Common views are:

- Attacker view: models the attacker with the attacks, threats and vulnerabilities of a system, or analyses the given model for flaws in the information flow [19, 31, 32, 35, 38–40, 43].
- Requirements & Implementation view: introduces elements to express requirements pertaining to security and privacy aspects and elements, which model security and privacy solutions [17, 18, 21–24, 26, 27, 30, 34, 36, 37, 43, 47].
- Verification view: allows users to check whether a model fulfils certain requirements by checking them against the model. This is realized, for example, with constraints, which are checked for correct implementation, or the verification of policies [18, 21, 24, 29, 34, 39–42].

The software architecture-oriented approaches realize the 'attacker view' by introducing an attacker with his capabilities. We found only one approach of this type in our analysis [19]. The business process-oriented side identifies flaws in the information flow, and thus privacy breaches. Both the software architecture-oriented approaches and the business process-oriented approaches are represented in the 'requirements & implementation view'. Here, elements are introduced to express security and privacy requirements or solutions. The difference in these approaches lies in the degree of abstraction. While the business process-oriented approaches are typically on a less technical and more abstract level, the software architecture-based approaches introduce both a non-expert view and, sometimes, a more technical, expert view. In both software architecture-oriented approaches and business process-oriented approaches, we identified the intention to verify whether the implementation or model is correct with respect to certain requirements. These approaches are part of the 'verification view'. While software architecture-oriented approaches verify the correctness of modelled solutions, business process-oriented approaches try to identify and verify security policies against a given model. In general, we recognized that, for the reviewed approaches, the software architecture-based approaches tended to model requirements or design solutions more often. They also had a stronger focus on verifying whether the model fulfils the requirements. The business process-based approaches had a stronger focus on the identification of flaws and the verification of policies.

6   Conclusion

As we have shown, there are some approaches to systematically modelling security and/or privacy aspects of organizations each from a specific perspective. However, no comprehensive approach integrates all aspects such as process, structural organization and data. Such approaches must be developed or further developed. Figure 1 illustrates the relationships between companies and enterprise software (as the origin of models), sent model types and views, as well as the implemented software, the implemented processes/structure and the people involved. The arrow shown between origin and model describes a mapping function. Dotted arrows describe influences between different original models or artefacts. Different models exist for a company (the model origin at the top of the figure). For the view Business Process Flow Models, for example, Petri Nets and/or BPMN models exists. For this purpose, we have drawn in a new integrated view, information security/privacy. This includes various other views and their models and integrates them in an appropriate manner. Appropriate links must be developed for this purpose. For example, you need to describe which organizational unit participates in a particular activity of a business process, and to determine whether the organizational unit is allowed access to the data that is also linked to the activity. In addition to this linking of existing views, an integrated view can further enhance the models (for example, by providing additional information on data protection, such as the purpose of an activity to check the purpose limitation of the data). Such an integrated view is currently not sufficiently developed for the Information Security/Privacy application case, as literature research has shown. However, approaches and concepts already exist (such as the concept modelling suites, a concrete implementation of which is, for example, the Horus Business Modeller, www.horus.biz), on the basis of which this integrated view was developed. Integrated views means that models from different views are linked together and consistency is enforced.

This integrated view describes the requirements of those responsible for the company software. These requirements of the enterprise models must be transferred into the software models to be implemented later. However, software engineers use other models (e.g. UML) to describe the requirements.

Nevertheless, traceability of the requirements must be guaranteed. A systematic and, as far as possible, automatic transformation of the requirements is therefore required. This is shown in Fig. 1 by the dashed line between the company models and the software. Here, it is necessary to derive an integrated view for the middle part of the illustration from the integrated view of the upper level. We therefore suggest an automated model transformation from enterprise to software modelling. Continuous modelling is a prerequisite for the traceability of the requirements. Therefore, it must be possible to transfer business requirements modelled in Petri nets to software requirements modelled in UML.

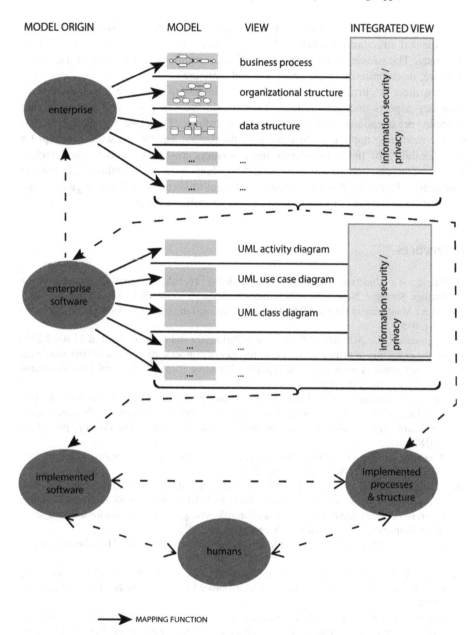

Fig. 1. Holistic modelling approach.

The arrow between enterprise software and the enterprise in Fig. 1 shows that standard software influences enterprises as well. The arrow between the company models in their entirety and the implemented processes/structure describes the influence of modelling on subsequent execution. The connection between the software models as a whole and the implemented software is also shown by a dashed arrow. Finally, implemented software and implemented processes (which can also be partly manual)/ implemented structure influence each other in terms of execution properties such as efficiency. The people involved are also affected or influence the concrete use of the software, or compliance to the processes and structures.

That there is currently no comprehensive modelling approach which covers the necessary aspects and perspectives. This should include processes as well as, for example, organizational and data structure questions. Therefore we suggest a new holistic modelling approach which includes the needed aspects and with a concept for the traceability of the requirements from business models to software architecture models. The new approach uses modelling languages and methods of existing approaches. To get a holistic view we linked them (different views and languages) and enriched them for the purpose of privacy and security modelling.

References

1. Reisig, W.: Understanding Petri Nets: Modeling Techniques, Analysis Methods, Case Studies. Springer, New York (2013). https://doi.org/10.1007/978-3-642-33278-4
2. Object Management Group. OMG Unified Modeling Language TM (OMG UML), Version 2.5 (2015)
3. Regulation (EU) 2016/679 of the European Parliament and of the Council of 27 April 2016 on the protection of natural persons with regard to the processing of personal data and on the free movement of such data, and repealing Directive 95/46/EC (General Data Protection Regulation), vol. 119 (2016)
4. Alpers, S., Pilipchuk, R., Oberweis, A., Reussner, R.: Identifying needs for a holistic modelling approach to privacy aspects in enterprise software systems. In: Presented at the 4th International Conference on Information Systems Security and Privacy, pp. 74–82 (2018)
5. Accenture. Cost of cyber crime study (2017). https://www.accenture.com/us-en/insight-cost-of-cybercrime-2017. Accessed 26 Jun 2018
6. Federal Financial Supervisory Authority (BaFin). Minimum Requirements for Risk Management (2005). https://www.bundesbank.de/Redaktion/EN/Downloads/Tasks/Banking_supervision/PDF/minimum_requirements_for_risk_management_mindestanforderungen_an_das_risikomanagement_marisk.pdf. Accessed 26 Jun 2018
7. Gesetz zur Erhöhung der Sicherheit informationstechnischer Systeme (IT-Sicherheitsgesetz) (2015)
8. Genz, A.: Datenschutz in Europa und den USA: Eine rechtsvergleichende Untersuchung unter besonderer Berücksichtigung der Safe-Harbor-Lösung. Deutscher Universitätsverlag (2004)
9. Hornung, G., Schnabel, C.: Data protection in Germany I: the population census decision and the right to informational self-determination. Comput. Law Secur. Rev. 25(1), 84–88 (2009)
10. Directive 95/46/EC of the European Parliament and of the Council of 24 October 1995 on the protection of individuals with regard to the processing of personal data and on the free movement of such data, vol. OJ L (1995)
11. ISO: ISO/ IEC 27000:2014(E) Information technology - Security techniques - Information security management systems - Overview and vocabulary (2014)
12. Bundesamt für Sicherheit in der Informationstechnik, 'IT-Grundschutz'. https://www.bsi.bund.de/DE/Themen/ITGrundschutz/itgrundschutz_node.html. Accessed 26 Jun 2018

13. Agutter, C.: ITIL Foundation Handbook, 3rd edn. The Stationery Office Ltd., London (2012)
14. COBIT 5: A Business Framework for the Governance and Management of Enterprise IT. http://www.isaca.org/cobit/pages/default.aspx. Accessed: 26 Jun 2018
15. Störrle, H.: How are conceptual models used in industrial software development?: a descriptive survey. In: Proceedings of the 21st International Conference on Evaluation and Assessment in Software Engineering, New York, NY, USA, pp. 160–169 (2017)
16. Aerts, A.T.M., Goossenaerts, J.B.M., Hammer, D.K., Wortmann, J.C.: Architectures in context: on the evolution of business, application software, and ICT platform architectures. Inf. Manag. **41**(6), 781–794 (2004)
17. Jutla, D.N., Bodorik, P., Ali, S.: Engineering Privacy for Big Data Apps with the Unified Modeling Language. In: 2013 IEEE International Congress on Big Data, pp. 38–45 (2013)
18. Basso, T., Montecchi, L., Moraes, R., Jino, M., Bondavalli, A.: Towards a UML profile for privacy-aware applications. In: 2015 IEEE International Conference on Computer and Information Technology; Ubiquitous Computing and Communications; Dependable, Autonomic and Secure Computing; Pervasive Intelligence and Computing, pp. 371–378 (2015)
19. Jürjens, J.: UMLsec: extending UML for secure systems development. In: Jézéquel, J.-M., Hussmann, H., Cook, S. (eds.) UML 2002. LNCS, vol. 2460, pp. 412–425. Springer, Heidelberg (2002). https://doi.org/10.1007/3-540-45800-X_32
20. Jürjens, J.: Model-based security engineering with UML. In: Aldini, A., Gorrieri, R., Martinelli, F. (eds.) FOSAD 2004-2005. LNCS, vol. 3655, pp. 42–77. Springer, Heidelberg (2005). https://doi.org/10.1007/11554578_2
21. Heldal, R., Schlager, S., Bende, J.: Supporting confidentiality in UML : a profile for the decentralized label model. In: Proceeding Workshop on Critical Systems Development with UML (2004)
22. Goudalo, W., Seret, D.: Toward the engineering of security of information systems (ESIS): UML and the IS confidentiality. In: 2008 Second International Conference on Emerging Security Information, Systems and Technologies, pp. 248–256 (2008)
23. Hatebur, D., Heisel, M.: A UML profile for requirements analysis of dependable software. In: Schoitsch, E. (ed.) SAFECOMP 2010. LNCS, vol. 6351, pp. 317–331. Springer, Heidelberg (2010). https://doi.org/10.1007/978-3-642-15651-9_24
24. Fernández-Medina, E., Trujillo, J., Villarroel, R., Piattini, M.: Extending UML for designing secure data warehouses. In: Atzeni, P., Chu, W., Lu, H., Zhou, S., Ling, T.-W. (eds.) ER 2004. LNCS, vol. 3288, pp. 217–230. Springer, Heidelberg (2004). https://doi.org/10.1007/978-3-540-30464-7_18
25. Triki, S., Ben-Abdallah, H., Feki, J., Harbi, N.: Modeling conflict of interest in the design of secure data warehouses, pp. 445–448 (2010)
26. Mouheb, D., Talhi, C., Lima, V., Debbabi, M., Wang, L., Pourzandi, M.: Weaving security aspects into UML 2.0 design models. In: Proceedings of the 13th Workshop on Aspect-oriented Modeling, New York, NY, USA, pp. 7–12 (2009)
27. Simons, C.: CMP: a UML context modeling profile for mobile distributed systems. In: 2007 40th Annual Hawaii International Conference on System Sciences, HICSS 2007, p. 289b (2007)
28. Shariati, M., Bahmani, F., Shams, F.: Enterprise information security, a review of architectures and frameworks from interoperability perspective. Procedia Comput. Sci. **3**, 537–543 (2011)
29. Huang, H., Kirchner, H.: Secure interoperation design in multi-domains environments based on colored Petri nets. Inf. Sci. **221**, 591–606 (2013)
30. Mixia, L., Qiuyu, Z., Dongmei, Y., Hong, Z.: Formal security model research based on Petri-net. In: 2005 IEEE International Conference on Granular Computing, vol. 2, pp. 575–578 (2005)

31. Akbarzadeh, M., Azgomi, M.A.: A framework for probabilistic model checking of security protocols using coloured stochastic activity networks and PDETool. In: 5th International Symposium on Telecommunications (IST), pp. 210–215 (2010)
32. Bouroulet, R., Devillers, R., Klaudel, H., Pelz, E., Pommereau, F.: Modeling and analysis of security protocols using role based specifications and petri nets. In: van Hee, Kees M., Valk, R. (eds.) PETRI NETS 2008. LNCS, vol. 5062, pp. 72–91. Springer, Heidelberg (2008). https://doi.org/10.1007/978-3-540-68746-7_9
33. Crazzolara, F., Winskel, G.: Events in security protocols. In: Proceedings of the 8th ACM conference on Computer and Communications Security, pp. 96–105 (2001)
34. Zhang, Z.-L., Hong, F., Liao, J.-G.: Modeling Chinese wall policy using colored Petri nets. In: The Sixth IEEE International Conference on Computer and Information Technology, p. 162 (2006)
35. Henry, M.H., Layer, R.M., Zaret, D.R.: Coupled Petri nets for computer network risk analysis. Int. J. Crit. Infrastruct. Prot. 3(2), 67–75 (2010)
36. Sun, H., Yang, J., Wang, X., Zhang, Y.: A verification mechanism for secured message processing in business collaboration. In: Li, Q., Feng, L., Pei, J., Wang, S.X., Zhou, X., Zhu, Q.-M. (eds.) APWeb/WAIM -2009. LNCS, vol. 5446, pp. 480–491. Springer, Heidelberg (2009). https://doi.org/10.1007/978-3-642-00672-2_42
37. Lai, H., Hong, J., Jeng, W.: Model e-contract update by coloured activity net. In: 2008 IEEE Asia-Pacific Services Computing Conference, APSCC 2008, pp. 488–493 (2008)
38. Accorsi, R., Wonnemann, C.: InDico: information flow analysis of business processes for confidentiality requirements. In: Cuellar, J., Lopez, J., Barthe, G., Pretschner, A. (eds.) STM 2010. LNCS, vol. 6710, pp. 194–209. Springer, Heidelberg (2011). https://doi.org/10.1007/978-3-642-22444-7_13
39. Accorsi, R., Lehmann, A., Lohmann, N.: Information leak detection in business process models: theory, application, and tool support. Inf. Syst. 47, 244–257 (2015)
40. Li, W., Wu, R., Huang, H.: Colored Petri nets based modeling of information flow security. In: 2009 Second International Workshop on Knowledge Discovery and Data Mining, WKDD 2009, pp. 681–684 (2009)
41. Knorr, K.: Multilevel security and information flow in Petri net workflows. In: Proceedings of the 9th International Conference on Telecommunication Systems, pp. 613–615 (2001)
42. Atluri, V., Huang, W.-K.: An extended Petri net model for supporting workflows in a multilevel secure environment. In: Samarati, P., Sandhu, R.S. (eds.) Database Security. IFIP Advances in Information and Communication Technology, pp. 240–258. Springer, Boston (1996). https://doi.org/10.1007/978-0-387-35167-4_15
43. Atluri, V., Huang, W.-K.: A Petri net based safety analysis of workflow authorization models. J. Comput. Secur. 8(2–3), 209–240 (2000)
44. Leitner, M., Miller, M., Rinderle-Ma, S.: An analysis and evaluation of security aspects in the business process model and notation, pp. 262–267 (2013)
45. Meland, P.H., Gjaere, E.A.: Representing threats in BPMN 2.0, pp. 542–550 (2012)
46. Wolter, C., Meinel, C.: An approach to capture authorisation requirements in business processes. Requir. Eng. 15(4), 359–373 (2010)
47. Mülle, J., von Stackelberg, S., Böhm, K.: Modelling and transforming security constraints in privacy-aware business processes. In: 2011 IEEE International Conference on Service-Oriented Computing and Applications (SOCA), pp. 1–4 (2011)
48. Labda, W., Mehandjiev, N., Sampaio, P.: Privacy-aware business processes modeling notation (PrvBPMN) in the context of distributed mobile applications. In: Matera, M., Rossi, G. (eds.) MobiWIS 2013. CCIS, vol. 183, pp. 120–134. Springer, Cham (2013). https://doi.org/10.1007/978-3-319-03737-0_13

A Critical Security Analysis of the Password-Based Authentication Honeywords System Under Code-Corruption Attack

Ziya Alper Genç, Gabriele Lenzini[(✉)], Peter Y. A. Ryan,
and Itzel Vazquez Sandoval[(✉)]

Interdisciplinary Centre for Security, Reliability and Trust (SnT),
University of Luxembourg, Luxembourg, Luxembourg
{ziya.genc,gabriele.lenzini,peter.ryan,itzel.vazquezsandoval}@uni.lu

Abstract. Password-based authentication is a widespread method to access into systems, thus password files are a valuable resource often target of attacks. To detect when a password file has been stolen, Juels and Rivest introduced the Honeywords System in 2013. The core idea is to store the password with a list of decoy words that are "indistinguishable" from the password, called honeywords. An adversary that obtains the password file and, by dictionary attack, retrieves the honeywords can only guess the password when attempting to log in: but any incorrect guess will set off an alarm, warning that file has been compromised. In a recent conference paper, we studied the security of the Honeywords System in a scenario where the intruder also manages to corrupt the server's code (with certain limiting assumptions); we proposed an authentication protocol and proved it secure despite the corruption. In this extended journal version, we detail the analysis and we extend it, under the same attacker model, to the other two protocols of the original Honeywords System, the *setup* and *change of password*. We formally verify the security of both of them; further, we discuss that our design suggests a completely new approach that diverges from the original idea of the Honeywords System but indicates an alternative way to authenticate users which is robust to server's code-corruption.

Keywords: Honeywords · Password-based authentication ·
Secure protocols design · Formal analysis · ProVerif

1 Introduction

Password-based authentication is a simple and widespread way to validate user identity [1]: it requires users to have a public login and a secret password. It is not the most secure though. For that, passwords must remain secret, users must chose them hard-to-guess, not to share them, and transmit them only over

© Springer Nature Switzerland AG 2019
P. Mori et al. (Eds.): ICISSP 2018, CCIS 977, pp. 125–151, 2019.
https://doi.org/10.1007/978-3-030-25109-3_7

encrypted channels. Servers, in turn, should not store passwords in cleartext but keep them hashed (usually with some "salt") in a file called the *password file*.

Such valuable files are naturally the target of hackers, who try to steal them from servers for then retrieve passwords by off-line dictionary attacks. A taste of the extension of the problem can be read from the news. In 2016, Yahoo! was reported to have had, in 2014, 500 million user accounts hacked, a number that was corrected, later, to be 1 billion accounts [2], and further to be 3 billion [3]. MySpace, Tumblr, and LinkedIn were also be reported to have had millions of login credentials stolen (64 million Tumblr accounts and more than 360 million MySpace accounts [4]). The theft would have passed unnoticed if it was not for someone who tried to sell the credentials in the black market.

These examples, in addition to the high number of passwords lost, surprise because of the time that has passed between the attacks and their detection. Such a delay is a problem as serious as the reason that led to the leak because puts off the application of countermeasures that could limit the damage.

To improve the awareness of passwords theft, computer security research has proposed solutions. For instance, Google monitors suspicious activities and invites users to review from what device and from which location they have accessed their account. But of course, it is more critical and valuable to ensure that a service becomes aware of the theft of a password file because, in such situation, a great deal of passwords is exposed at once. This problem is the starting point of some recent research.

2   Juels and Rivest's Honeywords System

Aiming to make password-cracking detectable, in 2013, Juels and Rivest proposed to modify the classical password-based authentication scheme with one called *Honeywords System* [5].

A Honeywords System hides and stores a user (hashed) password in a list of decoy words, called *honeywords*. Honeywords are chosen to be indistinguishable from the password, for instance "redsun3" is a good honeyword for "whitemoon5", a property which is called *flatness* [5,6]. Honeywords should also be chosen in such a way that is unlikely that a user types a honeyword purely by mistake. From those properties from any attempt to log in with a honeyword instead of the password one can soundly concludes that the password file must have been leaked. So does the Honeywords System, which flags the event and initiates some contingency procedure (e.g., system administrators are alerted, monitors are activated, user's execution rights are reduced, user's actions are run in a sandbox, and so on).

The Honeywords System's architecture is logically organized in two modules: (1) a "computer system" which, according to Juels and Rivest, is "any system that allows a user to 'log in' after she has provided a username and a password" (*ibid*) and which we call the *Login Server (LS)*; (2) an auxiliary *hardened secure* server that assists with the use of honeywords, which Juels and Rivest call the *Honeychecker (HC)*. For each registered user u, the LS keeps (in the password file) the ordered list of u's *sweetwords* (so are called collectively honeywords and password), denoted here by $[h(w_x)]_u$, with $x \in [1, k]$ where k is the fixed number of sweetwords. The HC stores c_u, the index of u's password in such list.

The system's behavior comprises three phases: (1) *setup*, (2) *authentication* (i.e., the login), and (3) *change of password*. Authentication is the most critical phase, so we describe it first. We leave the setup and modification for later sections. At authentication, the LS receives username and password (u, w) from the user; then, it searches the hashed version of w in the list $[h(w_1), \ldots, h(w_k)]_u$ of (hashed) sweetwords of u. If no match is found, login is denied. Otherwise the LS sends to the HC the message (u, j), where j is the found position. This communication occurs over dedicated and/or encrypted and authenticated channels. The HC checks whether $j = c_u$. In the case that the test succeeds, access is granted. In case the test fails, it is up to the HC to decide what to do. Juels and Rivest say: "Depending on the policy chosen, the honeychecker may or may not reply to the computer system when a login is attempted. When it detects that something is amiss with the login attempt, it could signal to the computer system that login should be denied. On the other hand it may merely signal a 'silent alarm' to an administrator, and let the login on the computer system proceed. In the later case, we could perhaps call the honeychecker a 'login monitor' rather than a 'honeychecker'."(*ibid*). Figure 1 illustrates the authentication protocol considering a responsive honeychecker.

The Honeywords System's goal is not to impede the stealing of a password file: an intruder who has retrieved by an off-line dictionary attack the sweetwords can still succeed in guessing the correct password but, assuming that the adversary has no other clue than the sweetwords, he has probability $(k - 1)/k$ to fail and reveal the leak.

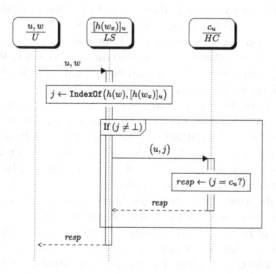

Fig. 1. Honeywords System authentication protocol. (Taken from [7]).

Juels and Rivest have left open several problems. One of them reads as follows "How can a Honeywords System best be designed to withstand active attacks e.g., malicious messages issued by a compromised computer system or code modification of the computer system?' (*ibid*).

In a conference version of this work [7], we took on the task to discuss the part of the problem regarding "*to withstand [..] code modification of the computer system*".

Generally speaking, awaiting to define in detail what "code modification" means (see next section), the corruption of the Honeywords System raises interesting questions. Juels and Rivest discuss in [5] that: "compromising only the honeychecker at worst reduces security to the level it was before the introduction of honeywords and the honeychecker". The situation worsens if the honeychecker *and* the module that we called the LS were both corrupted: we are inclined to believe that if the whole Honeywords System is compromised there is little to do to avoid that the intruder can get access unnoticed (although only a rigorous analysis, out of scope here but suitable for future work, can provide evidence to this claim). The last interesting case is to analyse the security of the Honeywords System against an adversary that has succeeded in "modifying the code of LS". In [7] we propose a solution, a new protocol that here we describe and analyze in full detail. We also extend the analysis to the two remaining protocols, the setup and the change of a password, which we also redesign and prove it be secure against a code modified LS.

3   Paper Outline

We first discuss the notion of "code modification". It was left informal in Juels and Rivest's work but so stated it does not help understand the real nature of the threat. We need to define it rigorously. So, in Sect. 4 we give our definition of "code modification" or, as we will call from now on, "*code corruption*": we prefer this term since it stresses the maliciousness of the act. We also state a few foundational assumptions before thoroughly giving the analysis of security of the original Honeywords System under the threat.

In Sect. 5 we prove the Honeywords System insecure, illustrating an attack that works when the LS's code has been corrupted according to our model and under our assumptions. The attack reveals that when confronted against the threat, the original Honeywords System has a core weakness. From studying the root cause of the attack we elicit a security requirement and by fulfilling it we are able to provide a solution to the problem.

In Sect. 7 we describe a new cryptographic protocol for authentication which we argue that removes the weakness and hence restores security. We sustain this statement formally in Sect. 7.2 by modeling in ProVerif the protocol together with the code-corrupting adversary and running an automatic analysis. The results of the verification confirm that the previous attack is no more possible. Actually, we prove that there are no more attacks against the new protocol, in the given model.

In Sect. 9 we discuss the Honeywords System's setup phase and extend our new protocol to cover this stage. The corresponding formal analysis addressing issues detected in a code corrupted Honeywords System follows in Sect. 9.1. Likewise, Sects. 10 and 10.1 are devoted to the change of password phase.

Our solution is meant to be primarily of theoretical interest, but because its cryptographic primitives rely on a generous use of exponentiation, we thought useful to implement the authentication protocol and benchmark its performance with respect to the original Honeywords System's authentication. The results are reported in Sect. 11: they show that although slower than the original Honeywords System, the loss in performance is linear in k, the number of sweetwords. Roughly speaking, our scheme can handle a few hundred authentication requests per second on a laptop with the service running on a virtual machine. It is reasonable to expect better results on more efficiently performing servers.

At the end, in Sect. 12, we discuss our solution in a wider perspective. We look at it from distance to conclude that, although it solves the open problem and works against the code-corruption threat that we have defined, it actually suggests a completely innovative design for password-based authentication that is far stronger to be used only as a fix for Honeywords System.

4 Code Corruption and Threat Model

What is a reasonable goal for an adversary that intends to code corrupt LS? What is *code corruption*? What levels of corruption are interesting to study? We have to answer all these questions to understand the threat.

We premise that if the meaning of code corruption should be taken literally, it suggested an ability to change the code at will. Stated in this way, it seems to be a very disruptive ability and not all its instances are interesting, in the sense that they do not bring to insights that help up understand the fundamental weaknesses of the system design. What understanding do we gain from a code corruption that, for instance, causes a shut-down of the entire system or that let anyone log in? It is necessary to establish specific *assumptions* to limit the extension of the threat.

We start with an obvious assumption, one that follows from the original Juels and Rivest's paper:

Assumption 1. The adversary, before corrupting the LS, knows the sweetwords but not the passwords.

Assumption 1 says that the adversary has stolen the password file and has retrieved all the k sweetwords of, say, user u: yet, s(he) does not know which one among the u's sweetwords is the password.

Let us call the fact of logging in without the HC's raising an alarm a "successful log-in". Assumption 1 states that the probability of a successful log-in for the intruder occurs when s(he) naïvely picks at random a sweetword. We exclude that the adversary have access to other sources to increase such probability, for instance, possessing social information about a specific user (e.g., relatives' birthdays, pets' names, etc.) which could be reflected in the password choice. Oppositely, for simplicity, we also exclude that the adversary failed to retrieve some sweetwords from the hashed values: all the sweetwords have been recovered.

"What is a reasonable goal for an adversary that intends to code corrupt the system?". We believe that a reasonable goal is to increase the intruder's probability of a successful log-in to a value higher than the one that (s)he would have by guessing the password and with an honest LS.

Definition 1. *The goal of a code corruption attack is to increase the adversary's probability to successfully log in with respect to the probability of guessing the password among the sweetwords retrieved from the passwords file.*

We answer the second question "What is code corruption?" together with "What levels of corruption are reasonable to consider"?

Definition 2. *Let* ls.exe *be the code of the LS's protocols. Code corruption of LS means changing* ls.exe.

With its code corrupted, LS can change completely its behavior. An intruder can reprogram it to do whatever, e.g., to play chess.[1] However, we are not interested in attacks that change the functionality of the LS, for the reason that they do not help the adversary to increase its probability of successfully logging in. For a similar reason, we are not interested in attacks that shut-down the systems or cause Denial-of-Service. These are important attacks from which to seek defense, but out-of-scope in this study.

We also exclude attacks such as those consisting in changing ls.exe to always grant access (but of course if would make sense to change ls.exe to grant access selectively e.g., to the adversary Mallory, if that were possible, see later).

But in excluding an access-for-all corruption we have also a technical reason. The original paper does not give full detail of the architecture of the "computer system", our LS, but it seems reasonable to assume that Honeywords System implements a *separation of duties* [8]. And if so the duty of LS is only to search the proffered password in the password file, to inform the HC, and possibly to report the decision to the user, but not to grant or deny accesses. So there is no simple to way to open access to anyone, unless LS can foul the HC and this is actually the core of the threat (see next section).

Assumption 2. A code corruption against LS does not change the LS's observable behaviour.

The rationale of this assumption is that, if the adversary changes the observable behaviour of LS, this would result in an anomaly that can be detected, triggering an alert in response to which a safe version of the ls.exe can be

---

[1] This is what R. Gonggrijp did when, in 2006, proved insecure a Dutch electronic voting machine.

restored. Since the adversary may have a once-in-lifetime opportunity to corrupt LS's code, he may not want to see his efforts vanishing in this way. Of course not all attackers will be so concerned about being undetected. They can be satisfied by managing to log in and say ex-filtrate sensitive data might be fine, even if this leaves a trail. But we decided to scope our analysis only within the context of Assumption 2.

However, even under Assumption 2 there are subtleties that need to be addressed. Interpreted strictly it does not allow the creation of any back door between the adversary and the LS that this last can use at anytime to leak information. This is because, interpreting strictly the term "undetectability", an exchange of messages from the LS towards the adversary and outside the protocol's message flow can be eventually detected (e.g., by monitoring the net traffic), leading to have a safe version of the ls.exe re-installed.

Thus according to this interpretation, Assumption 2 says that if the intruder wants to communicate with the corrupted LS, it must use the same channels from which legitimate users log in, and must respect the message flow of the honest protocol. This does not exclude that, when re-coding ls.exe, the adversary can use the knowledge he has gained from having hacked the password file and hard-code in the corrupted ls.exe a user's IDs, the sweetwords, or other information s(he) may have.

Still, if we take Assumption 2 less strictly, it admits that some information can flow back to the adversary, for example, in message *resp*. And, as we will discuss in detail in Sect. 5, letting LS to communicate back to the adversary leads to a powerful attack that breaks the original Honeywords System. In short, the attack works because LS can learn u's password (or the hash of it). This is a feature more than a vulnerability but a feature that a collusive adversary able to invert the hash can exploit to know the password. So, an incentive for code corrupting the LS is exactly to create this retroactive communication and we cannot exclude this possibility in our analysis.

We propose thus the following methodology: by default we interpret Assumption 2 strictly but, always, we discuss what happens if we relax this constraint and let LS leak information to the intruder.

Notably, the new protocols that we describe in Sects. 7–10, although designed to secure the Honeywords System under an Assumption 2 interpreted strictly turn out to be efficient also when we relax it. The new protocols will not impede the leak nor stop the adversary from learning u's password, but will make that information useless for the adversary. Somehow the ideas behind our protocols reduces considerably the role of the password as the only authentication token.

5   Attacks Against the Authentication Protocol

As future reference, we write down how ls.exe looks like for the authentication protocol. Algorithm 1 shows it in pseudo-code, using a notation whose commands are self-explanatory. Here, passwd is the password file, $passwd_u$ is the row of user u, and H is a hash function (e.g., SHA-3 [9]). We also assume that u is a legitimate user's name. The algorithms presented here were introduced first in [7].

Algorithm 1. Login Server Authentication.

```
1: procedure ls.exe(passwd)
2:     while true do;
3:         ReceiveFrom(U; (u, w));
4:         j ← IndexOf(H(w), passwd_u);
5:         SendTo(HC; (u, j));
6:         ReceiveFrom(HC; resp);
7:         SendTo(U; resp);
```

If the adversary can corrupt ls.exe, even under our Assumption 2 taken strictly, there is an obvious attack. The corrupted ls′.exe is reported in Algorithm 2. When LS notices a good user's password, it stores the valid pair of credentials (user, password) and then reuses that knowledge to let the adversary gain access, when (s)he reveals her/himself at the log-in with a specific user name (e.g., "Mallory").

Algorithm 2 represents an ideal attack. Actually, LS could just remember the valid index j (in step 11) and, in a next round, skip searching the $passwd_u$ (step 7) and send that j to the HC (step 8). But the corrupted ls.exe outlined mimics the behaviour of LS more faithfully and shows also that *LS gets knowledge of a user's valid password*. This, we will see, is the root of a serious vulnerability.

Algorithm 2. Code Corrupted LS.

```
1: procedure ls′.exe(passwd)
2:     (u′, w′) ← (⊥, ⊥)                                    ▷ init good (u, w)
3:     while true do;
4:         ReceiveFrom(U; (u, w));
5:         if (u′ ≠ ⊥) ∧ (u = Mallory) then
6:             (u, w) ← (u′, w′)
7:         j ← IndexOf(H(w), passwd_u);
8:         SendTo(HC; (u, j));
9:         ReceiveFrom(HC; resp);
10:        if (resp = granted) then
11:            (u′, w′) ← (u, w)                             ▷ good (u, w)
12:        SendTo(U; resp);
```

Note that not always, in instruction 10, the LS learns u's password with certainty. This may happen, for instance, when the HC follows a contingency policy that dictate to respond by granting access even when it receives a sweetword, as suggested in the original work (see also our quote about it in Sect. 2). However, the following strategy gives the LS at least a good chance to guess the password, especially when the strategy is coordinated with the adversary: since the adversary can submit honeywords on purpose, it refrains itself from trying to access for a certain time. During this interval, the only requests that arrive to the LS pretending to be from user u are actually from the legitimate u; all the w that come with the requests then must be the u's legitimate password. Surely, the user can sometimes misspell the password, but that will never collide with a honeyword (because honeywords are flat, see Sect. 2). It is therefore possible for the LS, purely by statistical analysis and by cross comparison between what u submits, to infer the u's real password and at that moment the LS can so help the adversary as we illustrated in our ideal version of the attack. The adversary has raised its probability to gain a successful access.

This attack is already serious but under a relaxed Assumption 2, LS can further send the password back to the adversary, who now can use the u's credentials at any time.

Discussion. The root cause of the attack seems therefore to lie in the fact that LS gets to know u's password. Only hashing the password will not help, since the LS can search for the position of such hash value in u's row in the password file or, under a relaxed Assumption 2, send the hash back to the adversary who can reverse it. The main problems seem then rooted into three concomitant facts: (a) LS knows username and password in clear (even if it receives them over a secure channel); (b) LS can query HC as an oracle to know whether the submitted password is the user u's valid password (in this way it also gets to know the hash of the password); (c) LS can retrieve the index of the password in passwd_u (and with that he can foul the HC to grant access).

So, if a solution exists that makes the system secure despite a corrupted ls.exe then it would be such that it impedes LS to perform all these three actions (a)–(c) together. We state this finding as a requirement:

Requirement 1. An authentication protocol resilient to code corruption should not (1) let the LS receive sweetwords in clear; (2) let it know when a sweetword is a valid password; (3) allow it to reuse that knowledge to retrieve a valid index at any moment that is not when the legitimate user logs in.

6 Towards a Solution

In searching for a solution we are not interested in pragmatic fixes such as checking regularly the integrity of `ls.exe` and reinstalling a safe copy. Our lack of interest is not because solutions like that are not fully effective (e.g., the intruder can still execute its attack before any integrity check is performed) but because such pragmatic fixes do not give any insights about intrinsic weakness. The same argument holds in relation to best practices like forcing users to change their password frequently.

If a solution exists then it must be searched in a strategy that satisfies our requirement's items (1)–(3).

One way to comply with them is by implementing the following countermeasures: (i) passwd_u is *shuffled each time* LS queries HC: this avoids that LS can reuse an index j that it has learned to be the index of u's password; (ii) passwd_u

is *re-hashed each time* LS queries HC: this avoids that LS can search again for the index of a typed password that it got to know being a valid u's password; (iii) let the *LS know what to search in* passwd$_u$ *only when user u is logging in*: this precaution is to avoid that LS can perform off-line searches on passwd$_u$.

The countermeasures (i)–(ii), and so requirements (1)–(2), can be implemented *leaving HC in charge of shuffling and re-hashing the password file each time that a user logs in and that the LS questions the HC about index j.*

The shuffling does not require particular explanation. It must be randomized but is a standard step: given a row $[w_1, \ldots, w_k]$, and a permutation π, it returns $[w_{\pi(1)}, \ldots, w_{\pi(k)}]$.

The re-hashing, instead, needs to be explained. It is implemented by *cryptographic exponentiation*. For each user, HC possesses g, a generator of a multiplicative subgroup $\mathbb{G}$ of order q (so, actually, g should be written g_u, but to lighten the notation we omit the index u). When first the list of sweetwords is generated, the file is initially hashed using g^{r_0}, where $r_0 \in \{1, \cdots, q-1\}$ is a random number. The u's row of the file is therefore $[g^{r_0 \cdot w_1}, \ldots, g^{r_0 \cdot w_k}]$, which we write $[h^{r_0(w_1)}, \ldots, h^{r_0(w_k)}]$ to stress that this is a hashing. More synthetically we also write it as $h^{r_0}(\overline{w})$.

To rehash the row and obtain $h^{r_1}(\overline{w})$, HC chooses a new random number $r_1 \in \{1, \cdots, q-1\}$ and, for each element w_i of the row, it calculates (introduced in [7])

$$h^{r_0}(w_i)^{\frac{r_1}{r_0}} = (g^{r_0 \cdot w_i})^{\frac{r_1}{r_0}} = g^{r_0 \cdot \frac{r_1}{r_0} \cdot w_i} = g^{r_1 \cdot w_i}$$

The process can be iterated: to re-hash token $h^{r_n}(\overline{w})$, HC selects another number $r_{n+1} \in \{1, \cdots, q-1\}$ and computes $(h^{r_n}(\overline{w}))^{r_{n+1}/r_n}$ which is the re-hashed token $h^{r_{n+1}}(\overline{w})$.

In fact, HC reshuffles and re-hashes passwd$_u$ in one single step as shown in Fig. 2.

So far, we are envisioning a message flow as follows: when HC receives from LS a check query, it also receives passwd$_u^{r_n}$, which it shuffles using a new ordering π', and re-hashes using a freshly generated r_{n+1}. The re-hashed, re-shuffled row of u, passwd$_u$, is therefore $[h^{r_n}(w_{u,\pi'(i)})]_{i \in \{1,\ldots,k\}}$, which we write compactly as passwd$_u^{r_{n+1}}$. HC *performs these three steps indivisibly*: the passwd$_u^{r_n}$ should not be accessed by concurrent versions of the HC before it has been shuffled and re-hashed.

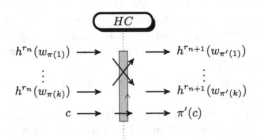

Fig. 2. Shuffling/re-hashing w's and updating c (Taken from [7]).

What explained so far implements countermeasures (i) and (ii). However, each nth time that a user u logs in and submits the password w, LS needs to calculate $h^{r_n}(w) = g^{r_n \cdot w}$ before being able to search for w's index in $\mathsf{passwd}_u^{r_n}$.

Letting LS to do this while avoiding that it gets to know u's password (i.e., by taking advantage of knowing the re-hashed password file $\mathsf{passwd}_u^{r_n}$ and the re-hashed $h^{r_n}(w)$, so anticipating the search and using HC as an oracle) is not obvious. We need to implement countermeasure (iii) and *prevent LS from searching the file at any time that is not when a legitimate user u logs in.*

Our final solution is explained in Sect. 7 and its workflow is illustrated in Fig. 3. The core idea is to inform the HC when a user is logging in, but without passing through the LS which may otherwise interfere with the communication. Because of the risk of man-in-the-middle attacks, this communication should not be over the Internet either. Instead, it *must happen on a secure second channel between the user and the HC*, which we suggest to be the *ether* and implement by letting them use a One-Time-Password (OTP) device. We are aware that, introduced without an adequate explanation, the need of a second channel and our suggestion to use an OTP may appear arbitrary and unjustified. They are not. In the rest of this section we briefly explain our reasons, but the reader interested only in the new protocol can skip it, and restart the reading from Sect. 7.

Why a Second Channel? Before concluding that we need a *second channel* between the user and the HC we tried to comply with countermeasure (iii) by other ways. One attempt was to add a module, called Keys Register (KR), to keep r_n. Abstractly, this suggests to outsource the calculation of the hash of the submitted password out from the LS. In particular, we let KR receive (u, w) and calculate the $h^{r_n}(w)$. The token is thus forwarded to the LS, who also receives the username u. Notably, KR's role cannot be played by LS itself. This would lead it to know the hash of the password and so its valid index, consequently enabling an attack as we have described previously. KR's role apart, the authentication process is not different from what we described before, with the HC that also shuffles, re-hashes, and returns the password file to the LS, but at the end the HC sends the new r_{n+1} only to the KR, which is ready for a new session.

This solution is secure, but only if KR cannot be code-corrupted. This is not an assumption that we intend to take easily. According to Juels and Rivest, the only component that is hardened secure is the HC. Thus, KR should be considered corruptible. And if it is so, the intermediate solution has a flaw. An adversary can compromise both kr.exe and ls.exe and, even under a strict Assumption 2 with no back doors, manage to successfully log in. The attack is implemented by the following corrupted code, presented first in [7], where we assume h' and passwd'_u to be updates of h and passwd_u. The corrupted instructions are in red:

Algorithm 3. Code Corrupted KR.

1: **procedure** kr$'$.exe(r_n)
2:    **while true do**;
3:       ReceiveFrom(U; (u, w);
4:       SendTo(LS; $h^{r_n}(w)$);
5:       ReceiveFrom(HC; r_{n+1});
6:       SendTo(LS; $h^{r_{n+1}}(w)$);

KR resends the last w, re-hashed using the new r_{n+1} received from HC. KR does not know whether w is a valid password, but a corrupted LS does. The attack works because LS gets pieces of information beforehand, using which, he can anticipate querying the new password file and get a valid j that can be used to let the adversary in.

Alternative ways to implement (iii), such as using timestamps from the user's side as a proof of freshness do not work either since LS stands in the middle and can compromise those messages. For all this follows our conclusion that if there must be a "synchronization" between users and the HC, it must be happening over a channel that is not under the control on any module of the Honeywords System nor of the adversary. We of course welcome, and we leave it as an open challenge, to find a secure solution that does not use a second channel between the user and the HC.

7   The New Authentication Protocol

One way to realize requirement's items (i)–(iii) in agreement with the Honeywords System solution, is to empower the user (i.e., the user's browser) with the ability to hash his password w with g_n^r using the same r_n that is generated by the HC. It is (almost) equivalent to let the user play the role of KR.

However, letting HC send r directly to the user over the Internet leaves the channel exposed to man-in-the-middle attacks and introduces other issues such as that of ensuring authentication of the user. The channel through which the HC "communicates" with the user must be a second channel and not in the Internet. We already justified this choice in the previous section.

The solution that we are about to discuss now and prove secure in the next section requires that the HC and the user share an OTP device. This is employed to generate a new seed r each time that the OTP is used, a seed which is also the same for the user and the HC. The protocol message sequence diagram is detailed in Fig. 3.

The OTP serves as pseudo-random generator but also as proof of freshness, since what it generates is synchronized with what the OTP generates by the HC. Here we talk of an OTP that generates a new seed each time that it is pressed.

In Fig. 3, we have indicated with OTP(n) the action of using the OTP for the nth time (step **1**). The user sends to the LS, the username u and the hashed version of its password, $h^{r_n}(w)$, where the hashing takes the nth OTP-generated number r_n as parameter (step **2**).

Then, the protocol follows as expected: the LS searches for an index in the password file (step **3**); the file has been reshuffled and re-hashed in a previous session by the HC, which has used in anticipation the same OTP number that the user has now used to hash the password (we will discuss in Sect. 7.1 how to handle when a user "burns" a generated number by pressing the OTP accidentally outside the login). The found index j is submitted together with the username and the row of the password file that LS has just used in the search (step **4**).

The HC checks first j against c_u (i.e., the index of the user's password) to determine whether to grant access or not (step **5**), then shuffles and re-hashes the password file's row. It also updates the c_u according to the index's re-ordering (steps in **6**). The shuffled and re-hashed file is returned to the LS (step **7**) and LS notifies the user (step **8**).

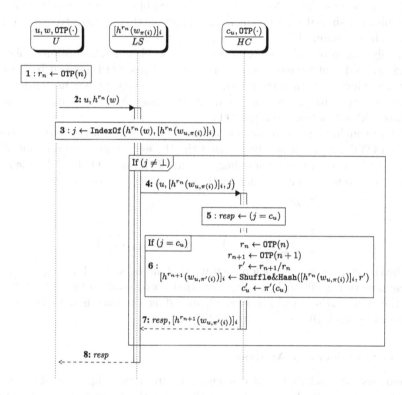

Fig. 3. New authentication protocol (Presented in [7]).

7.1 Informal Security Analysis

We argue that there is no corruption of the LS that under our assumptions can lead to a successful attack. In particular, even if the LS learns that a particular $h^{r_n}(w)$ is a valid password, LS cannot make any use of it to anticipate the index that w will have in the new reshuffled and re-hashed password file. LS could retain an old file, but the index retrieved from it would not correspond to the new c'_u that the HC holds. It could send to the HC the username and sweetwords file's row of another user and so have this later reshuffled and re-hashed. The only gain is that LS will likely have the request rejected without never getting to know whether that hashed honeyword (and consequently the j calculated) were good for access. Note that even if two users log-in with the same password, it is very unlikely that the hashes are the same if we assume that each user has its own OTP. LS can send the username u and password file's row of another user to know the answer about the correctness of j without having the file's row of u reshuffled and re-hashed. But then, HC changes c_u and so the LS will not be able to take advantage of what he has learned; besides, the effect seems to be disastrous in terms of compromising the integrity of a future check, when u logs in again. This counts as a Denial-of-Service (DoS) but not as an attack according to Definition 1 since it does not increase the probability of the adversary to gain access, which remains $1/k$.

Finally, our protocol is secure even under a relaxed Assumption 2. Even if the LS, learned that a particular $h^{r_n}(w)$ is a valid password, sends it back to the adversary which in turn retrieves the w, the adversary cannot use either w or the token $h^{r_n}(w)$ to gain access. He needs the token $h^{r_n+1}(w)$ which he cannot generate without holding also the OTP.

Before concluding, we comment on what to do if the user "burns" some of the valid OTPs. A classic solution is that the HC anticipates new versions of the password file using a certain number, say m, of the next OTPs. The file's row for user u becomes a matrix where each row is ordered with the same π':

$$\begin{bmatrix} h^{r_n}(w_{u,\pi'(1)}), & \cdots, & h^{r_n}(w_{u,\pi'(k)}) \\ & \vdots & \\ h^{r_n+m}(w_{u,\pi'(1)}), & \cdots, & h^{r_n+m}(w_{u,\pi'(k)}) \end{bmatrix}$$

The HC stores one c_u as before, but when shuffling and re-hashing the matrix for the new run, it discards all the rows that correspond to the OTP numbers that the user has accidentally burned, including the one used in the current submission (which HC receives from LS).

7.2   Formal Security Analysis

We modeled the original protocol and our proposal (Fig. 3) in the *applied-π calculus* and used ProVerif [10] to formally verify their compliance with authentication security goals. ProVerif is an automatic verifier for cryptographic protocols under the Dolev-Yao model.

Honeywords System Authentication. We start by analyzing the original Honeywords System. We know already that there is an attack, but our aim is to test the proper way to model a LS that has been code corrupted according to Assumption 2. Moreover, we need to correctly interpret the results, discarding attacks originated from stronger attackers than the one defined in our threat model.

We built our formal design upon the following considerations. There are three parties: the User (U), the LS and the HC. The LS is an active attacker since it is able to read and send messages from and to the HC; the channel between LS and HC is thus public. In contrast, the channel between U and LS is private, otherwise the attacker can learn a correct pair of user and password from the beginning, contradicting Assumption 1.

Note that this decision together with the fact that the password is never transmitted in the public channel, prevents the attacker to know the submitted password at any time. It also rules out the simplest guessing (password) attack, which is the first one that ProVerif finds in the analysis, allowing the verifier to find attacks more related to the protocol's flow. We know already that a guessing attack is always possible, since Honeywords System is not designed to avoid it.

The attack described in Sect. 5 violates the following security property, introduced in [7]:

$$correctIndex(u, j) \implies injct(indexFound(u, p, j)) \quad \&\& \quad injct(usrLogged(u, p))$$

It expresses that, whenever the HC sends a positive answer to the LS for a submitted pair of user and index (u, j), all of these three actions occurred: (1) a user logged in with a pair of credentials (u, p) (2) the index j found by the LS corresponds to (u, p) and (3) the value stored in HC for u is equal to j. Injectivity in the expression ($injct$) captures the fact of HC processing only once each request that LS submits after events (1) and (2), to prevent interaction between LS and HC in the absence of a user.

Result. As expected, the verification indicates that the property does not hold. The attack found shows how once the attacker (in this case the LS) gets a positive answer from the HC, it is able to send a new check request to HC with the correct user and index, gaining access to the system and thus contradicting injectivity, because there was not a new $usrLogged(u, p)$ event for that second request. These observations support our model design for code-corruption and provide formal evidence that a Honeywords System resilient to the flaw must satisfy Requirement 1.

New Authentication Protocol. We are now ready to apply the analysis to the new protocol. In this ProVerif model, all channels are public since the LS can send requests at any time and can learn the inputs from U and HC. We choose this design to discover any attack using any information available. Conversely, the LS's function that retrieves the index of a sweetword is private, because LS can get information from the password's file but cannot modify it.

Unlike in the original, in this protocol each instance of U is synchronized with a HC instance by a *seed*, representing that both parts generate the same OTP at the beginning of a round; the HC knows as well the index of the password. Then, to give LS the opportunity to attempt an attack using the knowledge gained during the run of the protocol, we model the fact that HC keeps running with the updated index after reshuffling. The LS is almost as in the original protocol, except that this time it receives a hashed password parametrized by the OTP, instead of a plain password. An index is a term determined by the hashed word searched and the row of sweetwords where it is searched. We introduced in [7] its representation in ProVerif as

$$indexOfHw(hashWord(w, getOTP(n)), \quad shuffleNhash(u, n))$$

where *hashWord* is the hash of the plain submitted word w calculated with the seed n; *shuffleNhash* is the sweetwords' row for user u hashed with seed n.

Our equational theory relies on the *checkEqual* function in the HC, which returns *true* only when all the parameters of the indexes under comparison are equal. After a successful match, the index hold by the HC is affected by the next seed value, becoming $indexOfHw(...getOTP(\mathbf{next(n)}), ...(u, \mathbf{next(n)}))$. Therefore, after this point the evaluation of *checkEqual* will be *false* for any submitted index not obtained with the new seed.

We verified in [7] that our protocol fulfills a property equivalent to the one which the Honeywords System does not:

$$correctIndex(u, j) \implies injct(usrLogged(u, p)) \quad \&\&$$
$$injct(indexFound(j, hashWord(p, x), shuffleNhash(u, y)))$$

It states that every time an index j is equal to the one in the HC's database for u, then (a) the owner u of j logged in with password p and (b) j corresponds to the index of the hashed value of p in the sweetwords row for u. The conjunction ensures the execution of every step in the protocol; the injectivity ensures that each is executed only once.

In addition, we introduce the property *event(unreachable)* to verify that LS cannot retrieve a sweetword's index of a word not submitted by a user; the event *unreachable* is triggered if the HC's check function returns *true* after shuffling and rehashing, when applied to a previously submitted hashed password.

The model also assumes, as we stated in Sect. 6, that HC must process LS's requests *atomically*, finishing a request before starting the next. Failing to implement HC this way, leads to an attack as we are going to explain in the next section, which prove that atomicity is in fact necessary.

Result. All properties were verified to be true almost immediately. It follows that even knowing that a certain $hashWord(p, getOTP(n))$ is a valid password, LS cannot use it to anticipate the new good index, since it depends on the seed value possessed only by U and HC.

The analysis also proves that event *unreachable* is indeed so; this implies that LS cannot get any advantage even if using HC as an oracle if using messages obtained from previous runs with U and HC.

We also verified the necessity for the HC to execute all its tasks (as an atomic block) concerning a request from user u before processing another request from the same u. Removing this constraint reveals an attack: let HC_1 and HC_2 be parallel runs of the HC, then (1) After a LS request, HC_1 verifies that the submitted index is correct and sends the answer to LS (2) LS submits again the correct index, HC_2 processes it, finishes the protocol and grants access (3) HC_1 continues its execution and grants access as well.

8   Discussion

The new authentication protocol just described ensures that an adversary cannot improve its chances to get access even if (s)he manages to corrupt the code of the LS, and we have demonstrated formally this claim. Nevertheless, at the eye of someone, the new design may seem overkilling and the use of the OTP unconventional. But the new protocol is simply and rightly fulfilling the requirements that we have determined at first: to avoid that the LS could retrieve a good index by processing, on- and off-line, the information it handles. Re-shuffling, for us, is the operation that makes the LS's previous knowledge of the index become obsolete; and the use of the OTP provides freshness to each re-hashing, nullifying any attempt of the LS to use the password file to calculate, off-line, a good user index. In our protocols, password authentication becomes one-time.

Our use of the OTP differs from what is common in authentication procedure: OTPs are proofs of possession of a device and, sometimes, of freshness of a session. We elevate them to become proof of possession of the password and of freshness of the session; at the same time, we use them as random seeds, achieving that no one, not even the server, can learn the password from the messages exchanged. The new reassignment of the OTP's role is a price we think is worth to be paid if one wants to be sure that no unauthorized log in ca happen despite a code-corruption of the server (under our assumptions).

Another consequence of our new design is that the Honeywords System changes considerably. It does up to a point that the use of honeywords becomes unnecessary. What the LS stores and what the HC handles are random bitstrings with no linguistic meaning. It will be self-evident in the new *setup* and *change of password* protocols (see next sections): in them, the orginal procedures suggested in Juels and Rivest to generate flat sweetwords do not make sense any more: our new protocols generate decoy words which are arbitrary, distinct, strings and are not honeywords anymore. Still, we preserve that is the user who begins the process by choosing a password; and we believe it is important that he chooses it in a way for him meaningful from a usability viewpoint: but our OTP is used to add randomness, and this seems compensating any poor choice of passwords, thus protecting from phishing and from shoulder-surfing attacks until the user remains in possess of the OTP device. More research is however required to give evidence to this last claim.

9   Setup Protocols

So far we have discussed only the authentication phase. In this section we extend our study to cover the setup phase. We introduce first the Honeywords System's setup protocol to later present how that phase operates for our protocol described in Sect. 7.

At registration of user u the Honeywords System creates an identifier uid for u and then generates a randomly ordered list $[w_x]_u$ of k sweetwords ($x \in [1, k]$), containing $k - 1$ honeywords based on the given password pwd and the password itself. Next, it retrieves the index c_u of pwd in such list and creates a new one with the hash value of each w_i. LS stores this list, $[h(w_x)]_u$, and securely notifies c_u to HC, who in turn stores the entry (uid, c_u). The protocol is depicted in Fig. 4.

A code corrupted LS completely invalidates the Honeywords System's registration process given that it obtains all the knowledge (password, user and even index) of every new user, hence, LS can evidently store any valid pair of credentials and directly use it during the login phase as described in Algorithm 2 in Sect. 5. On the contrary, the LS possessing this information does not represent a critical threaten in our solution since the OTP generated value is needed too; that the LS gets the password in clear opens nonetheless doors to attacks. We will discuss this after presenting our protocol's setup phase.

Our protocol requires the user to collect in person an OTP device. On its side, HC shares the OTP's generating algorithm which outputs the same r as the user's device.

The registration protocol (Fig. 5) then proceeds as follows: user u obtains the first number from the OTP device (1), which is used to send a hashed version of his/her password $h^{r_1}(pwd)$ (2). On reception, LS creates an identifier uid for u (3) and sends it to HC together with the password received (4). HC performs then all the registration tasks: retrieves r_1, the same OTP number obtained by u; creates a list of $k - 1$ random words and hashes them using r_1 as a parameter for the hash function (5); inserts $h^{r_1}(pwd)$ in the list and stores its index. At this point, HC has already the password hidden with decoy words, the rest of the actions prepare the system for the authentication phase: HC obtains the next OTP number and uses it to rehash and reshuffle the list of hashes (6), this is needed in order to rule out the chance of LS using the known hash $h^{r_1}(pwd)$; it also updates the index of the hash corresponding to the password, according to the reshuffling output (7). The referred index is stored as valid for uid in HC (8), who finally sends the reshuffled row back to LS (9).

An important feature of this protocol is that even if an adversary gets in possession of the password, (s)he still needs to get the OTP's number to generate the hash value that would eventually grant access. This leads us to remark that our new protocol achieve much more than to detect whenever a password's file has been stolen; it actually help us to detect whenever the LS has been corrupted. We verify these security claims in the following part.

Note that although the original idea of the honeywords seems to be invalidated in our solutions, it is not the case though; the use of decoy words to disguise the password, even if they are not related to the password itself anymore, still lowers the probability of an adversary that manages to reverse hashes.

9.1   Formal Security Analysis

Honeywords System Setup. Our model of a code corrupted LS follows the considerations detailed for the authentication protocol in Sect. 7.2. In this case though, the property to verify is:

$$storedHC(uId(u), j) \implies inject(submittedCred(u, p)) \quad \&\& \quad inject(indexOfPwd(uId(u), j))$$

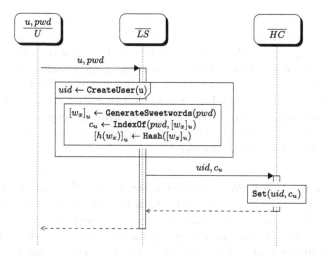

Fig. 4. Setup protocol in the Honeywords System.

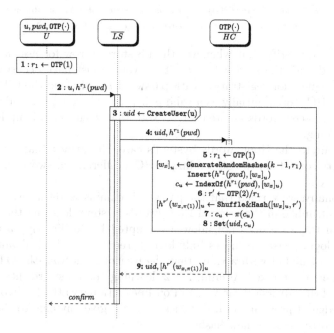

Fig. 5. New setup protocol.

It expresses that a pair of user identifier and index $(uId(u), j)$ is stored in the HC, only when both occur: (1) the user u submitted a registration request with password p and (2) the index of p in the row of u's sweetwords generated by LS is exactly that j.

The property is violated if the LS simply sends the HC a password different than the one submitted by the user. Another attack consists on the LS selecting and recording any index, then, sending it to the HC; since the only task for the HC is to store the values received, there is no risk for the attacker to be discovered of giving misleading information. Both attacks reflect as DoS to u. Here we are not interested in such kind of attacks, however, the attack trace found in the analysis confirms that even when the registration process is successful, a corrupted LS gets to know the password in clear, hence, it is able to use it in the login phase as previously discussed.

New Setup Protocol. We represent a corrupted LS in our setup protocol by making public the channel through which it sends messages to the HC; this reflects that the attacker is authorized to observe anything from and to send anything to the HC. The security property captures the same idea expressed for the Honeywords System, except that this time we need to consider as well the random seed used for hashing.

$$saveDecoys(u, shuffleNhash(row, nextOTP(s)))\ ^{(\mathbf{C})} \implies inject(setupRequest(u, hashWord(p, getOTP(s))))\ ^{(\mathbf{E1})}$$
$$\&\&\ \ inject(storedHC(u, indexOf(hashWord(p, getOTP(s)), row)))\ ^{(\mathbf{E2})}$$

In words, we verify that whenever the LS stores a row for user u reshuffled and rehashed with the seed $s + 1$ (**C**), two events must have occurred: (**E1**) u has sent a request for registration with password p and using the OTP number s, and (**E2**) HC stored initially as a valid pair (u, j) where j is the index of $h^s(p)$ in the list of decoy words created for u. Note that such index is updated after each reshuffling.

Analogous to the Honeywords System's case, the attack that we found for this property consists in the LS sending to HC a different password than the one submitted by u.

Additionally, we verified that the password remains secret at every moment. Remark that unlike in the original Honeywords System, learning the plain text password in this case does not allow a corrupted LS to directly obtain access during the login phase; to successfully login it requires the hashed value of such p, which is calculated with a value that the user obtains from the OTP device. However, under a relaxed Assumption 2, learning the password introduces the possibility of the adversary carrying out off-line dictionary attacks. In opposition, the knowledge of previous hashed values does not give any clue to the attacker about the corresponding new hashes.

10   Change of Password Protocols

The change of password phase involves a combination of the setup and authentication protocols. After a password update request, the user u is required to provide his credentials in order to validate that the modification attempt is authentic (as a side implementation note, carrying out the authentication in the first place assists to keep separated the management of OTPs between stages). On successful authentication, the protocol proceeds similarly to the setup phase, excluding the creation of a new user.

In the Honeywords System the LS creates and hashes sweetwords based on the new password $newW$, and then retrieves u's id and the index of $newW$ in the sweetwords' list. It sends the retrieved pair to the HC, which in turn updates the index value stored for u. Figure 6 represents this protocol, where $authentication(u, w)$ is the response from executing the authentication protocol in Fig. 1 and w is the old password.

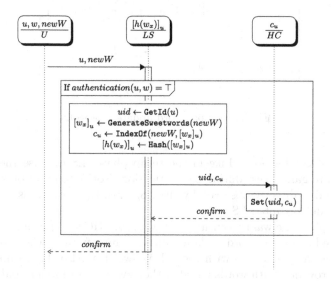

Fig. 6. Password's update protocol in the Honeywords System.

As for the new protocol, LS performs the authentication in Fig. 3 with the old password w (**1**); for this step it uses the OTP number n, i.e., the pair submitted for authentication is $(u, h^n(w))$. On a successful response, the user u is allowed to submit the new password $newP$ which is hashed with a freshly generated OTP number $n+1$ (**2**); LS gets u's identifier and proceeds sending the new credentials to HC (**3**). The tasks performed by HC are the same as for the setup, taking the current $n + 1$ instead of the first generated OTP. Also, in this case u' index is updated instead of inserted in HC. The protocol is displayed in Fig. 7.

10.1   Formal Security Analysis

Honeywords System Password Update. Given that the core of the protocols for password update and setup is essentially the same, both protocols are subject to identical attacks. A simple attack to the update in Honeywords System consists on the LS (remembering and) sending to the HC the password's

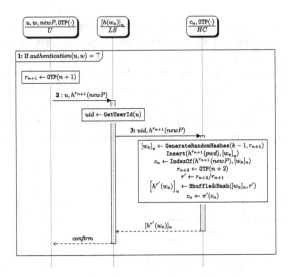

Fig. 7. New password update protocol.

index f of a selected user. Like in the setup phase, LS can use the recorded information to gain access during authentication. Notice too that once more the new password is directly observed by the LS, thus, the protocol is powerless in front of a code corrupted LS.

For this phase we want to ensure that whenever HC sets j as index of user u, it must have been a password update request coming from u, who was correctly authenticated in the system with the old password p. Also the LS updated the sweetwords row of u with words based in the new password $newP$ and the index of $newP$ in the sweetwords row is j. This is expressed by the property:

$$indexUpdated(uId(u), j) \implies injct(updateRequest(u, p, newP)) \quad \&\& \quad injct(authenticated(u, p))$$
$$\&\& \quad injct(passwordUpdated(u, newP)) \quad \&\& \quad injct(indexOfPwd(uId(u), j))$$

Our analysis found the attack trace corresponding to sending a self-selected index.

New Password Update Protocol. Similarly to the Honeywords System's case, the new setup protocol could be considered as an instance of the new update protocol executed with the first OTP number, with the only difference that, instead of updating, the LS stores the hashed row obtained from the HC. Besides, we abstract the OTP as a function parametrized by a counter. Therefore, our formal model is not significantly affected and changes consist merely in renaming functions.

The attacks stand hence according to the findings for the setup protocol and the analysis is to verify that whenever the LS stores a row for user u reshuffled and rehashed with the seed $s+1$, then (i) u has sent a change of password request with p and s as input parameters for password and OTP respectively and (ii) the valid index stored in HC is the index of $h^{s+1}(p)$ in the list of decoy words created for u. This is what the following formula captures:

$$updateDecoys(u, SandH(row, s+1)) \implies inject\,[updateRequest(u,\ hash(p, OTP(s)))]$$
$$\&\&\ inject\,[indexInHC(u,\ indexOf(hash(p, OTP(s+1)), SandH(row, s+1)))]$$

The code of all the formal models of the protocols presented here, as well as the results of the analysis, are available at https://github.com/codeCorruption/HoneywordsM.

11   Complexity and Performance

The contribution of this research is mainly theoretical but we judged useful to test the performance of what we propose. We sketch a complexity analysis and benchmark an implementation of both the original and our authentication protocols. We test them with respect to different implementations of the elliptic curve (EC) multiplication, which we used to execute the main operation of our protocol: exponentiation.

Although we implemented as well the setup phase, the analysis and benchmarks focus uniquely in the authentication phase.

Complexity Analysis. The analysis assumes that an elliptic curve multiplication takes constant time t_{CURVE} (which depends on the employed CURVE): this protects implementations against remote timing attacks [11].

Let us now consider the operations that affect the performance. Once received the password, LS calls IndexOf to search the index of the submitted password among the sweetwords. Given that the sweetwords are not ordered and also are constantly reshuffled, this is a linear search. In the worst case it can be done in $\mathcal{O}(k)$ time, where k is the number of sweetwords per user. In case of a match, the HC checks the validity of the index in $\mathcal{O}(1)$ time. Next, the HC calls Shuffle&Hash; this function shuffles the sweetwords in $\mathcal{O}(k)$ time and performs k times an EC multiplication in $k \cdot t_{\mathrm{CURVE}}$ time. The last equation is linear in k for a fixed CURVE. Since each of the previous operations takes at most $\mathcal{O}(k)$ time, the time complexity of the new protocol is $\mathcal{O}(k)$. As well, for a fixed k, the execution time increases linearly as t_{CURVE} grows. Moreover, EC multiplication is CPU intensive and dominates the total execution time. This is also confirmed by our empirical results (see Fig. 8(a)).

Communication Cost. In the original Honeywords system, the communication cost per login comes from messages (u, j) and *resp*. We denote the number of bytes required to encode (u, j) and *resp* by $|(u, j)|$ and $|resp|$ accordingly, and obtain the data transfer rate per login as $C = |(u, j)| + |resp|$. While the data flow remains the same, our protocol brings the following communication overhead to the original Honeywords system: LS sends the sweetword hashes $[h^{r_n+1}(w_{u,\pi'(i)})]_{i=1}^{k}$ and receives the updated ones. The number of bytes required to encode a password hash depends on the employed curve and is denoted by $\mathsf{H_{CURVE}}$. Thus, LS sends $|(u, j)| + k\mathsf{H_{CURVE}}$ bytes and receives $|resp| + k\mathsf{H_{CURVE}}$ bytes per login. As a result, the total data transfer rate per login between LS and HC is computed as $C + 2k\mathsf{H_{CURVE}}$ bytes.

Since k, the number of sweetwords, is a constant defined by the system, and $\mathsf{H_{CURVE}}$ is constant too, the overload in communication is bounded. We have not simulated nor evaluated how much this may affect a server's ability to process a great number of log-in attempts per unit of time, but we are inclined to believe that this loss in performance is not so dramatic. Of course one may will to discuss whether the solution that emerges from our analysis by fitting our requirements is not actually an overkill in itself. This is a legitimate question which we discuss in Sect. 12.

Implementation. We implemented our solution in `C#` at the Microsoft .NET framework.[2] Elliptic curve operations are performed using Bouncy Castle Cryptographic Library, although a faster version may be obtained by native language implementations or libraries.

In our implementation, u, j and *resp* are implemented as integers, hence C equals 12 bytes and $\mathsf{H_{CURVE}}$ takes 57, 65, 97, and 133 bytes for `P-224`, `P-256`, `P-384` and `P-521` accordingly. Figure 8(c) compares data transfer rates with different settings.

Performance Analysis. This section provides experimental results about the efficiency of our proposed authentication protocol with two questions in mind: *How does number of verifications per second correlates with the number of honeywords? What is the impact of the selected curve on verification speed?* The results presented have been performed on notebooks with Intel Core i7 CPU and 8 GB of RAM over an idle network. We measured the total execution time on server side computations and communication over the network separately. Roughly speaking, our prototype reaches a decision for each login request below 9 ms. Table 1 summarizes the overall performance with different settings.

Another performance consideration is the cost of avoiding login failures due to out-of-synchronization of OTPs. System policies may follow the strategy discussed in Sect. 7. The computational overhead of both, Login Server and Honeychecker, increases linearly on the number of copies in the password file.

It is reasonable to expect that the time required for re-encryption directly depend on the number of honeywords for a user. Figure 8 illustrates the time measurements. It can be seen that the time required for verifying a single user increases linearly with the number of honeywords per user. The Honeychecker performs one EC multiplication for each honeyword, which is the most expensive part of its function, and the result is aligned with our theoretical expectations. Our solution preserves the computational characteristics of the original honeywords protocol: performance is linearly dependent on the number of honeywords.

---

[2] Source code is available under GPLv3 at https://github.com/codeCorruption/HoneywordsM.

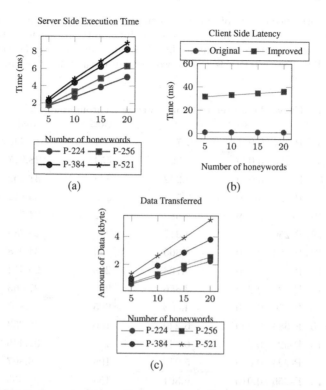

Fig. 8. (a) CPU time required to verify a user depending on the number of honeywords and employed curve. (b) Client side latency comparison between original protocol and our proposal with NIST Curve P-256. (c) The amount of the data (in kilobytes) transferred between the Login Server and the Honeychecker (Taken from [7]).

On the other hand, we can see from Fig. 8 (and from Table 1) that the time to run the employed curves increases with the number of honeywords.

Figure 8(b) compares our protocol with the reference implementation. The client side latency of both, original and improved protocols stays almost constant. Considering the delays caused by the network, the computational overhead of our protocol is relatively small. It might not be even noticed by the clients.

12   Conclusion

In this work we proposed a password-based authentication system motivated by a challenge left open by Juels and Rivest in [5]: how to protect a Honeywords System against a code corrupted login server (LS). A Honeywords System's architecture is intended to detect when a password file has been stolen.

We provided protocols for the three functionalities defined for a Honeywords System: the *setup* or registration, the *log-in* or authentication and the *change of password* or update. The study of the setup and the change of password extends the initial scope presented in the conference paper [7], where only the authentication protocol is addressed.

Table 1. Performance results of our implementation. Login Server and Honeychecker columns display the time in milliseconds for a single authentication on LS and HC, respectively. Throughput column shows the maximum number of verifications per second. Round-Trip Time (RTT) is the network delay during the experiments (Taken from [7]).

k	Curve	Login server (ms)	Honeychecker (ms)	Throughput (login/s)	RTT (ms)
5	P-224	0.011	1.709	581	24.446
5	P-256	0.009	1.796	554	28.917
5	P-384	0.009	2.242	444	31.502
5	P-521	0.010	2.541	392	30.812
10	P-224	0.009	2.680	372	24.534
10	P-256	0.009	3.317	301	29.885
10	P-384	0.010	4.365	229	34.918
10	P-521	0.010	4.793	208	29.414
15	P-224	0.009	3.856	259	27.063
15	P-256	0.010	4.868	205	30.896
15	P-384	0.009	6.240	160	36.253
15	P-521	0.010	6.842	146	31.445
20	P-224	0.009	5.016	199	26.867
20	P-256	0.010	6.301	158	29.355
20	P-384	0.010	8.220	122	32.724
20	P-521	0.011	8.965	111	31.944

We introduced a precise definition of code-corruption, according to which, the adversary model is less powerful than the Doloev-Yao model but powerful enough to correctly guess a users's password, hidden among a list of decoy words known by the adversary, with higher probability of success than with a honest LS. The flaw resides indeed in the LS knowing eventually the user's valid (hashed) password.

The solution that we propose prevents the LS to make, off-session, any good use of what he knows, but based on the requirements derived from studying attacks on the original Honeywords System, the new protocols consist in shuffling and rehashing the password (plus decoy words) after any user's attempt to log in. This solution impedes as well to the LS to interact with the HC in the absence of a legitimate user's message. In order to control such event, the user and the HC need some synchronization through a channel not controlled by the LS or by a man-in-the-middle. We propose OTPs for this purpose. Our protocols' security is supported by a formal analysis in Proverif.

Aiming to assess its feasibility, we implemented the setup and authentication phases in C#. A benchmark analysis on the authentication protocol shows that it performs reasonably well.

The new protocols invalidate until a certain point the need to detect when a password file is stolen because the adversary cannot gain access to the system without the OTP that creates the authentication token (i.e., the hash of the password). Of course leaking a password is still a serious weakness because users may reuse the same password across different sites. Yet, the strategy that we proposed suggests a completely new direction for password authentication, a procedure that is resilient even if a password is lost. In this sense, the proposed system's goal is not anymore to detect passwords' leakage but to detect whenever the code of a LS has been corrupted.

This approach puts in the table a password-based authentication process where users still type their passwords but where the token that the LS checks in the password file is one-time-valid. An implementation of this concept still differs from current OTP-based solutions used e.g., in home-banking, due to the assumption that it must work even when the LS has been code-corrupted. We consider this an open problem in password-based authentication and an interesting line for future work.

References

1. Furnell, S.M., Dowland, P., Illingworth, H., Reynolds, P.L.: Authentication and supervision: a survey of user attitudes. Comput. Secur. **19**, 529–539 (2000)
2. Goel, V., Perlroth, N.: Yahoo Says 1 Billion User Accounts Were Hacked. NT Times Online (2016). https://www.nytimes.com/2016/12/14/technology/yahoo-hack.html. Accessed 04 Sept 2017
3. Newman, L.H.: Yahoo's 2013 email hack actually compromised three billion accounts. Wired (2017). https://www.wired.com/story/yahoo-breach-three-billion-accounts/
4. Beck, K.: Hackers are selling account credentials for 400 million Tumblr and MySpace users. Machable (2016). http://mashable.com/2016/05/31/myspace-tumblr-hack. Accessed 04 Sept 2017
5. Juels, A., Rivest, R.L.: Honeywords: Making password-cracking detectable. In: Proceedings of the 2013 ACM SIGSAC Conference on Computer and Communications Security, pp. 145–160. ACM (2013)
6. Erguler, I.: Achieving flatness: selecting the honeywords from existing user passwords. IEEE Trans. Dependable Secure Comput. **13**(2), 284–295 (2016)
7. Genc, Z.A., Lenzini, G., Ryan, P.Y.A., Vazquez-Sandoval, I.: A security analysis, and a fix, of a code-corrupted honeywords system. In: Proceedings of the 4th International Conference on Information Systems Security and Privacy (2018)
8. Botha, R.A., Eloff, J.H.P.: Separation of duties for access control enforcement in workflow environments. IBM Syst. J. **40**, 666–682 (2001)
9. NIST: SHA-3 Standard: Permutation-Based Hash and Extendable-Output Functions (2015)
10. Blanchet, B.: An efficient cryptographic protocol verifier based on prolog rules. In: 14th IEEE Computer Security Foundations Workshop, pp. 82–96. IEEE (2001)
11. Brumley, B.B., Tuveri, N.: Remote Timing Attacks Are Still Practical. In: Atluri, V., Diaz, C. (eds.) ESORICS 2011. LNCS, vol. 6879, pp. 355–371. Springer, Heidelberg (2011). https://doi.org/10.1007/978-3-642-23822-2_20

GenVote: Blockchain-Based Customizable and Secure Voting Platform

Praneeth Babu Marella[1], Matea Milojkovic[2], Jordan Mohler[3],
and Gaby G. Dagher[1(✉)]

[1] Boise State University, Boise, ID, USA
gabydagher@boisestate.edu
[2] Winthrop University, Rock Hill, SC, USA
[3] University of Denver, Denver, CO, USA

Abstract. Electronic voting has been popularized in recent years as an alternative to traditional voting. Even though electronic voting addresses the problems that traditional voting brings, it is not a perfect solution. Electronic voting brings its own set of concerns which include: election fraud, voter privacy, data integrity, and confidentiality. To ensure fairness in electronic voting, a centralized system is required and the complete process has to be overseen by an authority. Due to these requirements it can be very expensive to roll-out on a large scale during every voting period. Blockchain, the distributed data structure popularized by Bitcoin, can be integrated into electronic voting systems to alleviate some the problems involved with them while being cost-effective. With the use of blockchain, we propose a voting system that is easily accessible, customizable, transparent, and in-expensive. GenVote is a distributed electronic voting system that utilizes Ethereum Blockchain, smart contracts, and homomorphic encryption to achieve a transparent voting process with non-authority based tallying and voter privacy. GenVote also allows the ballot creation and voting process to be customizable with different types of ballots and logic based voting. GenVote is currently a viable solution for university-scaled elections and has been deployed on Ethereum Ropsten testing network to evaluate its viability and scalability as an electronic voting system.

Keywords: Blockchain · Ethereum · Smart contracts · Voting · Privacy · Encryption.

1 Introduction

Voting is a fundamental part of every democratic process. It allows for us to have a voice in government process and be represented for issues that matter most to us. With the technology advancements we made, it could be assumed voting has become easily accessible for everyone and their votes are securely tallied. However, even at the university level, voter fraud has been a problem. In 2016, a fraud at Kennesaw State University brought forth the issues of voter

P. Mori et al. (Eds.): ICISSP 2018, CCIS 977, pp. 152–171, 2019.
https://doi.org/10.1007/978-3-030-25109-3_8

registration fraud. Students at the university believed they had signed up to vote in the 2016 Presidential Election without knowing that their registration forms were simply trashed. Due to this, the students were unable to cast their votes on the day of the election[1]. The same year city officials in Green Bay, Wisconsin refused to allow early voting on the University of Wisconsin's satellite campus[2]. So the only other option for students to vote was driving fifteen-minutes to a near-by voting location. But the location was only open during business hours so it was even more difficult for students to access the voting site. This led to a lot of students being excluded from voicing their opinions on the election. To make it even more difficult, student IDs are not considered a suitable identification for voter registration at many locations. Voter registration fraud and lack of access to voting sites for university students are important issues that must be addressed.

Secure and privacy preserving voting systems are necessary for university-scale elections. For instance, at many universities, one of the major objectives of the student government organization Associated Students (AS) is to "advocate for the interests of students at the University". To achieve this goal, they must provide a easily accessible platform for students to voice their choice on different matters. This is where electronic voting systems come in to fill the need. One such system, TIVI, uses digital authentication of voters through facial biometrics: specifically, selfies[3]. Although TIVI solves the accessibility issue previously mentioned, it does not completely stop fraudulent activity. Using public photos and 3-D rendering, malicious users can break into accounts[4]. Helios is the first online, open-audit voting protocol. The primary goal of Helios is data integrity but it also provides voter privacy to an extent. To ensure data integrity, any observer may audit the election process during its active voting period. At the start of the voting process, voters name and encrypted vote are posted. But after the election is completed, the votes are shuffled and then tallied to compute the end result. Helios claims to be the optimal voting system for small groups where coercion is unlikely but private voting is necessary [1]. Although Helios maintains data integrity, voter privacy is not preserved to the utmost. Another major limitation associated with current electronic voting systems is voting fraud in the form of database/platform manipulation [2]. With the use of centralized data storage, current implementations of electronic voting platforms are susceptible to vote altering. Our systems aims to address the security concerns of current electronic voting systems by incorporating blockchain elements to it. Due to the distributed nature of blockchains, voting systems that use a blockchain to record and tally their votes do not have a central point of failure [3]. Voters can also

---

[1] http://bettergeorgia.org/2016/09/11/a-different-kind-of-voter-fraud-one-to-actually-be-worried-about/.

[2] https://www.thenation.com/article/city-clerk-opposed-early-voting-site-at-uw-green-bay-because-students-lean-more-toward-the-democrats/.

[3] https://eandt.theiet.org/content/articles/2016/10/voting-online-made-possible-with-selfie-recognition-technology/.

[4] https://www.wired.com/2016/08/hackers-trick-facial-recognition-logins-photos-facebook-thanks-zuck/.

verify their vote has been recorded and not been tampered with by inspecting the blockchain. This can be achieved because every vote is recorded on the distributed ledger through transactions to the blockchain [4].

The blockchain is a distributed append-only data structure that grows through adding blocks. The blocks contain transactions submitted by participants, or nodes, of a peer-to-peer network. When a transaction is submitted, it goes into a pool that a validating node, also referred to as a miner, can extract. Miners can gather a set of transactions from the pool into a block and append it to the blockchain. In order for a miner to append his block to the blockchain, he must complete a consensus proof such as Proof-of-Work or Proof-of-Stake. Participating in the consensus proof process requires either computation power or a stake which is cost of participation. Once a transaction has been validated as part of a block and added to the chain, it cannot be altered. Because of these properties, the blockchain is considered an immutable, secure data structure. The Ethereum Blockchain expands this functionality by implementing smart contracts [5].

Smart Contracts are blocks of code written in specific languages, usually dictated by the blockchain being used, and contain methods/events. Methods contained within a Smart Contract allow for interaction with the blockchain through either external or internal calls. Smart Contracts are stored within the blockchain so once the code is deployed, it cannot be altered and is publicly available for anyone to interact with it. In Ethereum, to preserve the network, every interaction with a smart contract that changes its state needs to pay a computational fee, referred to as "gas". Gas is the unit of measure used to calculate amount of work a validating node will need to perform for an operation and the gas price, the amount user needs to pay, is measured in terms of ether in Ethereum [5]. Smart contracts are also extended to private implementation of blockchains; as opposed to public blockchains, private blockchains are implemented to be utilized within a single organization. While this sacrifices the decentralized nature of the blockchain, it enhances the privacy of the blockchain [6]. For the purpose of our system, GenVote implements a private blockchain. We believe that a private blockchain is best suited for maintaining the integrity and privacy of the ballots within an organization scale.

Our proposed system is an extension of our previous work [7]. We expand the functionality of our previous system by allowing voters to cast votes logically and giving ballot creators the freedom to create different types of ballots. Our system still uses similar concepts as [8–10], specifically in the areas of privacy and smart contracts. Votes in all those systems are encrypted and stored on the blockchain to achieve voter privacy and ballot transparency. These systems also utilize hashing to ensure strong data integrity within the voting process. In [8], the voting system may have an optional round in which voters hash and post their encrypted vote to the blockchain. Transactions consisting of votes are hashed before being stored on the blockchain in the system described in [9]. In addition, [8] uses the smart contracts as part of their voting system to allow for easy election process and perform cryptography functions.

1.1   Contributions

Our implemented system, GenVote, provides a secure and private electronic voting system that is easily accessible and customizable. GenVote is intended to be used in a university scale voting system. GenVote utilizes smart contracts in Ethereum and Paillier Homomorphic Encryption to achieve voter privacy and ballot integrity. Our system also allows elections to be customized with different types of ballots. Creators, of the ballots, have the freedom to create polls, standard elections, or first to X number of votes. Creators also have the option to either open voting for everyone or whitelist a certain set of voters to participate in the ballot. Voters have the option to vote in a traditional way or opt to vote logically using one of these options: vote for the current leading, vote for the runner-up, or vote for the losing candidate/choice. GenVote provides voter privacy on all our ballots by homomorphically encrypting every vote, tallying, and revealing the vote count using the Paillier cryptosystem. To maintain transparency, all ballot and voting data is publicly available as part of the smart contracts within the blockchain used in our system.

2   Preliminaries

2.1   Blockchain Mining

'Mining' is a process that is used in a trust-less blockchain network to reach a consensus about the state of the blockchain [11]. The role of a 'mining' node is to verify a group of transactions into a block by solving a computationally intensive puzzle. The puzzle involves the 'mining' node to find the hash of the block that begins with a certain number of zeros. To achieve this, a number called a 'nonce' is included in each block; each time miners hash the block without solving the computational problem, they increment the nonce and rehash the block [11]. The difficulty of solving the hashing problem is described as 'Proof of Work,' signifying the computational power and difficulty needed to append a new block to the blockchain [11]. Once the puzzle has been solved the block can be appended to the blockchain and the 'mining' node is rewarded with the appropriate cryptocurrency.

2.2   *Eth.calls*

Every valid transaction executed is stored on the blockchain [5]. Due to this, blockchains can suffer from scalability issues. Valid transactions sent to smart contracts in the Ethereum blockchain are considered state changeable calls and consume gas. To reduce gas consumption and the number of transactions on the blockchain, the Ethereum blockchain allows *eth.calls* to be utilized in addition to transactions. *Eth.calls* allow nodes to send messages to other nodes or smart contracts to retrieve its current state without storing the message on the blockchain[5]. Therefore, *eth.calls* are similar to simulations of transactions.

---

[5] https://github.com/ethereum/wiki/wiki/JSON-RPC.

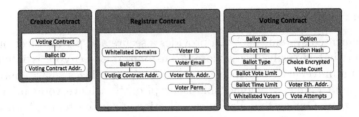

Fig. 1. Memory field structure of smart contracts in GenVote, where lines between fields represent relational data [7].

By executing *eth.calls* to send notifications/messages or to retrieve current states, the size of the blockchain can be greatly reduced [7].

2.3 Paillier Encryption

Full homomorphic encryption allows us to perform computations on encrypted data. The encrypted data can then be decrypted to reveal the same value as it would be if the computations were done on plain data [12]. However, fully homomorphic encryption requires fully modular multiplication which can be computationally intensive and very slow [13]. However, because of the advantages provided by homomorphic encryption, it is still a prominent encryption scheme and partial homomorphic encryption scheme has been introduced for faster encryption. One such scheme is the Paillier Homomorphic Encryption. This probabilistic public-key encryption method supports addition and multiplication [12]. Paillier system can homomorphically add two ciphertexts but it can only multiply a ciphertext with a plaintext integer. Since the Paillier system cannot homomorphically multiply two ciphertexts, it is considered partially homomorphic. The process of encryption is not completely intuitive: multiplying ciphertexts is equivalent to adding the plaintexts and raising a ciphertext to the power of another ciphertext is equivalent to multiplying the plaintexts [14]. To achieve the advantages of homomorphic encryption without the substantial reduction in processing speed, Paillier Encryption is one of the ideal encryption schemes.

2.4 MetaMask

MetaMask is a web broswer plugin that was created to make it easy for average users to interact with Ethereum blockchain based Dapps. MetaMask acts as an Ethereum browser, which allows the users to easily manage their Ethereum wallet and interactions with decentralized applications, or Dapps, and smart contracts. Using MetaMask removes the need for users to download a local copy of the blockchain. Users are also able to easily manage multiple accounts and switch between test or main network[6]. MetaMask facilitates the user transaction

---

[6] https://github.com/MetaMask/metamask-extension.

broadcasting by using a set of trusted nodes that relay the transactions to the pool. Since transactions are signed using the sender's private key, which is stored locally on the user's machine, MetaMask cannot impersonate the user and send transactions on the user's behalf or modify outgoing transactions. MetaMask makes it convenient and secure for average users to interact with Dapps on the blockchain using a simple web browser.

3   Proposed Solution: GenVote

3.1   Overview

Prior to discussing our proposed voting system, we would like to mention that the Ethereum blockchain used in our system has not been modified in any way and the standard proof-of-work was used for validating transactions. Our system, GenVote, uses existing functionality and features provided by Ethereum and Solidity to provide the ability for creating and voting on ballots. Our implementation consists of three smart contracts coded in Ethereum's Solidity language, two scripts written in JavaScript, and one HTML page. GenVote is an open source project and the entirety of the code is available for public use[7].

In order to participate in the system, the users have to utilize MetaMask plugin or become a node by downloading the Ethereum blockchain. We assume the administrator, creators, and voters have one of options setup and can create and

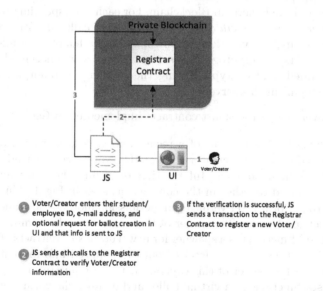

① Voter/Creator enters their student/ employee ID, e-mail address, and optional request for ballot creation in UI and that info is sent to JS

② JS sends eth.calls to the Registrar Contract to verify Voter/Creator information

③ If the verification is successful, JS sends a transaction to the Registrar Contract to register a new Voter/ Creator

Fig. 2. The process for registering a voter in GenVote, where black dotted line represent eth.calls and solid line represent transactions to the blockchain [7].

---

[7] https://bit.ly/2GEVtwk.

manage Ethereum accounts to interact with our system. We utilize Ethereum's Web3 framework internally, this allows our users to easily manage signed transactions and interactions with the Ethereum blockchain. The only action required of users when registering, voting, or creating ballots using MetaMask is to use their passwords/private keys to unlock their Ethereum accounts and securely interact with the blockchain. If the user decides not to utilize the Metamask plugin then they are responsible for running a node on their local machine and managing appropriate accounts to interact with our system using Web3 [7].

A brief description of all the user parts of GenVote follows:

- **Administrator** is responsible for deploying the initial Registrar and Creator smart contracts. The administrator also has the ability to grant or revoke ballot creation permission for registered voters/creators.
- **Voter** registers in our system with a valid student/employee ID and e-mail address to vote on given ballot ID numbers.
- **Creator** is a voter with ballot creation permission.

A brief description of the front/back-end pages implemented in GenVote follows:

- **VoteUI.html** page is the user interface for our users. This page allows users to enter necessary information for each of the different use cases. Once the user enters the necessary information, the corresponding click buttons will invoke functions in *App.js*.
- **VotingApp.js** gathers information from *VoteUI.html* and interacts with *Crypto.js* and the Ethereum Blockchain. For each corresponding request from *VoteUI.html*, it utilizes *eth.calls*, *Crypto.js* server calls, and Ethereum transactions to verify, encrypt/decrypt votes, and store ballot/vote information.
- **Crypto.js** acts as a cryptographic server. All votes are encrypted, homomorphically added, and decrypted using the Paillier homomorphic encryption system key pair in this server.

A brief overview of the smart contracts implemented in GenVote follows:

- **Registrar.sol** takes the role of a record and gate keeper. It keeps track of all registered voters and creators, ballot IDs, voting contract addresses, and whitelisted e-mail domains. Information regarding the voter and different ballots are linked together in the contract, as seen in Fig. 1. This allows the contract to perform voter verification, permission modification, and *Voting.sol* address retrieval easily. The owner of this contract is the administrator.
- **Creator.sol** functions as a spawner for new *Voting.sol* contracts. The Creator defines the voting contract details from the required information entered in *VoteUI.html*. The owner of this contract is the administrator.
- **Voting.sol** functions as a virtual ballot and handles the voting on the ballot. Another set of voter verification, including vote attempts and ballot time limit, is also conducted in this contract. As we can see in Fig. 1, ballot title and the choice encrypted votes are also stored here so that we can retrieve at later stages. The owner of this contract is the contract creator.

A brief overview of the types of ballots and voting styles implemented in GenVote follows:

- **Polling Ballot** lets you create a ballot that displays results live as users participate in this ballot and ends when the ballot reaches its end time. The choice that has most votes wins.
- **Election Ballot** is a traditional election style ballot that displays its results after the ballot end time has reached and the choice with the most votes wins.
- **First to X Ballot** is a hybrid ballot that displays its results live and when one of the choices reaches the required number of votes to win then the ballots ends. The winner is the one that reaches the X votes defined by the creator.
- **Vote Limiting on Ballot** can be imposed by the creator when creating any type of ballot. This will create a limit on the number of votes each voter/Ethereum address can send to a ballot.
- **Whitelisting on Ballot** can be utilized by the creator when creating any type of ballot. This will set a restriction on who can participate on a particular ballot. Currently the whitelisting is based on e-mail but can be customized to many different forms of identification whiteliting.
- **Traditional Voting** can be used on any type of ballot. The user manually decides which choice to vote for and submits the vote. The vote is then immediately processed and updated on the UI once its been verified.
- **Logical Voting** is a special type of voting. The user chooses from one of the three options: Winning Vote, Runner-Up Vote, and Losing Vote. Depending on which option is chosen, the system determines who to vote for and notifies the user once the vote has been verified. The user can also choose to allow the system to vote on their behalf at a later time with one of the options.

3.2 Initial Setup

The initial setup process needs to be kick-started by the administrator of the system. The administrator needs to deploy *Registrar* and *Creator* contracts to activate the system. The administrator is also responsible for including a set of e-mail domains that are permitted to be used for registering in our system. Once the system has been activated, the users can start registering, creating, and voting on ballots in our system.

3.3 Register Voter

Since GenVote was implemented with a university setting in mind, anyone with a student/employee ID number and a specific e-mail can register and use the system. The user has to have an e-mail that contains one of the whitelisted domains setup by the administrator to register as a voter and request ballot creation permission. Once the user has entered the ID number, e-mail address, and ballot creation permission fields in the registering section of *VoteUI.html*, the information is parsed by *VotingApp.js*. The parsed information is then used to make *eth.calls* to the *registrar* contract, as seen in step two of Fig. 2, to verify the user's e-mail and registration status. If the user passes the checks, then *VotingApp.js* sends a transaction to the *registrar* contract to store the new voter information, including the voter's ID, e-mail, and Ethereum address. The user's e-mail address and Ethereum address are linked so we can use it in the future to prevent the user from re-registering. Users that also requested access to create ballots are placed in a queue so that they can be manually reviewed by the administrator.

3.4   Create Ballot

Users with ballot creation ability can use the ballot creation section in *VoteUI.html* to spawn new voting contracts using the *Creator* contract. To create a new ballot, the creator must provide their registered e-mail address then choose whether this ballot will be a election, poll, or first to X votes type. Then determine the title of the ballot to let voters are aware of what they are voting on, voting options for the ballot, and the number of votes allowed per voter on this ballot. During this process, the creator can also opt to make it a whitelisted ballot. If the whitelisted ballot option is chosen, the creator is required to enter the list of e-mail addresses allowed to vote on the ballot. But if the creator chooses to not make it a whitelisted ballot, everyone with a registered e-mail address will be allowed to vote on the ballot. Lastly, the creator sets the ending date and time for the voting period for the ballot.

Once the creator has provided the necessary information to create a ballot, *VotingApp.js* parses the information and continues to step two in Fig. 3 to verify the creator status. To verify the status, *VotingApp.js* sends the two *eth.calls* to the *Registrar* Contract to verify the creator's provided e-mail address is registered in our system and whether the request originates from the registered Ethereum address linked to the e-mail address or not. If those two checks are passed, then *VotingApp.js* sends the third *eth.call* to determine if the user has the permission to create ballots. If it was determined that the user is allowed to create ballots, *VotingApp.js* gathers the parsed data and a randomly generated ballot ID number to include in a transaction to the *Creator* Contract. The *Creator* Contract uses the information provided in the transaction to create a new *Voting* Contract and deploy it onto the blockchain. Once the new *Voting* Contract has been deployed successfully, the contract address is returned to the *Creator* Contract.

VotingApp.js then sends a final *eth.call* to the *Creator* Contract to retrieve the new *Voting* contract address to register it in the system. Step six in Fig. 3 shows the transaction to the *Registrar* Contract for storing the newly linked ballot ID and contract address. The ballot ID is then displayed afterwards and the *creator* is reminded to write down this ballot ID since it will be the unique identifier for this ballot. The ballot identifier is then used by voters to load and vote on the ballot.

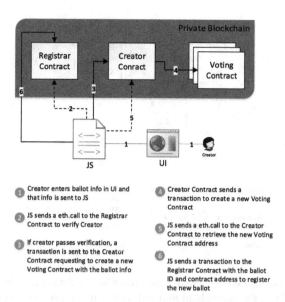

1. Creator enters ballot info in UI and that info is sent to JS

2. JS sends a eth.call to the Registrar Contract to verify Creator

3. If creator passes verification, a transaction is sent to the Creator Contract requesting to create a new Voting Contract with the ballot info

4. Creator Contract sends a transaction to create a new Voting Contract

5. JS sends a eth.call to the Creator Contract to retrieve the new Voting Contract address

6. JS sends a transaction to the Registrar Contract with the ballot ID and contract address to register the new ballot

Fig. 3. The process for creating a ballot as a creator in GenVote, where black dotted lines represent eth.calls and solid lines represent transactions to the blockchain [7].

3.5 Load Ballot

Users can load the ballot information by using the unique ballot identifier provided to the voters by the Creator of the ballot. After loading the ballot, the user can check the results of the ballot or vote on the ballot if the voting period has not passed. Once the voter enters the ballot ID in load ballot section of *VoteUI.html*, *VotingApp.js* sends an *eth.call* to the *Registrar* Contract to determine if the provided ballot ID is valid. If the ballot ID is valid, then the title, voting options, and the encrypted vote count for each choice are gathered from the *Voting* contract. If the voting period has ended or if the ballot is a poll or first to X type, the vote count is decrypted and displayed in *VoteUI.html*. In order for the decrypted vote count to be displayed, there is a step involved, which can be seen in Fig. 4 as step four, that send the encrypted vote count to the *Crypto.js* server. *Crypto.js* server will then decrypt the votes and send them back to *VoteUI.html*.

3.6 Vote (Traditional)

To vote on a ballot, the user needs to first load the ballot. Once the ballot has been loaded, the user types in the choice they want to vote for along with their registered e-mail address in the voting section of *VoteUI.html*. The voting information is parsed by *VotingApp.js* and sends an *eth.call* to the *Registrar* Contract to verify the voter as well as the Ethereum address linked to the e-mail. If the voter is verified successfully, then another *eth.call* is sent to the

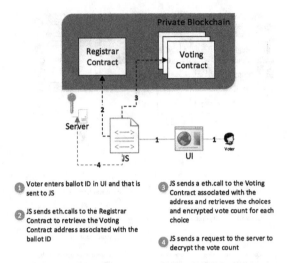

Fig. 4. The process for loading a ballot as a voter in GenVote, where black dotted lines represent eth.calls to the blockchain and red dotted line represents decryption calls to the server [7]. (Color figure online)

Voting Contract to check if this ballot is whitelisted. If the ballot is whitelisted then it checks if the voter's e-mail is part of the list or not. Once that check is completed then more *eth.calls* are made to the *Voting* Contract to check if the user has exceeded his/her voting limit and if the ballot voting period has passed. The voting period is checked by comparing the end time set by the creator with the current block timestamp. If those checks were passed then the vote for the chosen choice is set to one and the rest of the votes are set to zero for the other choices on the client side. Then those votes are sent to *Crypto.js* server, as we can see in step four of Fig. 5, to be encrypted using the previously generated public key in *Crypto.js* server. Once all the votes have been encrypted, the previously encrypted vote count for every choice is retrieved using an *eth.call*. Then the current encrypted votes and previously retrieved encrypted vote count are sent to the *Crypto.js* server to be homomorphically added together. Then the newly encrypted vote count for every choice is sent as an array in a transaction to the *Voting* Contract. Once the transaction has been verified, the *Voting* Contract has the updated encrypted vote count for each choice. Through this process we preserve voter privacy because we hide what their voting choice was by sending a encrypted vote to every single choice.

In the case of First to X wins ballot type, there are additional steps that need to be taken to verify and vote on the ballot. In between steps three and four of Fig. 5, *VotingApp.js* checks the status of the ballot by sending an *eth.call* to the *Voting* Contract. If the status returned as not closed then it checks to see if any of the choices have met the X to win condition. The check is done by getting every individual encrypted vote with an *eth.call* and decrypting them using the *Crypto.js* server. If none of the votes met the X to win condition then

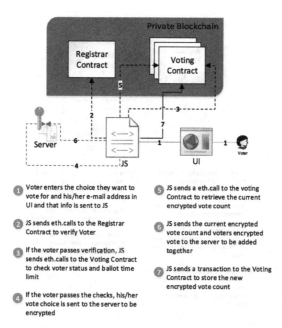

Fig. 5. The process for voting on a ballot as a voter in GenVote, where black dotted lines represent eth.calls, black solid lines represent transactions to the blockchain, and red dotted lines represent encryption calls to the server [7]. (Color figure online)

we proceed to step four in Fig. 5. But if the condition was met then we let the user know the ballot voting period has ended and we set the status of the ballot as closed in the *Voting* Contract.

3.7   Vote (Logical)

Logical voting allows the user to vote on a ballot using a calculated method. The user needs to first load the ballot. Once the ballot has been loaded, the user can choose between three options: Winning Vote, Runner-Up Vote, or Losing Vote and the option to case the vote now or at a later time. If the user chooses one of the choices and the vote now option, the process is simple. In this scenario there is only one extra step that is needed between step three and four in Fig. 5. That step would involve the *VotingApp.js* calculating what the current standing for all the voters are internally to choose the appropriate choice to vote for. After the choice has been calculated then it continues with the traditional process of voting. At the end the user gets a vote verified notification but not the choice that was chosen on their behalf. This prevents voters from gaining knowledge about the current standings in an election prematurely.

If the user chooses one of the choices and the vote later option, the process gets complex and its partially detailed in Fig. 6. In this process once the user has chosen the choice they want to use for voting, that choice is signed using

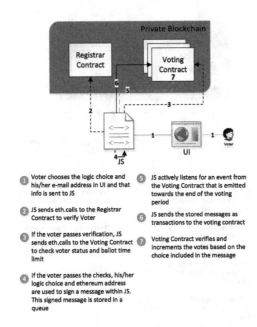

Fig. 6. The process for voting logically at a later time on a ballot as a voter in GenVote, where black dotted lines represent eth.calls, black solid lines represent transactions to the blockchain, and orange dotted lines represent listening events. (Color figure online)

ethsignedTypedData. ethsignedTypedData is a function that currently only available through *MetaMask* and it allows us to use the user's Ethereum address to sign a message. Once the message containing the users choice has been signed, it is then stored in a queue where it will reside until an event is emitted from the *Voting* Contract. In Solidity events are a mechanism to log that something has happened. When a function with an emit call gets invoked within the smart contract, then an event is triggered and that is logged. We can take advantage of this logging functionality by setting a function that listens for it on our front end, specifically using JavaScript. Since we need to wait until the close to end of the voting period, we setup a function that listens for the event from the *Voting* Contract. When that event is triggered, transactions are sent to the ballot using the Administrator Ethereum address with the user signed messages from the queue. The *Voting* Contract will verify the signed messages and increment the appropriate choice votes using separate functions. After the validation is complete, the ballot closes and when someone loads ballot the votes are retrieved to be decrypted to be displayed. Due to the experimental nature of the external libraries required to complete the Logical Vote Later process, we only provide the complete theoretical implementation. There are future plans to bring this functionality to Web3 so when that rolls out we will be able to complete the implementation.

3.8   Get Votes

getVotes acts as a data retrieval function. Whenever a user loads the ballot or successfully votes on a ballot, *getVotes* is invoked in *VotingApp.js*. *getVotes* sends an *eth.call* with the hashed choices to get the current total encrypted votes. Depending on the timelimit and election type, it would either decrypt the votes and display them or display the time when users can check back for the results. To decrypt the votes, *getVotes* sends the encrypted vote count to the *Crypto.js* server to be decrypted by the private key.

4   Testnet Experiment Analysis

In order to collect data and test the viability of our system, we deployed it onto the Ropsten Ethereum testnet and collected the gas cost for every use case. We chose to deploy it onto the testnet to simulate a mature blockchain and test the functionality on a blockchain that has enough validating nodes participating. Our primary focus for data collected was gathering gas costs for each process since it is closely related what the performance cost would be. By gathering the performance costs we can provide better estimates for resources that would be needed when the system is deployed onto a private blockchain. We conducted experiments on varying styles of ballots and specified the gas and time costs for every user, including Administrator (A), Creator (C), and Voter (V), involved in our system.

Contract (User):	Gas Cost:
Registrar (A)	755634
Creator (A)	2235815
Voting (A/C)	1944081*

Note: * = Base cost of creating a Voting contract

Fig. 7. Initial deployment gas costs for the Administrator to activate the system.

The Administrator deploys the Registrar, Creator, and a base Voting contract to activate the system on the blockchain. The deployment costs for this initialization step are shown in Fig. 7. The gas cost for deploying the Registrar contract can vary depending on the set of whitelisted domains the Administrator chose to include during initialization. We chose to whitelist three domains which contain an average of nine ASCII characters in length.

After the system has been deployed onto the testnet, our next step in experimentation was creating, loading, and voting on different types of ballots with varying sizes of voting options and whitelisted voters. We chose to use a poll style of ballot for all the tests but we did check other types and learned that

166 P. B. Marella et al.

	Register (V)	Create Ballot (C)	Load Ballot (C/V)	Vote (V)	Logic Vote (V)
Ballot Types (Poll):			**Gas Cost:**		
1a. 4 Voting Options and 0 Whitelisted Voters	106517	2093911	0	249056	248992
1b. 6 Voting Options and 0 Whitelisted Voters	106453	2310099	0	387966	390206
1c. 8 Voting Options and 0 Whitelisted Voters	106389	2496288	0	556564	556436
1d. 10 Voting Options and 0 Whitelisted Voters	106641	2697477	0	748131	748195
2a. 6 Voting Options and 4 Whitelisted Voters	106387	2477293	0	396180	396308
2b. 6 Voting Options and 6 Whitelisted Voters	106541	2542039	0	396451	396244
2c. 6 Voting Options and 8 Whitelisted Voters	106874	2621785	0	396244	396308
2d. 6 Voting Options and 10 Whitelisted Voters	106215	2671467	0	396308	396308
3a. 4 Voting Options and 10 Whitelisted Voters	106389	2470343	0	255094	255030
3b. 6 Voting Options and 10 Whitelisted Voters	106287	2671531	0	396244	396180
3c. 8 Voting Options and 10 Whitelisted Voters	106453	2872720	0	562730	562666
3d. 10 Voting Options and 10 Whitelisted Voters	106515	3073909	0	754233	754425

Note: (A) = Administrator. (C) = Creator. (V) = Voter

Fig. 8. Gas Costs for different types of ballots and use cases in our system.

there was no significant cost difference. The gas costs for those tests can be viewed in Fig. 8. The number of ASCII characters in the data being passed into the contracts has a noticeable effect on the gas cost so we used an average ASCII character length of 10 for ID numbers, 10 for voting choices, 25 for ballot titles and 18 for e-mail addresses. If we analyze the results in Fig. 8, we notice that it costs nothing to load ballot information because it sends no transactions to the blockchain. We also notice that the gas costs for a user to register into the system also stay fairly constant because it always a set of amount of information going to the blockchain. In our tests we chose to register all user with ballot creation permission but if the user chose to not opt for that then the gas cost would be lowered by roughly 10,000. In the test data we can also notice that the number of whitelisted voters doesn't affect the gas cost as significantly as the number of voting choices. This is because we set the whitelisted voters once whereas we need to manipulate the choices everytime to update vote count. We calculated that the average change in gas cost per increment of voting choice when creating a ballot is 100,000 whereas for voting it grows exponentially as voting choices increase. Finally, the difference between traditional voting and the logical voting we implemented in our extension has no significant cost difference as we can see in Fig. 8.

To better demonstrate the relationship of increasing gas cost as voting options increase, we create a graph (Fig. 9). The data used for the graph was derived from the use case data in Fig. 8. We calculated the average gas cost difference between creating and voting on non-whitelisted ballots. As we can see the increase in cost is linear when creating ballots with increasing options but voting on them starts to show signs of exponential growth in cost. Currently the Ropsten Ethereum testnet has a block gas limit of 4,700,000 gas so we were able to achieve a ballot with max ballot options of 28 without any whitelisted voters. If this system was deployed on a private blockchain with modified block gas limit then we could have larger ballots.

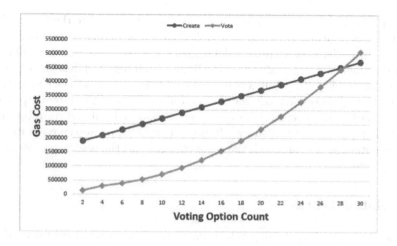

Fig. 9. Relationship between voting options and gas cost for creating and voting on ballots.

In our previous work we conducted a time cost analysis by calculating how long, in seconds, each use case would take. In this extension we chose to exclude that due to hugely varying times it can take to validate transactions for a single repeatable process. This happens due to the validating method, when the transactions are placed in a pool the validating node doesn't necessarily always include your transaction in the validation process right away. But even without actual time data we can say that in general time to complete will vary significantly on each of the use cases. Use cases that require sending transactions compared to the ones that only use *eth.calls* will take a longer time since they need to be validated. So the more transactions a use case utilizes the longer it would take to complete that specific process. For example, the Load Ballot would take the least amount time due to it only using *eth.calls*, which bypasses the mining requirement, to retrieve ballot information. But in the case of Create Ballot or Vote, they would take the longest on average since they require sending a few transactions to the smart contracts in order to complete their process.

5 Technical Difficulties

While implementing GenVote, we encountered a few technical difficulties. One such difficulty is support for cryptography: the maximum data value in Solidity is unsigned int of 256 bit. Many of the cryptosystems require large int numbers that the ones currently supported in the Solidity language. Therefore, GenVote cryptography is facilitated through a server, which can introduce new vulnerabilities. However, for the purpose of this paper, we assume the server is secure and cannot be compromised. Currently signed messages via users functionality is only limited to MetaMask but there are plans to expand it into the standard protocol[8]. Until then we are hindered in the ability to complete the Logical Vote at a later time feature. It can also be difficult to debug while coding in Solidity because, currently, it lacks proper debugging tools. To overcome that difficulty we chose to debug smart contracts using Remix, an integrated development environment for Solidity. To debug a transaction, Remix uses either the transaction's hash or the transaction's block number and index. From there, Remix provides details regarding the transaction's execution, including local and state variables, storage changes, and return values[9]. Remix allows users to step through the contract execution so we can check the state changes and the resulting global state in the system.

6   Related Works

Fair elections are heavily dependent on the privacy and correctness of the election process. Works by McCorry et al. [8], Zyskind et al. [15], Barnes et al. [9], Ernest [10], and Varshneya [16] explore different methods to utilize the blockchain for the purpose of data integrity. To protect the privacy of user data and to authenticate voters before the results are determined, [8] utilizes zero knowledge proofs. Whereas, [9,10] encrypt their voter data using symmetric encryption methods. In addition, [9] also stores segmented data on the blockchain. Follow My Vote and BitCongress are two seperate voting system analyzed by [16]. Follow My Vote is a voting protocol that is hosted online and encrypts voter data with symmetric encryption protcols. Voters in the Follow My Vote system are identified with unique addresses so their real identities are never revealed. But the system allows for third parties, like government officials, with permission to access the real identity of the voters. The second voting protocol, BitCongress, maintains data integrity with the use of two consensus methods, proof of work and proof of tally. In BitCongress, a voter is authenticated using the digital signatures of the votes cast by them. When a voter casts a vote for a candidate in BitCongress, the action is public but other participants cannot trace the vote to any voter in particular. This is achieved by creating a new key pair for voters when participating in a new election. GenVote applies partial homomorphic encryption to secure the privacy of voters and their votes on the blockchain [7].

[15] introduces a peer-to-peer network called Enigma. Enigma based implementations consist of three components: a public distributed ledger, a hash-table that refers to encrypted data off-chain, and a secure multi-party computation that is distributed among random participating nodes. Enigma is mainly used to connect to the blockchain for performing computationally sensitive data and store these records off-chain. Data integrity and privacy is achieved in the Enigma network by using the secure multi-party computation component. Secure multi-party computation is used to perform data queries without having to reveal the contents to the participating nodes. When a multi-party computation is needed,

---

[8] https://github.com/ethereum/EIPs/pull/712.
[9] https://media.readthedocs.org/pdf/remix/latest/remix.pdf.

data is distributed to a set of random nodes and the nodes process their part of the data without revealing to each other which part they have. Information leakage can only occur if the majority of the selected participating nodes collude [15]. The private blockchain employed by GenVote establishes a closed voting system to protect voters from outside privacy breaches. For internal privacy, homomorphic encryption mentioned above is used within the system [7].

With the use of smart contracts, voting processes can be automated. [8,15] utilize the smart contract components to enhance their voting systems. In [8] two smart contracts are implemented: a Voting Contract and a a Cryptography Contract. The Voting Contract is used to process the vote for different elections and the Cryptography Contract allows for the zero knowledge proof process used in the system. Since every participating node has a copy of the Smart Contract, they can reach an agreement on the contract output instead of having to rely on someone else. Similar to smart contracts, private contracts in [15] are applied to enhance the system's scalability. These contracts are designed to process the system's private information. Three smart contracts are utilized in GenVote: a Creation Contract, Voting Contract, and Registration Contract. The Creation Contract establishes the poll or election; once this contract is deployed, it can be used to create multiple, different ballots. The Registration Contract lists the eligible voters; and the Voting Contract allows eligible voters to vote for a candidate [7].

Providing a user interface for the voting process increases the ease of access for voters. Ease of access can help with mass adoption of the voting systems as well. [8] created three potential HTML5/JavaScript pages that the voters use to access the voting system through a web browser. BitCongress [16] utilizes an application called Axiomity as the graphical user interface through which users create elections and vote. Axiomity also keeps a voting record history for users to review on demand externally. Similarly, voters in the GenVote system cast their ballots through an HTML website [7] and Javascript is used to process the votes.

The voting processes in [8–10,16,17] are described below. The voting process is split into give stages in [8]. The first stage involves the election administrator creating a list of voters allowed and creates the election. The administrator also sets the election timers, deposit for registration, and toggle for optional commit stage. The second stage is when the voters register for the appropriate election. The third stage is the optional commit stage, the voters has to store a hash of their vote onto the blockchain before proceeding to the fourth stage. The fourth stage is where the voters publish their vote and a zero proof of knowledge onto the blockchain. Lastly, the final, fifth, stage computes the result of the election and reveals the outcome. It is important to note that in this system, voters can only vote for two options, typically "yes" or "no" [8].

BitCongress [17] follows a similar voting process in their system. In BitCongress, every "yes" or "no" is a token and candidate has an address. When the election is in progress, the voters cast their votes by sending their appropriate token. The tokens are then tallied and returned to voters at the end of the election process. In [9] the voting process is implemented in a hybrid way, it allows for online and offline voting. This is achieved by using two separate blockchains: one to store registered voters and one to store the actual votes. By using two separate blockchains, [9] ensures voter privacy and anonymity. Regardless of how a voter registers, the same information is required that uniquely identifies the voter. When the voter wants to vote online, they registration attempt is stored on the blockchain for government entities to mine for verification. Once verified, the voter is sent a ballot card and password to submit a vote, which is stored on the blockchain as a transaction. Some voting systems allow the voters to update their vote while it is active. This feature is implemented in both [10] and Follow My Vote discussed in [16]. Additionally, in Follow My Vote, voters can vote for multiple candidates. An election in GenVote is established when an administrator in the system deploys the Creation Contract in order to set up the ballot; this include defining the candidates of the election and the election timer. Next, the administrator defines within the Registrar Contract who is eligible to register. Lastly, the voters cast their ballots through the Voting Contract, which encrypts each ballot to provide security and privacy to the voters. Unlike the systems in [8,17], GenVote allows users to vote for multiple candidates with different styles of voting.

GenVote is currently a university-scaled voting system that is deployable on the Ethereum Blockchain. Voter privacy is handled through homomorphic encryption and the integrity of votes is ensured with the distributed ledger. To guarantee voter accessibility, voters cast their votes on an HTML website that can be accessed anywhere with Internet access. GenVote also has the ability to be used to conduct polls: similar to elections, polls allow individuals to voice opinions on matters. However, individuals are able to view poll statistics in real-time. Voters can also opt to let the system vote on their behalf for whoever is most (or least) favorable through logical voting. GenVote is a secure, economical voting system that is customizable and has the potential to be expanded from a university scale to a larger scale.

7   Conclusions and Further Work

In this paper, we have presented a proof of concept system for GenVote. We also deployed it on the test network for Ethereum blockchain to gather data for the purpose of showcasing the ease of deployment and the viability of the voting system. GenVote is setup to be used in a private blockchain within a university setting and utilizes the smart contracts in Ethereum blockchain to achieve voter privacy and ballot integrity. The smart contracts implemented in GenVote are multi-functional, they act as the record keeper for all the voters and ballots, perform access control duties to prevent voter fraud, and self tally the votes for each ballot. With the use of Pallier Homomorphic cryptosystem, blockchain, and smart contracts we were able to propose a system that alleviated some of the problems that were inherited from the current electronic voting systems.

In future work, we will investigate the possibility of allowing for logical voting at a future time using event triggers and raw transaction signing. We will also further explore the possibility of implementing a partial Paillier cryptosystem as a library contract in Solidity. With the implementation of that library smart contract, it will help us generate individual key pairs for each ballot so that we can make the ballot verification process more modular. This will help us achieve individual ballot audit without the risk of compromising the other ballots in the system.

References

1. Adida, B.: Helios: web-based open-audit voting. In: USENIX security symposium, vol. 17, pp. 335–348 (2008)
2. Tarasov, P., Tewari, H.: Internet voting using Zcash
3. Atzori, M.: Blockchain technology and decentralized governance: is the state still necessary? (2015)
4. Blockchain technology in online voting. Web (2016)
5. Buterin, V., et al.: Ethereum white paper (2013)
6. Buterin, V.: On public and private blockchains. Ethereum Blog 7 (2015)
7. Dagher, G.G., Marella, P.B., Milojkovic, M., Mohler, J.: BroncoVote: secure voting system using Ethereum's blockchain. In: Proceedings of the 4th International Conference on Information Systems Security and Privacy (ICISSP), pp. 96–107 (2018)
8. McCorry, P., Shahandashti, S.F., Hao, F.: A smart contract for boardroom voting with maximum voter privacy. IACR Cryptology ePrint Archive 2017, 110 (2017)
9. Barnes, A., Brake, C., Perry, T.: Digital voting with the use of blockchain technology (2016)
10. Ernest, A.K.: The key to unlocking the black box: why the world needs a transparent voting DAC (2014)
11. Nakamoto, S.: Bitcoin: a peer-to-peer electronic cash system (2008)
12. Yi, X., Paulet, R., Bertino, E.: Homomorphic Encryption and Applications. Springer, Cham (2014). https://doi.org/10.1007/978-3-319-12229-8
13. Wang, W., Hu, Y., Chen, L., Huang, X., Sunar, B.: Exploring the feasibility of fully homomorphic encryption. IEEE Trans. Comput. **64**, 698–706 (2015)
14. O'Keeffe, M.: The Paillier cryptosystem: a look into the cryptosystem and its potential application. College of New Jersey (2008)
15. Zyskind, G., Nathan, O., Pentland, A.: Enigma: decentralized computation platform with guaranteed privacy. arXiv preprint arXiv:1506.03471 (2015)
16. Varshneya, A.J., Poudel, S., Vyas, X.: Blockchain voting (2015)
17. Rockwell, M.: Bitcongress whitepaper (2015)

A Detailed Analysis of the CICIDS2017 Data Set

Iman Sharafaldin, Arash Habibi Lashkari$^{(\boxtimes)}$, and Ali A. Ghorbani

Canadian Institute for Cybersecurity (CIC), University of New Brunswick (UNB),
Fredericton, Canada
{Isharafa,A.Habibi.L,Ghorbani}@unb.ca

Abstract. The likelihood of suffering damage from an attack is obvious with the exponential growth in the size of computer networks and the internet. Meanwhile, intrusion detection systems (IDSs) and intrusion prevention systems (IPSs) are one of the most important defensive tools against the ever more sophisticated and ever-growing frequency of network attacks. Anomaly-based research in intrusion detection systems suffers from inaccurate deployment, analysis and evaluation due to the lack of an adequate dataset. A number of datasets such as DARPA98, KDD99, ISC2012, and ADFA13 have been used by the researchers to evaluate the performance of their proposed intrusion detection and intrusion prevention approaches. Based on our study of 16 datasets since 1998, many are out of date and unreliable. There are various shortcomings: lack of traffic diversity and volume, incomplete attack coverage, anonymized packet information and payload which does not reflect the current reality, or they lack some feature set and metadata. This paper focused on CICIDS2017 as the last updated IDS dataset that contains benign and seven common attack network flows, which meets real world criteria and is publicly available. It also evaluates the effectiveness of a set of network traffic features and machine learning algorithms to indicate the best set of features for detecting an attack category. Furthermore, we define the concept of superfeatures which are high quality derived features using a dimension reduction algorithm. We show that the random forest algorithm as one of our best performing algorithm can achieve better results with superfeatures versus top selected features.

Keywords: Intrusion detection · IDS dataset · DoS · Web attack · Infiltration · Brute force · Superfeature

1 Introduction

Intrusion detection plays a vital role in the network defense process by alerting security administrators about malicious behaviors such as intrusions, attacks, and malware. Having an IDS is a mandatory line of defense for protecting critical

---

The first two authors contributed equally to this work.

© Springer Nature Switzerland AG 2019
P. Mori et al. (Eds.): ICISSP 2018, CCIS 977, pp. 172–188, 2019.
https://doi.org/10.1007/978-3-030-25109-3_9

networks against ever increasing intrusive activities. Research on IDS has flourished However, researchers struggle to find comprehensive and valid datasets to test and evaluate their proposed techniques [14] and [developing—extracting—filtering out—isolating] a suitable dataset is a significant challenge itself [19].

Many datasets cannot be shared due to the privacy issues. Those that do become available are heavily anonymized and do not reflect current trends as evidenced by the lack of traffic variety and attack diversity A perfect dataset is yet to be realized [1, 19]. It should also be mentioned that benchmark datasets need to be updated periodically [Nehinbe 2011]. Due to malware evolution and the continuous evolution of attack strategies. Since 1999, Scott et al. [26], Heideman and Papadopulus , Ghorbani et al. [10], Nehinbe [19], Shiravi et al. [1], and Sharfaldin et al. [9] have tried to propose an evaluation framework for IDS datasets. According to the latest research and proposed evaluation framework, 11 characteristics are critical for a comprehensive and valid IDS dataset: attack diversity, anonymity, available protocols, complete capture, complete interaction, complete network configuration, complete traffic, feature set, heterogeneity, labelling, and metadata [9].

Our Contributions: We make three contributions in this paper First, we generate a new IDS dataset, named CICIDS2017, that has all 11 characteristics above with updated common attacks such as DoS, DDoS, brute force, XSS, SQL injection, infiltration, port scan and botnet. The dataset is completely labelled and has over 80 network traffic features extracted and calculated for all benign and intrusive flows using CICFlowMeter software which is publicly available at the Canadian Institute for Cyber Security website [12]. Second, the paper analyzes the generated dataset to select the best feature sets to detect different attacks. Finally we execute seven common machine learning algorithms to evaluate our dataset.

The rest of the paper is organized as follows. Section 1.1 surveys 16 datasets generated between 1998 and 2017. Section 2 describes 11 features to look for in datasets. Section 3 describes in more details the characteristics of the new dataset. Section 4 defines and describes superfeatures and an analysis of them.

This paper is an extension of the one published in the ICISSP proceedings [35] with defining the superfeatures as the high quality features that are made by linear or non-linear combination of set of basic features along with analysis and visualization of the generated dataset.

1.1   Available Datasets

In this section, we survey 11 IDS datasets made available since 1998 discussing their shortcomings that point to the need for a new comprehensive and reliable dataset.

DARPA (Lincoln Laboratory 1998–99): This dataset was constructed for network security analysis and exposed the issues associated with the artificial injection attacks and benign traffic. This dataset includes e-mail, browsing, FTP, telnet, IRC, and SNMP activity. It contains attacks such as DoS, guess password, buffer overflow, remote FTP, Synflood, Nmap, and Rootkit. Its shortcomings include: it does not represent real-world network traffic, it lacks false positives, and lacks actual attack data records. It is thus outdated for evaluating IDSs on modern networks both in terms of attack types and network infrastructure [2,16].

KDD'99 (University of California, Irvine 1998–99): This dataset is an updated version of DARPA98 and was made by processing the tcpdump portion. It contains different attacks such as Neptune-DoS, pod-DoS, Smurf-DoS, and buffer-overflow [6]. The benign and attack traffic are merged together in a simulated environment. It has a large number of redundant records and is studded with data corruptions that lead to skewed testing results [31]. NSL-KDD was created using KDD [31] to address some of KDD's shortcomings [16].

DEFCON (The Shmoo Group, 2000–2002): The DEFCON8 dataset created in 2000 contains port scanning and buffer oveflow attacks, whereas DEFCON10, created in 2002, contains port scan and sweeps, bad packets, administrative privilege, and FTP by telnet protocol attacks. In this dataset, the traffic produced during the capture the flag (CTF) competition is different from real world network traffic since it mainly consists of intrusive traffic as opposed to normal background traffic. This dataset was used to evaluate alert correlation techniques [11,18].

CAIDA (Center of Applied Internet Data Analysis 2002–2016): This organization has three datasets (a) CAIDA OC48includes different types of data observed on an OC48 link in San Jose (b) CAIDA DDOS which includes one-hour DDoS attack traffic split of 5-min pcap files, and (c) CAIDA Internet traces 2016 which is passive traffic traces from CAIDA's Equinix-Chicago monitor on the high-speed internet backbone. Most of CAIDAs datasets are very specific to particular events or attacks and are anonymized with their payload, protocol information, and destination. These are not useful benchmarking datasets due to a number of shortcomings, see [1,5,7,8,22] for details.

LBNL (Lawrence Berkeley National Laboratory and ICSI 2004–2005): The dataset is full header network traffic recorded at a medium-sized site. It does not have payload and suffers from heavy anonymization to remove any information which could identify an individual IP [17].

ISOT (Intrusion Dataset 2008): The dataset contains malicious and non-malicious datasets [36]. The benign part was created by combining (a) a dataset from the traffic lab at Ericsson Research which contain different benign traffic such as web browsing, gaming and torrent traffic; and (b) a dataset from the Lawrence Berkeley National Lab (LBNL) that contains different benign traffic such as traffic for web, email and streaming media applications. The malicious part contains Storm and Waledac botnet traffic. The three datasets were merged using their own method. It contains 23 subnets of normal traffic and one subnet for malicious traffic. Each flow has seven flow-based and four host-based features.

CDX (United States Military Academy 2009): This dataset captures network warfare competitions and can be utilized to generate modern, labelled datasets. It includes web, email, DNS lookups, and other service traffic. The attackers used attack tools such as Nikto, Nessus, and WebScarab to carry out reconnaissance and attacks automatically. It can be used to test IDS alert rules, but suffers from the lack of traffic diversity and volume [25].

Kyoto (Kyoto University 2009): This dataset was gathered from honeypots, so there is no labelling or anonymization, but it has a limited view of network traffic because only attacks directed at the honeypots can be observed. It has ten extra features, such as IDS_detection, malware_detection, and Ashula_detection, than previous datasets which are useful in NIDS analysis and evaluation. Normal traffic was simulated by only DNS and mail traffic data, which is not reflective of real world normal traffic. So there are no false positives which are important for minimizing the number of alerts [15, 23, 28].

Twente (University of Twente 2009): This dataset includes three services, OpenSSH, Apache web server and Proftp, using authtident on port 113 and captured data from a honeypot network by Netflow. There is some simultaneous network traffic such as authident, ICMP, and IRC traffic, which are not completely benign or malicious. Moreover, this dataset contains some unknown and uncorrelated alerts traffic. It is labelled and is more realistic, but the lack of volume and diversity of attacks is obvious [29].

UMASS (University of Massachusetts 2011): The dataset includes trace files, which are network packets, and some traces on wireless applications [UMASS 2011] [Nehinbe 2011]. It was generated using a single TCP-based download request attack scenario. The dataset is not useful for testing IDS and IPS techniques due to the lack of variety of traffic and attacks [30].

ISCX2012 (University of New Brunswick 2012): This dataset has two [CICIDS2017 5] profiles, the alpha-profile which carried out various multi-stage attack scenarios, and the beta-profile, which is the benign traffic generator and generates realistic network traffic with background noise. It includes network traffic with HTTP, SMTP, SSH, IMAP, POP3, and FTP protocols with full packet payload. However, since it does not contain any HTTPS traces, and HTTPS represents nearly 70% of todays network traffic, the distribution of the simulated attacks is therefore not realistic. Moreover, the distribution of the simulated attacks is not based on real world statistics [1].

ADFA (University of New South Wales 2013): This dataset includes normal training and validating data and 10 attacks per vector [4]. It contains FTP and SSH password brute force, Java based Meterpreter, add new superuser, Linux Meterpreter payload and C100 Webshell attacks. In addition to the lack of attack diversity and variety of attacks, the behaviors of some attacks in this dataset are not well separated from the normal behavior [32,34].

CTU-13 (CTU University 2013): This dataset was created by CTU University, Czech Republic [37]. The dataset contains botnet and benign traffic and background communication traffic. This dataset uses bidirectional Netflow records. They defined 13 different scenarios and captured specific malware traffic

Table 1. Comparing available IDS datasets based on the dataset evaluation framework [35].

	Network	Traffic	Label.	Interact.	Captu.	Protocols					Attack diversity							Ano.	Heter.	Features	Meta.
						HTTP	HTTPS	SSH	FTP	Email	Browser	Bforce	DoS	Scan	Bdoor	DNS	Other				
DARPA	YES	NO	YES	YES	YES	YES	NO	YES	YES	YES	NO	YES	YES	YES	NO	NO	YES	NO	NO	NO	YES
KDD'99	YES	NO	YES	YES	YES	YES	NO	YES	YES	YES	NO	YES	YES	YES	NO	NO	YES	NO	NO	YES	YES
DEFCON	NO	NO	NO	YES	YES	YES	NO	YES	NO	NO	NO	NO	NO	YES	YES	NO	YES	-	NO	NO	NO
CAIDAs	YES	YES	NO	NO	NO	-	-	-	-	-	NO	NO	YES	YES	NO	YES	YES	YES	NO	NO	YES
LBNL	YES	YES	NO	NO	NO	YES	NO	YES	NO	NO	-	-	-	YES	-	-	-	YES	NO	NO	NO
CDX	NO	NO	NO	YES	YES	YES	NO	YES	YES	YES	NO	NO	YES	YES	NO	YES	-	-	NO	NO	NO
KYOTO	YES	NO	YES	YES	YES	YES	YES	YES	YES	YES	YES	YES	YES	YES	YES	YES	YES	NO	NO	YES	YES
TWENTE	YES	YES	YES	YES	YES	YES	NO	YES	YES	NO	NO	YES	NO	NO	NO	NO	YES	-	-	NO	NO
UMASS	YES	NO	YES	NO	YES	YES	NO	NO	NO	NO	NO	NO	NO	NO	NO	NO	YES	-	-	NO	NO
ISCX2012	YES	NO	YES	YES	YES	YES	NO	YES	YES	YES	YES	YES	YES	YES	YES	NO	YES	NO	YES	NO	YES
ADFA2013	YES	YES	YES	YES	YES	YES	NO	YES	YES	YES	YES	YES	NO	NO	YES	NO	YES	NO	-	NO	YES
ISOT	YES	YES	YES	YES	YES	YES	NO	NO	NO	YES	NO	NO	NO	NO	NO	NO	YES	YES	NO	NO	YES
SSHCure	YES	YES	YES	YES	YES	NO	NO	YES	NO	NO	NO	YES	NO	YES	NO	NO	NO	NO	NO	NO	YES
CTU-13	YES	YES	YES	YES	YES	YES	NO	NO	NO	NO	YES	NO	YES	YES	YES	NO	YES	NO	NO	YES	YES
UGR'16	YES	YES	YES	YES	YES	YES	YES	YES	YES	YES	NO	NO	YES	NO	YES	NO	YES	YES	NO	NO	YES
CICIDS2017	YES	YES	YES	YES	YES	YES	YES	YES	YES	YES	YES	YES	YES	YES	YES	YES	YES	NO	YES	YES	YES

for each scenario. They used a Windows XP SP2 virtual machine as a guest and a Linux Debian as their host. All of them were connected to the university network. As for labeling, all traffic was initially labeled as background traffic. Traffic that originated from switches, proxies, and legitimate computers was labeled as benign. All traffic which came from infected machines was labeled as botnet.

SSHCure (University of Twente 2014): This dataset contains SSH attacks on a campus network [38]. SSHCure contains Netflow records that were exported from Cisco 6500 series routers. It has two parts which were collected over a month on the campus of the UT. Each part represents different scenarios. The first part contains SSH traffic targeting honeypots and the second part contains SSH traffic from normal servers. There are 11348 attack records.

UGR'16 (University of Granada 2016) This dataset was created by the University of Granada and is designed for the evaluation of cyclostationarity-based network IDSs [39]. The dataset was captured over four months in a tier-3 ISP. They anonymized Netflow records. The dataset offers little attack variety. Also, they mixed botnet captures in a controlled environment with background traffic that reduces the quality of the dataset.

CICIDS2017 (Canadian Institute for Cybersecurity 2017): The dataset was created by Canadian Institute for Cybersecurity. They proposed a novel systematic approach by defining two types of profiles to create a valid dataset. The dataset contains a variety of up to date multi stages attacks such as Heartbleed and different types of DoS and DDoS attacks. Furthermore, a variety of modern protocols are included. It has 80 features for each Netflow record and is in CSV format, making importing it into machine learning software easy [35].

2 Comparing Current Datasets

Finding a suitable IDS dataset is a significant challenge since many datasets cannot be shared due to privacy issues. Also, most of the available datasets are heavily anonymized and do not reflect the real-world trends. According to our last dataset evaluation framework published in 2016 [9], a dataset should meet 11 criteria.

Complete Network Configuration. Having a complete computer network is the foundation of an online dataset to represent the real world. Several attacks have only revealed themselves in a complete network with numerous PCs, servers, routers, and firewall. So it is necessary to have a realistic configuration in the testbed to capture the real effects of attacks.

Complete Traffic. Traffic is a sequence of packets from a source, which can be a host, router, or switch, to a destination, which may be another host, a multicast group, or a broadcast domain. Based on the traffic generation technique, it is possible to have real, pseudo-realistic, or synthetic traffic in a dataset. The pseudo-realistic has partially the real world traffic, such as having simulated human behavior traffics with real attack scenarios.

Labeled Dataset. While a dataset for evaluating different discovery mechanisms in this domain is important, tagging and labeling data are also important. If there are no correct [accurate—informative] labels, without a doubt, it is not possible to use a dataset and the results of any analysis is invalid and unreliable. For example, in network datasets, after converting pcaps to netflows, it is desireable to have [accurate—informative] labels which are informative, useful and understandable for users and not merely "benign" or "malicious".

Complete Interaction. For the correct interpretation of the results, one of the vital features is the amount of available information on anomalous behaviour. So, having all network interactions such as within or between internal LANs is one of the major requirements for a valuable dataset.

Complete Capture. It is essential to capture all traffic to calculate the false-positive percentage of an IDS system. It seems some of the datasets remove traffic which is non-functional or I s not labeled.

Available Protocols. There are many different types of traffic. Some are vital for testing an IDS system such as bursty traffic which is an uneven pattern of data transmission and can cover some protocols such as HTTP and FTP. Interactive traffic includes sessions that consist of short request and response pairs such as applications involving real-time interaction with users (e.g., web browsing, online purchasing). In latency-sensitive traffic, e.g. VOIP and video conferencing, the user has an expectation that data will be delivered on time. In non-Real-time traffic, such as news and mail traffic, timely delivery is not important. A complete dataset should have both normal and anomalous traffic.

Attack Diversity. In recent years, threats have expanded their scopes into intricate scenarios such as application and app attacks. The types of attacks are changing daily. So, having the ability to test and analyze IDS and IPS systems by these new attacks and threat scenarios is one of the most important requirements that an on-line dataset should support. We categorized attacks into seven major groups based on the 2016 McAfee report, browser-based, brute force, DoS, scan or enumeration, backdoors, DNS, and other attacks (e.g., Heartbleed, Shellshock, and Apple SSL library bug).

Anonymity. Most of the datasets removed their payload due to privacy issues which decreases [deminishes] the usefulness of the dataset for some detection mechanisms, especially deep packet inspection (DPI).

Heterogeneity. Ideally, for IDS research, network traffic logs from various sources, e.g., operating systems and network equipment, would be available as they could be used for a complete test covering all aspects of the detection process. A homogeneous dataset using a single source type can be useful for analyzing a specific type of detection systems.

Feature Set. The main goal of providing a dataset is to let other researchers test and analyze their systems. One of the main challenges is to calculate and analyze the features. It is possible to extract features from different type of data sources such as traffic or logs using feature extraction applications.

Metadata. Lack of proper documentation is one of the main issues with datasets. Most do not have documentation or, even if they do, it is incomplete. Insufficient information about the network configuration, operating systems for attacker and victim machines, attack scenarios, and other vital information detracts from the usefulness of a dataset.

As Table 1 shows, among the 16 publicly available IDS datasets since 1998, just CICIDS2017 [35] covers all 11 criteria.

3   Selecting a Dataset

We selected CICIDS2017 based on the evaluation table (Table 1). Only this dataset covered all 11 evaluation criteria [35]. It includes two networks, namely attack network and victim network. The victim network has a highly secure infrastructure with firewall, router, switches and most of the common operating systems along with an agent that provides the benign behaviors on each PC. The attack network is completely separated infrastructure designed by a router and switch and a set of PCs with public IPs and different operating systems for executing the attack scenarios. Table 2 shows the victim and attackers IPs and operating systems [35].

Table 2. Operating systems and IPs [35].

	Machine	OS	IPs
Victim-Network	Servers	Win Server 2016 (DC and DNS)	192.168.10.3
		Ubuntu 16 (Web Server)	192.168.10.50–205.174.165.68
		Ubuntu 12	192.168.10.51–205.174.165.66
	PCs	Ubuntu 14.4 (32, 64)	192.168.10.19–192168.10.17
		Ubuntu 16.4 (32-64)	192.168.10.16–192.168.10.12
		Win 7 Pro	192.168.10.9
		Win 8.1-64	192.168.10.5
		Win Vista	192.168.10.8
		Win 10 (Pro 32-64)	192.168.10.14–192.168.10.15
		Mac	192.168.10.25
	Firewall	Fortinet	
Attackers	PCs	Kali	205.174.165.73
		Win 8.1	205.174.165.69
		Win 8.1	205.174.165.70
		Win 8.1	205.174.165.71

Generating the realistic background traffic is one of the highest priorities on IDS/IPS datasets. This dataset, used a CIC-B-Profile system [35], which is responsible for profiling the abstract behavior of human interactions and generates natural benign background traffic. The B-Profile for this dataset extracts the abstract behavior of 25 users based on the HTTP, HTTPS, FTP, SSH, and email protocols.

Since CICIDS2017 is intended for network security and intrusion detection purposes, it simulates seven attack families, namely: brute force attack, heartbleed attack, botnet, DoS attack, DDoS attack, web attack and infiltration attack. Table 3 shows the attacks for one week [35]. (CICIDS2017 is publicly available at http://www.unb.ca/cic/datasets/IDS2017.html)

4   Superfeature

In this paper we define "superfeature" to mean a high quality feature that is made by a linear or non-linear combination of basic or derived features. One of the main methods to extract superfeatures is to use dimension reduction techniques. Although the ability of dimension reduction techniques (like t-SNE and PCA) to visualize anomalies has been proven, the problem is that it is not always possible to interpret the meaning of the different axes of the visualization. One can extract superfeatures by applying dimensional reduction techniques and mapping data-points from higher dimensions to lower dimensions. Not all dimensional reduction techniques can do this efficiently. For example neighbor embedding techniques are not suitable for our work because they ruin the structure of the space by optimizing their cost function. The most appropriate unsupervised dimensional reduction technique which we found was singular value decomposition (SVD). It was chosen because it can provide insights about the relation of superfeatures (reduced dimensions) and features and one can be aware of the most influential features in the selected superfeatures.

4.1   Singular Value Decomposition

The singular value decomposition (SVD) is a matrix factorization. If A is an $n \times m$ matrix, then we can decompose A as a product of three different factors [40]:

$$A = U\Sigma V^*, \tag{1}$$

Table 3. Daily label of dataset [35].

Days	Labels
Monday	Benign
Tuesday	BForce, SFTP and SSH
Wednes.	DoS and Hearbleed Attacks, slowloris, Slowhttptest, Hulk and GoldenEye
Thurs.	Web and Infiltration Attacks, Web BForce, XSS and Sql Inject, Infiltration Dropbox Download and Cool disk
Friday	DDoS LOIT, Botnet ARES, PortScans (sS, sT, sF, sX, sN, sP, sV, sU, sO, sA, sW, sR, sL and B)

where U represents an orthogonal $n \times n$ matrix, also, V is an orthogonal $m \times m$ matrix, V^* is the transpose of V, and Σ is an $n \times m$ sparse matrix with all zero values except for its diagonal entries, which are nonnegative real numbers. If σ_{ij} is the i, j entry of Σ, then $\sigma_{ij} = 0$ unless $i = j$ and $\sigma_{ii} = \sigma_i \geq 0$. The σ_i are the "singular values" and the columns of u and v are respectively the right and left singular vectors. Singular values are considered to be ordered so that

$$\sigma_1 \geq \sigma_2 \geq \cdots .$$

5 Analysis and Result

First we select two eigenvectors of SVD as our superfeatures. In order to show the efficiency of our selected superfeatures, we calculated them for each attack and then we compared them with the top two individual features from our feature selection in Table 4 on previous research [35]. In order to build the decomposition matrix, we used a set of 8000 randomly selected benign flows and 2000 attack flows for each attack (from our training dataset), which is considerably small in comparison to the whole dataset. Then we used a random forest classifier and 5 fold cross validation for the top two individually selected features for each attack and the top two selected superfeatures. We choose a random forest classifier because it is among the best classifiers in Table 5 [35]. As Table 8 shows, superfeatures outperform the top individual features in all selected attacks.

We can consider our dataset as a matrix that every row corresponds a Netflow and that column corresponds a feature. Now given this matrix we can decompose it by SVD and then interpret the result [33]. Matrix U is Netflow to superfeature similarity matrix. Also, matrix Σ represents strength of each superfeature. Finally, matrix V^* represents features to superfeatures similarity matrix.

In order to interpret "features to superfeatures" relation, we use matrix V^* in the SVD formula. Also, we defined a threshold of 0.1 to remove unimportant relations. Tables 6 and 7 represent relationships between superfeatures and features for all attacks. CICIDS2017 contains 80 features. In these tables we consider only meaningful relations: that means we removed all super-feature to feature relations with value zero for both top superfeatures. As is evident from Tables 6 and 7, the most influential features for generating superfeatures are flow duration, inter-arrival time related features (for flow, forward and backward categories) and idle time related features. One of the main reasons might be that all of these attacks contain same characteristics and they are all anomalies. Also, all of these attacks contains some bursty behaviors in comparison with benign traffic and because of this kind of behavior the flow duration, idle time and IAT related features are so pronounced as to indicate superfeatures.

Table 4. Feature selection [35].

Label	Feature	Weight
Benign	B.Packet Len Min	0.0479
	Subflow F.Bytes	0.0007
	Total Len F.Packets	0.0004
	F.Packet Len Mean	0.0002
DoS GoldenEye	B.Packet Len Std	0.1585
	Flow IAT Min	0.0317
	Fwd IAT Min	0.0257
	Flow IAT Mean	0.0214
Heartbleed	B.Packet Len Std	0.2028
	Subflow F.Bytes	0.1367
	Flow Duration	0.0991
	Total Len F.Packets	0.0903
DoS Hulk	B.Packet Len Std	0.2028
	B.Packet Len Std	0.1277
	Flow Duration	0.0437
	Flow IAT Std	0.0227
DoS Slowhttp	Flow Duration	0.0443
	Active Min	0.0228
	Active Mean	0.0219
	Flow IAT Std	0.0200
DoS slowloris	Flow Duration	0.0431
	F.IAT Min	0.0378
	B.IAT Mean	0.0300
	F.IAT Mean	0.0265
SSH-Patator	Init Win F.Bytes	0.0079
	Subflow F.Bytes	0.0052
	Total Len F.Packets	0.0034
	ACK Flag Count	0.0007
FTP-Patator	Init Win F.Bytes	0.0077
	F.PSH Flags	0.0062
	SYN Flag Count	0.0061
	F.Packets/s	0.0014
Web Attack	Init Win F.Bytes	0.0200
	Subflow F.Bytes	0.0145
	Init Win B.Bytes	0.0129
	Total Len F.Packets	0.0096

Table 4. (*continued*)

Label	Feature	Weight
Infiltration	Subflow F.Bytes	4.3012
	Total Len F.Packets	2.8427
	Flow Duration	0.0657
	Active Mean	0.0227
Bot	Subflow F.Bytes	0.0239
	Total Len F.Packets	0.0158
	F.Packet Len Mean	0.0025
	B.Packets/s	0.0021
PortScan	Init Win F.Bytes	0.0083
	B.Packets/s	0.0032
	PSH Flag Count	0.0009
DDoS	B.Packet Len Std	0.1728
	Avg Packet Size	0.0162
	Flow Duration	0.0137
	Flow IAT Std	0.0086

Table 5. The performance examination results [35].

Algorithm	Pr	Rc	F1	Execution (sec.)
KNN	0.96	0.96	0.96	1908.23
RF	0.98	0.97	0.97	74.39
ID3	0.98	0.98	0.98	235.02
Adaboost	0.77	0.84	0.77	1126.24
MLP	0.77	0.83	0.76	575.73
Naive-Bayes	0.88	0.04	0.04	14.77
QDA	0.97	0.88	0.92	18.79

Also, we visualized different attacks in Fig. 1 by using the top two selected superfeatures in two-dimensional planes. Red 'A' characters represent attack flows and blue 'B' characters represent benign flows. We can observe that brute force and web attacks tend to aggregate in the far left of figures. On the other hand, DoS attack is spread in space which might be due to being a low volume attack making it hard to distinguish from benign traffic. As well, the DDoS attack is the most difficult to distinguish because it is similar to benign flows. Moreover, except the DoS attack, there are no malicious flows in the upper right of visualizations.

Table 6. Web attack, FTP and SSH bruteforce attack superfeatures and features relations.

	Web attack		FTP bruteforce		SSH bruteforce	
	First SF	Second SF	First SF	Second SF	First SP	Second SP
Flow duration	0.5229	0.2536	0.5030	0.2882	0.5072	0.2800
Flow IAT Std	0	0.1487	0	0.1476	0	0.1462
Flow IAT Max	0.1787	0.2998	0.2037	0.2809	0.2015	0.2904
Fwd IAT Total	0.5190	0.2527	0.4983	0.2875	0.5025	0.2795
Fwd IAT Mean	0	0.2514	0.1126	0.2597	0.1072	0.2567
Fwd IAT Max	0.1780	0.2982	0.2025	0.2786	0.2003	0.2880
Fwd IAT Min	0	0.2661	0	0.2756	0	0.2709
Bwd IAT Total	0.4961	0.2602	0.4744	0.2979	0.4771	0.2966
Bwd IAT Mean	0	0.2481	0.1104	0.2495	0.1042	0.2437
Bwd IAT Max	0.1669	0.2725	0.1873	0.2510	0.1838	0.2537
Bwd IAT Min	0	0.2692	0	0.2707	0	0.2637
Idle Mean	0.1686	0.2883	0.1871	0.2666	0.1844	0.2718
Idle Max	0.1725	0.2912	0.1943	0.2682	0.1915	0.2743
Idle Min	0.1624	0.2908	0.1783	0.2697	0.1755	0.2743

SF: First Superfeature

Table 7. DDoS and DoS attack superfeatures and features relations.

	DDoS		DoS	
	First SF	Second SF	First SF	Second SF
Flow duration	0.4312	0.1139	0.3912	0.1705
Flow IAT Std	0.1045	0.1039	0	0
Flow IAT Max	0.3652	0.1913	0.3487	0.1833
Fwd IAT Total	0.4269	0.1070	0.3902	0.1663
Fwd IAT Std	0.1440	0	0.1391	0
Fwd IAT Max	0.3709	0.1738	0.3486	0.1843
Fwd IAT Min	0	0	0	0
Bwd IAT Total	0.1777	0.7727	0.1854	0.7413
BWD IAT Mean	0	0		0.121337
Bwd IAT Std	0	0.1451	0	0.1530
Bwd IAT Max	0.1322	0.4359	0.1479	0.4036
Bwd IAT Min	0	0.2692	0	0
Idle Mean	0.2872	0.1656	0.3426	0.1840
Idle Std	0.1086	0	0	0
Idle Max	0.3640	0.1918	0.3477	0.1966
Idle Min	0.2101	0.1419	0.3380	0.2075

SF: First Superfeature

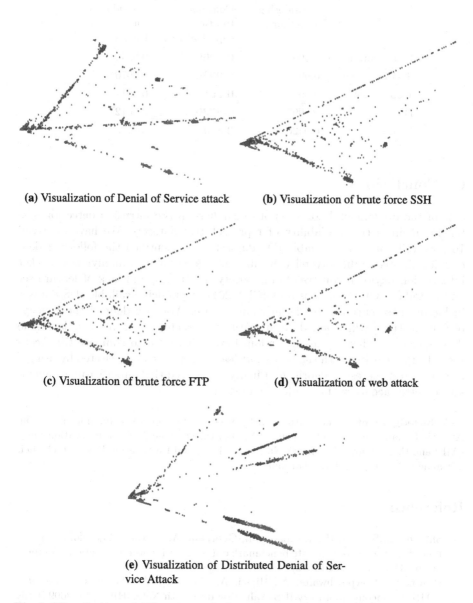

(a) Visualization of Denial of Service attack

(b) Visualization of brute force SSH

(c) Visualization of brute force FTP

(d) Visualization of web attack

(e) Visualization of Distributed Denial of Service Attack

Fig. 1. Visualization of different attacks by using superfeatures. (Color figure online)

Table 8. Accuracy of random forest using different feature selection and extraction scenarios.

	Considering all features	Considering top two superfeatures	Considering top two features
FTP brute force	0.9999	**0.9969**	0.9944
SSH brute force	0.9999	**0.9996**	0.9976
Web attacks	0.9998	**0.9982**	0.9911
DoS	0.9995	**0.9730**	0.9012
DDoS	0.9420	**0.8444**	0.6509

6   Conclusions

One of the fundamental concerns of researchers in the intrusion detection systems domain is the availability of representative datasets. We have analyzed 16 post 1998 publicly available IDS datasets and identified the following deficiencies: limited traffic diversity, insufficient traffic volume, anonymized packet information payload, constraints on variety of attacks, and lack of feature set and metadata. Our focus was on CICIDS2017, a publicly available IDS dataset including most current attacks in common use. Also, we defined the concept of superfeatures which are derived features extracted by using singular value decomposition. Then, we used random forest algorithm to compare the Accuracy of superfeatures with the best short feature set that were selected by using a random forest regressor algorithm. Finally, we proved that superfeatures demonstrate better accuracy than individual features.

Acknowledgements. The authors acknowledge the generous funding from the Atlantic Canada Opportunity Agency (ACOA) through the Atlantic Innovation Fund (AIF) and through grants from the National Science and Engineering Research Council of Canada (NSERC) to Dr. Ghorbani.

References

1. Shiravi, A., Shiravi, H., Tavallaee, M., Ghorbani, A.A.: Toward developing a systematic approach to generate benchmark datasets for intrusion detection. Comput. Secur. **31**(3), 357–374 (2012)
2. Brown, C., Cowperthwaite, A., Hijazi, A., Somayaji, A.: Analysis of the 1999 DARPA/Lincoln laboratory IDS evaluation data with NetaDHICT. In: 2009 IEEE SCISDA, pp. 1–7 (2009)
3. The Canadian Institute for Cybersecurity (CIC), CICFlowMeter: The network traffic flow generator and alanlyzer (2017). https://github.com/ISCX/CICFlowMeter
4. Creech, G., Hu, J.L.: Generation of a new IDS test dataset: time to retire the KDD collection. In: 2013 IEEE Wireless Communications and Networking Conference (WCNC), pp. 4487–4492 (2013)

5. T.C. Center for Applied Internet Data Analysis (CAIDA): The CAIDA OC48 Peering Point Traces Dataset, San Jose, California (2002)
6. I.U. University of California: KDD cup 1999 dataset (1999). http://kdd.ics.uci.edu/databases/kddcup99/kddcup99.html
7. T.C. Center for Applied Internet Data Analysis (CAIDA): CAIDA DDoS attack dataset (2007)
8. T.C. Center for Applied Internet Data Analysis (CAIDA): CAIDA anonymized internet traces 2016 dataset (2016)
9. Gharib, A., Sharafaldin, I., Habibi Lashkari, A., Ghorbani, A.A.: An evaluation framework for intrusion detection dataset. In: 2016 International Conference on Information Science and Security (ICISS), Thailand, pp. 1–6 (2016)
10. Ghorbani, A.A., Lu, W., Tavallaee, M.: Network Intrusion Detection and Prevention: Concepts and Techniques. Springer, Boston (2010). https://doi.org/10.1007/978-0-387-88771-5
11. T.S. Group: Defcon 8, 10 and 11 (2000). https://www.defcon.org/
12. Habibi Lashkari, A., Draper Gil, G., Mamun, M.S.I., Ghorbani, A.A.: Characterization of tor traffic using time based features. In: Proceedings of the 3rd International Conference on Information Systems Security and Privacy (ICISSP), Portugal, pp. 253–262 (2017)
13. Heidemann, J., Papdopoulos, C.: Uses and challenges for network datasets. In: Cybersecurity Applications Technology Conference For Homeland Security, CATCH 2009, pp. 73–82 (2009)
14. Koch, R., Golling, M.G., Rodosek, G.D.: Towards comparability of intrusion detection systems: new data sets. In: Proceedings of the TERENA Networking Conference, p. 7 (2017)
15. Sato M., Yamaki H., Takakura H.: Unknown attacks detection using feature extraction from anomaly-based IDS alerts. In: 2012 IEEE/IPSJ 12th International Symposium on Applications and the Internet (SAINT), pp. 273–277 (2012)
16. McHugh, J.: Testing intrusion detection systems: a critique of the 1998 and 1999 DARPA intrusion detection system evaluations as performed by Lincoln laboratory. ACM Trans. Inf. Syst. Secur. 3(4), 262–294 (2000)
17. Nechaev, B., Allman, M., Paxson, V., Gurtov, A.: Lawrence Berkeley National Laboratory (LBNL)/ICSI enterprise tracing project (2004)
18. Nehinbe, J.O.: A simple method for improving intrusion detections in corporate networks. In: Weerasinghe, D. (ed.) ISDF 2009. LNICST, vol. 41, pp. 111–122. Springer, Heidelberg (2010). https://doi.org/10.1007/978-3-642-11530-1_13
19. Nehinbe, J.O.: A critical evaluation of datasets for investigating IDSS and IPSS researches. In: IEEE 10th International Conference on CIS, pp. 92–97 (2011)
20. University of Massachusetts Amherst: Optimistic TCP hacking (2011). http://traces.cs.umass.edu
21. Pedregosa, F., et al.: Scikit-learn: machine learning in Python (2011)
22. Proebstel, E.P.: Characterizing and improving distributed network-based intrusion detection systems (NIDS): timestamp synchronization and sampled traffic. Master's thesis, University of California DAVIS, CA, USA (2008)
23. Chitrakar, R., Huang, C.: Anomaly based intrusion detection using hybrid learning approach of combining k-medoids clustering and Naive Bayes classification (2012)
24. Umer, M.F., Sher, M., Bi, Y.: Flow-based intrusion detection: techniques and challenges. Comput. Secur. 70, 238–254 (2017). In: 8th WiCOM, pp. 1–5
25. Sangster, B., et al.: Toward instrumenting network warfare competitions to generate labeled datasets. In: 2009 USENIX. USENIX: The Advanced Computing System Association (2009)

26. Scott, P., Wilkins, E.: Evaluating data mining procedures: techniques for generating artificial data sets. Inf. Softw. Technol. **41**(9), 579–587 (1999)
27. Sharafaldin, I., Gharib, A., Habibi Lashkari, A., Ghorbani, A.A.: Towards a reliable intrusion detection benchmark dataset. Softw. Netw. **2017**, 177–200 (2017)
28. Song, J., Takakura, H., Okabe, Y., Eto, M., Inoue, D., Nakao, K.: Statistical analysis of honeypot data and building of Kyoto 2006+ dataset for NIDS evaluation. In: Proceedings of the First Workshop on Building Analysis Datasets and Gathering Experience Returns for Security, pp. 29–36. ACM (2011)
29. Sperotto, A., Sadre, R., Vliet, F., Pras, A.: A labeled data set for flow-based intrusion detection. In: Proceedings of the 9th IEEE International Workshop on IP Operations and Management, IPOM 2009, pp. 39–50 (2009)
30. Prusty, S., Levine, B.N., Liberatore, M.: Forensic Investigation of the OneSwarm Anonymous Filesharing System. In: ACM Conference on CCS (2011)
31. Tavallaee, M., Bagheri, E., Lu, W., Ghorbani, A.A.: A detailed analysis of the KDD cup 99 data set. In: 2009 IEEE SCISDA, pp. 1–6 (2009)
32. Xie, M., Hu, J.: Evaluating host-based anomaly detection systems: a preliminary analysis of ADFA-LD. In: Proceedings of the 6th IEEE International Congress on Image and Signal Processing (CISP 2013), pp. 1711–1716 (2013)
33. Skillicorn, D.: Understanding Complex Datasets: Data Mining with Matrix Decompositions. CRC Press, Boca Rato (2007). Evaluating host-based anomaly detection systems: a preliminary analysis of ADFA-LD. In: 2013 6th International Congress on Image and Signal Processing (CISP), vol. 03, pp. 1711–1716
34. Xie, M., Hu, J., Slay, J.: Evaluating host-based anomaly detection systems: application of the one-class SVM algorithm to ADFA-LD. In: 2014 11th FSKD, pp. 978–982 (2014)
35. Sharafaldin, I., Habibi Lashkari, A., Ghorbani, A.A.: Toward generating a new intrusion detection dataset and intrusion traffic characterization. In: 4th International Conference on Information Systems Security and Privacy (ICISSP), Portugal, January 2018 (2017)
36. Szabó, G., Orincsay, D., Malomsoky, S., Szabó, I.: On the validation of traffic classification algorithms. In: Claypool, M., Uhlig, S. (eds.) PAM 2008. LNCS, vol. 4979, pp. 72–81. Springer, Heidelberg (2008). https://doi.org/10.1007/978-3-540-79232-1_8
37. Garcia, S., Grill, M., Stiborek, J., Zunino, A.: An empirical comparison of botnet detection methods. Comput. Securi. **45**, 100–123 (2014)
38. Hofstede, R., Hendriks, L., Sperotto, A., Pras, A.: SSH compromise detection using NetFlow/IPFIX. ACM SIGCOMM Comput. Commun. Rev. **44**(5), 20–26 (2014)
39. Maciá-Fernández, G., Camacho, J., Magán-Carrión, R., García-Teodoro, P., Therón, R.: UGR '16: a new dataset for the evaluation of cyclostationarity-based network IDSs. Comput. Secur. **73**, 411–424 (2018)
40. De Lathauwer, L., De Moor, B., Vandewalle, J., B.S.S. by Higher-Order: Blind source separation by higher-order singular value decomposition. In: Proceeding of the 7th European Signal Processing Conference (EUSIPCO 1994), Edinburgh, UK, pp. 175–178 (1994)

Personalising Security Education: Factors Influencing Individual Awareness and Compliance

Ismini Vasileiou[1(✉)] and Steven Furnell[1,2(✉)]

[1] Centre for Security, Communications and Network Research,
University of Plymouth, Drake Circus, Plymouth, UK
{ismnini.vasileiou, steven.furnell}@plymouth.ac.uk
[2] Centre for Research in Information and Cyber Security, Nelson Mandela
University, Port Elizabeth, South Africa

Abstract. Security education and awareness are frequently overlooked for users in both workplace and personal contexts, and even where some level of provision is offered it is rarely done in a manner that is matched specifically to the needs of the audience. However, by personalising the provision, and making the presentation and messaging more appropriate to the individuals receiving it, there is a greater chance of achieving understanding, engagement, and resultant compliance. This paper examines the gap that exists between the typical and desirable provision of security education. It highlights baseline areas of security literacy that ought to be applicable to all users, but then illustrates how variations in individuals' understanding of threshold concepts could complicate the task of delivering the related education. It is proposed that security education should be more tailored, recognising factors such as the user's role, prior knowledge, learning style, and current perception of security, in order to deliver a more personalised security education plan that is framed towards individual circumstances and can be delivered in a manner that suits their needs.

Keywords: Security · Education · Awareness · Threshold concepts · Behaviour · Risk perception · Peer learning · Security champions

1 Introduction

Understanding and working with cybersecurity is now a fundamental requirement for all users of IT, in both personal and workplace contexts. However, this is far from a guarantee that the issue actually receives the attention and resourcing that it deserves, and many users are consequently under-supported and ill-prepared in terms of what they should know to protect themselves and/or their organisation.

Security education, training and awareness (SETA) cannot currently be assumed as standard for personal users, and many current IT users are still from a generation that is often classed as digital immigrants [1]. However, even those who have grown up with the technology around them – the so-called digital natives – cannot be relied upon to be fully cognisant and compliant in terms of cyber security. Indeed, part of the challenge here is also that the range of related threats and required controls has become more

© Springer Nature Switzerland AG 2019
P. Mori et al. (Eds.): ICISSP 2018, CCIS 977, pp. 189–200, 2019.
https://doi.org/10.1007/978-3-030-25109-3_10

significant as time goes on, and so even someone who considers themselves IT literate can find it difficult to keep up-to-date. While we might hope that someone currently being schooled today would see security being covered, there are still various generations of current users that preceded them who will have varying levels of ability to recognise and deal with the issues they face.

Given the prevalence of technology and the resulting dependence upon it, modern organisations will clearly benefit from a security-aware workforce, However, much of the evidence suggests that they fail to devote attention towards it. For example, the UK's Cyber Security Breaches Survey 2018 reveals that only 30% of businesses provide user awareness and education [2]. This is in stark contrast to the level of attention given towards technology-based controls, such malware protection and network security where 90% and 89% adoption was suggested. Moreover, at the Board level, 68% indicate that they have received no training for cyber security incidents [3]. This picture of a lack of training is unfortunately commonplace, and in actual fact appears to be a fairly consistent picture across such various security surveys for the last couple of decades – the proportion of respondents indicating that awareness/training/education is provided is always limited to somewhere around a quarter to a third. Unfortunately, even where provision is made, it often fails to serve its purpose, and the rationale (or excuse) for not devoting more resource towards training is the belief that it makes no difference. However, the evidence is also there to show that lack of training contributes towards problems. Indeed, another result from the aforementioned Cyber Security Breaches Survey is that one of the most common actions taken in response to a breach (cited by almost a fifth of respondents) is 'additional staff training or communications'. One can only assume that if such action was taken proactively *in advance* then at least some level of breaches would have been prevented.

Another consideration is there are certain fundamentals of user education that ought to be provided irrespective of specific threats or actual breaches. Indeed, there are various aspects of baseline security literacy that everyone should be encouraged and enabled to have, irrespective of the particular devices, systems and data they use, and this in turn needs to build upon a solid foundation of basic IT and information literacy. Without this, users are unlikely to find that the cyber security lessons make sense, and may still lack the IT skills required to follow the advice and do what is needed.

Current SETA provision within many organisations is likely to rely upon a one-size-fits-all approach, where the same security training is made available to all staff (often via an e-learning package and/or other online resources). However, while this is clearly better than having nothing at all, the chances of it having the desired effect are arguably limited. It serves the purpose in terms of ensuring that staff have the opportunity to become acquainted with security issues, but it will be limited in terms of developing a true awareness and understanding of the topic because different people will benefit from different details and emphasis. To improve matters, the needs of the individual learner need to be considered, with the resulting SETA provision ideally being tailored accordingly.

The aim of this paper is to explore how we can more effectively address the issues around lack of security education, with particular focus upon the needs of end users. The core of the argument being made is that cybersecurity awareness, training and education programmes need to be designed and deployed with a clearer understanding of who is being addressed and how they are positioned to receive the material (e.g. in terms of factors such as their prior knowledge, their learning style, and their perception of and predisposition towards security). The discussion presented here is an extended version of that presented in an earlier position paper [4], with additional discussion of the educational approach that is proposed.

2 Background

Users are often highlighted as a weak link in cyber security, and criticised for a lack of awareness and a failure to follow good practice and use safeguards. However, this is often hardly surprising given the lack of SETA-related provision that is offered to support them. Understanding and accepting their cyber security responsibilities is often not the default position for many individuals, and there could indeed be several potential hurdles to overcome to get them to that point [5]:

- **Perception (What is It?):** how the threats and their associated security measures are viewed and understood by those that they may affect.
- **Priority (How Important is It?):** the ability to recognise the importance of security and protection aspects are when set alongside other activities and commitments.
- **Responsibility (What do I need to do?):** the extent to which relevant individuals accept, understand and undertake their security responsibilities
- **Capability (Can I do It?):** the extent to which users actually have   the knowledge and skills required to undertake their responsibilities.

Users clearly require related awareness and understanding if they are to answer the various questions here. Without such support, they will be potentially ill-prepared to do what is expected and required of them. However, as the survey results quoted earlier have already indicted, security managers often pay more attention to technical aspects, and tend to overlook (or entirely omit) human aspects and efforts toward reducing the related hazards.

Mechanisms are needed to boost awareness and understanding, and to help to ensure that end-users at all levels and from all backgrounds have the skills to make cyber security part of their everyday behaviour. However, many awareness often seems to become confused with simply ensuring publicity. It is easy (and perhaps convenient) to assume that having sent an email or delivered a presentation on a given security-related topic will be enough to have 'raised awareness' for those that may be affected. What this overlooks is attention towards associated behaviours. An individual's behaviour is the result of a decision-making process that informed by factors such as their knowledge, psychology, and cultural background. Simply promoting issues and technical controls without regard to this will be less likely to help the staff concerned to develop a security mind-set and culture.

The provision of SETA can be broken down into two categories; the content, and the framework within which it is delivered. The specifics of the content aspect will ultimately depend upon what the user needs to know, but even here there are generic issues that can be covered to the benefit of all users, and Sect. 3 gives some brief attention to this issue. Meanwhile, the framework element is arguably more challenging, insofar as it affects the potential for the content to reach and influence the target audience in the desired way. This consequently forms the basis for the majority of the overall discussion, as presented in Sects. 4–6.

3 Baseline Security Literacy

While the specifics of what one needs to know about security will depend upon the particular technology, systems and data that someone uses, there are equally a variety of baseline aspects that users should know in order to enable them to follow basic good practice and protect themselves from harm. As an example, prior work has proposed eight key areas of security in which users should have both an understanding of the importance as well as a suitable working knowledge of how to deal with them in practice [6]. These areas, and the associated understanding expected of users, are summarized as follows:

- **Authentication:** The role of authentication in preventing unauthorised access.
- **Backup:** The risks to systems and devices that may result in data loss, and the impact that such a loss may have for them.
- **Malware Protection:** The potential impacts of malware and the possible routes for infection
- **Mobile Devices:** The risks that devices can face from both technical threats and the physical environment.
- **Privacy and Data Leakage:** The sensitivity of different types of data, and the ways in which it could be misused (e.g. to support identity theft).
- **Safe Internet Access and Web Browsing:** The existence of threats such as phishing, malicious sites, and unsafe downloads.
- **Secure Networking:** The risks posed by using unprotected or unknown networks.
- **Software Updates:** The reason why software updates are released and the importance of patching vulnerabilities

Each topic also has a set of accompanying baseline tasks things that users will need to handle in order to achieve the related protection. In some cases, this will require more active involvement on the part of the user than others, as there are increasingly system-automated features that can cover basic safeguards (provided that they are enabled and permitted to work). For example, in the case of authentication, core skills would include the ability to choose and use suitable passwords, and then follow good practice in terms of managing them. So, in this case it requires the user to have some ability to discern and make the correct decisions. Meanwhile, for malware protection, the basic requirement is for the user to have the ability to check that appropriate antivirus protection is installed, enabled, and up-to-date (i.e. beyond this there is not much they will routinely be required to do in an active sense).

Unfortunately, while it may be easy to agree that these areas are indeed reasonable things to expect, it is less straightforward to determine how and where they should be acquired. For example, many organisations would seem to implicitly believe that such knowledge would be acquired elsewhere, and so provide little workplace support for developing them. In practice however, users are frequently not pre-equipped with a uniform and sufficient understanding of either the security basics or the underpinning IT aspects, and so still require support to operate effectively. A further complication to providing such support comes from how the variations in individuals' prior knowledge (or lack of it) may represent a barrier to their further learning. As such, it is relevant to understand how each person is positioned and what is potentially standing in their way, as discussed in the next section with the notion of threshold concepts.

4   The Role of Threshold Concepts

The ideas of threshold concepts and troublesome knowledge were introduced by Meyer and Land [7] as a means to help educators understand the barriers in people's learning cycle. They refer to characteristics learners have in any kind of learning environment that form the ontological concepts of that individual. Learners can often find that the integration of information, required to progress towards understanding of a subject, can becomes troublesome. Threshold concepts demand the integration of the concepts and deeper understanding the learner needs to acquire and develop their ideas. This results in learners accepting that their individual learning will transform.

The notion of threshold concepts is now recognised as a valuable tool to understand, facilitate and aid the development of learning and awareness across multiple fields and disciplines Within the current discussion, it is suggested that an approach that recognises threshold concepts could be beneficial as a basis for reconsidering the planning and delivery of security awareness training. By using the threshold concept approach, both the development and delivery of training materials should incorporate greater linkages between thinking and practicing. Meyer and Land identify the following key characteristics [7]:

- **Transformative:** When the idea is understood, a threshold concept can change the end user's views.
- **Irreversible:** Given their transformative potential, threshold concepts can be irreversible.
- **Integrative:** Once learned, it is more likely to bring together different aspects and opinions and become more related.
- **Bounded:** Identifying the conceptual space, serving a specific and limited purpose.
- **Discursive:** Crossing thresholds will incorporate a greater level of understanding and engagement in the field.

The characteristics of bounded and integrated collectively identify the episteme of the security awareness discipline. It can assist in exploring the particular behaviours and ways of thinking and practicing. One characteristic cannot happen without the other four. Concepts are, and need to be, integrative and transformative. Security managers need to aim for further change so continuous development of the training and re-training is highly needed. By using the threshold concepts approach, managers will be in a better position to identify and define the boundaries and make sense of specific problems. In short, it will help them to identify and understand why end users do not always apply security as expected and desired.

Table 1, based on [8], shows some differences between the conceptual change in the acquisition of basic and new concepts.

Table 1. Definition and exemplification of three types of conceptual change [4].

Type of conceptual change	Types of transformation and integration	Examples in Security Awareness
Basic	Understanding everyday experiences of security issues through integration of personal experiences with ideas	• Understanding the role of each of the baseline areas of cybersecurity literacy • Understanding the differences between basic security methods such as authentication, data encryption
Security awareness threshold concepts	Understanding of other subject ideas integrated and transformed through acquisition of theoretical perspective	• Understanding how to combine controls in order to ensure a holistic approach to security compliance (e.g. recognising what might meaningfully work together to provide a required form or level of protection) • Requires people to know the basic roles of the distinct elements of protection and be able to make the connections between them
Procedural (how awareness models are constructed + evaluated)	Ability to construct discipline-specific narratives and arguments, transformed through acquisition of ways of practising	• Users are able to continue and advance their understanding and application of security awareness well after their training • Identifying the need for security in situations that had not previously been introduced (e.g. identifying that the content of a document is sensitive, and then judging the appropriate protection to apply).

The need for a multi-disciplinary approach has not only been acknowledged in many different fields, but it is also recognised as empowering and helps to contextualise the involvement of the users with the systems. Recognising the importance of the employee's own role in adhering to security policies should be a key priority, and this can only be done by implementing policies that take the human factor into account.

Organisations should not only be looking to address technical aspects of security, but also the socio-cultural and educational aspects, and any related instructions and guidelines should be produced in an interdisciplinary manner. Although organisations may consider themselves to provide sufficient training, we often find that they forget the underlying human factors, and as a consequence, while training may be delivered, the content is seen as basic, and the lessons it attempts to offer make little transition into practice.

5 Establishing a Framework for Individual Security Learning

By understanding an individual's position in relation to the threshold concepts, we are better placed to support the development of their security-specific learning. As an example, if we can enable people to understand concepts around the interconnectedness of networks and the inability to properly recall, retract or cancel things once sent, then they will be better positioned to receive lessons about security and privacy aspects indiscriminate data sharing.

As previously indicated, another aspect the comes into play when considering security at the individual level is the diversity of learning styles that can be encountered. People learn in different ways, and so presenting the materials and framing the messages in ways that suit their individual preference is likely to yield better results [9]. As an example of the approaches underlying this, Fleming [10] proposes the VARK (Visual, Aural, Read/write and Kinaesthetic) model, reflecting four sensory modalities that may be used for learning information (e.g. some like to 'read' texts rather than look at 'diagrams', while others prefer to 'listen' to a lecture rather than 'doing' a practical session). Similarly, if we have an appreciation of the individual's prior knowledge and their existing predisposition towards security, then this could be used to further tailor the way in which things are presented to them. For example, are they already compliant with policy or tending toward disobedience? Are they risk averse or risk tolerant? Are they accepting of security or resistant towards it? Having appropriate insights here could affect the way in which the awareness and education messages are framed in order to reach different portions of the audience [11]. All of this, combined with a recognition of their role within the organisation, can help to tailor things more specifically to their needs.

While security is often recognised as important in concept, in practice many users see it as a chore or an overhead that is endured rather than embraced. If this is their stance when being exposed to security-related training and education, then there is clearly a different starting point to someone that has bought into the concept and is more actively ready to learn. Even if there is not active resistance, it is fair to say that cybersecurity itself is a topic area that may not naturally engage or excite the majority of the target audience. In this sense, those attempting to promote the issues are arguably disadvantaged from the outset.

Full adoption of the proposed approach would represent a significant contrast to the typical provision of security education, and this is illustrated in Fig. 1 The left-hand side of the diagram portrays a standard, one-size-fits-all approach, while the right-hand element presents the approach advocated here. The latter requires a variety of information to be gathered for each user in order to establish their individual circumstances (and hence associated effort to do so), but if this were to be done then it clearly has the potential to deliver a far more tailored security education experience (which in turn would be hoped to yield better results in terms of acceptance, understanding and compliance).

The requirement for upfront data gathering points towards the desirability of designing and evaluating a questionnaire that organisations could use as a diagnostic tool to determine where their staff members are currently positioned in relation to each of the factors that may affect their learning. This in turn will help to determine the most appropriate starting point for different staff members, both in terms of their pre-existing IT and/or security knowledge, as well as the delivery mode that maps best to their learning style. This would then be supplemented by the incorporation of peer-based support to further reinforce and enhance the learning and acceptance.

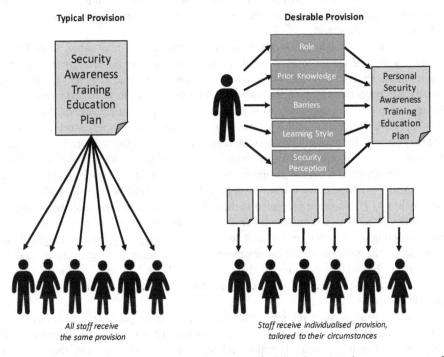

Fig. 1. Comparing current and proposed modes of delivering security awareness and education [4].

6   Extending and Enhancing Security Education with Peer Learning

Prior research acknowledges the fact that although training is widely offered within an organisation, users still do not comply. In [12], Bada and Sasse list various campaigns that took place in an attempt to get the users to comply with the training provided. In addition, they offer a variety of reasons why those campaigns failed and what stands out - and indeed what we focus on in this paper - is the people's behaviours and what influences them. Moreover, the ISF [13] concludes that just delivering a training programme is not enough and that we should be making our people/employees our strongest control. The ISF approach is to introduce a behaviour change programme that creates specific requirements that depend on the audience dynamics and cultures. They suggest that any security awareness training needs to target behaviour change rather than just a delivery of a programme. Such change can be achieved by engaging people at personal level and setting realistic expectations. To support this further, Furnell and Rajendran [14] discuss the behaviour users can present and/or adopt within an organisation or even at home. Both [15] and [16] suggest the notion of security champions. What they suggest is that within an organisation certain people can be identified that will continue promoting and ensuring users are compliant. They suggest that such people will be identified by having high level motivation and great understanding of the policies.

What we understand from the above is that there is a significant need to develop a community of good practice within various environments. Boud and Middleton [17] were amongst the first to identify that learning in workplaces can take an informal format, can be complex, and that there is a diverse range of people to work with. Although there is some published research discussing peer learning for organisations [18, 19], there has been little development across this area in general, and more specifically within security awareness, training and compliance.

Traditionally Peer Learning is where advanced learners provide support for learners at lower levels within educational establishments. Companies nowadays try to be innovative, and offer extensive training for their staff, but they forget they importance of the post-training phase. With the Peer Learning scheme, where in our case it will be highly motivated individuals acting as the initiators, knowledge transfer will not be a static phase but an ongoing development of diverse environments, where users will continue learning. There will also be some monitoring of compliance, and the results of this could in turn provide feedback into the points emphasised in the peer learning.

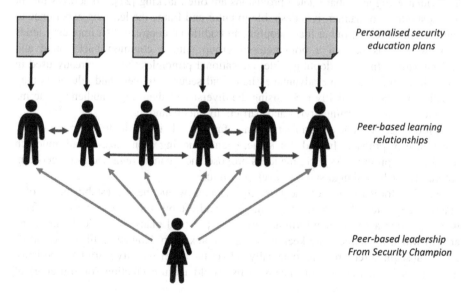

Fig. 2. Extending the personalised framework with peer learning and security champions.

Training itself is not enough. There are five key aspects that organisations should be focusing on: the trainee, the trainer, the content, the process and the environment [20]. In practice, however, organisations often focus more on how to develop and deliver an outstanding training programme, but often without taking into consideration these five aspects. With a peer learning approach within organisations, we are looking at a flexible solution to be applied in many different situations, taking into consideration what the organisation needs, the benefits of user compliance, and how to create a more diverse and inclusive environment. By such approaches an organisation is embedding the aforementioned five aspects and can benefit as follows:

1. Promoting ongoing learning among colleagues.
2. Offering a cost-effective approach at the post-training phase.
3. Involving real life examples and problem-based approaches, with on-the-spot answers provided.
4. Enhancing individuals' CPD and promoting the organisation in the sector in terms of providing security awareness and training for it's employees.

An illustrative depiction of the proposed concept, extending from the earlier concept of desirable provision, is presented in Fig. 2. This illustrates both the peer learning flows amongst individual employees, as well as the proactive steer that can be provided by a designated security champions (who are also part of the peer group, but are expected to be more particularly engaged in the promotion and advocacy of security to others).

7 Conclusions

Today's IT users undoubtedly require support in relation to SETA aspects, and much of the evidence suggests that related provisions are often lacking [21]. To address this in the most effective manner, it is desirable to tailor and frame the learning experience to suit individual needs, rather than adopting an traditional approach that implicitly tends to view staff as part of a homogenised group with a common background and understanding. Indeed, adopting wider educational principles that are already used in other disciplines will have advantages here, and security trainers and educators may benefit from more explicitly recognising the diversity of their target audience in terms of factors such as learning styles and barriers to understanding.

Unfortunately, many organisations are far from being able to offer a tailored experience in practice. Indeed, for some, even achieving a one-size-fits-all approach remains an aspiration. As such, the ideas proposed here can be regarded as longer-term ambitions for how things should develop in future.

Moving forward, one of the key requirements would be the establishment of a diagnostic tool/test that could profile the user and establish their learning needs. This would provide a basis for informing how their personal plans should look, and is an area in which the authors are keen to focus as a next step. However, this clearly leads into a subsequent requirement to actually deliver the cyber security learning experience in a manner that matches the needs. This would require creation (or sourcing) of suitable delivery materials to map onto the different requirements; an endeavour that clearly has the potential to be demanding in terms of time and resources.

One particular aspect that needs to be explored further is related to the quality of the peer learning offered and how it is monitored within the organisation. The organisations' quality assurance provisions and the strategies in place to implement high standards should incorporate the term peer learning. It is relevant to recognise that peer learning often happens without anything necessarily having been formalised. When the organisation develops a formal strategy around it then they can monitor the quality of the outcomes among the staff involved, and inform their policies and future training. Developing a culture and influencing it appropriately should be one of the priorities in any strategies around quality assurance. Security education has to be more than just providing and transferring knowledge and information to people. Security needs to target, action and do, whilst dealing with complex behaviours in an attempt to provide consistent rules. Personal handling abilities can often influence the effectiveness of compliance and as such organisations need to evaluate one's behaviour and how it is likely to affect or impact on the policies and to shape the future training needed.

In conclusion, the authors are in the process developing a framework and toolkit to support the development of the proposed peer learning scheme for organisations. The framework will offer clear links to organisational strategic priorities and how to design and incorporate the scheme within a training scheme on security awareness training that will empower compliance. The resultant approach and outcomes will then form the focus of future publications.

References

1. Prensky, M.: Digital natives, digital immigrants. Horizon 9(5), 1–6 (2001)
2. DCMS: Cyber Security Breaches Survey 2018. Main report. Department for Culture, Media & Sport, April 2018 (2018). https://www.ipsos.com/sites/default/files/ct/publication/documents/2018-04/cyber-security-breaches-survey-2018-main-report.pdf
3. HM Government, FTSE 350 Cyber Governance Health Check Report 2017, Department for Digital, Culture, Media and Sport, London, UK, July 2017 (2017). https://www.gov.uk/government/uploads/system/uploads/attachment_data/file/635605/tracker-report-2017_v6.pdf
4. Vasileiou, I., Furnell, S.: Enhancing security education - recognising threshold concepts and other influencing factors. In: Proceedings of ICISSP 2018 - 4th International Conference on Information Systems Security and Privacy, Funchal, Madeira, Portugal, 22–24 January 2018, pp. 398-403 (2018)
5. Furnell, S.: Jumping security hurdles. Comput. Fraud Secur. 2010, 10–14 (2010)
6. Furnell, S., Moore, L.: Security literacy: the missing link in today's online society? Comput. Fraud Secur. 2014, 12–18 (2014)
7. Meyer, J.H.F., Land, R.: Threshold concepts and troublesome knowledge – linkages to ways of thinking and practising. In: Rust, C. (ed.) Improving Student Learning – Ten Years On. OCSLD, Oxford (2003)
8. Davies, P., Mangan, J.: Recognising Threshold Concepts: an exploration of different approaches. In: European Association in Learning and Instruction Conference (EARLI), Nicosia, Cyprus, 23–27 August 2005 (2005)

9. Talib, S.: Personalising Information security education. Ph.D. thesis, University of Plymouth (2014). https://pearl.plymouth.ac.uk/bitstream/handle/10026.1/2896/2014talib10137661phd.pdf

10. Fleming, N.D.: Teaching and Learning Styles: VARK Strategies, 2nd edn. Neil D Fleming, Christchurch (2006)

11. Pattinson, M., Anderson, G.: Risk communication, risk perception and information security, security management, integrity and internal control in information systems. In: Proceedings of IFIP TC-11 WG11.1 and WG11.5 Joint Working Conference, Fairfax, Virginia, USA, December 2005, pp. 175–184 (2005)

12. Bada, M., Sasse, A.: Cyber Security Awareness Campaigns - why do they fail to change behaviour?, Draft Working Paper, Global Cyber Security Capacity Centre, July 2014 (2014). http://discovery.ucl.ac.uk/1468954/1/Awareness%20CampaignsDraftWorkingPaper.pdf

13. ISF: From Promoting Awareness to Embedding Behaviours - secure by choice, not by chance. Information Security Forum (2014). https://www.securityforum.org/uploads/2015/03/From-Promoting-Awareness-ES-2014_Marketing.pdf

14. Furnell, S., Rajendran, A.: Understanding the influences on information security behaviour. Comput. Fraud Secur. **2012**, 12–15 (2012)

15. Gabriel, T., Furnell, S.: Selecting security champions. Comput. Fraud Secur. **2011**, 8–12 (2011)

16. Beris, O., Beautement, A., Sasse, M.A.: Employee rule breakers, excuse makers and security champions: mapping the risk perceptions and emotions that drive security behaviors. In: Somayaji, A., Van Oorschot, P., Böhme, R., Mannan, M. (eds.) NSPW 2015: Proceedings of the 2015 New Security Paradigms Workshop, pp. 73–84 (2015)

17. Boud, D., Middleton, H.: Learning from others at work: communities of practice and informal learning. J. Work. Learn. **15**(5), 194–202 (2003)

18. Ashwin, P.: Implementing Peer Learning Across Organisations: the development of a model. Mentor. Tutoring Partnersh. Learn. **10**(3), 221–231 (2010)

19. Faysse, N., Sraïri, M.T., Errahj, M.: Local Farmers' Organisations: a space for peer-to-peer learning? The case of milk collection cooperatives in Morocco. J. Agric. Educ. Ext. **18**(3), 285–299 (2012)

20. Arthur Jr., W., Bennett Jr., W., Edens, P.S., Bell, S.T.: Effectiveness of training in organisations: a meta-analysis of design and evaluation features. J. Appl. Psychol. **88**(2), 234–245 (2003)

21. Furnell, S., Vasileiou, I.: Security education and awareness: just let them burn? Netw. Secur. **2017**, 5–9 (2017)

Managing Cybersecurity Break-ins Using Bluetooth Low Energy Devices to Verify Attackers: A Practical Study

Kenneth C. K. Wong and Aaron Hunter[(✉)]

British Columbia Institute of Technology, Burnaby, Canada
kkenwwong@gmail.com, kenwong@ecuad.ca,
aaron_hunter@bcit.ca

Abstract. We present a novel solution in tracking the behaviour of an attacker and limiting their ability to compromise a cybersecurity system. The solution is based on combining a decoy with a real system, in which a BLE controller will be embedded in the middle of the system, thereby acting like a fob that opens and closes the access of the server's BLE. If the first server wants to communicate with the second server, the BLE must be activated by the BLE controller in order for both servers to communicate with one another. This is a relatively low-cost solution and our aim is to lower the interruption to the live system, capture the attacker's position, and limit the damages the attacker can do to a live system. A second related goal is to lower the attacker's opportunity to detect that they are being monitored. A third goal is to gather evidence of the attacker's actions that can be used for further investigation. This work is significant in that it is implemented within a real physical system for testing and evaluation using Raspberry PI and Arduino boards to replicate servers that communicate wirelessly. Adding a specifically-designed Encryption Block Cycle Cipher can protect legitimate users and redirect attackers to a honeypot system. Several custom programs were written from scratch to monitor the attacker's behaviour and Bluetooth Low Energy is enlisted to verify users. When the device was disassembled, all of the Raspberry PI, which run the Linux servers, were discontinued and unable to communicate with other devices.

Keywords: Cybersecurity management · Bluetooth low-energy ·
Honeypot system · Encryption keys · Cryptography

1 Introduction

In the following article, we propose a solution in which a fictitious main system interacts with a monitoring system (the real system), representing good use of Bluetooth Low Energy (BLE) devices and a combination of a specifically designed Encryption Block Cycle to control the communication flow between each server. This approach of using the BLE devices and a specifically designed Encryption Block Cycle can limit the opportunity for an attacker to breach the real system. Each user must have a dedicated BLE built into their computer at 5 m distance in order for the master (main) BLE controller to verify the user [6]. This paper is an extended version of [6] that

© Springer Nature Switzerland AG 2019
P. Mori et al. (Eds.): ICISSP 2018, CCIS 977, pp. 201–214, 2019.
https://doi.org/10.1007/978-3-030-25109-3_11

introduces a novel architecture to mitigate the cybersecurity threats in a network environment. This paper is different from the original as it furthers the depth of the project, by adding a specifically designed Encryption Block Cycle Cipher that combines with the BLE devices to prevent attackers from penetrating through to the main system. This research makes several contributions to existing work on cybersecurity. First, without the proper BLE verification, even with the correct username and password, the system will direct the user to the decoy system and never to the real system. With the protection of a unique designed encryption block cycle lock that protects the entrance and access between each server and controlled by the master (main) BLE controller; this limits the attacker's vulnerability attack and penetrating activities on the real system.

Second, we provide python applications that can be installed in practice to detect and trace attackers' positioning in the system. Significantly, our solutions have been tested in a real, physical network environment. The correct username and password is verified by the BLE (Bluetooth Low Energy) device and gets filtered through the built-in encryption block cycle cipher system, where the credential is scanned before allowing legitimate users to enter into the real system. Alternatively, intruders are directed to the honeypot system.

2   Preliminaries

2.1   Background

Cybersecurity break-ins are a worldwide problem; governments and businesses can expect roughly $400 billion annual costs in damages and property loss due to such attacks [5]. A fundamental solution to such break-ins is to gather intelligence about adversaries and their methods [1]. Though, several problems can lead to break-ins, including weaknesses of firewalls and encryption enforcement schemes. An attacker can also use port-scanning techniques to scan both open and closed ports of unprotected firewalls. Port scanning helps in managing the networks, but it can also be destructive in nature as if someone is sniffing for a weakened access point to breach into the computer system with different critical attacks like DOS, Botnet and DDOS [7].

Likewise, the research concluded that there were mistakes in cryptographic software implementations, in which they found that 17% of mistakes occur in core cryptographic libraries (which often have devastating consequences), and the remaining 83% of mistakes are in individual applications. It has been proven that the use of an encryption scheme does not provide integrity, which means that an attacker is able to undetectably modify stored keys [7].

It is determined that low and high-interaction honeypots have limitations in preventing intruders [9]. First, low interaction does not track the follow-up actions of the attacker since there is no real system or service to break into [9]. The second issue is the low interaction honeypots reaction to queries can be fingerprinted and thus the systems can be readily identified and ignored by the attackers [9]. The issue with a high interaction honeypot is once it is compromised the attacker has a fully functional system to launch other attacks within the network [9].

At the same time, this can further assert that cyber-attacks are increasing in the real-world and they cause widespread damage in cyber-infrastructure and loss of information [8]. Likewise, they found a three-party password-only authenticated key exchange (PAKE) protocol that can run in only two communication rounds [8] which can resist attackers. Honeypots allow a victim to monitor an intruder in the act, revealing the tools and methods used [1]. However, inadequate monitoring of honeypot traffic and activities increases the risk of theft of any data stored on the actual production host [1]. For note, the articles and studies provided here contain a few methodological flaws from previous research that should not be replicated and improvements in research methodology must be made.

Furthermore, a Low Energy Bluetooth device should be implemented in honeypots because it has a 5 m range with less than 16% energy overhead gateway [3] than the traditional Bluetooth devices. A new device-agnostic system, called BLE-Guardian, protects the privacy of the users/environments equipped with BLE device [3]. Using Bluetooth Low Energy can achieve low power consumption that can communicate without being traced [4]. Additionally, [2] concluded that Bluetooth Low Energy devices are a solution for short-range communication but have outstanding challenges. In their study, they found that the Bluetooth Low Energy devices aim to eliminate unnecessary interaction with a third party, leveraging physical proximity and minimizing energy consumption, while providing strong privacy and anonymity guarantees [3]. To successfully enlist this method, there must be a cryptographic secret handshake that communicates through the Bluetooth Low Energy devices.

By building on existing weaknesses of firewalls, encryption keys, and honeypots, and the findings of the literature review, this study improves weak security architecture defenses that are currently incorporated in most network systems. The study's results are beneficial to commercial and government organizations in resolving their potentially weak security defenses in honeypots.

In the literature, several approaches are typically combined to protect against cyber break-ins. Many of these approaches involve the use of cryptographic methods and cryptographic software. It is worth noting however, that simply using cryptographic software to protect data is insufficient. One problem is that some cryptographic software has been demonstrated to have programming issues both in the core libraries and in specialized applications [4]. Moreover, encryption alone cannot provide data integrity while an attacker can sometimes undetectably modify stored keys. Overall, cryptographic software has limitations in terms of securing data, partially due to standard software issues and poor management of security schemes.

One common method for preventing break-ins is to use firewalls that block an intruder from accessing a machine remotely. However, using a firewall alone tends to be ineffective for several reasons. First, if security policies are mismanaged or inadequate, then the utility of a firewall is significantly decreased. Moreover, attackers can use port-scanning techniques to scan both open and closed ports of unprotected firewalls; in many cases, this scanning process will give the attacker enough information to get by the firewall [7]. One final limitation of a firewall includes the fact that it does not filter traffic on the protected side. Hence, everyone on the inside is largely trusted [7].

Another well-known technique to prevent break-ins is through a honeypot, which is essentially a fake system that appears to contain real data [9]. The idea is that an attacker will be deceived into exploring the honeypot. Nevertheless, it is well known that low-interaction honeypots alone cannot prevent break-ins because they do not track the actions of the attacker sufficiently [9]. Worse yet, attackers can often easily identify whether a system is a honeypot and choose not to explore it. In order to avoid this problem, we can implement a high-interaction honeypot that interacts with the real system. Unfortunately, this can give the attacker access to real system data. Inadequate monitoring of honeypot traffic can actually increase the risk of theft of data from the real system [1].

In summary, security professionals cannot rely solely on security firewalls, cryptographic software, and low-interaction honeypots to stop cybersecurity threats. Overall, firewall does not effectively protect system through policies and set rules. Cryptographic software has the capability to infect and lock-down available hosts in the system. Honeypots alone cannot capture valuable information from attackers and limit to retain the attacker.

2.2 Motivation

The situation outlined in the preceding suggests that there is still a need for new solutions to help prevent cyber security break-ins. One approach that has been suggested in the literature is the use of wireless (Bluetooth) communication between a honeypot and a real server [9]. The idea here is that the honeypot will have no hard-wired connections to the real server. As such, the attacker will not be able to access the main server through the honeypot. In effect, this idea is intended to produce a high-interaction honeypot without the inherent risks of system access. The master (main) controller acts like a verification bridge and controller, where all users must be verified before being taken to the real system. It has been shown that BLEs use low power consumption and can communicate without being traced [8]. The differences between classic Bluetooth and BLE revolve around three factors: power consumption, data throughput, and the simple implementation of sensors [3]. For example, BLEs have a communication rate of roughly 305 kbps, as opposed to 0.7 to 2.1 Mbps for classic Bluetooth. In terms of distance, a single data file can be transferred between BLE devices at less than 10 m. On the other hand, classic Bluetooth devices have a distance range spanning from 10 to 100 m. Moreover, in order to guarantee privacy of the communication with a BLE, a cryptographic secret handshake is required [8].

There are questions around the feasibility of using BLE devices to communicate between servers in a practical setting. Our goal in this paper is to demonstrate, in a practical setting, a system architecture that uses BLEs to verify users and transfer files between a decoy system and a real system in a manner that is hidden from attackers. As such, we want to use real, physical computing hardware to simulate an attacker, a decoy system, and a real server. We aim to demonstrate that it is possible to capture information about the attacker on the decoy server, while using a BLE device to send data to the real server in an undetectable manner. Setting this up in a real physical network is important. We are already aware of the advantages in principle, but it remains to be seen whether these advantages can be modelled, tested, and obtained in a physical demonstration setting. In order to develop a low-cost solution that demonstrates the desired features, we will use very simple hardware with limited computing power. Our demonstration could then easily be extended to more complex hardware and software with the same benefits.

3 The Proposed Infrastructure

3.1 Fundamental Questions

We are fundamentally interested in two main problems. First, we must determine what information needs to be secured. In order to secure the communication between the various components of a system infrastructure, one needs to place an appropriate security filter inside of the infrastructure itself. Attackers generally attempt to isolate the communication between the servers inside a system infrastructure. This makes it difficult for the System and Security Administrators to detect, trace and investigate the attacker's position. As such, we built a supplemental layer of security that relies on the BLE devices, and configured and developed a Python application (script) that will detect and trace the attacker's position with a high level of precision.

The network design is shown in Fig. 1. Our experimental system involves three Raspberry PI devices. One of the servers from the decoy system acts like a gateway, at the point where the attackers and legitimate users enter the system. The system verifies the username and password and is then additionally required to verify whether the user's computer has a unique BLE key that is assigned by the master (main) BLE controller. The master (main) BLE controller must verify if the user has a built-in BLE device that synchronize a given encrypted key in order to divert them to the real system. Otherwise, the system will drop the user to the decoy system, like a hydraulic pipe that connects to the high-interaction honeypot system. An Arduino electronic hardware device will be the master (main) BLE controller.

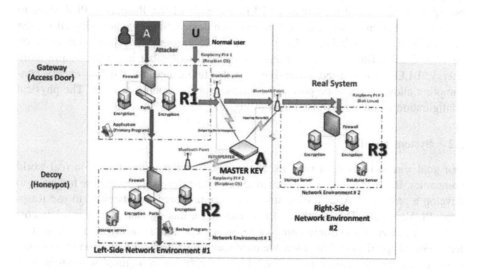

Fig. 1. Network connection.

Basically, our model comprises of two network environments. One network is a standard network with some fixed topology, which can be accessed in the typical way. The addition of the BLE node adds a second network with the topology depicted in Fig. 2. This network is completely separated into two environments. The BLE device controls the verification and communication between the servers.

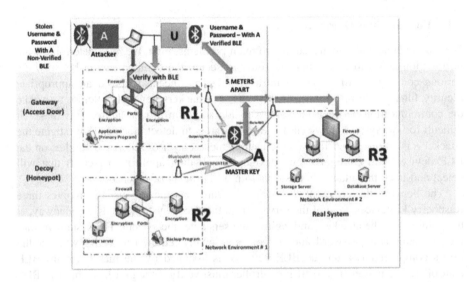

Fig. 2. Network connection indicating the BLE (Bluetooth Low Energy) device verification.

The second problem to address is how to implement the infrastructure as shown for testing purposes. As noted, we used Raspberry PI electronic hardware for the computing side. We tested a number of BLEs on each of the Raspberry PI devices to determine the appropriate distance between each device. Since we are using BLEs, the devices need to be relatively close; in testing we required less than 10 m between devices. Classic Bluetooth would allow greater distance, but it would require more energy. BLEs will be used increasingly in the future because the low energy consumption allows them to be powered continuously for months or years. The physical configuration of our system is shown in Fig. 3.

3.2   System Details

Our goal was to replicate a network environment similar to those used in real-world companies. In order to do so, we needed to determine the most appropriate hardware to develop a prototype. After testing several electronic boards, we decided to use Raspberry PI, Version 3. The Raspberry PI is suitable for this simulation as it is a low-cost item with powerful electronic components which can run a variety of operating systems. For this particular simulation, we used Kali Linux because it allowed us to secure the main server with closed ports. Each Linux server was configured with an internal firewall, user authentication privileges and cryptographic software.

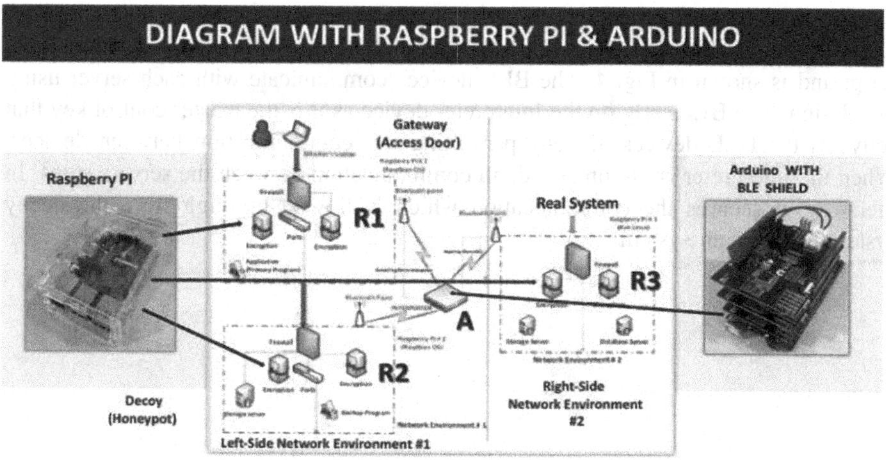

Fig. 3. Network connection with Raspberry PI and Arduino photograph.

The Arduino electronic board (main BLE) is placed in the middle, and acts as the master controller for the individual BLEs on each server. The master (main) BLE activates and deactivates the BLEs automatically if necessary to close the port connection. For example, if there is a need to send data between the Linux servers, this is enabled by the Arduino. The board we used was the Arduino UNO, primarily because it was only required to control the BLEs; it was not used for data transfer. If this board had been required to actually complete the data transfer, then a higher performance board would have been necessary.

Several Python programs were written to detect, trace and alert the presence of an attack by communicating with the monitoring system through the BLE devices. The main application is intended to handle the data transfer from the decoy server to the main server. In order to do, it performs several tasks:

- It checks for login sessions on the decoy machine. Since this machine has no legitimate purpose, all logins are likely to be attackers. We collect information for each session (Ex: information is collected at every session login/logout).
- The information is compiled into a single log file, indicating the user ID and passwords attempted and Session ID.
- The log file is sent to a separate program that controls the communication between BLE devices.

In fact, two "copies" of this program are installed: one as a primary and the other as a secondary that activates if the primary fails. This duplication is used to mitigate the risk of an attacker discovering and removing the communication program. It would be difficult for an attacker to remove both copies simultaneously, particularly given the fact that the secondary program will not be active until the primary program fails. As noted, a second Python program controls communication between the BLE devices. This program constantly scans for other BLE transmissions and then establishes a communication channel. This is a generic communication module that can be used for any transmitting and receiving BLE devices.

The third Python program only runs on the main server and is responsible for receiving the log file after it has gone through the interpreter. It runs on a very simple script and is shown in Fig. 4. The BLE devices communicate with each server using this design. The BLEs rely on the Interpreter device as it is the master control key that activates the BLE devices, thereby permitting intercommunication between devices. When the Interpreter is disconnected, all communication between the servers stops. In this way, it secures the communication which is flowing through from the decoy system to the main system.

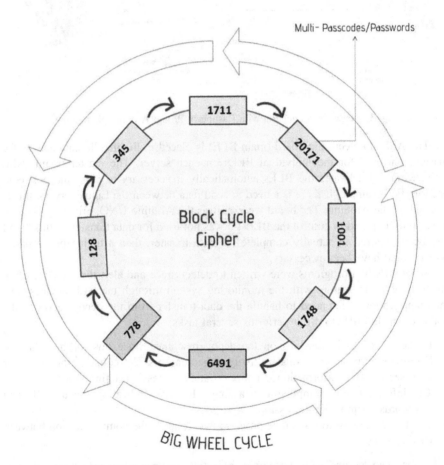

Fig. 4. Encryption block cycle cipher diagram [Securing the system].

This methodology allows us to limit the attacker's opportunity to compromise a system. It further allows us to investigate and gather precise information about the attacker's position. There are limits to the methodology with respect to protecting the system. The method of using the BLE devices is adopted so as to add an additional verification authentication to prevent attackers from compromising the real system.

3.3 Encryption Block Cycle Lock

The encryption cycle lock is one of the new improvements of cipher encryption key technology that already in use today. The encryption key that we created is called the block cycle cipher. It can be controlled by the BLE (Bluetooth low energy device), and it changes the user's password automatically when the wrong password is entered. The attacker will have a difficult time to grasp the correct password, as the cycle keeps switching the key password combination. The legitimate user's private key will match all the combinations on the block cycle cipher, in order for them to enter the system. The legitimate user must have the unique BLE (Bluetooth Low Energy) device in order to enter the system. A time lock encryption key has been used in the past, but it has never yet been added to a counter cycle encryption cipher lock. Most of the applications are consumes the cryptographic techniques for providing the security and confidentiality in data [10]. Unfortunately, they are implemented and built correctly to prevent attackers intruding in the system [10]. Furthermore, Efficiency concerned with the minimizing the computational resources in terms of memory consumption and execution time and the solution optimization and execution time and the solution optimization is leads to modifying the cryptographic technique using hybrid approach with their integrity check [10]. The solution to the problem is to implement a cycle that have the capability to change the password and reduces the cipher text in significant amount. The number cycles will improve the time complexity and restrict the attacker ability to gain access to the real system. The new generate password is always compatible with the legitimate user's private encryption key, because the user have an assigned BLE devices that gets verified through the master (main) BLE system.

Figure 4 shows the rotation of the Encryption Block Cycle Cipher and how the password changes. The password is encrypted by the user's private key. However, in this scenario it gives out a set of combinations that always match the user's public keys, as long as the user's BLE (Bluetooth Low Energy) devices are assigned by the master (main) BLE, no matter how many times this Encryption Block Cycle Cipher changes the password within the set of combinations. The user is able to securely log into the real system without any interruption. The attacker will not anticipate the password changes rapidly, and without the proper assigned BLE, the attacker will never be able to enter the real system.

4 Testing

4.1 Limitations

For our simulation, we required a data transfer device that can be run with the BLEs. We added an Arduino board to act like the master (main) controller to handle user verification and as well as a doorway to transfer log files between the servers. Due to difficulties we encountered using classical Bluetooth, we opted to replace and use BLE devices instead. This did not present a major obstacle.

While the choice of the Raspberry PI was effective in most respects, it did come with a restriction. The Raspberry PI can only set up two sets of authentication filters, thereby inherently limiting each board. To address this problem, we added Raspberry

Pi extension hardware connected to the existing boards in order to install more authentication filters.

Finally, the operating system chosen comes with some vulnerabilities. We selected Kali Linux because it is considered to be a reasonably secure stand-alone operating system. Nonetheless, one reason it is secure is because it has most of the vulnerability exploitation hacking tools listed in its system. This could allow attackers to use security tools on Kali to compromise the overall system. This limitation has been addressed to some degree by the extension boards, which can run Ubuntu Linux.

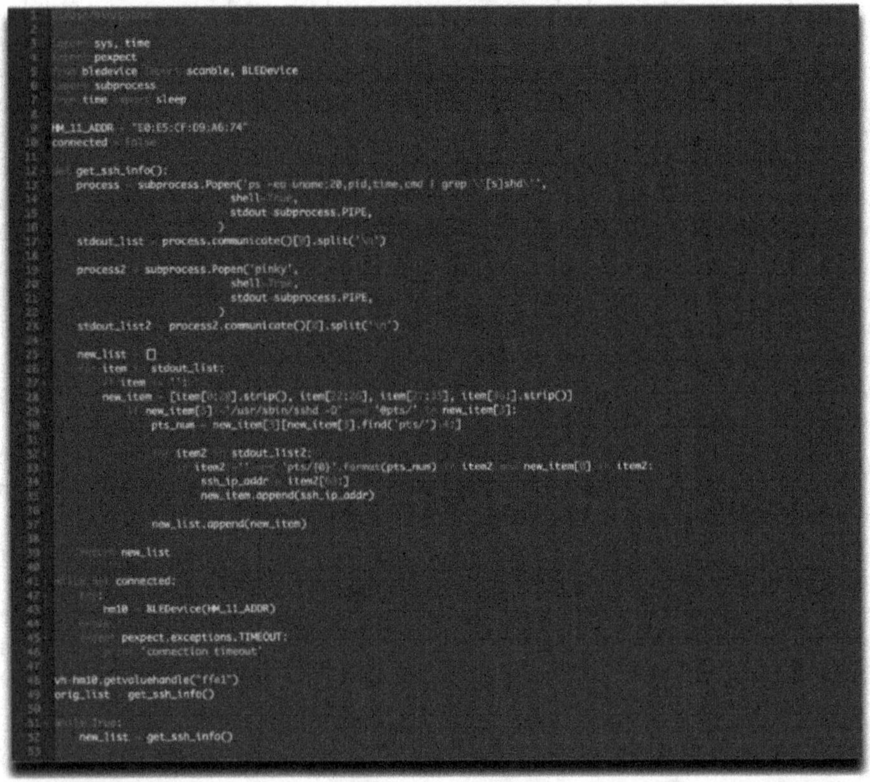

Fig. 5. Python programming language [Controls the BLE devices, located on the three servers]. (Color figure online)

4.2 Results

There are several kinds of findings that can be discussed from the development of this system. One entirely practical result rests in the fact that we were able to produce a working demonstration that uses BLEs for communication. This is not a true 'result' and it is essentially implicit in the discussion to this point. It is worth mentioning, however, that the physical configuration of the system was a technical challenge. We had to experiment with a variety of computing devices, a variety of BLE solutions, and a variety of physical configurations for the network. The result of this stage was a working system that includes the key features that were required for testing. Once the system was completely configured, we were able to simulate an attack in which the attacker accesses the decoy system. This involves four working components:

- The decoy system ran successfully with the Python event logger in place.
- The attacker system ran successfully, and it was able to access the decoy system.
- The main system ran successfully, and it was able to receive the log file from the decoy system.
- The BLE can verify legitimate users and attackers.
- The Encryption Block Cycle Lock is able to divert attackers to the honeypot and changing the password automatically, once the password is entered without a Bluetooth Low Energy to verify the unique encryption key.
- The Encryption Block Cycle Lock is able to communicate with each user's BLE (Bluetooth Low Energy) devices and the master (main) BLE (Bluetooth Low Energy) device. Changes and cycle the encryption key, but it will always be able to match the user's BLE devices.

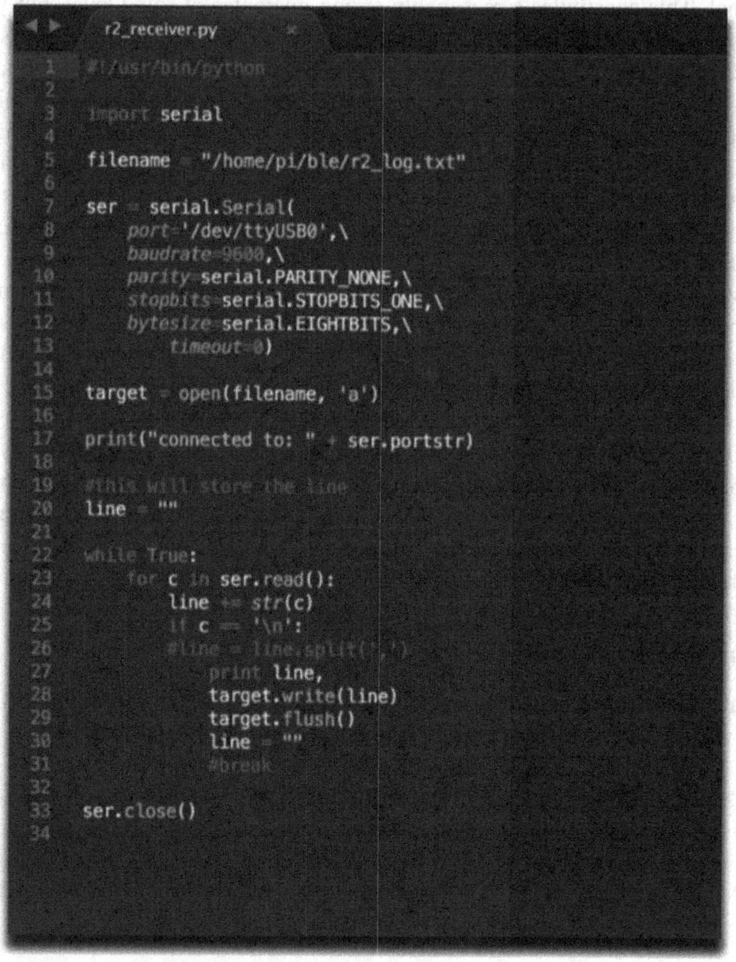

```python
r2_receiver.py

#!/usr/bin/python

import serial

filename = "/home/pi/ble/r2_log.txt"

ser = serial.Serial(
    port='/dev/ttyUSB0',\
    baudrate=9600,\
    parity=serial.PARITY_NONE,\
    stopbits=serial.STOPBITS_ONE,\
    bytesize=serial.EIGHTBITS,\
        timeout=0)

target = open(filename, 'a')

print("connected to: " + ser.portstr)

#this will store the line
line = ""

while True:
    for c in ser.read():
        line += str(c)
        if c == '\n':
            #line = line.split(',')
            print line,
            target.write(line)
            target.flush()
            line = ""
            #break

ser.close()
```

Fig. 6. Python programming languages [Controls the Master BLE Device]. (Color figure online)

In Fig. 6, the source code is named "R2 (Raspberry PI 2) Receiver". It receives the data log file from the Interpreter (Arduino electronic board) that is placed between the Raspberry PI 1, 2 and 3 electronic boards. Raspberry PI 2 receives the data log files that Raspberry PI 1 has sent to the Bluetooth Low Energy devices through the Interpreter.

4.3   Theoretical Verification

In this section, we briefly provide some theoretical grounds for the analysis and verification of the network architecture that we have introduced. Of these points, the first two are standard features of any honeypot-like scenario. The key issue that distinguishes our work here hinges on the third and fourth point. The reason we use BLE devices is to distinguish if the attacker is a legitimate user and BLE can cut all connection at the same time. It is also able to pass information about the attack to the main server to explicitly hide the communication from the attacker.

We were interested in having some sort of guarantee that the attacker will not know what is happening. At present, this guarantee comes from the physical properties of the BLE signal. This constitutes a reasonably strong guarantee at some level, but we still do not know what this level of ignorance on behalf of the attacker allows us to conclude. In addition, we do not know how to react in the case where the attacker discovers the communication. This is important to consider, as the attacker might be able to determine that a BLE is being used, either by some form of fingerprinting or by simply discovering the Python script on the system that is sending the information to the real server. Hence, even though the attacker will not know anything about the real server, they may become aware that it exists and they might know what information it is receiving.

We were able to make good use of the BLE devices to verify users and manage system portals, and were additionally able to transfer log files between the servers. When we disconnected the BLE Arduino (master), all communication through the server was ceased, thereby supporting the enhanced security measures and precautions outlined by the experimental model. The security solution is a low-cost and extreme advanced strategy of protecting and investigating a system infrastructure. In any event, this formalization would allow us to state formal properties about the system, and then formally prove them under flexible assumptions about the attacker's behaviour. This formal analysis will take our system from a practical demonstration to a provably secure architecture. We leave this aspect for future work.

4.4   Further Results and Development

Legitimate users are assigned a special authentication BLE key to enter to the real system, which is the R3 (Raspberry PI server 3). All legitimate users should have a physical BLE key and an assigned authentication code. Intruders or hackers do not have a physical BLE key on their machine (desktop/laptop), so the master BLE devices does not assign a special authentication key, but rather allows them to only access to the fake system, which is the R2 (Raspberry PI server 2). The data log files in Fig. 5 are the results that are captured from what is gathered about the user as it is logged by the system. For further results, we used colour coded text fonts in the terminal. If there was a legitimate user, the system generates green text log files whereas a hacker shows red text log files. See Fig. 6.

4.5   Future Work

Based on the results of the present research, future research would do well to enlist stronger filters such as adding additional authentication keys between each of the BLE devices on the servers that can strengthen security in the system. For instance, setting up an authentication key combination code which must be validated before entering the BLE master controller (Arduino) that is located between the Raspberry PI Linux servers. Not only will this strengthen the security of the system, but it will also prevent the attacker from being able to control the Arduino electronic board which is the master Bluetooth key controller. Once the attacker compromises the Arduino electronic board, they can have full access to control the BLE devices, allowing the attacker to control the main system.

4.6   Conclusion

The research project provides a successful approach towards securing a system infrastructure against threats or being compromised quickly. The results showed that the application programs utilized in the study's design are capable of gathering important information about the attacker. The use of BLE devices and shields on the Raspberry PI and Arduino electronic boards proved that the concept solution of data communication transfer does work between the Linux servers in two separate network environments. In the end, we successfully assembled and used the BLE devices and shields with the Raspberry PI and Arduino electronic boards to do the data communication transfer without interruption. These findings will help investigators in gathering useful information about the attacker and a solution in protecting the data.

References

1. Brown, A., Andel, T.: What's in your honeypot? In: The 11th International Conference on Cyber Warfare and Security, Boston, USA, pp. 370–377 (2016)
2. Cho, K., et al.: Analysis of latency performance of Bluetooth Energy (BLE) networks. Nat. Cent. Biotechnol. Inform. **15**(1), 59–78 (2015)
3. Fawaz, K.: Protecting privacy of BLE device users. In: The 25th USNIX Security Symposium, Austin, USA, pp. 1205–1221 (2016)
4. Gogic, A., Mujcic, A., Ibric, S., Suljanovic, N.: Performance analysis of Bluetooth low energy mesh routing algorithms in case of disaster prediction. Int. J. Comput. Electr. Autom. Control Inform. Eng. **10**(6), 929–935 (2016). World Academy of Science, Engineering and Technology
5. Hiller, J., Russell, R.: Modalities for cyber security and privacy resilience: the NIST approach. Int. J. Disaster Risk Reduct. **10**, 213–215 (2015)

6. Hunter, A., Wong, K.: Decoy systems with low energy Bluetooth communication. In: Proceedings of the 4th International Conference on Information Security and Privacy (ICISSP), Madeira, Portugal, pp. 404–409 (2018)

7. Lazar, D., Chen, H., Wang, X., Zeldovich, N.: Why does crypto-graphic software fail? A case study and open problems. In: The 5th Asia-Pacific Workshop on Systems, New York, USA, pp. 1–7 (2014)

8. Nam, J., Choo, K-K.R., Paik, J., Won, D.: Two-round password-only authenticated key exchange in the three party setting. In: Multidisciplinary Digital Publishing Institute (MDPI), pp. 393–396 (2014)

9. Rutherford, J., White, G.: Using as improved cybersecurity kill chain to develop an improved honey community. In: 49th Hawaii International Conference on System Science, pp. 2624–2632 (2016)

10. Kapoor, V., Yadav, R.: A hybrid cryptography technique to support cyber security infrastructure. Int. J. Adv. Res. Comput. Eng. Technol. 4(11), 3995–4002 (2015)

On Building a Visualisation Tool for Access Control Policies

Charles Morisset[1(✉)] and David Sanchez[2]

[1] Newcastle University, Newcastle Upon Tyne, UK
charles.morisset@ncl.ac.uk
[2] Northumbria University, Newcastle Upon Tyne, UK
david.sanchez@northumbria.ac.uk

Abstract. An access control policy usually consists of a structured set of rules describing when an access to a resource should be permitted or denied, based on the attributes of the different entities involved in the access request. A policy containing a large number of rules and attributes can be hard to navigate, making policy editing and fixing a complex task. In some contexts, visualisation techniques are known to be helpful when dealing with similar amounts of complexity; however, finding a useful visual representation is a long process that requires observation, supposition, testing and refinement. In this paper, we report on the design process for a visualisation tool for access control policies, which led to the tool VisABAC. We first present a comprehensive survey of the existing literature, followed by the description of the participatory design for VisABAC. We then describe VisABAC itself, a tool that implements *Logic Circle Packing* to pursue the reduction of cognitive load on Access Control Policies. VisABAC is a web-page component, developed in Javascript using the D3.js library, and easily usable without any particular setup. Finally, we present a testing methodology that we developed to prove usability by conducting a controlled experiment with 32 volunteers; we asked them to change some attribute values in order to obtain a given decision for a policy and measured the time taken by participant to conduct these tasks (the faster, the better). We obtained a small to medium effect size ($d = 0.44$) that indicates that VisABAC is a promising tool for authoring and editing access control policies.

Keywords: Visualisation · Attribute-based Access Control ·
User study · Circle Packing

1 Introduction

An *access control policy* can be seen as a compendium of authorisations that regulate the use of a particular set of resources. They are defined by *security administrators* and are processed by a trusted software module called *access control mechanism* or *reference monitor* [8].

© Springer Nature Switzerland AG 2019
P. Mori et al. (Eds.): ICISSP 2018, CCIS 977, pp. 215–239, 2019.
https://doi.org/10.1007/978-3-030-25109-3_12

The first access control model is usually considered to be the *Access Matrix* [21], in which a head-rows indicate subjects, head-columns represent objects and the interception-cells, the access rights granted. This approach could be inconvenient for systems requiring a large number of subjects and objects, and may lead to policy misconfigurations [6]. As a consequence, alternative access control models have been introduced[1] over the years that not only provide more convenient methods for designing policies in specific contexts but also aim for more expressivity. In that quest, *General policy languages* have subsequently been created, including, but not limited to, *ExPDT* [43], *EPAL* [2] and the standard XACML (eXtensible Access Control Markup Language) [45]. The latest version, XACML 3.0, was released in 2013, and standardizes *Attribute-based Access Control*, within which an *access request* can be seen as a set of attribute values, an *access rule* as a decision (e.g., permit or deny) returned when a boolean expression (i.e., target and/or condition) holds for a request, and an *access policy* as combining the decisions returned by a collection of rules using a composition operator (e.g., deny-overrides or permit-overrides). Although XACML is a very general and powerful framework, its underlying format is XML, which makes XACML policies machine readable, but arguably harder to author and edit by hand.

The need for including human factors —which involve human-software interaction [22]— in security is recognised as an important problem; in the UK, for instance, 50% of the worst 2015 breaches were caused by "inadvertent human error" (up from 31% in 2014) [36] and there has been an increasing effort on *usable security* (see, e.g., [1,17,20,48]). In fact, human cognitive capacity has been overflowed to such extend by the need of regulatory mandates [4] that typical Security Administrators cope with such entanglement by obviating irrelevant data, causing inadvertently security risks in the process [49]. Recent privacy breaches along with experiments, such as Trudeau et al. [48] corroborates this, showing that users (including experienced policy engineers) easily oversee details. There is therefore a clear case to build tools helping security administrators author and edit access control policies.

Reducing complexity is an essential stage in any kind of analysis and it is perfectly possible to simplify a system without loosing essential functional properties. *Information visualisation* [9] comprises techniques that allow humans to understand and manipulate huge quantities of abstract data by simplification and it is being actively investigated by security researchers [7,47,49]. Languages such as `Mir6` [15] have demonstrated that it is even possible to specify security visually, albeit with very limited complexity. In particular, visualisation techniques have been proposed in the context of access control [15,42], including the tools ALFA[2] (Axiomatics Language for Authorization), which proposes a much simplified textual syntax for describing XACML policies, or VisPE [29], which proposes a Sratch-based interface. However, these approaches tend to enhance

---

[1] See for instance [3] for an account on the variety of access control models introduced over the past decades.

[2] https://www.axiomatics.com/pure-xacml.html.

the textual representation of the policy, rather than offer a visualisation of the evaluation of a policy.

In this paper, we fully report on the design process we followed to design VisABAC [26], which provides an interface for evaluating access control policies represented by Circle Packing drawing technique[3]. Whereas our previous work [26] focuses on the result of a usability study we conducted to validate VisABAC, this paper focuses on the different steps of the design process as well as the description of the tool itself. More specifically, the contributions of this paper are:

- A comprehensive description of the design process for VisABAC was created. A considerable amount of time was invested into exploring concepts and ideas that have been detailed in the background section (Particularly in Sect. 2.2); we detailed early prototypes in Sect. 3.1.
- A comprehensive description of VisABAC and its inner workings. VisABAC is a client-side browser application that given an attribute-based access control policy, provides a textual representation of that policy (inspired by XACML 3.0 and ALFA), a graphical visualisation using the Circle Packing method, and an interface allowing a policy designer to change policy and attribute values. VisABAC is, to the best of our knowledge, the first visualisation tool to support the XACML 3.0 extended decision set, which includes multiple indeterminate decisions (indicating missing information).
- An explanation of the methodology we designed to measure usability of a visualisation tool, as well as the report of a controlled experiment with 32 participants, which showed that, compared to the controlled group, the tested group was, in average, faster to answer the questions (with an effect size of $d = 0.44$ over the monitored questions), and more likely to interact with the tool (subjective preferences measured at the end of the test showed that 76.47% of participants who tested the visualisation tool manifested they felt more confident operating the policy.)

These contributions can be particularly helpful to those intending to design a visualisation tool for access control policies, as we highlight the key problems we have encountered in the design process. In particular, to the best of our knowledge, there is no standard benchmark for evaluating the efficiency and usability of policy authoring/editing tool, and we believe the results of the controlled experiments could pave the way towards establishing such a benchmark.

The rest of this paper is structured as follows: we first introduce in Sect. 2 the background on Attribute-Based Access Control and related work on access control visualisation. We then present VisABAC in Sect. 3, how it was developed and inner workings essentials; the experiment in Sect. 4; results are discussed in Sect. 5 and conclusions in Sect. 6.

---

[3] VisABAC is open-source and available at https://gitlab.com/morisset/visabac.

2   Background and Related Work

2.1   ABAC

As briefly described in the Introduction, ABAC consists in considering an access request as a set of attribute values. To illustrate our approach, let us consider a health-care policy, regulating the access to a medical record, where, informally speaking, access is permitted when there is no explicit disagreement from the patient and when either the hospital or the concerned surgeon agrees for the access, and access is denied otherwise.

We present here a simplified version of ABAC, aligned with the current version of VisABAC, and we leave for future work the implementation of more complex ABAC languages, such as PTaCL [11,12]. This simplified version is nevertheless expressive enough to model missing information, which is a key aspect of XACML 3.0 and PTaCL. In a nutshell, we consider here five key concepts:

- An *atomic target* consists of an attribute name and an attribute value;
- An *access request* provides a valuation of atomic targets to a 3-valued logic;
- A *composite target* is a logical composition of atomic targets;
- An *access rule* consists of an access decision and a composite target;
- An *access policy* composes rules and policies using a composition operator.

Intuitively speaking, we can define the policy described above using the following syntax (we provide a formal definition below):

```
R1: Deny if PATIENT_disagrees
R2: Permit if OR(HOSPITAL_agrees, SURGEON_agrees)
P: DOV(R1,R2)
```

where PATIENT_disagrees, HOSPITAL_agrees and SURGEON_agrees are atomic targets, OR(HOSPITAL_agrees, SURGEON_agrees) is a composite target, Permit and Deny are access decisions, R1 and R2 are access rules, DOV is the deny-overrides composition operator, and P is an access policy.

More formally, we consider a set of attribute names $\mathcal{A}$, a set of attribute values $\mathcal{V}$, and a set of atomic targets $\mathcal{T} \subseteq \mathcal{A} \times \mathcal{V}$. In the example above, we have $\mathcal{A} = \{$PATIENT, HOSPITAL, SURGEON$\}$, $\mathcal{V} = \{$agrees, disagrees$\}$, and $\mathcal{T} = \{$(PATIENT, disagrees), (HOSPITAL, agrees), (SURGEON, agrees)$\}$ (we use the underscore notation in the textual representation to limit the number of parentheses). It is worth noting that we do not associate each attribute with each value. In practice, this can be quite significant, for instance with the encoding of the patient consent: in this example, we model an explicit disagreement instead of an explicit agreement.

A request is then defined as a function $q : \mathcal{T} \rightarrow \{1, 0, \bot\}$, such that, given an atomic target $t = (a, v)$, $q(t) = 1$ indicates that a has the value v in q, $q(t) = 0$ indicates that a does not have the value v in q, and $q(t) = \bot$ indicates that we do not know whether a has the value v in q or not. Here, we interpret 1, 0, and $\bot$ as the XACML elements Match, NoMatch and Indeterminate, respectively.

A composite target is defined as a proposition of atomic targets. Since, in the controlled experiment presented in Sect. 4, we targeted participants with no specific knowledge of access control, we only considered the conjunction ($\land$) and disjunction ($\lor$) operators, corresponding to the XACML AllOf and AnyOf elements, respectively. We leave the study of more complex logical operators for future work. We use a strong Kleene interpretation for the logical operators, following the PTaCL and XACML semantics: given a request q, and two targets t_1 and t_2, the target $t = t_1 \land t_2$ evaluates to 1 if both t_1 and t_2 evaluates to 1, to 0 if either t_1 or t_2 evaluates to 0, or to $\bot$ otherwise. Similarly, the target $t = t_1 \lor t_2$ evaluates to 1 if either t_1 or t_2 evaluates to 1, to 0 if both t_1 and t_2 evaluates to 0, or to $\bot$ otherwise.

An access rule is defined as a tuple (d, t), where d is a decision (either Permit or Deny) and t is a target. Given a request q, a rule (d, t) evaluates to d if t evaluates to 1, to NA (Not-Applicable) if t evaluates to 0, to Indet(P)[4] if $d =$ Permit and t evaluates to $\bot$, or to Indet(D) if $d =$ Deny and t evaluates to $\bot$.

Table 1. Evaluation of the healthcare policy example on some selected values for each atomic target, where each row corresponds to a different access request [26].

Targets				Rules		Policy
t_1	t_2	t_3	$t_2 \lor t_3$	r_1	r_2	p
1	1	1	1	Deny	Permit	Deny
0	1	1	1	NA	Permit	Permit
0	0	0	0	NA	NA	NA
0	$\bot$	0	$\bot$	NA	Indet(P)	Indet(P)
$\bot$	1	1	1	Indet(D)	Permit	Indet(PD)
$\bot$	0	0	0	Indet(D)	NA	Indet(D)

An access policy is a collection of rules, composed together with a composition operator. We implemented in VisABAC the six main XACML operators: permit-overrides (POV), deny-overrides (DOV), permit-unless-deny (PUD), deny-unless-permit (DUP), first-applicable (FA), only-one-applicable (OOA). We refer to the main documentation of XACML or for instance to [27] for the full definitions of these operators[5].

The example policy given above can be formally defined as follows: let $t_1 =$ (PATIENT,disagrees), $t_2 =$ (HOSPITAL,agrees) and $t_3 =$ (SURGEON,agrees) be atomic targets, $r_1 =$ (Deny, t_1) and $r_2 =$ (Permit, $t_2 \lor t_3$) be access rules, and $p =$ DOV(r_1, r_2) the access policy. The evaluations of these elements are presented

---

[4] For the sake of compactness, we abbreviate the XACML Indeterminate extended decisions to Indet.

[5] Also available with VisABAC documentation: http://homepages.cs.ncl.ac.uk/charl es.morisset/visabac/visualiser/resources/pages/help.html.

220   C. Morisset and D. Sanchez

in Table 1. It is worth observing that this simple policy can in practice evaluate to every possible XACML decision, depending on the values of the atomic targets.

2.2 Visualisation for Access Control

As previously stated, cognitive overload is a major issue in access control policy design, deployment and maintenance and visualisation techniques could ease those processes; unfortunately, not all visualisation mechanisms are helpful since many of them grow too large for human cognition[6]. There exist a rich literature for visualisation in security, however, few approaches deal with Attribute-based Access Control, and these approaches tend to work on the structure of the policy itself, such as VisPE [29], rather than on policy evaluation.

In the following subsections we summarise different visualisation techniques, some of them actively applied into access control, that were considered in the process of building VisABAC.

Euler Diagrams [13] visually represent containment, intersection and exclusion using closed curves. They are largely used in math to represent set operations and deductive reasoning [41,44] and were the first kind of diagrams considered as VisABAC framework. Security lends naturally to this kind of visualisation since policies can be represented in terms of relationship sets and they have proved [38] to effectively visualise thousands of elements if the set intersection are simple; however, the method becomes almost unreadable when a low count of elements have complex relationships among them. Euler diagrams prove to be very inspiring in the prototype designed but they were not implemented since they could be particularly difficult to draw automatically [46].

Grids are matrices with policies along rows and resources as columns; results of the evaluation of access to resources are placed in intersections. For example, [37] propose the use of multi-level grids to visualise results of multiple types of access control policy analysis and authoring. This approach is very simple to implement yet very powerful; however it does not take advantage of many visualisation concepts and it is very space consuming.

Graphs are used to represent access policies. [25] explores them visually in operational situations with its RubaViz prototype; however, its main use has been as memory structures. [18], for instance, uses Multi-Terminal Binary Decision Diagrams (MTBDDs), as a way to model XACML policies in Margrave (a proposed software tool developed in Scheme). Even though it heavily uses

---

[6] As a side note, the abstractions and simplifications commonly used in visual techniques designed for humans, can also be useful to computers, presenting even formal proof of the correctness and normalisation of policies. For example, in [35] Graph theory is used to validate policies and in [30] decision diagrams are used to accelerate XACML speed evaluation; none of them show any visuals to users.

graphs, no visual representation is derived from its internal structure since even the memory arrangement of a very simple policy can generate a confusing graph for humans. As a consequence, a standard Graph visualisation was discarded in the early stages of the process, even though there are many interesting tools such as Gephi [5] which are worth to be considered in future research.

Shortcomings of the Graph approach can also be appreciated in PRISM (PRIvacy-Aware Secure Monitoring), a software tool that proposes an architecture to mediate between information sources and entities on a network presented by [28]. Access Policies controlled with this interesting visual editor provides user-friendly administration of complex X.509 certificates[7] by users with no particular expertise [28]. The interface lays out many instruments to interact with the graph, being possible zoom-in/out, rotate and navigate. As a drawback this kind of representation can become unreadable as the number of policies increases and the user can easily get lost inside the graphical representation. PRISM tries to minimise this by including a birds-eye view.

Trees are being timidly studied as a way to visually find conflicts inside access policies; this seems surprising since trees are used to create XACML policies itself and it is the preferred method for explaining XACML policies in the OASIS specification [39]. [42] explore this approach for very light graphs in its XACML Viz prototype. [35] uses trees (Matching tree and Combining Tree) to optimise the evaluation of applicable rules in an access policy engine called XEngine. This tool is not aimed at visualisation but uses visual concepts and matches internal structures directly to trees representations. Illustrations were used as inspirations for the prototype.

Semantic Substrates   [9] uses spatial representation to group common attributes by regions. [33, 34] propose a visualisation toolkit called "Policy Visualisation Framework (PVF)" which extends XACML to support RBAC. It aims at providing a clearer representation than a conventional role-permission tree graph, and it seems particularly useful when combining different policies. This visualisation technique mimics three electronic breadboards that represents user, role and permission. Nodes inside each breadboard are drawn as circles, squares and triangles; they are interconnected by red, green and blue lines (wires) which assign user-role, role-permission and role-mapping relationship respectively. Hierarchy is achieved by arrows in the relationships [33, 34]. This technique has been successful when dealing with a relatively small number of policies but it has been insufficient with heavily dense policy graphs [51]. As a consequence, [51] propose complementing it with another techniques such as adjacency matrices.

---

[7] [28] indicates that future works is necessary in order to make PRISM a general purpose access control administration tool capable to support alternatives representations such as XACML.

Adjacency Matrices are widely used in graph visualisation because they allow a clear understanding of dense relationship structures. However, according [51] do not favoured them when dealing with hierarchical security relationships. As a consequence, [51] use them as a complementary representation to Semantic Substrate when visualising compliance of security policies in SELinux. Adjacency Matrices were discarded as a technique since they are not expressive enough.

Treemaps [16] visualise hierarchical tree structures using a root rectangle that contains all nodes of a given tree. Each subsequent level of the tree structure divides the above square according to a particular attribute of a node, such as size. [34] proposes treemaps to complement Semantic Substrates instead of adjacency matrices to form macro and micro vision respectively. It aims at the analysis of access control polices of RBAC model when multi-domain information is exchanged. Treemaps offer a perfect match between access policies and efficient space utilisation. They are pleasant to the eye and can provide interactivity. They were proposed for the prototype and survived along the first stages of implementation; unfortunately, they became difficult to understand as the number of policies increased and were finally discarded after pilot testing. Pictures of animated treemaps can be seen in Figs. 2 and 3.

Circle Packing [50] is very similar in concept to Treemaps, as it was inspired by them. As a marked difference, it uses circles instead of rectangles which give them a lower space efficiency ratio; however, they express more clearly the hierarchy they represent. Figure 1 shows a three-level Circle Packing diagram.

Even though Circle Packing may seem at first glance as Euler diagrams (or a type of Euler diagram like Venn), they are different in concept as well as in properties. For example, Circle Packing do not comply with many of the mathematical Euler characteristics, such as the presence of unique labels or crossing policies (Circle Packs do not intersect lines, while Euler diagrams do) [46]. However, for the purpose of VisABAC they provide the understandability of Euler representation with the ease of use and programmability of Treemaps. Additionally, Circle Packing provides clear containment —as Euler diagrams— but are space efficient. This is a huge benefit when comparing them with Trees, Grids and Graphs. [50] have shown with a file visualisation tool (FVT) that it is possible to handle efficiently thousands of nodes with this method. However, to the

Fig. 1. Simple Circle Packing Diagram [50]. Level 0 is painted light grey. Level 1 is painted green. Level 3 is painted red. (Color figure online)

best of our knowledge, Circle Packing has never been used in the context of access control priory to the VisABAC [26] implementation.

3   VisABAC

In this section, we first explain the process with which we have designed VisABAC, after which we describe the tool itself[8].

3.1   Creating VisABAC

In general, visualisation is not only a set of techniques but also a process [24] therefore, in order to achieve a successful representation, it is important to work closely with users affected by the shortcomings of traditional analysis. Hence, we work closely with 5 members of our research group using a *participatory design* [40]. That expertise targeted essential usability aspects and the feedback acquired (*heuristic approach* [40]) was complemented by *heuristic evaluation* and informal/formal evaluation by recruited participants.

VisABAC was developed using rapid-prototyping methodology [19]. The process involved three stages: throw-away, evolution and refinement.

The *Throw-away stage* involved the creation of over 70 prototypes with no functionality using presentation software to explore almost all ideas explained in the Sect. 2.2. Some approaches, such as: graphs, hierarchical graphs, hypergraphs, Euler diagrams, and binary decision diagrams (BDD), have already been identified as too complex to implement, visualise or unsuitable to be of any practical use [14,15,18,25]. Some candidates, on the other hand, were particularly promising, including trees and treemaps, which have been applied previously to security visualisation. Figure 2 shows an early prototype. In this stage, as well as the next one, we used simplified access control policies expressed as logical boolean algebra.

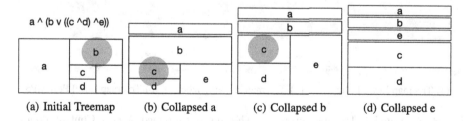

(a) Initial Treemap   (b) Collapsed a   (c) Collapsed b   (d) Collapsed e

Fig. 2. Early prototype: (a) shows the initial stage with a logic equation representing an access control policy. Tapping on (a) advances to (b) and successively.

---

[8] VisABAC is available for demonstration at http://homepages.cs.ncl.ac.uk/charles. morisset/visabac.

The *Evolutionary stage* was started once some ideas were identified as possibly useful. Under this stage many limited functional prototype were created over a quick iteration process. These high-fidelity prototypes were developed on Javascript using the D3 library, coded using NetBeans 8.1 and displayed on a web browser (primarily Mozilla Firefox 47). These prototypes did not evaluate a full ABAC policy and instead used a simplified access control policy handcrafted in JSON. During this stage two very interesting prototypes emerged based on treemaps and trees. However, some limitations were found during the participatory process, even after trying to refine them as *zoomable treemaps* (Fig. 3) and *collapsible trees* (Fig. 4). The most relevant limitations were:

- Users easily forgot the evaluation result of a particular policy they were inspecting and had to waste time by going back to a previous level.
- The relationship between screen state utilisation and navigability was highlighted as very important by participants. Screen utilisation for collapsible trees was very low (more than 50% is background)[9] and caused excessive panning when dealing with large policies; on the other hand, zoomable treemaps proposed a full screen state utilisation but users got lost inside the policy quickly.

A tradeoff between efficiency and usability was found in *circle packing*, a visualisation technique criticised [50] for not being as space efficient as treemaps but praised for providing a better hierarchy illusion than those obtained by, for

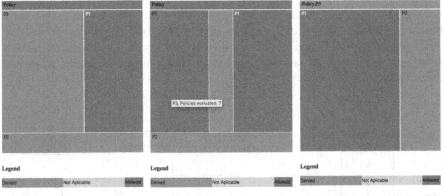

(a) Treemap Level Policy   (b) Treemap showing label   (c) Treemap Level Policy.P3

Fig. 3. Zoommable Treemap prototype showing a simplified Access Control Policy (Policy) composed of 3 sub-policies (P1, P2 and P3). (a) shows the initial Treemap level O. (b) Hovering over P3 rectangle policy, the label reveals information about was performed the evaluation for this policy (How the colour was obtained). (c) tapping on P3 shows the immediate interior P3 level (Policy.P3).

---

[9] A prototype version of VisABAC with collapsible trees is available alongside the main tool, illustrating the poor screen utilisation.

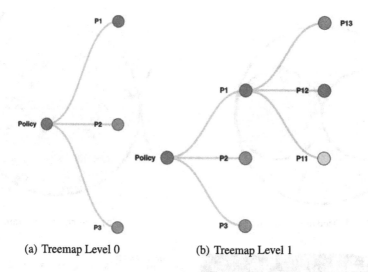

(a) Treemap Level 0   (b) Treemap Level 1

Fig. 4. Collapsible Tree prototype showing a simplified access control policy (Policy) composed of 3 sub-policies (P1, P2 and P3) (a) shows Policy with first level displayed (P1, P2 and P3). (b) shows P1 policy sublevel with their corresponding sub-sub-policies (P11, P12 and P13).

example, treemap representations. A late prototype of this stage was embedded into a FileMaker Pro application to combine an early version of the testing module with a database.

The *refinement stage* was started once the feasibility of the app was determined as well as a testing procedure could be applied. In this stage full access control policies could be edited and evaluated. Also, the FileMaker testing module was superseded by a Javascript one, making the new application completely web based. This final prototype became VisABAC and will be described in Sect. 3.2.

3.2   VisABAC Interface

The VisABAC interface is designed as a web page component and, as such, runs on any web browser. The interface consists of four main components, which we now detail, using the visualisation of the policy described in Sect. 2.1 as an example (Fig. 5).

The *Policy component* (Fig. 5(d)) is a textual box, directly editable from the browser, which contains the definition of the policy following the syntax described in Sect. 2.1. This definition can either be typed in, loaded from a set of existing samples, or loaded from a file. These rules are automatically parsed into JavaScript Object Notation (JSON), where the text of each rule is identified by its name. For instance, the policy described in Sect. 2.1 would correspond to the object:

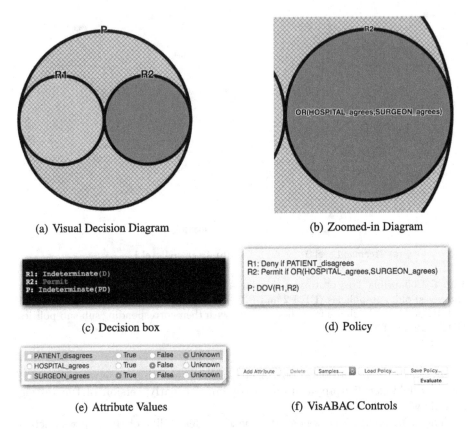

(a) Visual Decision Diagram

(b) Zoomed-in Diagram

```
R1: Indeterminate(D)
R2: Permit
P: Indeterminate(PD)
```

```
R1: Deny if PATIENT_disagrees
R2: Permit if OR(HOSPITAL_agrees,SURGEON_agrees)

P: DOV(R1,R2)
```

(c) Decision box

(d) Policy

(e) Attribute Values

(f) VisABAC Controls

Fig. 5. (a) and (c) show the evaluation of the policy P, represented in (d), when attributes are set as (e) (fifth row of Table 1). The largest circle (P) is filled in with a grey pattern, since it evaluates to Indet(PD), the circle for R1 is filled in with a red pattern, since it evaluates to Indet(D), and the circle for R2 is filled in green, since it evaluates to Permit. (f) shows the screen section that provides common controls, such as Add Attribute, Delete Attribute, Samples, Load Policy, Save Policy and Evaluate. (Color figure online)

```
policyRules=
{"R1": "Permit if PATIENT_disagrees",
 "R2": "Permit if OR(HOSPITAL_agrees,
                     SURGEON_agrees)"
 "P": "DOV(R1,R2)"}
```

The *Attributes component* (Fig. 5(e)) allows the user to set the value for each attribute value: true, false, or unknown. For instance, Fig. 5(e) corresponds to a request where we do not know if the patient disagrees to the access, we know that the hospital does not agree to the access, and that the surgeon agrees, which corresponds to the fifth row of Table 1.

The *Decision component* (Fig. 5(c)) lists, for each rule in the Policy component, the decision obtained for that rule. These decisions are obtained by iterating through the `policyRules` object, following the evaluation rules established in [12]. The evaluation returns an object with the same structure, but where each rule has been replaced by its decision. In the case where a rule is not well-formed (e.g., missing reference, syntax error), it evaluates to Indeterminate(PD). Note that cycles in rule definitions are not currently detected, and an error would occur.

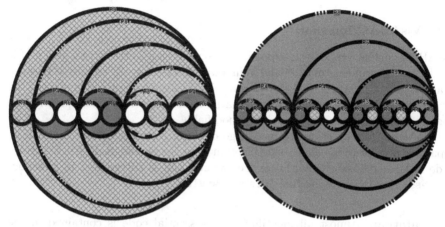

(a) Policy with 9 atomic rules and 9 binary poli- (b) Variation of 6(a) with sub-policies used
cies.   multiple times.

Fig. 6. Circle packing visualisation of complex policies in VisABAC [26].

Finally, the *Visual component* (Fig. 5(a)) uses Zoomable Circle Packing to visually explore access control policies, using the D3.js library[10]. The zoomable aspect is a crucial one, as it allows the space occupied by the visualisation to remain constant. A *circle* is either a rule or a composition of rules grouped by a composition operators. As a consequence, a policy comprised of sub-policies is represented by circles containing sub-circles in a similar hierarchy as the given policy. The visual diagram is dynamic, and is updated when the policy or the attributes are updated and a new evaluation is calculated. Each circle is defined by two characteristics:

- The colour, which matches the result of the policy/rule they represent: green is for Permit, red for Deny, white for NA, patterned-green for Indet(P), patterned-red for Indet(D), and patterned-grey for Indet(PD). We have also developed a colour deficiency mode, which caters for different types of colour deficiencies. In addition, since these colours are set through a simple CSS (Cascading Style Sheet), they could be user configurable.

---

[10] https://d3js.org.

- The line pattern which matches the operator used. In particular, we use full lines for Deny-overrides and dashed lines for Permit-overrides. The lines for the other operators can be found in the online help of the tool.

For instance, Fig. 5(a) shows that *Level 0* (P) represents the whole policy by the most outer circle line; *Level 1* (R1 and R2) represent the first level of the tree policy with smaller circles inside. A zoom on the inner circles would display their respective targets, since they are atomic policies. Figure 6 illustrates more complex examples of ABAC policies.

3.3 VisABAC Internals

VisABAC current version was coded in Javascript using NetBeans 8.2 on a multi-platform environment (macOS and Windows). Javascript was employed because it allows code transparency —source code could be easily explored and corrected by anyone who uses the application in a modern browser—. Consequently, the code is heavily commented and easily modifiable.

VisABAC follows standard web page creation conventions and, as such, it separates presentation elements description from the engine itself. All VisABAC code is located inside `visualiser/resources` and is categorised in `classes`, `images`, `libraries`, `pages`, `scripts` and `styles`.

Presentation. Almost all identifiable non-essential code is contained in the folders `images`, `pages`, `scripts` and `styles`. Files contained in each one of them are pretty much self explanatory and provide web page structure and non-essential elements (such as about, help, preferences, etc.); especial consideration is required only to the following items:

- `pages/VisualiserForm.html` contains the essential visual framework of the pilot VisABAC application and it could be modified to apply the engine to different products.
- `scripts/visualiserForm.js` contains the scripts that send messages to the VisABAC engine.
- `styles/logicCirclePacking.css` contains common styles used in the logic Circle Packing visualisation technique regardles of colour deficiency preferences; this is an essential VisABAC component.
- `styles/ visualiserForm.css`, `visualiserForm_ColorNormal.css` and `visualiserForm_ColorDeficiency.css` are used by visualiser Form.html.

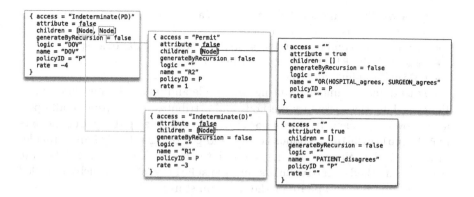

Fig. 7. Internal Tree structure formed by recurrent `Node` objects (`JSON` objects). The tree structure corresponds to the same sample shown in Fig. 5.

Engine. Essential code is contained in the folder `libraries` (only carrying `d3.v3.js`) and `classes`; the latest contains the following:

- Visualiser.js This is the class that creates the visualiser object. It stores all code that creates on screen the interface elements. It starts by `parsinPol-icyRules` and storing as an internal attribute the policy passed by the user (`policyRules` and `policyAttributes`). The code also draws the screen components according to the preferences, picking the right colour mode.
- LogicCirclePacking_d3v3.js Very important class in which *zoomable circle packing* happens; it receives a JSON tree that represents the policy previously evaluated (Fig. 7 shows a sample representation). The evaluation are rates in the domain $[-5, -4, -3, -2, -1, 0, 1]$ to be corresponded by the D3 library into the range [indeterminateDColour, indeterminatePColour, indeterminatePDColour, indeterminateDColour, notApplicableColour, denyColour, permitColour]. These colours, as well as additional patterns are defined in this class to correctly represent permits, denies and indeterminations (indeterminate permit, indeterminate deny and indeterminate permit-deny), (Fig. 9 shows the indeterminate patterns). D3 uses a `svg` to plot the circle packing using very concise instructions, applying the same presentation function to all nodes of the tree almost simultaneously. Appearance functions are appended to lines as well and according to each `rate`, a particular stroke is use to draw a circle line. Figure 8 shows lines and its significance. This class also contains the zoom parameters required by the D3 library that allows policy navigation.
- Node.js is a class that specifies a non reducible element that recursively combined creates the policy tree. Figure 7 shows five samples of them forming a simple tree; most important attributes are:
  - `access` e.g. `Permit, Deny, IndeterminatePD`...
  - `attribute` used to mark if it is an attribute node `true` or `false`.
  - `children` array of dependant node operations.

- generateByRecursion flag (true or false) to mark an auxiliar node created by a recursive evaluation.
  - logic stores composition operators, e.g. DOV, POV, FA, OOA, etc.
  - name e.g DOV, R1, etc. or any attribute name.
  - policyID unique identifier.
  - rate domain number resulting from node and its children evaluation.
- Policy.js This class provides methods and attributes to encapsulate all operations over a policy. It stores policy, policyRules, policyAttributesByRule, policyRulesOrCompositions and policyTreeInJSON and provides means to update them according to user interactions. The gist of the class are two main methods resolveRules and parsePolicyToTree which are called whenever there is an update or the program starts.
  resolveRules iterates through all policy rules (keys) to "solve" values, e.g.

```
policyRules={"PA": "Permit if attribute1",
             "PB": "Deny if attribute2",
             "PC": "DOV(PA,PB)"}
```

will be transformed into:

```
_policy={"PA": "Permit",
         "PB": "Deny",
         "PC": "Permit"}
```

```
_policyAttributesByRule={"PA": "attribute1",
                         "PB": "attribute2",
                         "PC": "DOV(PA,PB)"}
```

These two objects _policy and _policyAttributesByRule allow direct addressing either to results or attributes when parsePolicyTree is called. resolveRules also encapsulates a series of procedures (resolveLogic, resolveRule, resolveRuleOrComposition, resolveAttributesByRule) that handle the policy evaluation according to user inputting.
parsePolicyToTree is the entry point to a series of methods, starting by parseCompositionToTree that creates a tree using the policy. parseCompositionToTree uses a series of stacks and recursion to evaluate fragments of the policy. Stacks have to be used in order to respect parenthesis hierarchy that might exist in a complex policy. Depending on complexity, also recursive procedures could be called. During this procedure, numeric rates are assigned to the nodes that are being created.
- Sample.js is a support class used to store attribute values and logic inside the Policy.js class.

4   Evaluation

VisABAC, presented in the previous section, is relatively easy to use, since it is defined as an in-browser application. The input language for policies is relatively straight-forward from an Attribute-based Access Control perspective.

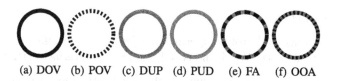

(a) DOV   (b) POV   (c) DUP   (d) PUD   (e) FA   (f) OOA

Fig. 8. Line conventions used by VisABAC to represent operations: (a) Deny overrides (b) Permit overrides (c) Deny unless permit (d) Permit unless deny (e) First applicable (f) Only one applicable. (c) and (d) may look similar in printing due to scale but they are clearly different in the application.

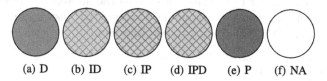

(a) D   (b) ID   (c) IP   (d) IPD   (e) P   (f) NA

Fig. 9. Operations colour conventions used by VisABAC: (a) Deny (b) Indeterminate deny (c) Indeterminate permit (d) Indeterminate permit deny (e) Permit (f) Not applicable.

More importantly, the D3.js library for Circle Packing is particularly fluid, making the tool very responsive. Our participatory design elicited Circle Packing as the preferred visualisation technique, compared with other techniques such as foldable trees or treemaps. However, we are also interested in understanding whether VisABAC is effectively *usable*, i.e, whether its proposed graphical representation could help users in their tasks.

Nielsen and Levy argue that usability should be measured according to *subjective user preferences* and *objective performance measures*, since, in some cases, users have favoured interfaces that are measurably worse for them [32]. Similarly, MacLean et al. [23] found that subjects inclined towards a proven slower data entry method would still prefer it as long as it was not 20% slower than the faster method.

Hence, in addition to a subjective user preference questionnaire, we want to design an objective performance measure for using VisABAC. To the best of our knowledge, there is no standard benchmark for the usability of tools for access control policies, and therefore we define a new method in this paper. Roughly speaking, we give the user a fixed policy, a valuation for the attributes, and ask the user to change this valuation in order for the policy to evaluate to a specified decision. Our hypothesis is that the faster the user is able to do this task, the more they understand the policy, and thus the better is the tool with which the user interacts. We now describe this experimental settings, and we discuss the limitations of our approach in Sect. 6.

4.1 User Interface

We conduct a controlled-group experiment, where users in different groups see a different user interface. We define two different user interfaces (UI):

- The *Graphics UI* is an extension of the VisABAC interface, described in Sect. 3.2, with the addition of two main elements: the *context* box, which introduces the context of the policy, in English; and the *question* box, which specifies the expected decision. The boxes for the policy, the attributes, the decision box, and the visual decision diagram, are as described in Fig. 5[11].
- The *Text UI* is similar to the Graphics UI, as the notable exception that the visual decision diagram box is missing. However, the user still has access to the evaluation of the policy with the decision box.

4.2 Policy Question

The aim of either UI described above is to answer a question, given a context and a policy. Ideally, we would like to ask questions related to any aspect of the editing or maintenance of a policy. However, we believe that this would introduce too many different dimensions to control, and we focus instead on questions related to policy evaluation. We leave for future work the study of more complex questions. The context is a simple description of the motivation behind the policy, for instance, for the policy described in Sect. 2.1 and Fig. 5, the context is:

Releasing medical records in a certain hospital requires compliance with an access control policy. The system checks events with statements that return True or False if the forms have been filled and validated by the corresponding departments.

The attribute values are initially set so that the policy evaluates to Indet(PD), and the question is:

Can you change the radio buttons so that PC evaluates to Deny?

The user can change any radio button, and then click on a button *Evaluate*, which refreshes the different boxes with the new policy evaluation. There is no limit on the authorised number of evaluation per question, and they can go to the next question by clicking on the *Submit* button. They were also instructed they could go to the next question at any time if they did not wish to submit an answer for the current question, and this would be recorded as a wrong answer.

The experiment consists of a total of 32 sub-questions, grouped in 8 main questions. All sub-questions within a single main question have the same context, and only differ on minor details. For instance, a sub-question in the same group than the policy above use the First-Applicable (FA) operator to combine R1 and R2 instead of the Deny-Overrides (DOV). The main questions are denoted from Q1 to Q8, the sub-questions for the main question Q_i are denoted from Q_ia to Q_id.

---

[11] The full test with both interfaces is available from the front page of the tool.

4.3   Protocol

Each recruited participant P_i goes through the following steps:

1. After reading and signing the participant consent form, P_i is randomly assigned to either the *Text group* (the control group) or the *Graphics group* (the tested group).
2. P_i is presented with a short introduction about ABAC, going through a simple policy example (similar to that described in Sect. 2.1). At this stage, they can use the Text UI on the introduced example (the Graphics UI is only introduced in Step 4 for the Graphics group) and ask any question. They are also explained what is expected of them and informed that their time will be recorded. They are also informed that some policies are on purpose hard to analyse, and that we are measuring how the interface helps them, rather than assessing them. This step takes in average 10 min.
3. Once they feel confident about using the tool, they start answering the first series of main questions, Q1 and Q2 (8 sub-questions in total), using the Text UI, regardless of their assigned group.
4. After Q2, if P_i is in the Text group, they keep answering Q3 to Q8 (24 sub-questions in total); if P_i is in the Graphics group, they switch to the Graphics UI, and they are briefly introduced with the specifics of the Circle Packing representation; they then answer Q3 to Q8 using the Graphics UI.
5. After Q8, P_i is debriefed, and explained the purpose of the experiment. According to recommended practices [31], a £10 Amazon voucher is given as compensation for their time.

The entire protocol was designed to take, in average, between 30 to 45 min, including 20 min of actual assessment. The time to answer each question was visible to the participant, and although there was no strict countdown, to avoid adding time pressure, participants were encouraged to move on to the next question if they were spending more than 5 min on a sub-question (which happened in only one instance). The experiment took place in the same office and the same computer (a 27″ iMac), in order to control environmental changes. Participants were asked about colour deficiency, but none was indicated in our experiment.

4.4   Objective Performance Measure

Intuitively, we want to compare the time taken by users in the two different groups, in order to evaluate whether the Graphics UI was beneficial. However, performance measure among different individuals varies according to the capabilities of each one, and the nature of the experiment makes it hard to ensure the distribution of users in the groups is consistent with user capabilities. As a consequence, a procedure of normalisation had to be performed in order to compare data.

The selected normalisation value was the inverse of the number of seconds each participant spent on solving Q2 (i.e., the total time spent on subquestions

Q2a, Q2b, Q2c and Q2d). We denote this as the *normalisation coefficient* α_i, for each participant P_i. Subsequently, the time taken by P_i to answer each question is normalised by multiplying it by α_i. If this value is lower than 1, this implies the subject performed a particular question faster than Q_2 while a larger value represents the opposite. For instance, if P_1 took 4 s to complete Q2 ($\alpha_1 = 0.25$) and 6 s to complete Q3, their normalised time for Q3 is 1.5; if P_2 took 16 s to complete Q2 ($\alpha_2 = 0.0625$) and 23 s to complete Q3, their normalised time for Q3 is 1.4375. In other words, even though, absolutely speaking, P_2 was slower than P_1 for Q3, they were comparatively faster.

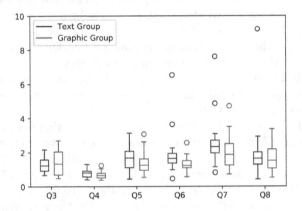

Fig. 10. Boxplots comparison of normalised times for questions Q3 to Q8 between the Text and Graphics groups (lower is better). The body of each box represents the intervals between the first (q_1) and third quartiles (q_3), the bar represents the mean, the whiskers represent the maximal and minimal values between $q_3 + 1.5(q_3 - q_1)$ and $q_1 - 1.5(q_3 - q_1)$, fliers represent points outside of this range.

This choice for the normalisation function comes from the fact that we have designed different questions with different levels of difficulty, Q7 being the most difficult for the full details of Q7). Hence, we expect that all users will spend more time to answer Q7 than Q2, and we want to measure this difference, rather than measuring directly the difference between users. Q2 was selected as the normalisation value since all participants, regardless of their group, had to do it with the Text UI, and it was assumed some familiarity was already gained by the user after performing Q1, since Q1 and Q2 have a similar complexity level.

4.5   Subjective User Preferences

Subjective Testing was performed on users who were exposed to the visualisation technique. A relatively standard questionnaire was presented to collect their impressions using a *Likert scale* [32] after finishing the objective testing.

5   Results

We recruited 32 participants over 4 weeks, mostly among undergraduate Computer Science students, with no formal knowledge of ABAC, and randomly assigned to the groups (16 participants each). The aim of this study was to assess the impact of circle packing, so we targeted a relatively uniform group in terms of prior knowledge, rather than experts in Access Control. Figure 10 shows the normalised time average of participants for each question, including wrong answers (there are 8 wrong answers in each group). The mean for the Graphics group is lower (i.e., better) from Q4 to Q8 (comparatively to the time taken for Q2) compared to the Text group. The mean of Graphics group is higher for Q3, which could indicate a small learning curve with the Graphics UI.

Altogether, the normalised mean time for participants in the Text group to answer all questions from Q3 to Q8 is $m_t = 10.38$ (with a confidence interval of $[7.88, 12.88]$ and a standard deviation of $\sigma_t = 5.10$). In comparison, the normalised mean time for participants in the Graphics group is $m_g = 8.58$ (with a confidence interval of $[7.33, 9.83]$ and a standard deviation of $\sigma_g = 2.55$). This allows us to conclude that the effect size[12] is 0.44, which is traditionally seen as a small to medium effect size [10].

In addition, the results of the user preferences survey showed that 82.35% of participants described the presence of the visualisation as useful; 76.47% of participants felt more confident operating the policy with the presence of the graph and 47.06% agree and 35.39% agree to some extent that the presence of the graph makes them feel they understand the policy better. Some questions were however very conclusive, e.g. if complex mental operations were needed, which could indicate this question was not well formulated.

6   Conclusions

Building a usable visualisation tool for access control policies is a challenging task, as it requires: (i) to have a good understanding of the existing literature on visualisation; (ii) to be based on a clear semantics for the access control language; (iii) to use a participatory design process; (iv) to be validated with a user study. We have successfully followed these steps in the design of VisABAC, which is the first visualisation tool for attribute-based access control policies, where composition operations seems to be adequately represented and details are disclosed on demand thanks to the zooming and progressive disclosure of tags. VisABAC also provides interactivity to the user and increments the exploring of the policy in a graphical manner. The extensive literature survey presented in Sect. 2.2 is, to the best of our knowledge, the first survey on visualisation technique for access control policies.

The participatory design process was positive, and most users liked the concept very much, found it intuitive and easy to use, although they remarked that

---

[12] Cohen's effect is computed as $(m_t - m_g)$ divided by $\sqrt{(\sigma_t^2 + \sigma_g^2)/2}$.

some training could have decrease their response time. Crucially, the experiment showed a small to medium effect size [26], allowing us to conclude that VisABAC improves the handling of attribute-based access control policies for a population with no formal training. Of course, at this stage, it is not yet clear whether VisABAC can provide a significant contribution to access control experts, but we believe the tool as presented here and our results pave the way towards an experiment at a larger scale.

Future Work. VisABAC is specifically designed to be open and easy to extend. The underlying infrastructure uses HTML (for the basic interface), JSON (for the encoding of the policies), and Javascript (for the evaluation of policies and the visualisation elements), making it possible to consider other visualisation techniques. In particular, the collapsible tree approach (see Sect. 3.1) has received some positive response during the participatory design phase of VisABAC (policies tend to be naturally seen as trees), but suffers from a space occupation issue. The textual input for VisABAC can also be straightforwardly extended, for instance by parsing directly XACML policies, making it possible to compare real XACML cases against their visualisation (and not synthetic ones), and include authoring tools such as VisPE [29].

Acknowledgements. This work was partially supported by the UK National Centre for Cyber-Security, in the context of the Research Institute in the Science of Cyber-Security. The authors would also like to thank Nick Holliman from Newcastle University for very useful discussions on visualisation techniques.

References

1. Alavi, R., Islam, S., Mouratidis, H.: A conceptual framework to analyze human factors of Information Security Management System (ISMS) in organizations. In: Tryfonas, T., Askoxylakis, I. (eds.) HAS 2014. LNCS, vol. 8533, pp. 297–305. Springer, Cham (2014). https://doi.org/10.1007/978-3-319-07620-1_26
2. Ashley, P., Hada, S., Karjoth, G., Powers, C., Schunter, M.: Enterprise privacy authorization language (EPAL). IBM Research (2003)
3. Barker, S.: The next 700 access control models or a unifying meta-model? In: SACMAT, pp. 187–196. ACM (2009)
4. Barrett, R., Kandogan, E., Maglio, P.P., Haber, E.M., Takayama, L.A., Prabaker, M.: Field studies of computer system administrators: analysis of system management tools and practices. In: Proceedings of the 2004 ACM Conference on Computer Supported Cooperative Work, CSCW 2004, pp. 388–395 (2004). https://doi.org/10.1145/1031607.1031672
5. Bastian, M., Heymann, S., Jacomy, M.: Gephi: an open source software for exploring and manipulating networks. In: Third International AAAI Conference on Weblogs and Social Media (2009)
6. Bauer, L., Garriss, S., Reiter, M.K.: Detecting and resolving policy misconfigurations in access-control systems. In: SACMAT, pp. 185–194. ACM (2008)

7. Becker, J., Heddier, M., Öksüz, A., Knackstedt, R.: The effect of providing visualizations in privacy policies on trust in data privacy and security. In: 2014 47th Hawaii International Conference on System Sciences, pp. 3224–3233 (2014). https://doi.org/10.1109/HICSS.2014.399

8. Benantar, M.: Access Control Systems: Security, Identity Management and Trust Models. Springer, Boston (2005). https://doi.org/10.1007/0-387-27716-1

9. Card, S.K., Mackinlay, J.D., Shneiderman, B. (eds.): Readings in Information Visualization: Using Vision to Think. Morgan Kaufmann Publishers Inc., San Francisco (1999)

10. Cohen, J.: Statistical Power Analysis for the Behavioral Sciences, pp. 20–26. Lawrence Earlbaum Associates, Hillsdale (1988)

11. Crampton, J., Morisset, C.: PTaCL: a language for attribute-based access control in open systems. In: Degano, P., Guttman, J.D. (eds.) POST 2012. LNCS, vol. 7215, pp. 390–409. Springer, Heidelberg (2012). https://doi.org/10.1007/978-3-642-28641-4_21

12. Crampton, J., Morisset, C., Zannone, N.: On missing attributes in access control: Non-deterministic and probabilistic attribute retrieval. In: SACMAT, pp. 99–109. ACM (2015)

13. Euler, L.: Lettres a une princesse d'allemagne. Sur divers sujets de physique et de philosophie, vol. 2. Birkhauser, Basel (1761)

14. Fisler, K., Krishnamurthi, S., Meyerovich, L.A., Tschantz, M.C.: Verification and change-impact analysis of access-control policies. In: Proceedings of the 27th International Conference on Software Engineering, ICSE 2005, pp. 196–205. ACM, New York (2005). https://doi.org/10.1145/1062455.1062502

15. Heydon, A., Maimone, M.W., Tygar, J.D., Wing, J.M., Zaremski, A.M.: Miro: visual specification of security. IEEE Trans. Softw. Eng. 16(10), 1185–1197 (1990). https://doi.org/10.1109/32.60298

16. Johnson, B., Shneiderman, B.: Tree-maps: a space-filling approach to the visualization of hierarchical information structures. In: Proceedings of the 2nd Conference on Visualization 1991, Los Alamitos, CA, USA, pp. 284–291. IEEE (1991)

17. Kirlappos, I., Sasse, M.A.: What usable security really means: trusting and engaging users. In: Tryfonas, T., Askoxylakis, I. (eds.) HAS 2014. LNCS, vol. 8533, pp. 69–78. Springer, Cham (2014). https://doi.org/10.1007/978-3-319-07620-1_7

18. Kolovski, V.: Logic-based access control policy specification and management. Technical report, Department of Computer Science, University of Maryland, College Park (2007)

19. Kordon, F.: An introduction to rapid system prototyping. IEEE Trans. Softw. Eng. 28(9), 817–821 (2002). https://doi.org/10.1109/TSE.2002.1033222

20. Lacey, D.: Managing the Human Factor in Information Security: How to Win over Staff and Influence Business Managers. Wiley, Hoboken (2009)

21. Lampson, B.W.: Protection. Oper. Syst. Rev. 8(1), 18–24 (1974). https://doi.org/10.1145/775265.775268

22. Licht, D.M., Polzella, D.J., Boff, K.R.: Human factors, ergonomics and human factors engineering: an analysis of definitions. Crew System Ergonomics Information Analysis Center (1989)

23. MacLean, A., Barnard, P., Wilson, M.: Evaluating the human interface of a data entry system: user choice and performance measures yield different tradeoff functions. People Comput. Des. Interface 5, 45–61 (1985)

24. Meyer, M.: Information visualization for scientific discovery, April 2011. https://www.youtube.com/watch?v=Sua0xDCf8MA

25. Montemayor, J., Freeman, A., Gersh, J., Llanso, T., Patrone, D.: Information visualization for rule-based resource access control. In: Proceedings of International Symposium on Usable Privacy and Security (SOUPS), p. 24 (2006)

26. Morisset, C., Sanchez, D.: VisABAC: a tool for visualising ABAC policies. In: Proceedings of the 4th International Conference on Information Systems Security and Privacy - Volume 1: ICISSP, pp. 117–126. INSTICC, SciTePress (2018). https://doi.org/10.5220/0006647401170126

27. Morisset, C., Zannone, N.: Reduction of access control decisions. In: SACMAT, pp. 53–62. ACM (2014)

28. Mousas, A.S., Antonakopoulou, A., Gogoulos, F., Lioudakis, G.V., Kaklamani, D.I., Venieris, I.S.: Visualising access control: the prism approach. In: 2010 14th Panhellenic Conference on Informatics (PCI), pp. 107–111, September 2010. https://doi.org/10.1109/PCI.2010.52

29. Nergaard, H., Ulltveit-Moe, N., Gjøsæter, T.: ViSPE: a graphical policy editor for XACML. In: Camp, O., Weippl, E., Bidan, C., Aïmeur, E. (eds.) ICISSP 2015. CCIS, vol. 576, pp. 107–121. Springer, Cham (2015). https://doi.org/10.1007/978-3-319-27668-7_7

30. Ngo, C., Makkes, M.X., Demchenko, Y., de Laat, C.: Multi-data-types interval decision diagrams for XACML evaluation engine. In: 2013 Eleventh Annual International Conference on Privacy, Security and Trust (PST), pp. 257–266, July 2013. https://doi.org/10.1109/PST.2013.6596061

31. Nielsen, J.: Usability Engineering. Morgan Kaufmann Publishers Inc., San Francisco (1993)

32. Nielsen, J., Levy, J.: Measuring usability: preference vs. performance. Commun. ACM 37(4), 66–75 (1994). https://doi.org/10.1145/175276.175282

33. Pan, L., Liu, N., Zi, X.: Visualization framework for inter-domain access control policy integration. China Commun. 10(3), 67–75 (2013). https://doi.org/10.1109/CC.2013.6488831

34. Pan, L., Xu, Q.: Visualization analysis of multi-domain access control policy integration based on tree-maps and semantic substrates. Intell. Inf. Manag. 4(5), 188–193 (2012)

35. Pina Ros, S., Lischka, M., Gómez Mármol, F.: Graph-based XACML evaluation. In: Proceedings of the 17th ACM Symposium on Access Control Models and Technologies, SACMAT 2012, pp. 83–92. ACM, New York (2012). https://doi.org/10.1145/2295136.2295153

36. PwC: 2015 information security breaches survey. Technical report, HM Government and PwC Consulting and Infosecurity Europe, April 2015

37. Rao, P., Ghinita, G., Bertino, E., Lobo, J.: Visualization for access control policy analysis results using multi-level grids. In: IEEE International Symposium on Policies for Distributed Systems and Networks, pp. 25–28 (2009). https://doi.org/10.1109/POLICY.2009.29

38. Riche, N.H., Dwyer, T.: Untangling Euler diagrams. IEEE Trans. Vis. Comput. Graph. 16(6), 1090–1099 (2010). https://doi.org/10.1109/TVCG.2010.210

39. Rissanen, E., Lockhart, H., Moses, T.: XACML V3.0 administration and delegation profile version 1.0. Committee Draft 1 (2009)

40. Ritter, F.E., Baxter, G.D., Churchill, E.F.: Foundations for Designing User-Centered Systems. Springer, London (2014). https://doi.org/10.1007/978-1-4471-5134-0

41. Rodgers, P.: A survey of Euler diagrams. J. Vis. Lang. Comput. 25(3), 134–155 (2014). https://doi.org/10.1016/j.jvlc.2013.08.006

42. Rosa, W.D.: Toward visualizing potential policy conflicts in eXtensible Access Control Markup Language (XACML). Theses and dissertations, University of New Orleans, New Orleans, May 2009
43. Sackmann, S., Kähmer, M.: ExPDT: Ein policy-basierter ansatz zur automatisierung von compliance. Wirtschaftsinformatik **50**(5), 366–374 (2008)
44. Sato, Y., Mineshima, K., Takemura, R.: The efficacy of Euler and Venn diagrams in deductive reasoning: empirical findings. In: Goel, A.K., Jamnik, M., Narayanan, N.H. (eds.) Diagrams 2010. LNCS (LNAI), vol. 6170, pp. 6–22. Springer, Heidelberg (2010). https://doi.org/10.1007/978-3-642-14600-8_6
45. OASIS Standard: eXtensible Access Control Markup Language (XACML) version 2.0 (2005)
46. Stapleton, G., Zhang, L., Howse, J., Rodgers, P.: Drawing Euler diagrams with circles. In: Goel, A.K., Jamnik, M., Narayanan, N.H. (eds.) Diagrams 2010. LNCS (LNAI), vol. 6170, pp. 23–38. Springer, Heidelberg (2010). https://doi.org/10.1007/978-3-642-14600-8_7
47. Stepien, B., Matwin, S., Felty, A.: Strategies for reducing risks of inconsistencies in access control policies. In: 2010 International Conference on Availability, Reliability and Security, pp. 140-147 (2010)
48. Trudeau, S., Sinclair, S., Smith, S.W.: The effects of introspection on creating privacy policy. In: WPES 2009: Proceedings of the 8th ACM Workshop on Privacy in the Electronic Society, pp. 1–10. ACM, New York (2009). https://doi.org/10.1145/1655188.1655190
49. Vaniea, K., Ni, Q., Cranor, L., Bertino, E.: Access control policy analysis and visualization tools for security professionals. In: SOUPS Workshop (USM) (2008)
50. Wang, W., Wang, H., Dai, G., Wang, H.: Visualization of large hierarchical data by circle packing. In: Proceedings of the SIGCHI Conference on Human Factors in Computing Systems, CHI 2006, pp. 517–520. ACM, New York (2006). https://doi.org/10.1145/1124772.1124851
51. Xu, W., Shehab, M., Ahn, G.J.: Visualization based policy analysis: case study in SELinux. In: Proceedings of the 13th ACM Symposium on Access Control Models and Technologies, SACMAT 2008, pp. 165–174. ACM, New York (2008). https://doi.org/10.1145/1377836.1377863

Survey and Guidelines for the Design and Deployment of a Cyber Security Label for SMEs

Christophe Ponsard[✉] and Jeremy Grandclaudon

CETIC Research Center, Charleroi, Belgium
{christophe.ponsard,jeremy.grandclaudon}@cetic.be

Abstract. Cyber Security risks and attacks are on the rise, especially at the light of the recent events in the geopolitical landscape. Cyber attacks are not longer targeting big organisations such as governments, institutions or global companies. Smaller businesses and even citizens are now also being hit by cyber attacks, either directly or as a result of side effects. At the same time, the regulation and legislative pressure to prevent cyber attacks is increasing, especially in Europe. In order to protect Small and Medium Enterprises (SMEs), different labels, specific standards or practical guidelines are being developed. This papers makes a comparative survey of such initiatives with the aim to initiate such an approach in Belgium in a consistent way with other existing approaches and also to enable longer term convergence with a possible European scheme. Our goal is to reach enough SMEs with a basic level of cyber security and engage them in continuous improvement to keep a sustainable but efficient level of security. At a more practical level, we report about how to set up the overall organisational structures, basic management processes and some supporting tools.

1 Introduction

Our hyper-connected world has become a dangerous place for companies as any cyber incident can seriously impact their business. Cyber attacks and data breaches have been ranked as the top two threats for the past three years, according a long term survey by the Business Continuity Institute [1]. This report also reveals that large companies are more aware about those threats with about 57% of respondents showing concern. In contrast, only about one third of Small and medium-sized enterprises (SMEs) are feeling threatened.

This lack of awareness raises a lot of concerns because SMEs cannot hide any more behind the fact they are just too small to be worth being attacked as the situation has completely changed over the past few years [2]. Various sources consistently report that about half of cyber attacks actually target SMEs [3]. The main reasons are that SMEs show a good value vs risk ratio as they often underestimate the value of their data (e.g. high-tech start-up) [4]. SMEs can also be used as relays to direct attacks towards bigger targets [5].

P. Mori et al. (Eds.): ICISSP 2018, CCIS 977, pp. 240–260, 2019.
https://doi.org/10.1007/978-3-030-25109-3_13

To make things worse, SMEs are often the most eager to adopt new technologies, given the high potential of value creation through new business models (e.g. SaaS) or simplified IT management (e.g. Cloud hosted). However, adopting such technologies often means a new kind of cyber security threat, which is often overlooked or not yet fully understood. The 2016 report of the US-CERT to congress has revealed that over the last decade, the number of reported incidents has been multiplied by 14 with an annual grow of around 30% [6, 7].

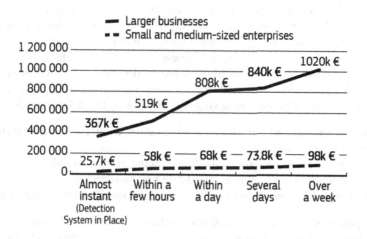

Fig. 1. Financial impact of cyber breaches according to detection time [8].

It is critical to protect our SMEs because they are known to play a key role in the worldwide economy. In European countries they employ two thirds of the workforce and generate about 60% of the total added value [9]. Moreover, SMEs are a lot more fragile than bigger companies. Although the impact is lower in absolute value as shown in Fig. 1, it is very high when compared to their revenues and it will also have an higher detection time, meaning an higher impact. In case of attack, most SMEs will not get a second chance: about 60% of companies go out of business within six months after an attack [10].

Of course, the market has not left such risks unanswered and SMEs are already being regularly challenged about their cyber security maturity in calls for tender, or need to have specific clauses added to their contracts [11]. However, this is not always beyond the reach of SMEs. For example, ISO27000 compliance requires about 25 mandatory documents [12]).

Public authorities have also identified the need to help and even to force SMEs to become more mature in the way they address cyber security threats. At European level, many organisation such as ENISA, SME Alliance, the European Commission, European Cybersecurity Organisation (ECSO) are active in this area. At national or even regional scale, the need to support SMEs to face cyber security challenges has given birth to a number of initiatives aiming at defining and deploying specific labelling schemes. Those are usually operated by a network of third party expert companies, supported by specific public funding that are also setting up the rules to operate in such a network. For example the cyberessentials is supported by cyber security vouchers in United Kingdom [13]. Of course such a work should not be done in isolation as stressed by Digital Europe [14]. It should be as much as possible aligned with strategic directions defined at the European level or in international standards. It should also learn from similar on-going work carried out in other countries.

The aim of this paper is to outline the main directions to build a realistic cyber security labelling approach addressing the needs of SMEs. Its overall goals also include raising awareness and helping them reach a first level of assurance and maturity. This paper is an extended version of our initial work that identified and analysed a number of existing frameworks and emerging national labels. Those were ranked against a number of required criteria for their adoption by SMEs. It also sketched a first high level scheme for setting up a label [15]. This paper is a significant extension of this earlier work in the following directions:

- it provides an updated but also more exhaustive, deeper and better structured survey of existing initiatives.
- it proposes a more concrete labelling scheme that also takes into account specific guidelines such as from the ECSO meta-scheme.
- it details specific tool support such as a self-assessment questionnaire.

This paper is structured as follows. Section 2 identifies relevant constraints and needs SMEs have to face when dealing with cyber security and summarises the main European organisations active in this field. Section 3 gives an overview of the existing approaches in the light of those needs. Based on this, Sect. 4 highlights the main organisational feature to set up and proposes some tooling support adapted for SMEs use. Finally, Sect. 6 concludes by discussing the next steps of our roadmap in Belgium and more general challenges to progress towards a common labelling at European level.

2   SME Cybersecurity Needs and European Landscape

2.1   SMEs Needs About Information/Cyber Security

A survey made in 2014 amongst UK SMEs shows some interesting findings about their perception and approach of cyber security [5]:

1. Only 21% of the respondents have shown a low awareness about basic security guidelines.
2. To the (open) question "What do you find the most difficult with cyber security?", one of the main reported barriers is the lack of trust and quality regarding available information, amongst others such as the lack of resources or knowledge.
3. 39% have done an in-depth risk analysis including cyber security, and 48% keep the company's risk analysis, policies and backups up to date.

4. Despite these low percentages (compare to bigger businesses), most SMEs are aware of the reasons why cyber security measures are necessary.
5. The cost is still the main barrier for implementing cyber security solutions and standards, as those are often designed·for bigger companies.

The bottom line is that most SMEs already have a good level of awareness and are ready to devote resources to cyber security. However, they lack "simple effective measures that are not too time-consuming and require a great in depth knowledge of IT systems". This lack of reliable sources of truth and guidance is a huge hindrance for them and the perceived incentives are not sufficient to break that barrier. We give here a short summary of the main requirements gathered from different surveys [5,16,17] and our own interactions with local SMEs. The following list is structured according to the FFIEC Cybersecurity domains [18].

- Management and oversight: the whole organisation should be committed with management support. A dedicated person should be identified and given resources. Roles could be aligned with risk management process to make the link with the company assets. Some internal training/awareness should be organised. A plan-do-check-act type of governance should be set up.
- Intelligence and collaboration: guidelines should be available for classical SMEs network architecture (e.g. with/without central office).
- Controls: easy to implement controls should be available. They must be easy to operate internally with limited amount of outside expertise (e.g. to help select and install adequate controls).
- External Dependency Management: external interfaces should be clearly identified and related to the assets to help identifying the protection level.
- Incident management and resilience: basic business continuity actions should be available (including backup strategy, alternative processes,...)

2.2 European Initiatives Addressing SME Cybersecurity

At European level, the main on-going initiatives tackling with SMEs needs are the following:

- The European Union Agency for Network and Information Security (ENISA) is conducting security surveys and publishing dedicated cyber security guides for SMEs. ENISA is also making recommendations to foster the level of adoption of security standards by SMEs. This includes actions targeting SMEs to ease their access to relevant knowledge and include them in the development and review process of relevant standards. Moreover it also proposes to define certification schemes and standards that are specifically tailored for SMEs, stressing the the need to have low cost and lightweight approaches fitting SMEs capabilities and risk profiles [19].
- The European Digital SME Alliance supports the SME ecosystem by developing a "EU trusted solution" label. The goal is more general: it is to emphasise on European high standards related to data protection and security. Another benefit is to accelerate the development process across the ecosystem and

act as a differentiator especially for increasing the international visibility of European SMEs [20].

- The European Commission is also investigating a certification framework for ICT products and services. This would include a complementary labelling scheme for the security of ICT products [21].
- The European Cyber Security Organisation (ECSO). Is is the contractual counterpart to the European Commission for the implementation of the Cyber Security contractual Public-Private Partnership. ECSO members include a wide variety of stakeholders such as large companies, SMEs and start-ups, research centres, universities, end-users, etc. ECSO has issued a full state of the art of cyber security standard but not specifically addressing SMEs needs and with a sectorial focus [22]. It has also proposed a meta-certification scheme providing interesting guidelines [23].
- Last but not least, to improve the protection of personal data, the EU has issued a new General Data Protection Regulation (GDPR) in full application since May 2018 [24]. It requires strict data protection processes with severe penalties. Demonstrating cyber security maturity is thus required as be part of measures to avoid data breaches.

3   Existing Labels and Frameworks for SMEs

This section reviews a number of emerging labels with a focus on SMEs. It is also considering bigger frameworks, generally based on international standards, when those can be adapted to SMEs needs as described in the Sect. 2. In the rest of this section, the general term "SME-oriented approach" will be used to cover all those labels and frameworks. Note also that some approaches were discarded because targeting a specific domain (e.g. IEC-62443 for industrial automation) or lacking enough track records about their use in an SME context. The section will detail each approach in a turn based on a set of criteria detailed hereafter. The final part of the section gives a global summary and comparative discussion.

- *Name* of the reference framework considered
- *Type:* label, standard or guidelines
- *Country:* where it was issues (if country specific). For a standard, some scope may be mentioned (e.g. US, Europe)
- *Date:* when the reference framework was first officially released
- *Website:* on-line reference website or entry point
- *SME:* indicate relation with SMEs: it can be specifically designed for SMEs or adapted to it in some way (e.g. through guidelines)
- *Controls:* overview of the kind of controls that are available.
- *Available tools:* from white papers and guidelines to software tools either online or downloadable.
- *Scheme:* details about the process to evaluated SMEs are selected, typically through officially recognised third parties and how those are selected. Renewal frequency is also identified when available.

– *Maturity:* details how the reference framework deals with the need to progressively rise in maturity level or to show a specific level of maturity for more critical business.

3.1   Cyber Essentials (UK)

Cyber Essentials is a UK government scheme launched in 2014 to encourage organisations to adopt good practices in information security [13]. It includes an assurance framework and a simple set of security controls to protect information from threats coming from the Internet. It was developed in collaboration with industry organisations combining expertise in Information Security (ISF), SMEs (IASME) and standardisation (BSI).

There are five main controls, respectively covering: boundary firewalls/internet gateways, secure configuration, access control, malware protection and patch management.

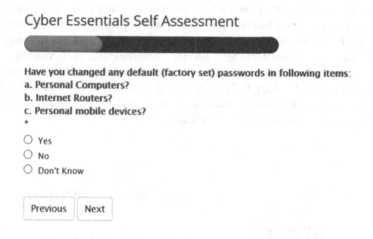

Fig. 2. Cyber essentials self-assessment proposed by [25].

Cyber Essential is organised in two levels of certification which must be renewed yearly. The first level is a basic level based on a self-assessment which is independently verified. Figure 2 shows part of the proposed self-assessment questionnaire. The second "Plus" level provides higher assurance through certifying the external testing of the organisation's cyber security. Certifying bodies are licensed (either for the basic or both levels) by five Accreditation Bodies which are currently appointed by UK government. The certifying bodies must demonstrate appropriate levels of quality assurance processes, security controls, and security assessment methodologies. They must also sign a code of conduct and provide technical competent and qualified staff to be mandated.

In order to support SMEs in adhering to the approach, the UK government has deployed a specific voucher scheme including coaching, documentation and certification. It was quite successful: more than 2000 Cyber Essentials and Cyber Essentials Plus certifications have been issued since the launch. Once certified, the SME can also advertise about the fact it takes cyber security seriously – boosting its reputation and providing a competitive selling point.

3.2   BSI and VdS (Germany)

A German cyber security act has been issued in 2010 to face the rise of cyber crime. A concern is the impact of certification on companies. Compliance measures have to reflect the "current state of the technology" and this work has to be carried out by the German Federal Office for Information Security (BSI) for each sector. BSI has developed the "IT-Grundschutz", an extensive modular catalogue on Information Security Management for several years. It is proposed to public authorities and companies. The focus is however mainly to facilitate ISO 27001 certification and the experience has shown that this is still beyond the reach of the vast majority of SMEs.

To our knowledge, initiatives for SMEs are originating from the private sector, e.g. by "Vertrauen durch Siecherhiet" (VdS) which is major independent testing institute with a focus on corporate security and safety. VdS has developed certifications targeting manufacturers, service providers and end consumers. VdS controls are structured in four domains: organisation (responsibilities, guidelines, staff and entries), technology (IT systems networks, mobile devices and data carriers), prevention (environment, backup, breakdown and incident handling) and management (of IT outsourcing and Cloud).

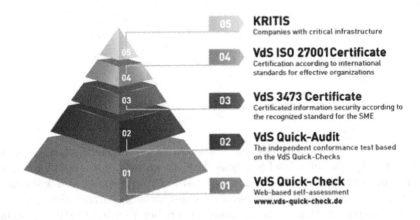

Fig. 3. Different levels of certification proposed by VdS [26].

The VdS scheme has five levels depicted on Fig. 3 with four certified levels built on top of a self-assessment level of about 40 questions and which is available on-line as shown on Fig. 4. The ISO27001 is at level 4 while level 5 is addressing the need of critical infrastructures. Once a company has the so-called 'basic security' audited and certified by VdS, it is allowed to transfer the security risk (to some extend) to an insurance company.

The certification body approves service providers for the consultancy of information security/cyber security for a limited time.

3.3 ANSSI Certification (France)

The French government announced in 2015 their new digital security strategy, led by the ANSSI (The French Network and Information Security Agency) and designed to support the digital transition of French society. The ANSSI certification process is based on the Common Criteria for Information Technology Security Evaluation (CC) [27]. The CC are primarily designed to support the certification of security oriented product with a well-defined boundary. It defines evaluation assurance level based on a growing set of mandatory processes to follow to ensure the targeted level. Level 1 is the most basic and cheapest and level 7 the most stringent and expensive. In practice, most security systems target level 4 with some additions (named EAL4+). Although the spirit of CC has been studied for its adaptation to SMEs [28], it is not suited for helping SMEs to manage the cyber security of their infrastructure, as their business is only indirectly impacted by security issues at the boundaries of their organisation.

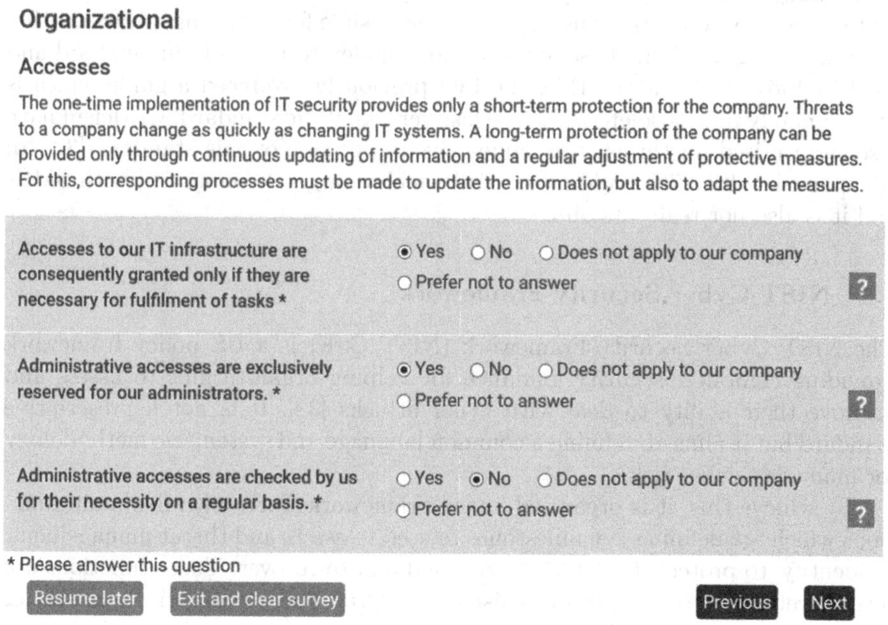

Organizational

Accesses

The one-time implementation of IT security provides only a short-term protection for the company. Threats to a company change as quickly as changing IT systems. A long-term protection of the company can be provided only through continuous updating of information and a regular adjustment of protective measures. For this, corresponding processes must be made to update the information, but also to adapt the measures.

Accesses to our IT infrastructure are consequently granted only if they are necessary for fulfilment of tasks *	⦿ Yes ○ No ○ Does not apply to our company ○ Prefer not to answer `?`
Administrative accesses are exclusively reserved for our administrators. *	⦿ Yes ○ No ○ Does not apply to our company ○ Prefer not to answer `?`
Administrative accesses are checked by us for their necessity on a regular basis. *	○ Yes ⦿ No ○ Does not apply to our company ○ Prefer not to answer `?`

* Please answer this question

Resume later   Exit and clear survey   Previous   Next

Fig. 4. Self-assessment proposed by VDS [26].

To cope with SMEs needs, the approach is rather to rely on guidelines which are regularly updated [29] and to promote training on cyber security. This can take the form of an off-line guide for internships to educate a reference person in cyber security or a massive on-line course (MOOC) aiming at making cyber security accessible for all [30]. This course was quite a success with about 60.000 registrations over one year and is ranked among the best MOOCs in the world.

Note also that for SMEs developing products or services with strong security requirements, a French cyber security label was also created to attest and promote the French quality of the developed solution [31].

3.4 ISO27001 Standard and Its Adaptation for SMEs

The ISO 27001 family of standards has grown quite large over the last years. It now includes some 40 standards which makes it difficult to address for a SME without guidance [12]. The ISO 27001 is the best-known standard in the family providing requirements for an information security management system (ISMS). It sets out more than 130 individual security controls grouped into 11 key areas. Not all controls have to be implemented, as they can be selected on the basis of a professional risk assessment. A SME will find that such a standard contains many controls that are not relevant or appropriate to their circumstances, but might occasionally be required by a large customer or business partner to demonstrate their level of compliance.

Although the ISO 27002 provides best practice recommendations on information security controls for use by those responsible for initiating, implementing or maintaining a ISMS, those are still too complex to be easily understood and used by SMEs. To address this, the ISO previously produced a guide which is unfortunately now obsolete w.r.t. the last version of the standard. Criticism have also been raised on the lack of value-driven approach of this standard [32]. In summary, the ISO27K could never really achieve a good connection with SMEs and it is also not really its aim.

3.5 NIST Cyber Security Framework

The NIST Cyber Security Framework (NIST CSF) is a US policy framework providing computer security guidance for helping organizations to assess and improve their ability to deal with cyber attacks [33]. It is not a prescriptive standard but it aims at defining a common language and systematic methodology for managing cyber risk.

To achieve this, it is organised in the Framework Core, with five main functions which are defining key milestones related to assets and threat management: to identify, to protect, to detect, to respond and to recover. Those functions are further refined into 22 categories listed in Fig. 5. Those categories are further refined in subcategories down to about 100 security controls which are actually mapped to other standards like the ISO 27001, COBIT, NIST SP 800-53, ISA 62443. So using the NIST CSF is really a reference framework unifying various approaches and also helping in moving from one to the other. Its aim is to give a broad and stable base in cyber security and the users have to adapt it to their

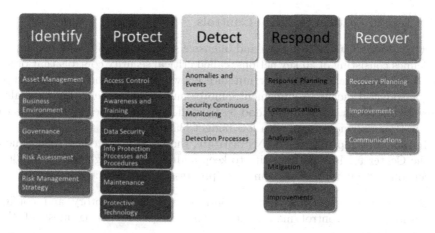

Fig. 5. The NIST cyber security framework [33].

needs. It will not give to the board the acceptable amount of cyber risks the company can tolerate or not, neither a mythical "all in one" formula to banish cyber attacks. However it clearly enables best practices to become standard practices for everyone, via a common lexicon to share actions across diverse stakeholders.

The NIST CSF also provides progressive implementation tiers depicted in Fig. 6. It provides context on how and organisation views cyber security risks and the processes in place to manage those risk. The framework can realistically be used by SMEs [34] and is actually used by the Italian framework described just after.

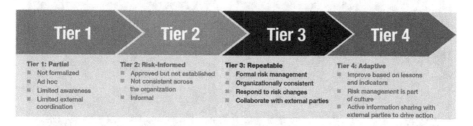

Fig. 6. NIST cyber security framework tiers [33].

3.6 Italian Cyber Security Framework

The Italian government has published their Framework in 2015, largely inspired from the framework for improving critical infrastructure cyber security (NIST) and targeting critical infrastructures. Their main modifications can be found in a strong focus on the Italian economic context (large numbers of SMEs) and a dedicated part on the contextualization. A company willing to use the document should first establish its context before selecting the right subcategory and Framework Core, as in the "vanilla" NIST. This a not a standard but a common reference to identify existing and future sector standards and regulations.

3.7   Top 20 Critical Security Controls

In 2008, a consensus of defensive and offensive security practitioners developed guidelines consisting of 20 key actions, called critical security controls that organizations should take to block or mitigate known attacks. Those controls support automated means to implement, enforce and monitor them. They are also expressed in terms easily understood by IT staff. Specific guides are available to help SMEs implement them with low budget [35].

Initially developed by the SANS Institute, those controls are now maintained by the Center for Internet Security to keep addressing the highest threats [36]. In version 7, they are organised in three progressive sets depicted in Fig. 7:

- *Basic CIS Controls:* the first 6 controls focus on inventory and configuration/access control management. They help eliminating most of the vulnerabilities.
- *Foundational CIS Controls:* the next 10 controls focus on more specific protection (email, data), defense (malware, boundary), monitoring and recovery.
- *Organizational CIS Controls:* the four last controls are of organisational nature and include: awareness, training, incident management and "red team" exercise.

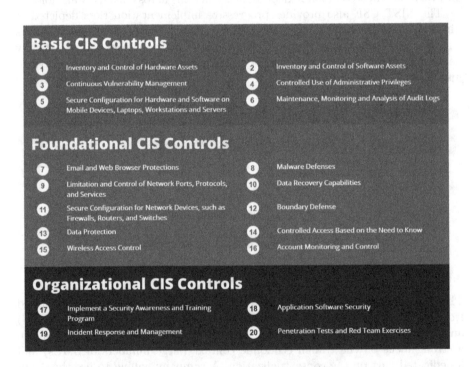

Fig. 7. Three levels of controls of the CIS20 [36].

3.8   ISSA5173 (UK)

The ISSA 5173 encourages SMEs to secure their customers and employees data. It also raises awareness of the relevant legislation that applies to them w.r.t. data security. Although the standard does not seem to be actively developed, it defines an interesting prioritization scheme depicted in Fig. 8 [37].

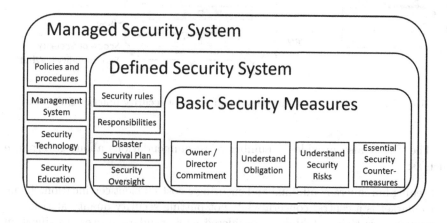

Fig. 8. Prioritization of security measures in ISSA5173 [37].

3.9   European Cyber Security Organisation (ECSO)

The ECSO is not proposing a concrete labelling scheme nor it is specifically focusing on SMEs needs. However it has surveyed a larger set of available standards [22] and has also proposed an interesting meta-scheme enabling to abstract away from specific certification and to combine the advantages of different schemes [22]. It starts by formulating a number of key objectives that can also be applied to our SME context such as: the need to perform threat analysis and risk assessment, the involvement of the risk owner, the minimisation of the certification burden, the need for regular reassessment, the standard use of patching and the use of security/privacy by design techniques.

A proposed meta-scheme template is depicted in Fig. 9. It is structured in two key levels:

- *Base levels* which is largely sector agnostic and can provide two level of assurance: Entry (self-assessment) and Basic (assessment through an accredited third party). The Basic level matches the lowest level of VdS while the second is VdS level 2 and the first level of Cyber Essentials.
- *Advanced levels* with more advanced assessment performed by an accredited third party with three different levels where the minimum scope of security functionality is sector specific and with approaches ranging from black-box (Enhanced-Basic) to grey-box (Moderate) and white-box (High).

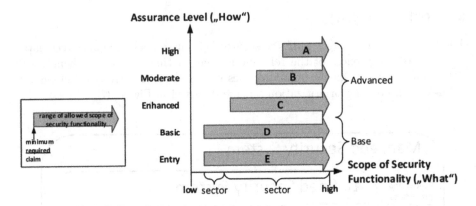

Fig. 9. Link between assurance level and scope of security functionality [23].

The ECSO also provides a number of recommendations about governance such as:

- keeping bureaucracy minimal and ensuring a cost-efficient certification. Time-to-market is a central concern while not putting security quality at risk.
- making sure that patching is considered as a standard process certification flow.
- making sure sector-specific security requirements and evaluation and certification procedures are optimized by a dedicated Expert Group.
- implementing maximum re-use of certified items across sectors
- ensuring that evaluation and certification bodies are working on a mutually consistent quality level to have good operational capabilities.
- making sure cheating participants are blacklisted if detected.

3.10 Comparison Summary

Table 1 summarises previous approaches. It helps in comparing and combining them to build a dedicated approach without reinventing the wheel and staying aligned with existing works.

Looking at the table, what looks interesting is to:

- instantiate the meta-scheme to have at least the entry level (for awareness) and the basic level while provisioning other levels for future growth in maturity
- rely on CIS20 for a simple set of well defined security controls, given the Cyber Essentials and VdS are not explicitly available. The NIST CSF can still be used as reference as the CIS20 is mapped on it.
- implement governance recommendations for the ECSO and also borrow some concrete support from various labels like awareness questionnaire and good practice guides.

Table 1. Comparison of main SME-oriented approaches.

Name	Type	Country	Organi-sation	SME	Controls	Tools	Scheme	Maturity	Since
Cyber Essentials	Label	UK	Gov.	Yes	5 main controls	Online self assess.	Accreditation and certification	2 levels	2013
ANSSI Certif.	Label	France	ANSSI	Yes	Unknown	Unknown	Based on Common Criteria	2 levels	2015
BSI	Advice	Germany	Gov.	Yes	ISO27K based	Threat catalogue			2008
VdS	Certif.	Germany	Private	Yes	4 areas 39 quick checks	online- self-assess.	Approved service providers	4 levels	2017
Italian Frame-work	Frame-work	Italy	ISCOM	Yes	CSF based 11 guidelines	Unknown	Unknown	4 levels	2015
ISO27K	Standard	Intl	ISO	No	11 areas 130 controls	Many ISMS tools	Accreditation and certification	No (scope based)	2013 (lat-est)
NIST CSF	Frame-work	US/Intl	NIST	Some	5 functions exhaustive mapping	CSF Reference Tool	Not Applicable	4 tiers	2015
ISSA 5173	Standard	UK	ISSA	Yes	10 categories	Unknown	Unknown	3 levels	2011
CIS Top 20	Good prac-tices	US/Intl	Center of Internet Security	Yes	20 controls	Support for control automation	Informal use	3 levels (6+10+4)	2008
ECSO	Meta-Schema	Europe	NPO	Some	N/A	N/A	Governance aspects	2 key levels with tunable sub-levels	2018

4 Setting up a Label

4.1 Global Organisation

Our label is aimed at any SME wishing to demonstrate a level of maturity in information security. Its purpose is to define the level of cyber security maturity for an enterprise on a relevant scale. It would reflect a level reached by the company in terms of cyber security and could be used by actors outside the company such as customers, suppliers, subcontractors, insurers or even computer crime investigators.

The envisioned approach is based on a framework both strong and adaptable to SMEs needs like the NIST CSF, similarly to the Italian approach. It would rely on the NIST Framework Core and the five functions and for each function use the Tier approach as detailed in Sect. 3.6 which enables a maturity scale. The global organisation is depicted in Fig. 10, it includes both the certification of provider that will be allowed to deliver the label. To encourage SMEs to better protect themselves and engage in the label, the public authorities have also launched cyber security vouchers that can be used for consultancy and labelling by certified companies.

The combination of these categories and tiers in the label will give a clear overview for the SMEs situation and its context. This is the real challenge in the galaxy of existing frameworks, recommendations and controls. The label has to be smart and flexible, designed and/or adapted for tight resources and budget. A small bakery and a sensible data processing company do not have the same budget and are not confronted to the same threats, the approach obviously has to be tailored without sacrificing the security.

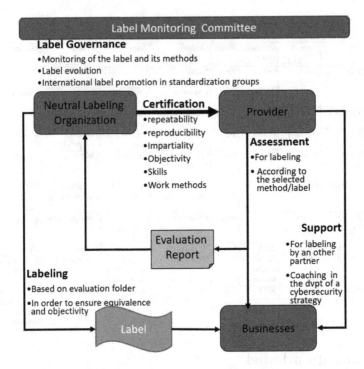

Fig. 10. Proposed labelling scheme [15].

4.2   Raising Awareness

In order to raise awareness a number of actions can be identified. Based on the experience reported by others, we have identified and implemented the following actions which are further detailed in the rest of the section:

- defining and refining the label with stakeholders
- communication actions through events, website, etc.
- proposing a self-assessment questionnaire
- training SMEs

A. Defining and Refining the Label with Stakeholders. Setting up a label is a long process during which several difficulties have to be addressed. A major issue is to succeed in defining a new structure with an official recognition and a secured recurrent funding. In order to ensure the endeavour has a chance to succeed, a key point is to make sure all key stakeholders are fully taking part to the process and will get value out of it, for example:

- public authorities will help SMEs to secure their business and hence be more competitive.
- companies of the IT security field will have access to a well-defined market with well-defined rules to access and deliver.

– specialised organisations independent from the market like research centre, quality reference centre or accreditation centre will need to authorise IT companies on a regular basis.

To help in defining the label and its governance, a number of means can be used. Sectorial meeting of cyber security actors are a good place to discuss the current practices, define the global requirements and discuss the roadmap. More specific meetings among market independent actors also need to take place to set up the whole organisation structure. As far as public funding is concerned, a call for tender for filling up the required roles may also take place.

B. Communication Actions. In order to reach out interested SMEs different communication channels are available and can be used in turn, starting from more targeted actions to more general actions:

– SMEs with urgent need are known by IT security companies and they can directly be informed about the label through their networks.
– specialised events dedicated to security or with a security track are regularly organised in different towns and can host a specific slot presenting the label.
– a dedicated website can be set up and provide a general presentation and complementary materials such as frequently asked questions, a white paper, guidelines, etc. It can also give access to a self assessment questionnaire.
– specific communications like radio, television or press can also take place to reach a wider audience.

C. Self-assessment Questionnaire. A self-assessment questionnaire can be set up on-line using different means. However given the sensible nature of the information, Cloud-based questionnaires are not a good option. In our case, we relied on Lime Survey which is an Open Source tool based on PHP and MySQL that can be deployed on a well controlled infrastructure [38].

The design process is as follows. First the CIS20 logic is analysed and encoded into a spreadsheet. This document is used to capture the various questions and the chain of decision leading from a general question to more detailed ones. It is also divided into three main sections corresponding to the basic, foundational and organisation levels of the CIS20. Clarifying comments can be captured at this stage as well as some practical recommendations. Figure 11 shows the form design for the second CIS control which covers the inventory and control of software assets.

The information can then be injected (either manually or possibly using an automated process) into a Lime Survey server. Figure 12 shows the resulting questionnaire that can be filled by a end-user. The system automatically maps relevant controls for collecting different kind of answers (yes/no, select among a list, number, etc).

CIS Control 2: Inventory and Control of Software Assets				
CIS Sub-Control	Asset Type	Security Function	Title	Descriptions
2,1	Applications	Identify	Maintain Inventory of Authorized Software	Maintain an up-to-date list of all authorized software that is required in the enterprise for any business purpose on any business system.
			IF YES GOTO 2.2 / ELSE STOP	
2,2	Applications	Identify	Ensure Software is Supported by Vendor	Ensure that only software applications or operating systems currently supported by the software's vendor are added to the organization's authorized software inventory. Unsupported software should be tagged as unsupported in the inventory system.
			GOTO 2.3	
2,3	Applications	Identify	Utilize Software Inventory Tools	Utilize software inventory tools throughout the organization to automate the documentation of all software on business systems.
			GOTO 2.4	
2,4	Applications	Identify	Track Software Inventory Information	The software inventory system should track the name, version, publisher, and install date for all software, including operating systems authorized by the organization.
			GOTO 2.5	

Fig. 11. Design of the self-assessment questionnaire in a spreadsheet.

CIS Control 2: Inventory and Control of Software Assets

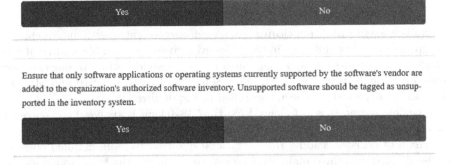

Maintain an up-to-date list of all authorized software that is required in the enterprise for any business purpose on any business system.

Yes	No

Ensure that only software applications or operating systems currently supported by the software's vendor are added to the organization's authorized software inventory. Unsupported software should be tagged as unsupported in the inventory system.

Yes	No

Fig. 12. Resulting interactive form for CIS Control 2.

At the end of the questionnaire, a complete summary is provided with a global score and some recommendations as shown in Fig. 13. The collected data is only processed for statistical purposes and the identity of the participant is never recorded.

Lime Survey has some built-in analysis and display capabilities for processing statistics over the collected answers. Figure 14 shows a few of them. Data can also be easily exported to performed more detailed analysis or even be presented to the end user so he can position himself.

Questions	Answers
CIS Control 1: Inventory and Control of Hardware Assets	
Utilize an active discovery tool to identify devices connected to the organization's network and update the hardware asset inventory.	Yes
Utilize a passive discovery tool to identify devices connected to the organization's network and automatically update the organization's hardware asset inventory.	Yes
Use Dynamic Host Configuration Protocol (DHCP) logging on all DHCP servers or IP address management tools to update the organization's hardware asset inventory.	No
CIS Control 2: Inventory and Control of Software Assets	
Maintain an up-to-date list of all authorized software that is required in the enterprise for any business purpose on any business system.	Yes
Ensure that only software applications or operating systems currently supported by the software's vendor are added to the organization's authorized software inventory. Unsupported software should be tagged as unsupported in the inventory system.	Yes

Fig. 13. Global summary.

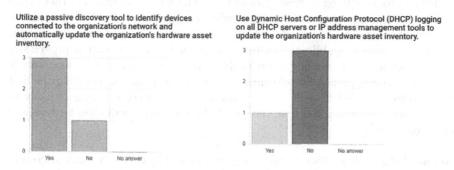

Utilize a passive discovery tool to identify devices connected to the organization's network and automatically update the organization's hardware asset inventory.

Use Dynamic Host Configuration Protocol (DHCP) logging on all DHCP servers or IP address management tools to update the organization's hardware asset inventory.

Fig. 14. Statistics.

D. Training SMEs and Service Providers. At this stage only a few end-user SMEs have been directly involved in the process in order to check their training needs. In the process of reviewing existing labels, we have collected and consolidated a large set of reference and training material that is being adapted to the training need. Specialised training will be delivered by specialised IT companies provided it is not the company performing the security audit. But before this occurs, those service providers will also have access to the reference material and to the label guidelines which will ensure a common background. Periodic meeting to share good practices are also planned.

5   Conclusions and Perspectives

The threats raised by cyber security on SMEs are not new. However attacks have shifted to smaller and more vulnerable targets, i.e. SMES. Hence, it is increasingly important to help them protect their assets and business from cyber threats. Unfortunately, standards and frameworks were designed in the first place with large companies in mind and are not tailored to the needs and resources of SMEs. By definition SMEs are also very heterogeneous and a single solution cannot fit them all. Consequently, the need for a comprehensive, flexible and cost-minded framework is clear and main actors such as European union and major standards are beginning to work on it. At a more local level, more concrete and closer-to-the-market approaches are now emerging. In this paper we have reviewed both kinds of approaches and compared them. Based on this, we have proposed an mixed approach that also relies on guidelines issues by the ECSO to combine them in a consistent and evolutionary label. Our aim was primary to set up a label at the Belgian level but we believe our approach can be useful for other countries engaging in the same process and for all in the perspective of an emerging common European scheme.

Going one step further than the design of our label, we have also identified a number of tools helping in raising awareness. The most elaborated of them is an on-line self-assessment questionnaire providing a fairly good level of automation.

After having defined our labelling scheme together engaged with the relevant IT cluster and our public authorities, our work is now to start a progressive deployment if our label using the available awareness material. Our next step is to validate the approach by selecting our first auditors and monitoring the first SMEs being labelled. Based on the collected feedback some tuning is likely to occur before launching the first version of the label with will then be reviewed on a yearly basis.

Acknowledgements. This research was partly funded by IDEES research projects of the Walloon Region. We thanks Infopole and companies of the cyber security cluster for their support. We also thanks Sébastien Bal (HELHA) for prototyping the on-line questionnaire.

References

1. Business Continuity Institute: BCI Horizon Scan Report 2018 (2018). https://www.bsigroup.com/LocalFiles/en-GB/iso-22301/case-studies/BCI-Horizon-Scan-Report-2018-FINAL.pdf
2. Smith, M.: Huge rise in hack attacks as cyber-criminals target small businesses (2016). http://bit.do/sme-attack-rise
3. Symantec: 2017 Internet Security Threat Report (2017). https://www.symantec.com/security-center
4. Hayes, J., Bodhani, A.: Cyber security: small firms under fire [information technology professionalism]. Eng. Technol. **8**, 80–83 (2013)

5. Osborn, E., Creese, S., Upton, D.: Business vs technology: sources of the perceived lack of cyber security in SMEs. In: Proceedings of the 1st International Conference on on Cyber Security for Sustainable Society (2015)
6. Donovan, S.: Annual Report to Congress, Federal Information Security Modernization Act. Office of Management and Budget (2016). http://bit.do/fisma-report-15
7. Slye, J.: Federal Cybersecurity Incidents Continued Double-Digit Growth (2016). http://bit.do/cybersecurity-incidents
8. Kaspersky Lab: Measuring Financial Impact of IT Security on Businesses (2016)
9. Muller, P., et al.: Annual Report on European SMEs 2014/2015. European Commission (2015)
10. Leclair, J.: Testimony of Dr. Jane Leclair before the U.S. House of Representatives Committee on Small Business (2015). http://bit.do/sme-leclair
11. CybSafe: Enterprise IT leaders demanding more stringent cyber security from suppliers (2017). http://bit.do/cybsafe
12. ISO: ISO/IEC 27000 Family - Information Security Management Systems (2013). https://www.iso.org/isoiec-27001-information-security.html
13. UK Government: Cyber Essentials (2016). https://www.cyberaware.gov.uk/cyberessentials
14. Whalen, A.: Digital Europe's views on cybersecurity certification and labelling schemes (2017). http://bit.ly/2m3dyLV
15. Ponsard, C., Grandclaudon, J., Dallons, G.: Towards a cyber security label for SMEs: a European perspective. In: Proceedings of the 4th International Conference on Information Systems Security and Privacy, ICISSP 2018, Funchal, Madeira, Portugal, 22–24 January 2018, pp. 426–431 (2018)
16. Boateng, Y., Osei, E.: Cyber-Security Challenges with SMEs. Developing Economies: Issues of Confidentiality, Integrity & Availability. Aalborg University (2013)
17. Padfield, C.: Issues of IT Governance and Information Security from an SME & Social Enterprise Perspective. MSc Edinburgh Napier University (2015)
18. FFIEC: Federal Financial Institutions Examination Council. https://www.ffiec.gov
19. ENISA: Information security and privacy standards for SMEs (2015). https://www.enisa.europa.eu/publications/standardisation-for-smes
20. Digital SME Alliance: European Cybersecurity Strategy: Fostering the SME Ecosystem (2017). http://bit.do/digital-europe
21. EU: Strengthening Europe's Cyber Resilience System and Fostering a Competitive and Innovative Cybersecurity Industry (2016). http://eur-lex.europa.eu/legal-content/EN/TXT/?uri=COM%3A2016%3A410%3AFIN
22. ECSO: State of the Art - Overview of existing Cybersecurity standards and certification schemes v2 (2017). https://www.ecs-org.eu/documents/publications/5a31129ea8e97.pdf
23. ECSO: European Cyber Security Certification: A Meta - Scheme Approach v1.0 (2017). https://www.ecs-org.eu/documents/publications/5a3112ec2c891.pdf
24. EU: General data protection regulation (2016). http://eur-lex.europa.eu/eli/reg/2016/679/oj
25. Certification Europe: Cyber essentials self assessment (2018). https://www.cyberessentials.ie/self-assessment
26. Vertrauen durch Siecherhiet: A Brief Assessment for SMEs - Quick Check for Cyber Security (2017). http://vds-quick-check.de
27. ISO/IEC: 15408–1:2009 Common Criteria for Information Technology Security Evaluation (2009). https://www.commoncriteriaportal.org

28. Ponsard, C., Massonet, P., Molderez, J.F.: Bringing the Common Critera to Business Enterprise. ERCIM News, Special Issue on Security and Trust Management (2005)
29. ANSSI: Charte d'utilisation des moyens informatiques et des outils numériques - guide d'élaboration en 9 points clés pour PME et ETI (2017). https://www.ssi.gouv.fr/uploads/2017/06/guide-charte-utilisation-moyens-informatiques-outils-numeriques_anssi.pdf
30. ANSSI: MOOC SecNumacadémie (2018). https://www.secnumacademie.gouv.fr
31. ANSSI: France Cybersecurity Label (2014). https://www.francecybersecurity.fr
32. Lieberman, D.: Practical advice for SMBS to use ISO 27001 (2011). http://www.infosecisland.com
33. NIST: Cybersecurity Framework (2014). https://www.nist.gov/cyberframework
34. Sage, O.: Every Small Business Should Use the NIST CSF (2015). https://cyber-rx.com
35. Eubanks, R.: A Small Business No Budget Implementation of the SANS 20 Security Controls. SANS Institute InfoSec Reading Room (2011)
36. CIS: CIS Controls V6.1 (2016). https://www.cisecurity.org/controls
37. ISSA: 5173 Security Standard for SMEs (2011). http://www.wlan-defence.com/wp/ISSA-UK.pdf
38. Schmitz, C., Chenu, D., et al.: Lime survey (2003). https://www.limesurvey.org

Privacy Preserving Collaborative Agglomerative Hierarchical Clustering Construction

Mina Sheikhalishahi[1]($\boxtimes$), Mona Hamidi[2], and Fabio Martinelli[1]

[1] Istituto di Informatica e Telematica, Consiglio Nazionale delle Ricerche, Pisa, Italy
{mina.sheikhalishahi,fabio.martinelli}@iit.cnr.it
[2] Dipartimento Ingegneria dell Informazione e Scienze,
Universita di Siena, Siena, Italy
mona.hamidi@student.unisi.it

Abstract. Sharing information brought by governments, companies, and individuals, has created fabulous opportunities for knowledge-based decision making. However, the main challenge in collaborative data analysis returns back to the privacy of sensitive data. In current study, we propose a general framework which can be exploited as a *secure* tool for constructing any agglomerative hierarchical clustering algorithm over partitioned data. We assume that data is distributed between two (or more) parties either horizontally or vertically, such that for mutual benefits the participated parties are interested in obtaining the clusters' structure on whole data, but for privacy concerns, they are not willing to share the original datasets. To this end, in this study, we propose general algorithms based on *secure scalar product* and *secure hamming distance* to securely compute the desired criteria for shaping the clusters' scheme. Our proposed approach covers the private construction of all possible agglomerative hierarchical clustering algorithms on distributed datasets, including both numerical and categorical data.

Keywords: Privacy preserving ·
Agglomerative hierarchical clustering · Data sharing

1 Introduction

Facing the new challenges brought by a continuous evolving Information Technologies (IT) market, large companies and small-to-medium enterprises found in *Information Sharing* a valid instrument to improve their key performance indexes. Sharing data with partners, authorities for data collection and even competitors, may help in inferring additional intelligence through collaborative information analysis [16,25]. Such an intelligence could be exploited to improve revenues, e.g. through best practice sharing [3], market basket analysis [22], or prevent loss coming from brand-new potential cyber-threats. Other applications

P. Mori et al. (Eds.): ICISSP 2018, CCIS 977, pp. 261–280, 2019.
https://doi.org/10.1007/978-3-030-25109-3_14

include analysis of medical data, provided by several hospitals and health centers for statistical analysis on patient records, useful, for example, to shape the causes and symptoms related to a new pathology [1].

Information sharing, however, independently from the final goal, leads to issues and drawbacks which must be addressed. These issues are mainly related to the information privacy. Shared information might be sensitive, potentially harming the privacy of physical people, such as employee records for business applications, or patient records for medical ones [16]. Hence, the most desirable strategy is the one which enables data sharing in a secure environment, such that it preserves the individual privacy requirement while at the same time the data are still practically useful for analysis.

Clustering is a very well-known tool in unsupervised data analysis, which has been the focus of significant researches in different studies, spanning from information retrieval, text mining, data exploration, to medical diagnosis [2]. Clustering refers to the process of partitioning a set of data points into groups, in a way that the elements in the same group are more similar to each other rather than to the ones in other groups.

The problem of data clustering becomes challenging when data is distributed between two (or more) parties and for privacy concerns the data holders avoid to publish their original dataset, but still they are willing to shape more accurate clusters, identified on richer sets of data.

In all this study it is assumed that clustering on joint datasets, as in general cases, produces better result rather than clustering on individual dataset. The following scenarios present the motivation of current study:

- *Vertical data distribution:* suppose that two organizations, an Internet marketing company and an on-line retail company, own datasets with different attributes for a common set of records. These organizations are interested in sharing their data for clustering to find the optimal customer targets to maximize return on investments. How can these organizations learn about their clusters using each other's data without learning anything about the attributes' values of each other [23]?
- *Horizontal data distribution:* suppose that a hospital and a health center hold different datasets with the same set of attributes. Both centers are interested to shape clusters on whole data, which brings the benefits of identifying the trends and patterns of diseases on the larger set of samples. How would it be possible to learn about clusters without disclosing patients' records [26]?

To address this issue, in this study, we first solve the problem of secure construction of hierarchical clustering algorithms between two parties. Both scenarios of data being described through either *numerical* or *categorical* attributes are addressed in this study. For each scenario, we propose secure two-party computation protocols which can be exploited as a general tool to construct securely all possible agglomerative hierarchical clustering algorithms between two parties. At the end, each data holder finds the structure of hierarchical clusters on the whole data, without knowing the records of other party. Afterwards, we extend the proposed approach to the scenarios of data being distributed among more than two parties. Again it is assumed that the data holders are interested in detecting the structure of hierarchical clusters on all of their records without revealing their dataset.

In all proposed methodologies for identifying the clusters, two secure computation protocols, named *secure scalar product* and *secure hamming distance* protocols are exploited to propose new algorithms such that each party is able to find the closest points (or clusters) for agglomeration.

The contribution of this paper can be summarized as the following:

- A framework is proposed which serves as a tool for two parties to detect the clusters' structures on the whole dataset, in terms of agglomerative hierarchical clustering, without revealing their data, in two different scenarios of data being distributed horizontally and vertically, when data is described either numerically or categorically;
- We extend the proposed approach to the scenarios of data being distributed among several (more than two) parties;
- The communication cost, security analysis, and the experimental results of the proposed approaches are presented.

This paper completes and extends the work presented in [11] with the following novel contributions:

- We generalize the architecture of previous work which was only applicable for two parties, to the situation where data is partitioned horizontally among more than two parties.
- We extend the previous study, which was only a platform for horizontal distributed data, to the scenario in which data is partitioned vertically between two (or more) parties.
- We compute the communication cost of the proposed framework.
- We also present the security analysis of our architecture in both horizontal and vertical distributed data.
- Finally, we present the experimental analysis of our mechanism to evaluate the time complexity.

The rest of the paper is structured as follows. Related work is presented in Sect. 2. Section 3 presents some preliminary notations which are exploited in this study. Section 4 presents in detail the system model. In Sect. 5 we describe the proposed framework, detailing the secure computation protocols for hierarchical clustering construction when data is distributed between two (or more) parties. In Sect. 7, the communication costs of the proposed algorithms are evaluated. Section 8 reports the experiments to evaluate the efficiency of the proposed approach. Finally, Sect. 9 briefly concludes proposing future research directions.

2   Related Work

The problem of privacy preserving data clustering is generally addressed for the specific case of k-means clustering, either when data is distributed between two parties [6,13] or more than two parties [15].

In [27], *document clustering* has been introduced, and a cryptography based framework has been proposed to do the privacy preserving document clustering between two parties. It is assumed that each party has her own private documents, and wants to collaboratively execute agglomerative document clustering without disclosing their private content. In the proposed approach, differently from our technique, the problem when data are described through numerical attributes, is not addressed. In [8] a secure hierarchical clustering approach over vertically partitioned data is provided which increases the accuracy of the clusters over the existing approaches. However, in our study, we address the problem of hierarchical clustering construction when data is distributed horizontally and vertically. In [24] and [17], the problem of *divisive* hierarchical clustering is addressed when data is distributed between two parties (or more) horizontally and vertically. However, the criteria for divisive hierarchical clustering, discussed in their study, is different from agglomerative hierarchical clustering algorithms. In [12] the problem of secure agglomerative hierarchical clustering construction has been discussed when data is distributed between two parties.

In all aforementioned studies, differently from ours, one out of all possibilities have been focused on. However our proposed approach covers all possibilities of horizontally and vertically partitioned data with both numerical and categorical attributes between two parties and multi parties. To the best of our knowledge the problem of secure clustering algorithm construction, when data is partitioned, is a topic which is required to be explored deeper.

3   Preliminary Notations

In this section, we present some background knowledge which are exploited in our proposed framework.

3.1   Hierarchical Clustering

Clustering algorithm partitions a set of objects into smaller groups such that all objects within the same group (cluster) are more similar or close rather than the objects in different clusters [14]. *Hierarchical clustering* generates a hierarchical decomposition of the given set of data objects, which can be either *agglomerative* or *divisive* based on how the hierarchical decomposition is formed. In agglomerative approach, which is the focus of current study, the objects or clusters which are close to one another are successively merged, until all of the clusters are merged into one or until a termination condition holds. The termination conditions are generally either the *number of clusters* or *clustering accuracy*. In the former case, clusters are agglomerated till a preidentified number of clusters is achieved. In the latter case, an accuracy evaluation technique, e.g. *Dunn index*, is exploited to measure the precision of clusters in each step of agglomeration. In the step that the accuracy reaches to the required threshold, the agglomeration process stops [8].

3.2 Secure Scalar Product

Scalar product is a useful technique in data mining such that many data mining algorithms can be reduced to computing the scalar product. For secure two-party scalar product computation, assume that two parties, named *Alice* and *Bob*, each has a vector of cardinality n, e.g $X = (x_1, \ldots, x_n)$ and $Y = (y_1, \ldots, y_n)$, respectively. Then, both are interested in securely obtaining the scalar product of the two vectors, i.e. $\sum_{i=1}^{n} x_i \cdot y_i$, without revealing their own vectors. Among different approaches for secure scalar product extraction, in this study we exploit the one proposed in [29], in which the key is to use linear combinations of random numbers to make vector elements, and then do some

---

Algorithm 1. *Sec.Scalar()*: Secure Scalar Product

    Data: *Alice* and *Bob* have vectors $X = (x_1, \ldots, x_n)$ and $Y = (y_1, \ldots, y_n)$, respectively.

    Result: *Alice* and *Bob* obtain securely $s = X \cdot Y$

1 initialization;

2 *Alice* and *Bob* together decide on random $n \times n$ matrix C

3 **for** Alice **do**

4   *Alice* generates a random vector R of cardinality n, e.g. $R = (r_1, \ldots, r_n)$

5   *Alice* generates $n \times 1$ matrix Z, where $Z = C \times R$

6   *Alice* computes $X_1 = X + Z$ and sends X_1 to *Bob*

7 **end**

8 **for** Bob **do**

9   *Bob* computes the scalar product $S_1 = \sum_{i=1}^{n} x_{1i} \cdot y_i$

10   *Bob* also generates the $n \times 1$ matrix, where $Y_1 = C^T \times Y^T$

11   *Bob* sends both S_1 and Y_1 to *Alice*

12 **end**

13 **for** Alice **do**

14   *Alice* generates $S_2 = \sum_{i=1}^{n} Y_{1i} \cdot R_i$

15   *Alice* computes the scalar product $S = S_1 - S_2$ and reports S to *Bob*

16 **end**

---

computations to eliminate the effect of random numbers from the result. Algorithm 1 details the process.

3.3 Secure Hamming Distance Computation

In the case that *Alice*'s and *Bob*'s vectors are described through categorical attributes, the distance between vectors is computed with the use of secure hamming distance. The secure communication between two parties for obtaining hamming distance is on the base of *oblivious transfer*. A 1-out-2 *oblivious transfer*, denoted by OT_1^2, is a two party protocol where one party (the sender) inputs n-bit strings $X_1, X_2 \in \{0, 1\}^n$, and the other party (the receiver) inputs a bit b. At the end of the protocol, the receiver obtains X_b but learns nothing about X_{1-b}, while the sender learns nothing about b [4]. The secure computation of the Hamming distance has been presented based on oblivious transfer in [5]. It is assumed that two parties, say *Alice* and *Bob*, hold bit strings of the same length n, $X = (x_1, \ldots, x_n)$ and $Y = (y_1, \ldots, y_n)$, respectively. Both are interested in jointly computing the *Hamming Distance* between X and Y, i.e. $D_H(X, Y) = \sum_{i=1}^{n}(x_i \oplus y_i)$ without revealing X and Y. Algorithm 2 details the process.

4   System Model

Suppose that some data holders are interested in detecting the structure of clusters through an agglomerative hierarchical clustering algorithm on their datasets as a whole. However, for privacy concerns, they are not willing to publish or share the main datasets. To address this issue, in what follows, we present how the distance between two records (described numerically or categorically) can be computed when data is distributed either horizontally or vertically between two parties.

Algorithm 2. *Sec.Hamming()*: Secure Hamming Distance Computation [4]

Data: *Alice* and *Bob* have n-bit strings $X = (x_1, \ldots, x_n)$ and $Y = (y_1, \ldots, y_n)$, respectively.

Result: *Alice* and *Bob* obtain the hamming distance between X and Y

1 initialization;
2 *Alice* generates n random values $(r_1, \ldots, r_n) \in_R Z_{n+1}$ and computes $R = \sum_{i=1}^{n} r_i$
3 **for** *each $i = 1, \ldots, n$, Alice and Bob engage in a OT_1^2* **do**
4 | *Alice acts as the sender and Bob as the reciever*
5 | *Bob's selection bit is y_i*
6 | *Alice's input is $(r_i + x_i, r_i + \bar{x}_i)$ where x is a bit value and $\bar{x}$ denotes $1 - x$*
7 | *The output obtained by Bob is consequently $t_i = r_i + (x_i \oplus y_i)$*
8 **end**
9 *Bob computes $T = \sum_{i=1}^{n} t_i$ and sends T to Alice*
10 *Alice computes and outputs $T - R$*

4.1   Horizontal Data Distribution

Let's assume that data is distributed horizontally between two parties. This means that each data holder has information about all the features but for different collection of objects. More precisely, let $\mathcal{A} = \{A_1, A_2, \ldots, A_n\}$ be the set of n attributes all used to express each record of data. Therefore, each record is an n dimensional vector $X_i = (v_{i_1}, v_{i_2}, \ldots, v_{i_n})$, where $v_{i_j} \in A_j$. Figure 1 depicts a higher level representation of hierarchical clustering construction on horizontal distributed framework. *Alice* and *Bob*, holding respectively datasets D_A and D_B, are the two parties interested in constructing hierarchical clustering on $D_A \cup D_B$, without knowing the data information of the other party. As it can be observed, the two tables are described with the same set of attributes, but on different objects.

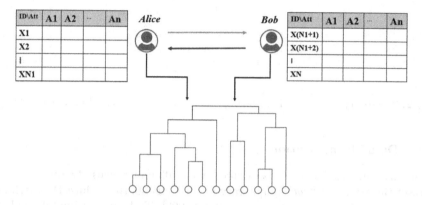

Fig. 1. Two-party hierarchical clustering construction over horizontal partitioned data [11].

4.2   Vertical Data Distribution

Now let us consider that *Alice* and *Bob* are interested in detecting the clusters' schemes on whole of their datasets, when data is partitioned *vertically* between two parties. This means that *Alice* and *Bob* each holds the same set of objects, but described with two different sets of attributes in each side. More precisely, let $\mathcal{A} = \{A_1, A_2, \ldots, A_n\}$ be the set of attributes used to describe each record of data. However, having the same set of objects, *Alice* and *Bob* each holds excluded parts of attributes describing the data. Since in reality, it is possible they also have some common attributes, we assume that the common attributes to be shared with one of them, say *Bob*. Without loss of generality, let consider *Alice* has the description of data based on $\mathcal{A}_A = \{A_1, \ldots, A_k\} \subset \mathcal{A}$, and consequently *Bob* owns the set $\mathcal{A}_B = \{A_{k+1}, \ldots, A_n\} \subset \mathcal{A}$, describing the same set of objects D. For instance, *Alice* may have the information about the "*size*" of records, while *Bob* has the information about the "*age*" of the same records. Figure 2 depicts a higher level representation of hierarchical clustering construction when data is divided vertically between two parties. As it can be observed, both tables contain the same set of objects but expressed with different features. At the end, both *Alice* and *Bob* obtain the structure of clusters on whole of data information, without knowing each others' data. After obtaining the final hierarchical clustering structure, it is exploited in each side for grouping their data.

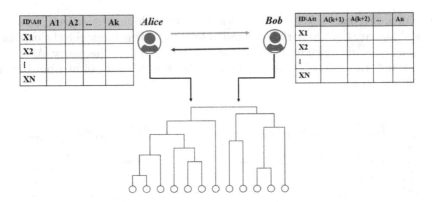

Fig. 2. Two-party hierarchical clustering construction over vertical partitioned Data.

4.3 Data Normalization

Generally, numerical data are described with different ranges of values, e.g in a dataset the attribute *"age"* might vary in the range $[0, 100]$, whilst the attribute *"salary"* gets its values in the range $[0, 100, 000]$. To have meaningful result in data clustering, it is required to normalize the numbers in the same range $[0, 1]$ by dividing them to the maximum value of that attribute. In horizontal partitioned data, we suppose that the data holders are aware about the maximum value that each attribute might reach. Hence, all parties simply divide each value of an attribute to the known maximum value.

When data is distributed vertically between two parties, then each party has a complete information of a specific attribute. This means that it is enough that the data holders participate in communication when they have already normalized the data values by dividing them to the maximum value. In the rest of this study we assume that data have been normalized before that the data holders start communication. Morepver, it is supposed that all numbers have been multiplied to big number (say 10^5), which result that all numbers to remain integers.

4.4 Horizontal Distance Computation

Depending on whether data is described through *numerical* or *categorical* attributes, secure *Euclidean* and *Hamming* distance computations are exploited inside communication algorithms, respectively.

Suppose that *Alice* and *Bob* own vectors $X = (x_1, \ldots, x_n)$ and $Y = (y_1, \ldots, y_n)$, respectively. We assume that $n > 2$, and both participated parties are interested in obtaining securely the distance between X and Y. Algorithm 3 details the process of secure distance computation in which for numerical data there is a call of *secure scalar product* (Algorithm 1), and for categorical data there is a call of *secure hamming distance* (Algorithm 2).

Algorithm 3. *Sec.Horizontal()*: Secure Horizontal Distance Computation

---

Data: *Alice* and *Bob* own vectors $X = (x_1, \ldots, x_n)$ and $Y = (y_1, \ldots, y_n)$, $n > 2$, respectively.

Result: *Alice* and *Bob* compute securely the distance between X, Y

1 initialization;
2 **if** *X and Y are numerical* **then**
3   *Alice* reports $X \cdot X$
4   *Bob* reports $Y \cdot Y$
5     $X \cdot Y \leftarrow Sec.Scalar(X, Y)$
6   **return** $D_E(X, Y) = (X \cdot X + Y \cdot Y - 2X \cdot Y)^{\frac{1}{2}}$
7 **else**
8     $D_H(X, Y) \leftarrow Sec.Hamming(X, Y)$
9   **return** $D_H(X, Y)$
10 **end**

4.5 Vertical Distance Computation

In the case that data is distributed vertically between two parties, independently from the fact that data is expressed numerically or categorically, it is enough that each party computes the distance of two records in the part which is described with the use of her own set of attributes, and then she reports the result. For example, suppose that *Alice* and *Bob* have information about the attributes "*age*" and "*salary*" of the same records, respectively. For computing the distance of two records, *Alice* reports the difference of the *age* of the records, say $D_E^2(age_1, age_2) = (age_1 - age_2)^2$, and *Bob* reports the difference of the *salaries*,

---

Algorithm 4. *Sec.Vertical()*: Secure Vertical Distance Computation

---

Data: Two records $X_1 = (x_{11}, \ldots, x_{1k}, x_{1(k+1)}, \ldots, x_{1n})$,
       $X_2 = (x_{21}, \ldots, x_{2k}, x_{2(k+1)}, \ldots, x_{2n})$ where *Alice* has the information of the first k values, and *Bob* has the rest

Result: *Alice* and *Bob* compute securely the distance of X_1, X_2

1 initialization;
2 **if** *if X_1 and X_2 are numerical* **then**
3   *Alice* reports
    $D_A(X_1, X_2) = D_E^2((x_{11}, \ldots, x_{1k}), (x_{21}, \ldots, x_{2k})) = \sum_{i=1}^{k}(x_{1i} - x_{2i})^2$
4   *Bob* reports $D_B(X_1, X_2) = D_E^2((x_{1(k+1)}, \ldots, x_{1n}), (x_{2(k+1)}, \ldots, x_{2n})) = \sum_{i=k+1}^{n}(x_{1i} - x_{2i})^2$
5   **return** $D_E(X_1, X_2) = (D_A(X_1, X_2) + D_B(X_1, X_2))^{\frac{1}{2}}$
6 **else**
7   *Alice* reports $D_A(X_1, X_2) = D_H((x_{11}, \ldots, x_{1k}), (x_{21}, \ldots, x_{2k}))$
8   *Bob* reports $D_B(X_1, X_2) = D_H((x_{1(k+1)}, \ldots, x_{1n}), (x_{2(k+1)}, \ldots, x_{2n}))$
9   **return** $D_H(X_1, X_2) = D_A(X_1, X_2) + D_B(X_1, X_2)$
10 **end**

---

say $D_E^2(salary_1, salary_2) = (salary_1 - salary_2)^2$. Then, the Euclidean distance of two records is equal to $(D_E^2(age_1, age_2) + D_E^2(salary_1, salary_2))^{\frac{1}{2}}$. The same solution is applicable for hamming distance computation in vertical distributed data. Algorithm 4 details the process.

5   Secure Agglomerative Hierarchical Clustering Construction

In this section we explain how all possible agglomerative hierarchical clustering algorithms can be constructed securely between two parties with the use of algorithms presented in Sect. 4. We address the issue in different scenarios (1) when data is expressed either numerically or categorically, (2) when data is partitioned between two or more than two parties.

In the beginning of agglomerative hierarchical clustering, each element is in a cluster by its own. Afterwards, the set of N objects to be clustered are grouped into successively fewer than N sets, arriving eventually at a single set containing all N objects [7]. According to different distance measures between clusters, all agglomerative hierarchical methods have been divided into seven methods with the use of a formula named *Lance-Williams* [19]. These seven categories of agglomerative hierarchical clustering algorithms are named *single link, complete link, average link, weighted average link, Ward's method, centroid method,* and *the median* [10].

More precisely, in agglomerative hierarchical clustering algorithms, *Lance-Williams* formula is used to calculate the dissimilarity between a cluster and a cluster formed by merging two other clusters [10]. Formally, if objects i and j are agglomerated into cluster $i \cup j$, then the new dissimilarity between the cluster and all other objects of cluster k is required to be specified as the following:

$$d(i \cup j, k) = \alpha_i \ d(i, k) + \alpha_j \ d(j, k) + \beta \ d(i, j) + \gamma \ |d(i, k) - d(j, k)|$$

where α_i, α_j, β and γ defines the agglomerative parameters [19]. The value for each of these coefficients in different algorithms has been listed in Table 1. The *Lance-Williams* formula is the key concept in current study which allows us to generalize the process of secure construction of any agglomerative hierarchical clustering algorithm to the process of secure construction of *dissimilarity matrix*. Dissimilarity matrix is a square and symmetric matrix which express the pairwise difference (distance) between samples. In what follows we show that in two party scenario, if *Alice* and *Bob* are able to find securely the distance between each pair of elements (dissimilarity matrix), they are both able to construct all possible agglomerative hierarchical clustering algorithms without revealing their data.

Table 1. Specification of hierarchical clustering methods [19].

Hierarchical clustering	Lance-Williams	Distance metric
Single Link	$\alpha_i = 0.5$ $\beta = 0$ $\gamma = -0.5$	$d(i \cup j, k) = \frac{1}{2}d(i, k) + \frac{1}{2}d(j, k) - \frac{1}{2}|d(i, k) - d(j, k)|$
Complete Link	$\alpha_i = 0.5$ $\beta = 0$ $\gamma = 0.5$	$d(i \cup j, k) = \frac{1}{2}d(i, k) + \frac{1}{2}d(j, k) + \frac{1}{2}|d(i, k) - d(j, k)|$
Group average (UPGMA)	$\alpha_i = \frac{|i|}{|i|+|j|}$ $\beta = 0$ $\gamma = 0$	$d(i \cup j, k) = \frac{|i|}{|i|+|j|}d(i, k) + \frac{|i|}{|i|+|j|}d(j, k)$
Weighted group average (WPGMA)	$\alpha_i = 0.5$ $\beta = 0$ $\gamma = 0$	$d(i \cup j, k) = \frac{1}{2}d(i, k) + \frac{1}{2}d(j, k)$
Median method	$\alpha_i = 0.5$ $\beta = -0.25$ $\gamma = 0$	$d(i \cup j, k) = \frac{1}{2}d(i, k) + \frac{1}{2}d(j, k) - \frac{1}{4}d(i, j)$
Centroid method	$\alpha_i = \frac{|i|}{|i|+|j|}$ $\beta = -\frac{|i||j|}{(|i|+|j|)^2}$ $\gamma = 0$	$d(i \cup j, k) = \frac{|i|}{|i|+|j|}d(i, k) + \frac{|i|}{|i|+|j|}d(j, k) - \frac{|i||j|}{(|i|+|j|)^2}d(i, j)$
Ward method	$\alpha_i = \frac{|i|+|k|}{|i|+|j|+|k|}$ $\beta = -\frac{|k|}{|i|+|j|+|k|}$ $\gamma = 0$	$d(i \cup j, k) = \frac{|i|+|k|}{|i|+|j|+|k|}d(i, k) + \frac{|i|+|k|}{|i|+|j|+|k|}d(j, k) - \frac{|k|}{|i|+|j|+|k|}d(i, j)$

Theorem 1. *For constructing securely any agglomerative hierarchical clustering algorithm between two parties, it is enough to find the dissimilarity matrix securely.*

Proof. From *Lance-Williams* formula, depending on that which agglomerative hierarchical clustering algorithm is desired to be constructed, the distance of the elements in a cluster and other elements should be computed. This means that if the participated parties have the distance of all elements, they are both able to discover the hierarchies of the clusters on their own side through the formula of the desired agglomerative hierarchical clustering. Hence, a dissimilarity matrix, which reports the distances of all pair of records, is the one that if it has been obtained securely can be exploited to securely construct the desired algorithm.

It is noticeable that in the last two formulas in Table 1, the number of elements in each cluster is required to be known. However, in our approach for creating dissimilarity matrix, the ID of each object is recorded. Thence, in horizontal scenario the number of elements in each cluster can be obtained for both *Alice* and *Bob* through counting the number of ID's belonging to a cluster. In vertical scenario, both parties know the ID's of all elements beforehand. □

5.1   Secure Two-Party Hierarchical Clustering Construction

Following the Theorem 1, we present in Algorithm 5 how *Alice* and *Bob* are able to construct securely the dissimilarity matrix on all of their records, when data is distributed horizontally between them, without revealing their own data.

In the case that data is distributed vertically between *Alice* and *Bob*, through Algorithm 6 both are able to obtain securely the dissimilarity matrix.

Algorithm 5. *Sec.H.Matrix():* Secure Horizontal Dissimilarity Matrix Construction

---

    Data: *Alice* and *Bob* have information of records $X_1, \ldots, X_k$ and
        $X_{k+1}, \ldots, X_N$, respectively.
    Result: Horizontal dissimilarity matrix.

1 initialization;
2 **for** $1 \leq t, t' \leq k$ **do**
3   **if** $X_t, X_{t'}$ *are numerical* **then**
4 | *Alice* reports $(M(t,t') \leftarrow D_E(X_t, X_{t'}))$
5   **else**
6 | *Alice* reports $(M(t,t') \leftarrow D_H(X_t, X_{t'}))$
7   **end**
8 **end**
9 **for** $k+1 \leq s, s' \leq N$ **do**
10   **if** $X_s, X_{s'}$ *are numerical* **then**
11 | *Bob* reports $(M(s,s') \leftarrow D_E(X_s, X_{s'}))$
12   **else**
13 | *Bob* reports $(M(s,s') \leftarrow D_H(X_s, X_{s'}))$
14   **end**
15 **end**
16 **for** $1 \leq t \leq k$ **do**
17   **for** $k+1 \leq s \leq N$ **do**
18 | $M(t,s) \leftarrow$ *Sec.Horizontal*(X_t, X_s)
19   **end**
20 **end**
21 **for** $1 \leq t, s \leq N$ **do**
22 | **return** $M(t,s)$
23 **end**

5.2   Secure Multi-party Hierarchical Clustering Construction

In this section, we present how the problem of secure two-party hierarchical clustering construction can be extended to the scenario of data being distributed among more than two parties horizontally and vertically.

Multi-party Data Normalization. In the case that data is distributed *horizontally* among more than two parties, then again we assume that all know the maximum value that each attribute might reach, then they all divide the attributes' values to the maximum value. When data is distributed *vertically* among several parties, then the problem is more simpler addressed. This is resulted from the fact that each data holder has completed information about a subset of attributes. Thence, it is enough that the data holder to divide the values of her own attributes to the maximum value of that attribute, and then she participates in communication. After normalization, all numbers are multiplied to a big number for having them all as integer, for secure computation protocols to be applicable.

Algorithm 6. *Sec. V.Matrix():* Secure Vertical Dissimilarity Matrix Construction

---

> **Data**: *Alice* has the information of the first k values, and *Bob* has the rest
> values of the records $X_1, \ldots, X_N$, respectively.
> **Result**: Vertical dissimilarity matrix
> 1 initialization;
> 2 **for** $1 \leq i, j \leq N$ **do**
> 3 $M(i,j) \leftarrow$ *Sec. Vertical*(X_i, X_j)
> 4   **return** $M(i,j)$
> 5 **end**

Multi-party Horizontal Data Distribution. In the case that data is distributed *horizontally* among more than two parties, the problem can be deduced to the construction of a secure two-party dissimilarity matrix between each pair of parties. More precisely, assume that data is distributed *horizontally* among l parties $(l > 2)$, say $P_1, P_2, \ldots, P_l$, such that they own the information of the records $\{X_1, \ldots, X_{k1}\}, \{X_{k1+1}, \ldots, X_{k2}\}, \ldots, \{X_{k(l-1)+1}, \ldots, X_{kl}\}$, respectively. Each record is an n dimensional vector described with the same set of attributes $\mathcal{A} = \{A_1, \ldots, A_n\}$. All participated parties are interested in obtaining the structure of an agglomerative hierarchical clustering on the whole of their data, without revealing their original datasets. To this end, it is required to compute the dissimilarity matrix that reports the distance of each pair of records. This problem can be solved by finding the distance of each pair of elements, say X_i and X_j, as (1) if both records belong to the same data provider, she will report the distance, (2) if party P_i owns X_i and party P_j owns X_j, then the distance between these two records, i.e. $D(X_i, X_j)$, is securely computed through Algorithm 5. Figure 3 shows how the problem of secure multi-party dissimilarity matrix computation, over horizontal partitioned data, is deduced to the secure two-party dissimilarity matrix computation.

Multi-party Vertical Data Distribution. Suppose that data is distributed *vertically* among l parties $(l > 2)$, say $P_1, P_2, \ldots, P_l$. This means that each party holds the same set of objects $X_1, X_2, \ldots, X_N$, but described with different sets of attributes. Let's assume that parties $P_1, P_2, \ldots, P_l$ own the information of data described based on the set of attributes $\mathcal{A}_1 = \{A_1, \ldots, A_{k1}\}, \mathcal{A}_2 = \{A_{k1+1}, \ldots, A_{k2}\}, \ldots, \mathcal{A}_l = \{A_{k(l-1)}, \ldots, A_k\}$, respectively. All participated parties are interested in constructing an agglomerative hierarchical clustering on whole of their data, without revealing their original datasets. To this end, it is required to compute the dissimilarity matrix that reports the distance of each pair of records. In vertical distributed data, the communication cost reduces due to the fact that each party computes the distance of two records on the part described on her own set of attributes. More precisely, assume that we want to compute the distance of the records $X_i = (X_{i\mathcal{A}_1}, X_{i\mathcal{A}_2}, \ldots, X_{i\mathcal{A}_l})$ and $X_j = (X_{j\mathcal{A}_1}, X_{j\mathcal{A}_2}, \ldots, X_{j\mathcal{A}_l})$, where $X_{i\mathcal{A}_t}$ is the part of X_i which is described

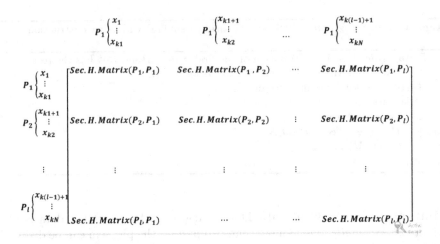

Fig. 3. Multi-party dissimilarity matrix computation over horizontal partitioned data.

by the set of attributes $\mathcal{A}_t$ owned by party P_t. To this end, the distance of X_i and X_j is computed, as the following, when data are described *numerically*:

$$D_E(X_i, X_j) = (D_E^2(X_{i\mathcal{A}_1}, X_{j\mathcal{A}_1}) + \ldots + D_E^2(X_{i\mathcal{A}_l}, X_{j\mathcal{A}_l}))^{\frac{1}{2}}$$

where $D_E^2(X_{i\mathcal{A}_t}, X_{j\mathcal{A}_t}) = \sum_{x_{i\mathcal{A}_t} \in X_{i\mathcal{A}_t}, x_{j\mathcal{A}_t} \in X_{j\mathcal{A}_t}} (x_{i\mathcal{A}_t} - x_{j\mathcal{A}_t})^2$ is computed by party P_t, and then the result is shared with the others. In the case that data are described *categorically*, the distance of two records X_i and X_j is computed as follows:

$$D_H(X_i, X_j) = D_H(X_{i\mathcal{A}_1}, X_{j\mathcal{A}_1}) + \ldots + D_H(X_{i\mathcal{A}_l}, X_{j\mathcal{A}_l})$$

where $D_H(X_{i\mathcal{A}_t}, X_{j\mathcal{A}_t})$ is the hamming distance of records X_i and X_j in the part described with the set of attributes $\mathcal{A}_t$ $(1 \leq t \leq l)$ owned by party P_t.

6   Security Analysis

In all the current study it is assumed that the participated parties are honest but curious (semi-honest model). Secure horizontal distance computation as proposed in Algorithm 3 does not reveal the value of each party's data, but the distance. This security is resulted from the fact that it is supposed that $n > 2$, hence in numerical scenario $X \cdot X$ and $Y \cdot Y$ will not reveal something about the specific amount of each component of the vectors X and Y. Moreover, $X \cdot Y$ is computed through secure scalar product protocol proven to be secure in [29]. In categorical scenario, the distance is computed by a call of secure hamming distance computation, proven to be secure in [5]. In this study, it was assumed that what can be inferred from the distance of two records is not considered as privacy violation. Secure vertical distance computation as proposed in Algorithm 4 does not also reveal the value of each party's data, but the distance.

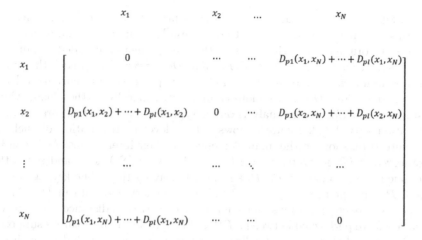

Fig. 4. Multi-party distance matrix computation over vertical partitioned data.

This security is resulted from the fact that non of *Alice* and *Bob* report the values of the records, but just the distance of records in the part expressed with their attributes. The privacy of dissimilarity matrix, which is filled with the above information, is guaranteed from the security of distance computations. The privacy of multi party scenario, in semi honest model, is resulted from the fact that we deduced the problem to the situation of data being distributed between two parties. Moreover, we assume that the participated parties follow the protocols and they do not collude (Fig. 4).

It is noticeable that although *Alice* and *Bob* will not reveal their own vectors, but the result of distance might reveal some information about records. In current study we supposed that what can be inferred from the distance of two records is not considered as privacy violation. But if it is not the case, still both *Alice* and *Bob* can solve the problem in two different ways:

- Both parties can always add *systematic noise* [18] to the final result. *Systematic noise* mechanism through adding noise to output, which is dependent to an *utility* function, preserves the utility of revealed data, while also increase the privacy in terms of differential privacy. However, it should be kept in mind that adding noise in clustering algorithms might change the correct decision for which records are closer to be agglomerated. The following solution is completely accurate and secure, but extremely heavy in terms of communication and computation.
- To securely evaluate the distance of two sensitive records through Euclidean or Hamming distance, considering that any of the data providers might be an adversary, it is not possible for any of them to be the generator of encryption keys. This means that a component, out of participated parties, is required to generate public and private keys. However, to avoid this component to have access to original information by decrypting the data, we add another component to this system which stores encrypted data for analysis.

The latter component adds noise to encrypted data before communicating with key generator component. Under these hypotheses, no component has access to original data. Hence, two other components are added to our system, say *Secure Trusted Party (STP)* and *Data Server (DS)*, such that *STP* is a semi-honest component which follows the protocols, but curious to learn about data, and *DS* is a remote component, generally in the cloud, which stores and performs the analysis on encrypted data through secure communication with *STP*. Figure 5 shows a high level representation of such an architecture, showing the main elements and their interactions. As it can be observed, *STP* generates public (P_k) and private (S_k) keys, and sends the public key P_k to parties P_1, P_2 and *DS*. Receiving the public key, agents P_1 and P_2 encrypt their records and upload the encrypted data in *DS*. Afterwards secure computations for evaluating the statistical distance between two datasets are performed between *STP* and *DS*. If this architecture is supposed to be utilized then secure *Euclidean* distance can be computed through the mechanism proposed in [9], the Hamming distance can be computed through secure *Equality* test proposed in [20], and without revealing the outputs, the minimum distance can be obtained through *Comparison* protocol proposed in [21].

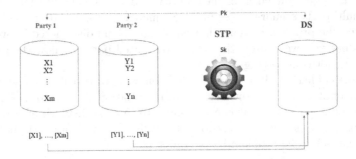

Fig. 5. Reference architecture.

7   Communication Cost

In this section we present the communication cost between two parties to construct the dissimilarity matrix.

Suppose that numerical data is distributed *horizontally* between *Alice* and *Bob*, such that they own N_1 and N_2 records, respectively. In this scenario, *Alice* and *Bob* need to obtain securely the *Euclidean* distance of each pair of records. To this end, we first compute the communication cost of computing the Euclidean distance of two vectors $X = (x_1, \ldots, x_n)$ and $Y = (y_1, \ldots, y_n)$ owned by *Alice* and *Bob*, respectively. *Alice* reports the number $\sum_{i=1}^{n} x_i^2$, and *Bob* reports the number $\sum_{i=1}^{n} y_i^2$, which leads to constant communication cost (1 for each side).

In the next step, they both need to call the secure scalar product protocol to obtain securely $X \cdot Y$. It has been shown in [29] that the bitwise communication cost of scalar product of two vectors, with the length ℓ, equals to $2\ell + 3$. This means that the total communication cost for Euclidean distance computation between two vectors equals to $n(2\ell + 3)$.

Thence, for dissimilarity matrix construction, when numerical data is distributed horizontally between two parties, $\frac{1}{2}(N_1 N_2)(n(2\ell + 3))$ communication cost is required. The division by 2 is because the dissimilarity matrix is symmetric.

Now let us to compute the communication cost of dissimilarity matrix construction when *categorical* data is distributed between two parties. Let κ and ℓ be the symmetric security parameter and bit length, respectively. Then, the communication cost for secure hamming distance computation (Algorithm 2) between the two vectors X and Y owned by *Alice* and *Bob*, respectively, equals to $\ell(\log_2 \ell + \kappa)$ [4]. Now suppose that *Alice* and *Bob* own N_1 and N_2 records, respectively. Thence, for constructing the dissimilarity matrix, first $\frac{1}{2}N_1 N_2 \ell(\log_2 \ell + \kappa)$ communications are required for computing the hamming distance of records. The division by 2 is because the dissimilarity matrix is symmetric.

After having the dissimilarity matrix with $N_1 + N_2$ records, the time complexity for constructing an agglomerative hierarchical clustering equals to $\mathcal{O}((N_1 + N_2)^2 \log(N_1 + N_2))$.

8 Experimental Analysis

To give an additional insight on the proposed framework, in this section we present the experimental analysis of our proposed framework.

We implemented secure *Euclidean* distance algorithm, and consequently the construction of dissimilarity matrix, when data is distributed *horizontally* and *vertically* between two (or more) parties (Algorithms 3, 4, 5 and 6).

Experiments have been run on a PC with Intel(R) Core (TM) i3-4030U CPU 1.90 GHz, RAM 4 GB, using Visual Studio on a 64 bit, Windows 10 operating system.

In our experiments, we employed *Wholesale Customers* dataset[1], which contains 8 numerical attributes, divided between two parties horizontally, each owning 200 instances. We first execute the scalar product as proposed in Algorithm 1, and then we computed secure Euclidean distance. The time needed for creating dissimilarity matrix was equivalent to 225×10^{-1} s.

In the case which data is *vertically* distributed between two parties, the *sales transactions weekly* dataset [28] from *UCI* machine learning repository has been selected to compute the required time for obtaining secure *Euclidean* distances and as a result the dissimilarity matrix. The dataset contains weekly purchased quantities of 200 products over 52 weeks. We have divided the attributes in a way that 20 attributes belong to *Alice* and the remaining 32 attributes are owned

---

[1] http://hdl.handle.net/10071/4097.

by *Bob*. As presented in Algorithm 4, the secure *Euclidean* distances between each two vectors has been computed, which required 10^{-2} s for constructing each element of the dissimilarity matrix. The whole secure vertical dissimilarity matrix of size 200×200 was built in 18 s.

9 Conclusion

In this work we proposed a framework which can be exploited for data holders to construct any agglomerative hierarchical clustering algorithm on their data as a whole, without revealing the original datasets. To this end, secure two-party computation algorithms are proposed to obtain the required criteria for detecting the clusters on whole data, when (numerical or categorical) data is distributed either horizontally or vertically between two parties. Afterwards, we extended the proposed protocols to the scenarios of data being partitioned among more than two parties. Finally, we presented the security analysis of the proposed approach, we calculated the communication cost, and we analyzed the efficiency of our methodology on benchmark dataset.

References

1. Artoisenet, C., Roland, M., Closon, M.: Health networks: actors, professional relationships, and controversies. In: Collaborative Patient Centred eHealth, vol. 141. IOSPress (2013)
2. Berkhin, P.: A survey of clustering data mining techniques. In: Kogan, J., Nicholas, C., Teboulle, M. (eds.) Grouping Multidimensional Data, pp. 25–71. Springer, Berlin Heidelberg (2006). https://doi.org/10.1007/3-540-28349-8_2
3. Bogan, E., English, J.: Benchmarking for Best Practices: Winning Through Innovative Adaptation. McGraw-Hill, New York (1994)
4. Bringer, J., Chabanne, H., Favre, M., Patey, A., Schneider, T., Zohner, M.: GSHADE: faster privacy-preserving distance computation and biometric identification. In: Proceedings of the 2nd ACM Workshop on Information Hiding and Multimedia Security, New York, NY, USA, pp. 187–198 (2014)
5. Bringer, J., Chabanne, H., Patey, A.: SHADE: secure hamming distance computation from oblivious transfer. In: Adams, A.A., Brenner, M., Smith, M. (eds.) FC 2013. LNCS, vol. 7862, pp. 164–176. Springer, Heidelberg (2013). https://doi.org/10.1007/978-3-642-41320-9_11
6. Bunn, P., Ostrovsky, R.: Secure two-party k-means clustering. In: Proceedings of the 14th ACM Conference on Computer and Communications Security, CCS 2007, pp. 486–497. ACM, NY, USA (2007)
7. Day, W.H.E., Edelsbrunner, H.: Efficient algorithms for agglomerative hierarchical clustering methods. J. Classif. **1**(1), 7–24 (1984)
8. De, I., Tripathy, A.: A secure two party hierarchical clustering approach for vertically partitioned data set with accuracy measure. In: Thampi, S., Abraham, A., Pal, S., Rodriguez, J. (eds.) Recent Advances in Intelligent Informatics. Advances in Intelligent Systems and Computing, vol. 235. Springer, Cham (2014). https://doi.org/10.1007/978-3-319-01778-5_16

9. Erkin, Z., Franz, M., Guajardo, J., Katzenbeisser, S., Lagendijk, I., Toft, T.: Privacy-preserving face recognition. In: Goldberg, I., Atallah, M.J. (eds.) PETS 2009. LNCS, vol. 5672, pp. 235–253. Springer, Heidelberg (2009). https://doi.org/10.1007/978-3-642-03168-7_14

10. Gan, G., Ma, C., Wu, J.: Data Clustering: Theory, Algorithms, and Applications. ASA-SIAM Series on Statistics and Applied Probability. Society for Industrial and Applied Mathematics, Philadelphia (2007)

11. Hamidi, M., Sheikhalishahi, M., Martinelli, F.: Secure two-party agglomerative hierarchical clustering construction. In: Proceedings of the 4th International Conference on Information Systems Security and Privacy, ICISSP 2018, Funchal, Madeira, Portugal, 22–24 January 2018, pp. 432–437 (2018)

12. Hamidi, M., Sheikhalishahi, M., Martinelli, F.: Secure two-party agglomerative hierarchical clustering construction. In: the 4th International Conference on Information Systems Security and Privacy (ICISSP). SciTePress (2018)

13. Jagannathan, G., Pillaipakkamnatt, K., Wright, R.N.: A new privacy-preserving distributed k-clustering algorithm. In: SDM, pp. 494–498. SIAM (2006)

14. Jagannathan, G., Wright, R.N.: Privacy-preserving distributed k-means clustering over arbitrarily partitioned data. In: Proceedings of the Eleventh ACM SIGKDD International Conference on Knowledge Discovery in Data Mining, KDD 2005, pp. 593–599. ACM, New York, NY, USA (2005)

15. Jha, S., Kruger, L., McDaniel, P.: Privacy preserving clustering. In: di Vimercati, S.C., Syverson, P., Gollmann, D. (eds.) ESORICS 2005. LNCS, vol. 3679, pp. 397–417. Springer, Heidelberg (2005). https://doi.org/10.1007/11555827_23

16. Martinelli, F., Saracino, A., Sheikhalishahi, M.: Modeling privacy aware information sharing systems: a formal and general approach. In: 15th IEEE International Conference on Trust, Security and Privacy in Computing and Communications (2016)

17. Sheikhalishahi, M., Martinelli, F.: Privacy preserving hierarchical clustering over multi-party data distribution. In: Wang, G., Atiquzzaman, M., Yan, Z., Choo, K.-K.R. (eds.) SpaCCS 2017. LNCS, vol. 10656, pp. 530–544. Springer, Cham (2017). https://doi.org/10.1007/978-3-319-72389-1_42

18. Mohammed, N., Chen, R., Fung, B.C., Yu, P.S.: Differentially private data release for data mining. In: Proceedings of the 17th ACM SIGKDD International Conference on Knowledge Discovery and Data Mining, KDD 2011, pp. 493–501, ACM, New York, NY, USA (2011)

19. Murtagh, F., Contreras, P.: Algorithms for hierarchical clustering: an overview. Wiley Interdisc. Rew. Data Min. Knowl. Discov. **2**(1), 86–97 (2012)

20. Nateghizad, M., Erkin, Z., Lagendijk, R.L.: Efficient and secure equality tests. In: 2016 IEEE International Workshop on Information Forensics and Security (WIFS), pp. 1–6 (2016)

21. Nateghizad, M., Erkin, Z., Lagendijk, R.L.: An efficient privacy-preserving comparison protocol in smart metering systems. EURASIP J. Inf. Secur. **2016**(1), 11 (2016)

22. Oliveira, S.R.M., Zaïane, O.R.: Privacy preserving frequent itemset mining. In: Proceedings of the IEEE International Conference on Privacy, Security and Data Mining, CRPIT 2014, vol. 14, pp. 43–54 (2002)

23. Oliveira, S.R.M., Zaiane, O.R.: A privacy-preserving clustering approach toward secure and effective data analysis for business collaboration. Comput. Secur. **26**(1), 81–93 (2007)

24. Sheikhalishahi, M., Martinelli, F.: Privacy preserving clustering over horizontal and vertical partitioned data. In: 2017 IEEE Symposium on Computers and Communications, ISCC 2017, Heraklion, Greece, 3–6 July 2017, pp. 1237–1244 (2017)

25. Sheikhalishahi, M., Martinelli, F.: Privacy-utility feature selection as a privacy mechanism in collaborative data classification. In: The 26th IEEE International Conference on Enabling Technologies: Infrastructure for Collaborative Enterprises, Poznan, Poland (2017)

26. Sheikhalishahi, M., Mejri, M., Tawbi, N., Martinelli, F.: Privacy-aware data sharing in a tree-based categorical clustering algorithm. In: Cuppens, F., Wang, L., Cuppens-Boulahia, N., Tawbi, N., Garcia-Alfaro, J. (eds.) FPS 2016. LNCS, vol. 10128, pp. 161–178. Springer, Cham (2017). https://doi.org/10.1007/978-3-319-51966-1_11

27. Su, C., Zhou, J., Bao, F., Takagi, T., Sakurai, K.: Two-party privacy-preserving agglomerative document clustering. In: Dawson, E., Wong, D.S. (eds.) ISPEC 2007. LNCS, vol. 4464, pp. 193–208. Springer, Heidelberg (2007). https://doi.org/10.1007/978-3-540-72163-5_16

28. Tan, S.C., San Lau, J.P.: Time series clustering: A superior alternative for market basket analysis. In: Herawan, T., Deris, M., Abawajy, J. (eds.) DaEng-2013. LNEE, vol. 285, pp. 241–248. Springer, Singapore (2014). https://doi.org/10.1007/978-981-4585-18-7_28

29. Vaidya, J., Clifton, C.: Privacy preserving association rule mining in vertically partitioned data. In: Proceedings of the Eighth ACM SIGKDD International Conference on Knowledge Discovery and Data Mining, KDD 2002, pp. 639–644. ACM, New York, NY, USA (2002)

Insights into Unsupervised Holiday Detection from Low-Resolution Smart Metering Data

Günther Eibl$^{(\boxtimes)}$, Sebastian Burkhart, and Dominik Engel

Center for Secure Energy Informatics, Salzburg University of Applied Sciences,
Urstein Süd 1, 5412 Puch/Hallein, Austria
{guenther.eibl,sebastian.burkhart,dominik.engel}@en-trust.at
http://www.en-trust.at

Abstract. Recently, first methods for holiday detection from unsupervised low-resolution smart metering data have been presented. However, due to the unsupervised nature of the problem, previous work only applied the algorithms on a few typical cases and lacks a systematic validation. This paper systematically validates the existing algorithm by visual inspection and shows that numerous cases exist, where implicit assumptions are not met and the methods fail. Moreover, it proposes a new, very simple rule-based method which is in principle able to overcome these problems. This method should be seen as a first step towards improvement, since it is not automated and needs a moderate amount of human intervention for each household.

Keywords: Privacy · Smart grids · Smart metering

1 Introduction

Privacy concerns have been raised by the planned large-scale rollout of Smart Meters [10]. Several methods exist that analyze energy consumption profiles. Especially NonIntrusive Load Monitoring (NILM) is an area of active research [4,7,11] where the goal is to divide (disaggregate) the (aggregate) signal that results from summing up consumption of different devices into the individual summands. While it is clear that such techniques have high potential to improve or generate new services, one could learn private information like habits from information about device usage. Typically, these approaches use a time resolution in the range of a second which is much lower than the time resolutions that occur in the Smart Grid. For example in Austria, the planned rollout foresees Smart Meters that only have a time resolution of 15 min.

Another branch of methods aim at detection of occupancy, i.e., at determining for each point in time, if a household is occupied by at least one person or not [1,2,5,8,9]. These methods are typically tested using laboriously collected ground truth for a low number of places. Also there, typically time resolutions of seconds or a minute are smaller than the time resolution in Smart Metering.

© Springer Nature Switzerland AG 2019
P. Mori et al. (Eds.): ICISSP 2018, CCIS 977, pp. 281–302, 2019.
https://doi.org/10.1007/978-3-030-25109-3_15

In a recent study [3] holiday detection from low resolution has been investigated for the first time. Inspired by ideas from occupancy detection several methods have been developed that aim at detecting holidays. Note that there and in this paper a holiday is defined as a day without electricity consumption that is triggered by a human. The methods have been described and investigated for several typical households. However, since the paper was intended as a first, explorative step towards holiday detection, no systematic validation of the methods has been performed.

This paper aims at filling this gap. The performed validation discovered several weaknesses of the existing methods and proposes a first step towards a better method.

2 Related Work

2.1 NIOM

NIOM is a rule-based algorithm that classifies households as occupied or unoccupied for time intervals containing T measurement points. For each time interval the following features are calculated: the average value, the standard deviation and the range (maximum-minimum). For each feature, thresholds need to be found for classifying the time interval as unoccupied, if the feature is below the threshold. Otherwise the time interval is classified as occupied. All the time intervals where occupancy is determined that way occur during daytime $\mathcal{D} = [6\,\mathrm{h},\ 23\,\mathrm{h}]$ and not during nighttime.

The thresholds themselves are determined as the maximum values during the previous night between 1 h and 4 h ($\mathcal{N} := [1\,\mathrm{h},\ 4\,\mathrm{h}]$). Gaps between time intervals detected as occupied are filled using a plausible heuristic. The authors themselves already pointed out that their results are sensitive to the choice of the threshold.

2.2 MaxOnly

MaxOnly has been developed in [3] as a simple extension of NIOM for holiday detection. As done by NIOM, the maximum value of the measurements of household i, but now only one value per 15 min, is determined for the nighttime $\mathcal{N}$ of day d. Then the maximum of the day values $x_{i,d}^t$ is compared with this value. In order to not underestimate the number of holidays a tolerance δ is added to the night maximum yielding the *MaxOnly* holiday detection rule

$$h_{i,d} = \begin{cases} 1 & \text{if } \max_{t \in \mathcal{D}} x_{i,d}^t < \max_{t \in \mathcal{N}} x_{i,d}^t + \delta \\ 0 & \text{otherwise.} \end{cases} \tag{1}$$

For practical tests, δ has been set to 0.1 kW.

2.3   LogReg

While MaxOnly is a simple extension of NIOM, LogReg has been developed in [3] especially for holiday detection. The idea of LogReg is to reformulate the problem as follows: For a holiday, both, the night and the day values of a day, should resemble night values. This reformulation enables one to train and use a classifier f_i that distinguishes night values from day values of household i. Thus, in a first step a classifier f_i is learned for each household using logistic regression which is a common classification method. Logistic regression has been used because it not only outputs the class but also the estimated probability to be in a class.

Given the learned classifier, a new day to be classified is then treated as follows: if the classifier classifies both, its day values and its night values, as likely being night values using again a threshold τ_i then the day is classified as a holiday. The threshold τ_i is heuristically determined from the 25% quantile of the estimated probability of the night measurements to be a night measurement.

So far it is still open which features should be used as the input to the classifier, i.e., how to describe the day and night values, respectively. Two variants have been studied in [3] and will also be studied here. The first set of features summarizes the day and night values simply by their maximum, the corresponding overall method is called *LogRegMax*. In order to possibly exploit more details of the distribution the second set of features summarizes the day and night values by quantiles. More precisely the 25%, the 50%, the 75% and the 99.9% quantile are used. The corresponding overall method is called *LogRegQuant*.

3   Validation

3.1   Initial Comparison of Results

It has already been stated in [3] that the differences in the predicted number of holidays can be large. Now, it is investigated where this differences come from and which of the methods yields the better prediction. The proceeding for this task is as follows: First the households where the largest differences in the

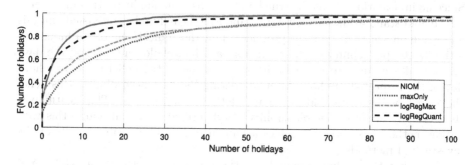

Fig. 1. Comparison of the results of the methods proposed in [3].

predictions occur are detected, then validation plots were created and visually compared. Essentially the result of this section is a complete failure of all the existing methods for a variety of households.

By looking at the distribution of the number of holidays, it can be shown that NIOM and LogRegQuant yield to lower number of holidays than MaxOnly and LogRegMax (Fig. 1).

It is clear that NIOM yields fewer holidays than MaxOnly because its threshold is lower by the chosen tolerance (chosen as 0.1 kW). We explain the underestimation by LogRegQuant by the conjecture that the maximum is the best feature for the description of human activits. More details will be shown in Sect. 5.1.

Preliminary examinations of validation plots provided first evidence that MaxOnly and LogRegMax are favoured over NIOM and LogRegQuant. Consequently the subset of households that are investigated are based on the differences between these two methods which is shown in Fig. 2. In order to easily recognize households where differences occur the points of the scatterplot are labeled by the household ID.

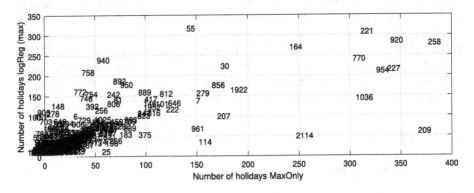

Fig. 2. Comparison between the results of MaxOnly and LogRegMax.

3.2   Validation Plots

Since no information about the true holidays exists human inspection must serve as the gold standard here. Therefore, validation heavily relies on visual analysis and common sense. In order to produce a plot that quickly enables a human to estimate the plausibility of the result for each household and method the days are ranked according to the quantity that represents the belief in being a holiday of the respected method. After reordering the days according to this belief the values of the household are again plotted as a heatmap. This heatmap is then visually analyzed for plausibility. As described below, although this validation method is simple, it enables a human to find implausible results of the investigated methods.

Note that the ranking depends on the prediction method: for NIOM and MaxOnly holiday score s_d^{MaxOnly} is calculated as the according to the difference between the maximum value during nighttime and the maximum value during the daytime. Note that while the score is the same for NIOM and MaxOnly, the threshold is set higher for MaxOnly.

For the logReg methods the holiday score $s_{i,d}^{\text{logReg}}$ for day d of household i is the predicted probability for day d to be a holiday

$$s_{i,d}^{\text{logReg}} = p_d^i = y_d^{i,\text{day}} \cdot y_d^{i,\text{night}}$$

While the formula for the score is the same for the two variants, the difference lies in the inputs of the trained classifiers f^i that tries to distinguish between the day and the night values.

In order to better visualize the differences between the night and the day values for the heatmap values that exceed 1 kW were set to 1 before visualization. More details about this choice is given in Sect. 5.1. An additional vertical separation line with numbers of 1 kW is added in order to separate days which were detected holidays (left) from days where no holiday was detected (right).

The reordering has an additional beneficial effect. While longer periods of holidays such as in Fig. 3 can easily be detected in the original heatmap, single holidays can easily get overlooked. Due to the reordering, single holidays are put to the left of the separation line and can thus be compared with other detected holidays.

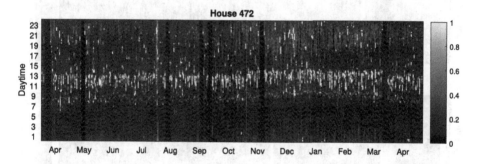

Fig. 3. Household 472: holiday periods can be easily identified as vertical black stripes.

Based on the visual inspection of the validation plots the following categories were found to be suitable for describing the results: "plausible", "too few holidays detected", "too many holidays detected" and "bad ranking". Since the number of holidays is not known the best category to achieve is plausible. This means that the sorting of days in the heatmap and the distinction between holidays and non-holidays look reasonable. "Bad ranking" means that the ordering of days in the heatmap does differs from the expected ordering. An example for bad ranking is shown in the upper panel of Fig. 4. There, many days with high consumption especially during night are rated as most likely being a holiday. This is far from being plausible since during a holiday low consumption is expected throughout the day. An example for too many found holidays is shown in the lower panel of Fig. 4. While the ranking is plausible there, only the days with consistently very low energy consumption that constitute the black part at the leftmost part of the figure should be labeled as holidays.

Due to the high number of households, not all validation plots were looked at. Instead, in spirit of estimating the performance from properly selected samples four different regimes of households were investigated: two kinds of households, where the two methods agree and two kinds, where the two methods disagree. For the latter two cases households with an extremely high number of predicted holidays by at least one method were investigated. More precisely it is looked at households for which

- both methods estimate around 30 holidays: 7 selected households
- both methods estimate around 0 holidays: 6 selected households
- MaxOnly predicts more than 150 holidays: 18 selected households
- logRegMax estimates more than 150 holidays but MaxOnly estimates less than 100 holidays: 7 selected households

While it is not possible to even show all these plots, typical households are shown in order to demonstrate the key issues.

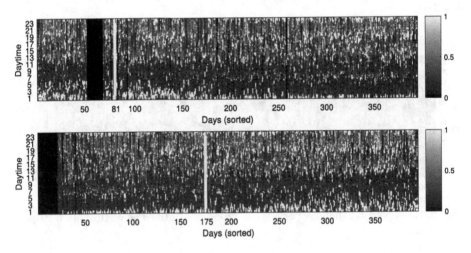

Fig. 4. Household 892: both MaxOnly (top) and LogRegMax (bottom) overestimate the number of holidays. In the panel above, the false positives of MaxOnly that occur from high night values can be seen most clearly.

3.3   Households with About 30 Detected Holidays

First, cases that may be considered normal for Austria (with 25 free days per year) are analyzed now. A subsample consisting of households 1, 112, 194, 334, 551, 552, 472 was investigated. Except household 551 all of them had at least one longer period with a holiday. Both algorithms showed plausible results with the one exception when MaxOnly wrongly assigns a day a holiday when larger values occur during night time. As a typical example the consumption of household 472 is shown in Fig. 3.

The validation plots for the same household 472 are shown in Fig. 5. As already described in [3], both methods yield plausible results for such cases: in this case 25 holidays are detected by MaxOnly, 21 by LogRegMax.

3.4   Households with About 0 Detected Holidays

Considering households with near zero assigned holidays it is studied, if the methods also tend to underestimate the number of holidays. Visual inspection of households 73, 422, 452, 460 and 968 confirm that no longer holiday exist and only a small number of single holidays may exist. Thus also for this regime the algorithms yield plausible results.

Out of these households, household 769 is the only one that has a short holiday period (Fig. 6) in January. For this household logRegMax shows a plausible ranking but too few holidays: days with low consumption throughout the day are right to the separation line (Fig. 7). MaxOnly shows more holidays.

This household is also an interesting case where a pool exists. This pool causes high values of a rectangular shape both during day and night. In fact, one of MaxOnly's detected holidays has a considerable part of the day affected by the pool pump. Because the remaining values of this day are small, this may indeed be a day where no one is at home and only the automatic pool pump is running as the only device with high energy consumption. This household demonstrates that detection methods must find a way to deal with automatic appliances like swimming pools.

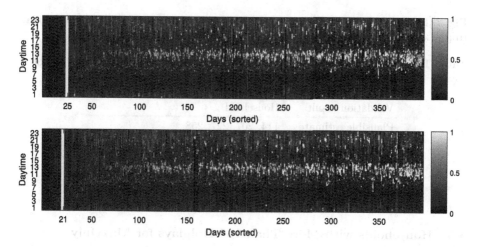

Fig. 5. Household 472: both algorithms show plausible results: MaxOnly (top): 25, LogRegMax (bottom): 21 holidays.

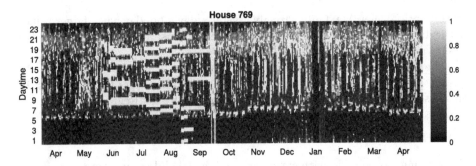

Fig. 6. Household 769 has one holiday in January and rectangular patches of higher values that are caused by a pump of a swimming pool.

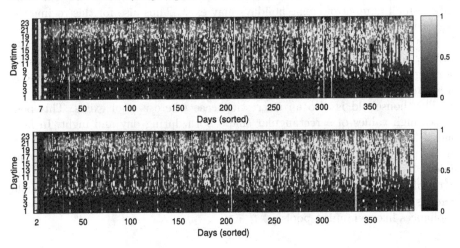

Fig. 7. Household 759: MaxOnly shows a plausible result with one questionable holiday (top), LogRegMax underestimates the number of holidays (bottom).

Table 1. Validation of MaxOnly for households where MaxOnly estimates ≥150 holidays.

Validation result	Household
Plausible estimate	114, 207, 227, 258
Bad ranking	7, 30, 164, 279, 770, 856
Estimated too many	221
Estimated too few	209, 920, 954, 961, 1036, 1922, 2114

3.5   Households with More Than 150 Holidays for MaxOnly

Now households where MaxOnly estimated more than 150 holidays are visually validated. The IDs of these households can also be identified in the scatter plot in Fig. 2. The validation result for MaxOnly is shown in Table 1.

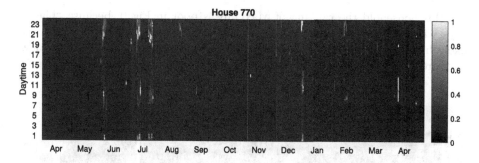

Fig. 8. Household 770: the regular, "oscillating" behaviour is supposed to be caused by the refrigerator. This background signal is not there the whole year.

Since the estimated number is so high the authors expected an overestimation of MaxOnly. However, this turned out to be not the case. The validation plots even more showed that more often both methods still underestimated the number of holidays. In the best case results looked plausible, however this did not happen often.

MaxOnly mainly also suffered from an inadequate ranking. Bad ranking of MaxOnly occurs for days with low values during daytime and at least on high consumption value during nighttime. Since MaxOnly compares the maximum during daytime with the maximum during nighttime, the difference is negative which is considered as a holiday by MaxOnly. However, such a day is likely not a holiday resulting in erroneously detected holidays where the consumption during day was low but consumption during night was high. An example household, where bad ranking clearly occurs, is shown in Fig. 12.

The validation result for LogRegMax shown in Table 2 demonstrates that for these households LogRegMax in most cases underestimates the number of holidays.

Table 2. Validation of LogRegMax for households where MaxOnly estimates ≥ 150 holidays.

Validation result	Household
Plausible estimate	7, 164
Bad ranking	221
Estimated too many	30
Estimated too few	114, 207, 209, 227, 258, 279, 770, 856, 920, 954, 961, 1036, 1922, 2114

As an example, household 770 is shown in Fig. 8. The figure clearly demonstrates that the background signal can vary over the time of the year. This property makes the determination of suitable thresholds more complicated.

For this household the ranking of MaxOnly is poor in Fig. 9, because "black" days with nearly zero consumption are not consistently ranked as extremely likely holidays. While the ranking of days of logRegMax is plausible, too few days are detected as holidays because the threshold for p_d^i is set too low.

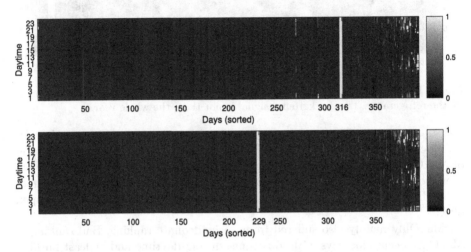

Fig. 9. Household 770: both MaxOnly (top) and LogRegMax (bottom) underestimate the number of holidays.

It is remarkable that even though households with a high number of holidays detected by MaxOnly have been selected for this section, still the number of holidays detected has often been too small. In order to demonstrate that such cases exist, as an example Fig. 10 shows the validation plots of household 952 where occupancy is obviously extremely rare. From a privacy perspective such households could be secondary residences that are only occupied for a small part of the year. Since in parts of Austria secondary residences are restricted finding such households as possible secondary residences could be a use case for government.

3.6   Households with Most Holidays for LogRegMax

Now households are analyzed, where logRegMax estimates more than 150 holidays but MaxOnly only estimates less than 100 holidays.

Households with 2 different characteristics occur. Households 55 and 892 have a high (where high here means near 1 kW) energy consumption for rather large parts of the day and also during parts of the night. While household 55 has no obvious holiday, household 892 has a clear holiday at the end of the measurement time. The validation plot of household 892 in Fig. 4 shows that both MaxOnly and logRegMax strongly overestimate the number of holidays. MaxOnly again fails because of the considerable energy consumption during night. LogRegMax

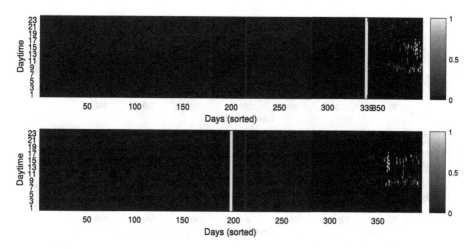

Fig. 10. Household 954: both MaxOnly (top) and LogRegMax (bottom) underestimate the number of holidays which is very large.

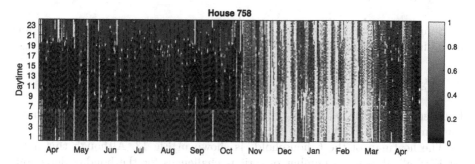

Fig. 11. Household 758: energy consumption shows vertical lines in winter which are possibly caused by an electric heater.

fails because the differences between the day and the night values are rather small. While the ranking makes more sense than for MaxOnly, the threshold is clearly set wrong resulting in an overestimation of the number of holidays.

The second set of households (758, 772, 940, 950) have the characteristic feature that vertical lines occur during winter time. As an example household 758 is shown in Fig. 11. Because of the primary occurrence in winter we suspect that these vertical lines stem from electrical heating systems that run throughout the day. Since it would make sense to turn the rather expensive electrical heating off during a holiday days with such vertical lines are likely not holidays.

Here, for both methods the bad distinction between night and day values lead to a failure of both methods as can be seen in Fig. 12. While the ranking of logRegMax is more plausible it still overestimates the number of holidays since many days with high consumption are left to the separation line.

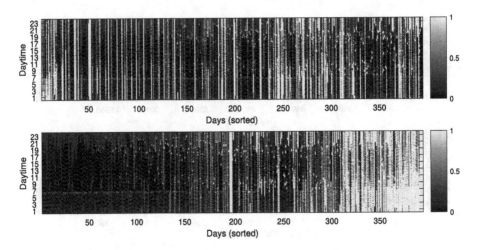

Fig. 12. Household 758: MaxOnly (top) has a bad ranking of the days (top) and estimates 50, LogRegMax (bottom) overestimates 197 holidays.

Summarizing, in this regime, both methods suffer from overestimation for both kinds of household characteristics.

4   Validation for ECO Data

In order to build the validation on a stronger basis, another source of household consumption, the ECO dataset [9], is considered.

The heatmap of the 6 households is shown in Fig. 13. Although this data set is small, it poses a number of serious challenges for the holiday detection method. While houses 1 and 2 look typical and show longer periods of holidays, houses 3 and 4 have high average consumption throughout the year. Houses 3, 4 and 5 have a horizontal line of high values which is likely to stem from an automatic appliance. However, even though automatic appliances are not triggered by inhabitants, they can indicate occupancy. One example for such an appliance is automatic electrical heating. Houses 4 and 6 also show vertical lines that extend into the night. As seen before, using algorithms that rely too much on the distinction between day and night values will have problems there. Household 3 has an automatic appliance running during night between August and October. The behavior that it runs during night is expected to negatively affect algorithms that estimate thresholds from night values. The fact that is does not run through the whole year is an additional challenge, because the night values can be treated equally for all days. In the ideal case the regular structure of automatic appliances could be used to filter them out. However, such a method is currently not available. While the structure is rectangular it is not the same for all days which would certainly require a non-trivial removal method. The ECO data set illustrates a challenging diversity of load profiles, a detection should be able to deal with.

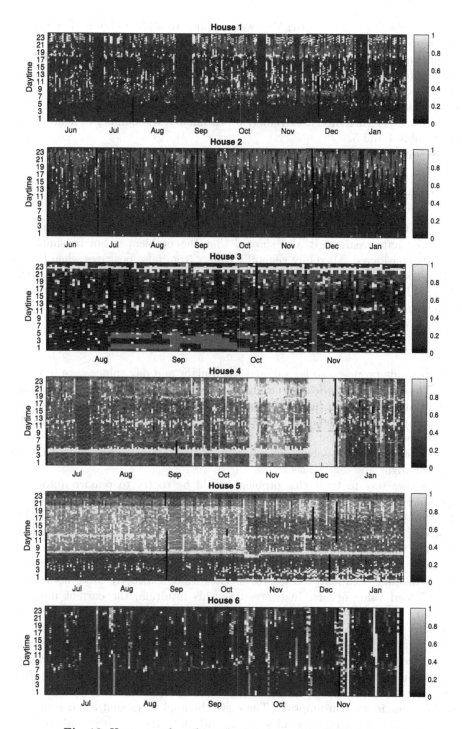

Fig. 13. Heatmaps describing the 6 houses of the ECO dataset.

Both MaxOnly and LogRegMax were applied to all households. The validation plots are shown in Figs. 14 and 15, respectively. MaxOnly showed plausible results for houses 1, 2 and 6 with a slight overestimation again for days with high night values (leftmost part of the plot). The overestimation was moderate for household 3, it was extreme for households 4 and 5. LogRegMax showed a plausible ranking for households 1, 2, 3 and 6 with underestimation for households 1, 2, and 6. As MaxOnly, it extremely overestimated the number of holidays for households 4 and 5.

In summary, both methods showed big weaknesses for the ECO data set.

5   Towards a New Model

The validation of the existing methods in Sects. 3 and 4 showed that there is much for improvement. It also showed that the problem is not as simple as initially considered. MaxOnly generally suffers from false positives when higher values occur during night. LogRegMax mainly suffered from the setting of the threshold especially when most of the days are holidays or when consistently high values also occur during night.

5.1   Use Only Maximum Values: MaxTol

The methods proposed so far suffered when night and day values were too similar. This characteristic leads to a big error because the number of holidays are overestimated. While it has been clear that this is an explicit assumption naturally arising from the adaption of the occupancy detection approach in [2], the experiments showed that the distinction between day and night may introduce more problems than it solves. Therefore, here we propose to skip the distinction between night and day values.

Another way to treat this problem would be to try to remove automatic appliances that also run during night time thus decreasing the difference between daytime and nighttime consumption. However, such methods are not yet readily available for all kinds of appliances, especially for low resolution data. Therefore, we leave this way as a topic for future research.

Especially houses 4 and 5 of the ECO data showed a clear overestimation. For a human, occupancy seems to be clear that somebody is at home, if a "high" load value occurs. In contrast to this intuition, the current methods all only compared day values with night values, but no method compared the *absolute* value with a threshold. Therefore it seems reasonable to consider a fixed threshold for the maximum of the whole day. Using such a threshold is supported by the results about the determinants of electricity consumption [6], where it is stated that "most high consumption, intermittent appliances such as electric water heater, electric clothes dryer, and Spas/Pools primarily contribute to daily maximum consumption. These are the appliances that are not "always on" and their operating schedules are dependent on the activities and habits of the occupants". The power consumption of the class of ohmic devices that need

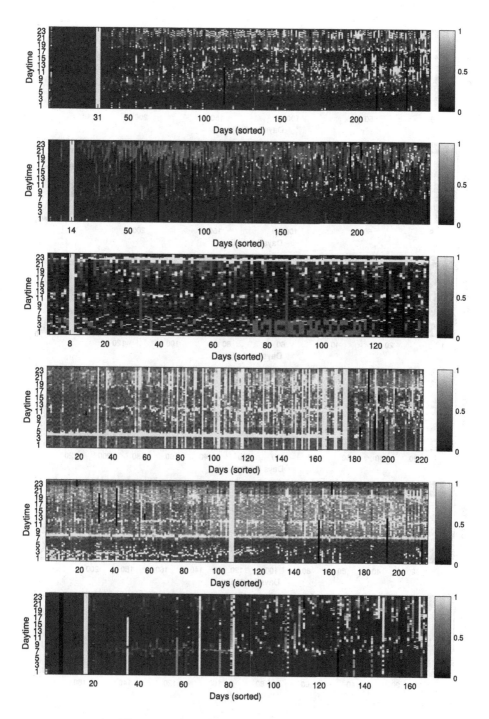

Fig. 14. Validation of MaxOnly for ECO data.

296   G. Eibl et al.

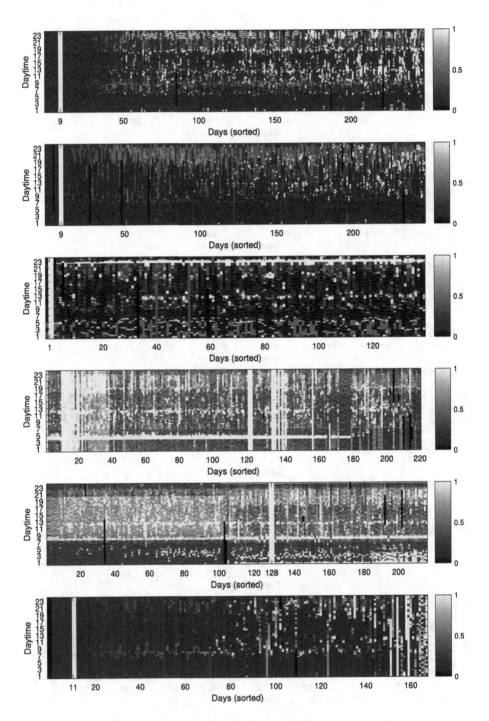

Fig. 15. Validation of LogRegMax for ECO data.

to produce heat have power values above $1\,\mathrm{kW}$. Therefore, we used $1\,\mathrm{kW}$ as an upper limit for a value where we can be quite sure that it stems from an activity of a human in the household. Consequently, all values entering a heatmap have been clipped from above at $1\,\mathrm{kW}$ so that the heatmaps are suitable to show the low maxima that are interesting for developing thresholds. The fact that this clipping enabled us to conduct the validation analysis based on the heatmaps supports the usefulness of considering values above $1\,\mathrm{kW}$ as likely human-driven.

Using these considerations as a guideline, we next study the following, extremely simple rule-based classifier that compares the maximum value of the *whole* day with a constant, household-dependent threshold. Consider a whole day d of household i. Denoting the 96 quarterly-hour power values of as $\boldsymbol{x}_{i,d} = (x_{i,d}^1, \dots, x_{i,d}^{96})$, the binary holiday variable $h_{i,d}$ is assigned by the following simple rule using a single tolerance value Tol_i for a household

$$ h_{i,d} = \begin{cases} 1 & \text{if} \quad \max_{t \in \{1,\dots,96\}} x_{i,d}^t < \mathrm{Tol}_i \\ 0 & \text{if} \quad \max_{t \in \{1,\dots,96\}} x_{i,d}^t \geq \mathrm{Tol}_i \end{cases} \qquad (2) $$

For future reference, this simple rule is called MaxTol. From (2) it is clear that more holidays will result from choosing a bigger value of Tol_i.

Two questions immediately arise. First: is such a simple rule flexible enough to get a reasonable holiday detection mechanism? Second: how should the threshold be determined? For these 2 questions preliminary answers will be given in the next two subsections based on trials for the diverse ECO data set.

5.2   Threshold Selection

Before demonstrating how the threshold is chosen, the effect of the threshold on the outcome is illustrated in Fig. 16 for first, bigger dataset. There, the threshold has been set to the same value for all households.

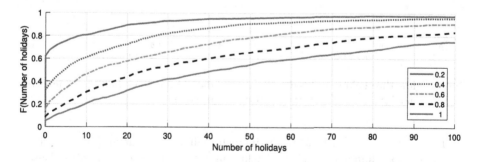

Fig. 16. Effect of different thresholds on the holiday distribution.

From Fig. 16 two conclusions can be drawn: first, the threshold has a huge effect on the distribution of the number of holidays. Second, the range between

0.2 and 1 suffices for realistic, typical households. If Tol would be set to 1 for all households, around 30% of households would have 80 holidays or more per year. This seems unrealistically high for Austria.

Threshold selection is done manually for each household based on the heatmap of a household and the cumulative distribution of the night values (Fig. 17). In the first step, the night time is determined based on the heatmap. For all households of the ECO dataset the night time was set to the time span between 2 h and 4 h, only for house 4 the time span between 0 h and 2 h was selected in order to avoid the values of the "horizontal line". Then the cumulative plot of the night values was created (Fig. 17).

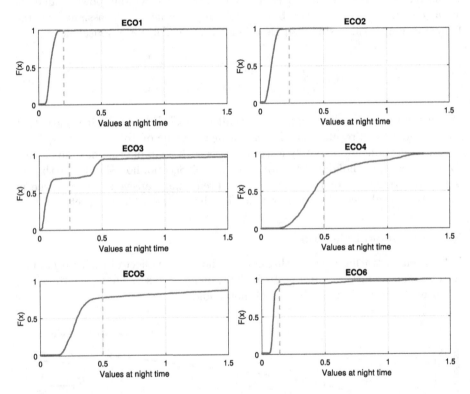

Fig. 17. How threshold have been selected (red, dashed line) based on the cumulative distribution of the night values (blue). (Color figure online)

This plot serves as a basis to distinguish high values that indicate activities stemming from humans from the background of automatic appliances. Based on inspection of the heatmap (Fig. 13), if no high values occur during night, the threshold was set high enough to include nearly 100% of the night values (houses 1 and 2). If a considerable amount of high values exist, the threshold should be chosen to sort these values out. For example, house 3 contains a considerable amount of high values. The plot of the cumulative distribution shows that these high values account for about 30% of the night values that can be seen in the plot as the second increase after the plateau. The threshold (red line) was set to just exclude these values. In a similar way the threshold can be achieved for houses 4 to 6. Only for household 4 the position of the threshold stays rather unclear since no clear flat intermediate region occurs. Based on several manual trials it turned out that for house 4 the result was insensitive to the exact setting of the threshold.

As already can be seen in Fig. 17 the thresholds are well below 1 kW but changed considerably between houses. The thresholds used are also listed in Table 3.

Table 3. Results of MaxTol for ECO data.

House ID	1	2	3	4	5	6
Used thresholds Tol_i	0.2	0.2295	0.2395	0.496	0.5	0.13
Detected number of holidays	27	11	0	0	0	11

5.3 Application to ECO Data

Finally, using the thresholds derived in Sect. 5.2, MaxTol was applied to the ECO dataset. The corresponding validation plot in Figs. 18 and 19 ordered the days by increasing maximum values, now using values from the *whole* day for the determination of the maximum.

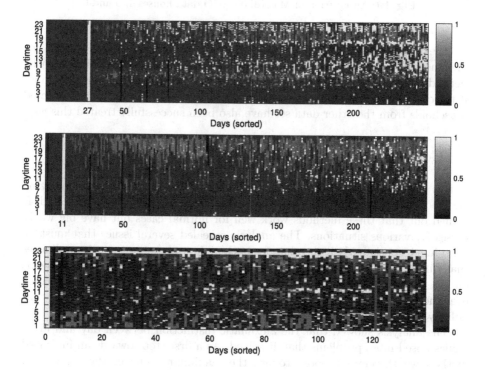

Fig. 18. Application of MaxTol on ECO data houses 1, 2 and 3.

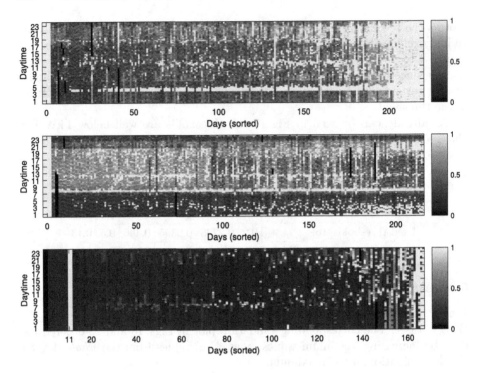

Fig. 19. Application of MaxTol on ECO data houses 4, 5 and 6.

The figures shows that reasonable results can be achieved by MaxTol for all households although it is in principle simpler than the other investigated methods, which performed weak for this dataset. However, this good result comes at the cost of needed manual intervention. It should be noted that a few selected households from the other data set have also been successfully treated this way.

6   Conclusion and Outlook

In this paper, previously developed methods that detect holidays by analyzing low frequency smart metering energy consumption data have been evaluated. It turned out that these methods work well for normal cases but have big weaknesses for various situations. The analysis revealed several issues that must be considered: consistently high values for both night and day, automatic appliances that run for parts of the day or night but not all year, background that depends on the time of the year or also households with unexpectedly rare occupancy over the year. From a privacy perspective, it can be considered good news that holiday detection is not as simple in general as one would think at first.

The analysis showed that the automatic distinction between day and night values posed more problems than it solved. As a first step towards an improved method we therefore propose to use the maximum value of the *whole* day.

There is also evidence that it is better to only use the maximum without additional quantiles of the load values. The absolute value of thresholds should be restricted to be in a certain range that is below consumption values of known human-driven appliances like ohmic heaters. Based on these principles a more suitable, very simple method is proposed. It is shown that using this simple method in principle the houses of the ECO dataset can be treated in a plausible way. However, the method comes at the cost of human intervention in estimating the threshold.

Holiday detection from electric load profiles is still in its infancy. Therefore many extensions are possible. A particular challenge will be to find thresholds automatically. It could also be challenging to develop more flexible models that are based on modeling of human habits and activities. Validation currently needs visual inspection which is both laborious and error-prone. Because labeled data will be hard to achieve, validation by household simulations could be a viable alternative.

Acknowledgement. The financial support by the Federal State of Salzburg is gratefully acknowledged. Furthermore, the authors would like to thank the Energieinstitut at the Johannes Kepler University Linz for providing the data set.

References

1. Becker, V., Kleiminger, W.: Exploring zero-training algorithms for occupancy detection based on smart meter measurements. Comput. Sci. Res. Dev **33**(1–2), 25–36 (2018). https://doi.org/10.1007/s00450-017-0344-9
2. Chen, D., Barker, S., Subbaswamy, A., Irwin, D., Shenoy, P.: Non-intrusive occupancy monitoring using smart meters. In: Proceedings of the 5th ACM Workshop on Embedded Systems For Energy-Efficient Buildings - BuildSys 2013, pp. 1–8 (2013). https://doi.org/10.1145/2528282.2528294
3. Eibl, G., Burkhart, S., Engel, D.: Unsupervised holiday detection from Low-resolution smart metering data. In: 2018 Proceedings of the 4th International Conference on Information Systems Security and Privacy, ICISSP, pp. 477–486. SciTePress (2018). https://doi.org/10.5220/0006719704770486
4. Hart, G.W.: Nonintrusive appliance load monitoring. Proc. IEEE **80**(12), 1870–1891 (1992)
5. Jin, M., Jia, R., Spanos, C.: Virtual occupancy sensing: using smart meters to indicate your presence. IEEE Trans. Mob. Comput. **16**(11), 3264–3277 (2017). https://doi.org/10.1109/TMC.2017.2684806. http://ieeexplore.ieee.org/document/7882676/
6. Kavousian, A., Rajagopal, R., Fischer, M.: Determinants of residential electricity consumption: using smart meter data to examine the effect of climate, building characteristics, appliance stock, and occupants' behavior. Energy **55**, 184–194 (2013). https://doi.org/10.1016/j.energy.2013.03.086
7. Kim, H., Marwah, M., Arlitt, M.F., Lyon, G., Han, J.: Unsupervised disaggregation of low frequency power measurements. In: The 11th SIAM International Conference on Data Mining, pp. 747–758 (2011)

8. Kleiminger, W., Beckel, C., Santini, S.: Household occupancy monitoring using electricity meters. In: Proceedings of the 2015 ACM International Joint Conference on Pervasive and Ubiquitous Computing, pp. 975–986 (2015). https://doi.org/10. 1145/2750858.2807538

9. Kleiminger, W., Beckel, C., Staake, T., Santini, S.: Occupancy detection from electricity consumption data. In: Proceedings of the 5th ACM Workshop on Embedded Systems For Energy-Efficient Buildings - BuildSys 2013, pp. 1–8 (2013). https:// doi.org/10.1145/2528282.2528295, http://dl.acm.org/citation.cfm?doid=2528282. 2528295

10. Lisovich, M.A., Wicker, S.B.: Privacy concerns in upcoming residential and commercial demand-response systems. In: Clemson Power Systems Conference. IEEE (2008)

11. Zoha, A., Gluhak, A., Imran, M.A., Rajasegarar, S.: Non-intrusive load monitoring approaches for disaggregated energy sensing: a survey. Sensors (Switzerland) **12**(12), 16838–16866 (2012). https://doi.org/10.3390/s121216838

Author Index

Printed in the United States
By Bookmasters